COLLECTING THE AMERICAN WEST

IN MEMORIAM

AITA HAMBER (née SELL)

17th December 1923 – 11th November 2010

Kuus, Kuus Kallike

Collecting the American West

The Rise and Fall of William Blackmore

Anthony Hamber

First published in the United Kingdom in 2010
by The Hobnob Press, PO Box 1838, East Knoyle, Salisbury, SP3 6FA
www.hobnobpress.co.uk

British Library Cataloguing in Publication Data
A catalogue record for this book is available from the British Library

ISBN 978-1906978-10-5
Typeset in Scala 11/15 pt. Typesetting and origination by John Chandler
Printed by Lightning Source

For details of the cover illustration see caption on page 187.

Contents

Preface and Acknowledgements

MY FIRST ENCOUNTER with William Blackmore took place as a young boy in the late 1960s when a family friend working at the Salisbury & South Wiltshire Museum showed me the empty interior of the Blackmore Museum. I never considered that one day I would be researching the story of the mid-Victorian polymath behind it.

It was through a personal research project examining the early history of photography in Salisbury during the mid 19th century that I came across William Blackmore once more. This link was through the examination of the possible use of photography at the Salisbury Museum. I quickly became aware of William Blackmore's extensive and significant use of photography within his own eponymous museum, not specifically within the field of collections management, but to document North American Indians.

It has been generally accepted by those who have written about William Blackmore (such as Brayer, Taylor, McEvansoneya, and Fleming) that the scale and scope of his professional and personal interests defy documenting by a single biographer. Indeed probably William himself was likely to be the only person to do this justice and his untimely and problematic death resulted in their being no autobiography or contemporary biography. As Fleming pointed out to me in an email (April 2010), 'Blackmore is a fascinating but frustrating subject. I doubt we will ever have primary evidence to answer our questions, so the best we can do is speculate intelligently'.

This study is the result of an iterative circle; excavating tit-bits of the life and career of William Blackmore from mid 19th century and other sources; assembling these "artefacts" into a coherent whole; and then interpreting the matrix of Blackmore's complex life. While this may appear to be the generic norm for a researcher, the nature of the primary evidence that does exist adds to the complexity. Artefacts from the Blackmore Museum and William Blackmore's papers and archival material are distributed across numerous collections covering a wide and highly fragmented geographic orbit. Added to this is the extraordinary spread of references to Blackmore in secondary sources. The advent of the Web has enabled such data to be mined in a way that Blackmore's only previous biographer, Herbert Brayer, could only have dreamt of.

Thus while this book aims to bring together for the first time an overview of the professional, business, and scholarly activities of a little appreciated mid-Victorian polymath, it is but a small contribution to Blackmore Studies; and there remains much work still to be done.

Many individuals have been generous with their time and shared their knowledge with me as I have researched William Blackmore. However, all errors in this book should be placed at my door with the hope that others will correct them and contribute further to the study and evaluation of the life and achievements of William Blackmore.

My thanks go to:

Peter Saunders , Curator Emeritus, and Jane Standen, former Assistant Curator, Salisbury & South Wilts Museum

Adrian Green, Director, and Jane Schon-Ellis, Collections Manager, of Salisbury & South Wilts Museum

Bruce Purvis, former Local Studies Librarian, Salisbury Reference and Local Studies Library

Jane Howells, Salisbury historian

Ann Ferriera, local family historian of Salisbury

Paula Richardson Fleming, former Senior Archivist, National Anthropological Archives, Smithsonian Institution

Harry Persaud, Curator, Library Collections, Department of Africa, Oceania and the Americas, British Museum

Tomas Jaehn, Fray Angélico Chávez History Library, Palace of the Governors, Santa Fe

Dr Chris Morton, Curator of Photographs and Manuscripts, Pitt Rivers Museum, University of Oxford

Dr. Wendel Cox, Denver Public Library

Elizabeth Edwards, Senior Research Fellow, University of the Arts, London

Philip McEvansoneya, Trinity College Dublin

John Cresswell, Curator of the Bournemouth Natural Sciences Society

Peter Daniels, historian of photography in Salisbury

Roddy Stevens, a direct descendent of Edward Thomas Stevens, who shared his research into the Stevens family in Salisbury

Dr. Alexander Bastek, Kulturstiftung Hansestadt Lübeck

Pat Shawcross, Borough Archivist & Local Studies Manager, London Borough of Sutton Local Studies Centre

Liz Green, Archivist , Cheshire Archives and Local Studies Kevin Balster, UCLA Young Research Library

Amanda Claunch, Associate Archivist, Missouri History Museum

Brian Dippie, University of Victoria, Canada

Abel Alexander, Argentinean photographic historian

Lucie Carreau and Sandra Camarda have been generous in sharing their doctoral research material with me.

The staff of a number of libraries have helped immeasurably; the London Library, the library of the Royal Society, London, the City of Westminster Archives and the Westminster Abbey Muniments.

John Chandler, local historian and publisher of the Hobnob Press, has been generous and supportive in enabling my research to reach a wider audience through this book.

I should also thank my wife Katharina and my sons Alexander and Nicholas for their patience during enumerable family meals as I enthused over the life and times of William Blackmore. They may consider publication of this book a merciful release from what they termed the 'dreaded WB'!

1
Introduction

FROM THE PERSPECTIVE of the early 21st century it seems more than curious that the legacy of the remarkable career and achievements of William Henry Blackmore so rapidly disappeared. He represents a prime example of the mid-Victorian polymath; a philanthropist with a wide range of business and scholarly interests. However, he also fell victim to a set of social mores that dropped an immediate shutter that took some seventy years to begin to lift. The starting point for the rehabilitation of William Blackmore began with the publication in 1949 of Herbert O. Brayer's two volume biography.[1]

Blackmore became a successful lawyer based in Liverpool and subsequently an international financier involved in numerous American land grants in New Mexico and Colorado; he was principal financier of the Denver & Rio Grande Railroad; his reputation by the mid 1870s within London financial circles was that 'everyone knows him and he knows everyone' and that he 'has means of obtaining information in the City such as very few men possess'; he visited Salt Lake City and met Brigham Young (1801-1877), president of The Church of Jesus Christ of Latter-day Saints, and wrote a confidential report on the 'Mormon Empire' for the Cabinet of the British government and independent industrial leaders; he was prominent enough to be invited in April 1872 to dine at the White House with United States President Ulysses S. Grant (1822-1885); he acted as the British representative of the Samoan Government in highlighting the various political troubles suffered by

1 Herbert O. Brayer, *William Blackmore: A Case Study in the Economic Development of the West*, Bradford-Robinson, Denver, 1949 (2 vols.).

the island in the mid 1870s; he created, funded and populated with artefacts perhaps the leading ethnographic museum in 19th century Great Britain, located in his home town of Salisbury; he was an early patron of the leading Pre-Raphaelite artist Dante Gabriel Rossetti (1828-1882) and the commissioner of an influential set of watercolours of the Yellowstone region by Thomas Moran (1837-1926), now the most sought after American 19th century painter;[2] and he was acknowledged by contemporaries to have so effectively exploited photography to document the North American 'Indians' that in the late 1860s his photographic collection was copied to form the basis of the holdings of the Smithsonian Institution in Washington, D.C.

Yet Blackmore's legacy was to be comparatively limited. Shortly after his untimely death in 1878, his papers and other materials were consigned to storage. There they lay apparently unused for almost half a century. Elements of William's other art collections were subsumed within those of his brother and loyal ally, Humphrey. Following Humphrey's death in 1929 a major dispersal campaign began in earnest. While some of William's business documents were saved, a significant number were apparently destroyed and artefacts were subsequently dispersed through donation, auction and sale to other public and private institutions. The Blackmore Museum, whose name had become incorporated with that of the Salisbury & South Wiltshire Museum after his death – and was amalgamated in 1902 – remained something of a place of pilgrimage to American archaeologists until the early 20th century. While a new gallery was built in 1933 linking the buildings of the Blackmore Museum to the Salisbury Museum, William's museum was already in terminal decline and its collections were to be broken up and dispersed over a period of over four decades.

From 1929 the majority of the collections of the Blackmore Museum were auctioned, sold or donated directly to other British institutions. Another round of de-accessioning took place after the death in 1949 of

2 At the Christie's auction of *Important American Paintings, Drawings and Sculpture* held in New York on 22nd May 2008, Thomas Moran's monumental American West landscape *Green River of Wyoming*, realized a remarkable US$17.74 million, more than doubling the previous record for a 19th century American painting.

Frank Stevens (1868-1949), William's nephew, who had been appointed the museum's first professional curator – a role titled 'Controller' – in 1913. The Blackmore Museum fell into comparative disuse by the 1960s and finally disappeared as a legal entity in 1968, a year in which further 'remnants' were sold. What appears to be the final 'remnants' of the Blackmore Museum were offered for sale in 1975. Those artefacts that remained from William's museum moved from its purpose built setting adjoining the Salisbury & South Wiltshire Museum in St. Ann Street to The King's House in the Cathedral Close in 1981 and the original building was subsequently converted into residential apartments.

Very little has been written in detail about William Blackmore himself and his multi-faceted life, though in more recent years his name appears in a wide range of literature on anthropology/ethnography cross-cultural histories. However, Blackmore is far from a mainstream figure in the early 21st century study of either the history of collecting or the early use of photography in the fields of anthropology and ethnology, one of his most noticeable achievements.[3] In many respects he remains one of Salisbury's most significant and yet unheralded 19th century 'sons'.

The starting point for 'Blackmore studies' is Herbert Oliver Brayer's monumental two volume *William Blackmore: A Case Study in the Economic Development of the West; Volume I – The Spanish Land Grants of New Mexico and Colorado 1863-1878; Volume II – Early Financing of the Denver & Rio Grande Railway and Ancillary Land Companies 1871-1878* that was published in 1949 in an edition of a mere 500 numbered copies.[4] Brayer's focus was primarily on Blackmore's business dealings in North America and this highly detailed account is unlikely ever to

3 For instance, Blackmore is not included in Hermione Waterfield and J.C.H. King, *Provenance: Twelve Collectors of Ethnographic Art in England in England 1760-1990*, Paul Holberton, London, 2009. The twelve collectors discussed are Sir Ashton Lever (1729-1788), Pitt Rivers (1827-1900), William Downing Webster (1868-1913), William Ockelford Oldman (1879-1949), Harry Geoffrey Beasley (1881-1939), Captain Alfred Walter Francis Fuller (1882-1961),William Ohly (1883-1955), James Thomas Hooper (1897-1971), James Keggie (1901-1985), Herbert F Rieser (1902-1978), Kenneth Athol Webster (1906-1967) and Kenneth John Hewett (1919-1994).

4 Brayer was working in the Department of Agriculture in Albuquerque when he started work on this biography. Letter to the Curator of the S&SWM dated 9th September 1941. Salisbury & South Wiltshire Museum (S&SWM) Blackmore archives.

be surpassed. However, Brayer (1913-1984), a Canadian, who in 1943 became the first State Archivist of the Colorado State Archives, was fortunate to have had direct access to a number of members of William Blackmore's immediate family, notably two of his nephews; Frank Stevens (1868-1949) and Robert Vanderveer Boyle (1885-after 1949), whose father, Arthur Boyle (1840-1910) had moved with his family to the Colorado and New Mexico area in 1871 to act as William's agent, finally settling in Santa Fe.[5]

Frank Stevens was a ten year old boy in the year in which his uncle William committed suicide and his father died. He was in his early seventies when he wrote a four page 'Biographical Notes of the Blackmore Family' for Brayer (dated 28th October 1941)[6] and also provided Brayer with information via a number of letters. Brayer and his wife and co-researcher visited England in 1947 to undertake research though he may have been unaware of relevant archival material still extant within William Blackmore's immediate family. Whether he might have gained access to such material remains a matter of conjecture.

Frank Stevens had been educated at Hurstpierpoint College in West Sussex and in early adult life had been the private secretary to the Rajah of Vizianagram (Pusapati Ananda Gajapati Raju (1879-1897)).[7] On the Rajah's death, Stevens became a lecturer on botany and zoology on which he wrote a number of books and articles and developed a significant professional reputation.[8]

5 Brayer was a significant professional archivist and was elected a vice-president of the Society of American Archivists in 1947. He was considered by contemporaries in the Colorado State Archive to be more focussed on his personal research than in his day job. In 1942 he was archivist and historian of the Denver and Rio Grande Railroad. By at least 1947 he had been appointed a 'Consultant for Archives' for UNESCO and was working in London as the Director of the Co-operative Project for Research in Western Americana in Europe (based in the Library of Congress). The following year he was hired for the Business History Writing Project at Northwestern University, Evanston, Illinois. Brayer's career at Northwestern was troubled.

6 A copy of this typescript document is in the S&SWM.

7 There was another Indian connection in that Frank's brother Alfred was at one time the private secretary to Fateh Jang Nawab Mir Mahboob Ali Khan Siddiqi, Asaf Jah VI (1869-1911) , the sixth Nizam of Hyderabad.

8 These included *Adventures in Hiveland*, Hutchinson, London, 1903; *Adventures in Pondland*, Hutchinson & Co., London , 1905; *By-Paths in Nature*, Religious Tract

Comparatively little is known about Frank Stevens' cousin, Robert Vanderveer Boyle who acted as a host to Brayer while he researched Arthur Boyle's relatively small collection of letters, ledgers, bills and miscellanea in the family Santa Fe home.

Brayer appears to have been sufficiently informed to piece together and place in the public domain the background and events leading to William Blackmore's suicide, an event that clearly was to dominate William's legacy. William's untimely demise clearly caused the family to close ranks and it was only some sixty years later that acknowledgement of his suicide and the basic details of his demise were first published. In a letter to Frank Stevens dated 12th May, 1942 Brayer wrote 'I deeply appreciate your courtesy and frankness in the matter of the Blackmore information which I requested. You may be certain that any information which you indicate as confidential will be so treated.'[9] Brayer wrote of his account of William's suicide that it 'was taken from written statements to the author by three descendants of the financier who gave permission to use the story, but requested that their names be withheld.' [10] Brayer noted that after William Blackmore's death his archives and papers had 'remained intact and untouched in the basement of the Blackmore Museum, Salisbury, Wiltshire, England. In 1935 [*sic*] these papers were carefully sorted and the greater portion of those dealing with Mr. Blackmore's American activities were secured for the State Historical Society of New Mexico. Unfortunately that portion dealing with William Blackmore's European activities was retained by the family and subsequently destroyed.'[11]

Society, London, 1906. Roddy Stevens, the great, great grandson of Edward Thomas Stevens, has informed the author that the Stevens family understood that Frank and his brother Alfred struggled to find employment in England and thus secured positions in India.

9 Letter dated 12th May, 1942. S&SWM Blackmore archives.

10 Brayer *op.cit.* volume 1, p.318 footnote 8. While Frank Stevens and Vanderveer Boyle were two sources, the third source has yet to be established, though was probably a member of Henry Blackmore's family. It seems that Brayer did not examine the publically available inquest verdict and related documents on William's death. These are still held in Westminster Abbey Muniments and conclusively indicate that William shot himself.

11 Brayer, *op.cit.*, Volume 1. p.351. The description of the collection [available at http://

Brayer may not have been given full access to surviving documents and papers. Some thirty years later, the Wiltshire Record Office (now the Wiltshire & Swindon History Centre in Chippenham) acquired a significant number of documents relating to William's business dealings in Europe and South America together with his brother Humphrey's household and practice papers. These were deposited, probably following probate administration, on 25th August 1965 by Jonas & Parker, later Parker Bullen, solicitors, of 45 Castle Street, Salisbury.[12] Could these be part of the material Brayer had previously stated had been destroyed? If so, probate for which member of the Blackmore or Stevens family? Possibly Frank Stevens' wife Jean Campbell Stevens who died aged 91 on the 8th March 1963 at the Spero Nursing Home in Salisbury.[13]

It is unclear whether the material relating to William's business dealings on Continental Europe during the 1850s and up to the early 1860s that was allegedly destroyed in the early 1930s held any 'family skeletons' for the Blackmore family. After Humphrey's death in 1929, a significant part of the archive of William Blackmore's material was acquired by the Historical Society of New Mexico through the intervention of the anthropologist Barbara Aitken (1879-1967) who in 1928 had bought a cottage in Broughton, Hampshire, some 13 miles east of Salisbury.[14] The date of acquisition by the Historical Society of

elibrary.unm.edu/oanm/NmSm/nmsm1%23ac018/] states; 'In 1932 Barbara Aitken, an anthropologist who worked with Edgar Lee Hewett (1865-1946), secured the Blackmore Papers for the Historical Society of New Mexico. The collection was transferred to the Museum of New Mexico History Library by the Historical Society of New Mexico.' It is probable that Humphrey Blackmore kept all William's papers in his home at Vale House since there was no 'basement' at the Blackmore Museum.

12 I thank Ben Daubney of Wiltshire & Swindon History Centre for this information. Parker Bullen have no surviving records related to these documents. The Blackmore papers formed only part of a larger set of papers of a number of Salisbury families donated by Jonas & Parker to the Wiltshire Record Office.

13 For an obituary of Jean Stevens, known at the Salisbury Museum as 'Mrs Steve', see the *Annual Report of the Salisbury & South Wilts Museum 1962-1966*, Salisbury, pp.8-9. She played an important and significant role in the museum. The obituary states the date of death was 3rd March 1963. Jean Stevens' effects were valued at £1021 2s. 7d. Alan Meek Barker, solicitor, was the sole executor. Probate Volume for 1963 p.800.

14 Brayer, *op.cit*, volume 1, p.47 footnote 45. Barbara Freire Marreco Aitken (1879-

New Mexico was 1932 and there is reference to Barbara Aitken acting on behalf of the executors of the Blackmore estate.[15] Brayer noted that Aitken 'was permitted to make a series of notes from Blackmore's European papers before they were destroyed by the heirs and executors of the estate of Dr. Humphrey Purnell Blackmore' and subsequently supplied a summary to Brayer in a letter dated 25th November 1938 [*sic* – for 1948?] though the location of Aitken's notes is currently unknown to the author.[16] Given Aitken's professional background as an anthropologist quite whether she was adequately equipped to make a comprehensive assessment of a substantial set of complex business documents remains open to question. Clearly, the Blackmore family trusted her judgement, though some references in William's diaries to his complex love life after his wife's death slipped through and might have been redacted by a more scrupulous editor.

Humphrey Blackmore also bequeathed, on the death of his wife Augusta, his house in St. Ann Street and some of his collections to the Salisbury Museum. In July 1929 Sotheby's held a number of auctions that included a wide range of items from Humphrey Blackmore collections.[17] Augusta Blackmore died in 1931 following which bulk of her husband's notable porcelain collection was sold in London though a

1967), née Freire Marreco, was a student at Lady Margaret Hall, University of Oxford and one of the first students to take the Diploma in Anthropology, for which she was awarded a distinction. She then became a Research Fellow at Somerville College, Oxford. Between 1910 and 1913 Friere Marreco made two field trips to the South West USA where she worked amongst the Tewa of Hano on behalf of the Pitt-Rivers Museum (to which she would later donate part of her collections). This 'important work' in ethnobotany was considered of sufficient significance that in 1914 it was reported in the 'University Intelligence' column of *The Times*. For a biography of Barbara Aitken, see Mary Ellen Blair, *A Life Well Led: The Biography of Barbara Friere-Marreco Aitken British Anthropologist*, Sunstone Press, Santa Fe, 2008.

15 *New Mexico Historical Review*, Volume 9, University of New Mexico, 1934 p.246.

16 Brayer, *op.cit*, Volume I, p.47 footnote 45.

17 Frank Stevens, *The Salisbury Museums 1861-1947*, Bennett Brothers, Salisbury [1948] p. 12. The British Museum web site refers to a donation by Blackmore to the British Museum found in the 1921-2 Report for the museum, p.8. The original valuation of Humphrey's estate at £1588 7s. 7d. was challenged and later resworn at £9,806 4s. 3d. This may have reflected the value of the items the executors sold at Sotheby's in July 1929.

gift of pottery and porcelain from his collection was made to the British Museum in this year. In 1932 Woolley & Wallis held a house sale of the remainder of his estate held at Humphrey's home, Vale House beside the Blackmore Museum.

More recently, an Englishman, the late Colin F. Taylor (1937-2004), wrote a number of articles about Blackmore. These were focussed on Blackmore's interest in North American Indians and his use of photography.[18] Just prior to his untimely death, Taylor had put forward a synopsis and sample chapter for a full biography on William Blackmore but unfortunately this project was never fulfilled.

In turn, during the late 20th century a number of photographic historians have highlighted Blackmore's key role in the use of photography to document North American Indians, notably Paula Richardson Fleming.[19] Blackmore's photographic publications are now highly prized and achieve significant sums at auction or when appearing amongst the stock of antiquarian book dealers.

Recently, all of the photographs from William Blackmore's collection held at the British Museum have been catalogued and placed online on the museum's web site. Comparison between similar web catalogues such as at the Newberry Library in Chicago and the Beinecke Library at Yale University have enabled cross referencing of Blackmore's

18 "Ho, for the Great West!' Indians and buffalo, exploration and George Catlin: the West of William Blackmore' in Barry C. Johnson, '*Ho for the Great West!' and other original papers to mark the 25th Anniversary of the English Westerners' Society*, Eatome Ltd. for The English Westerners' Society, London 1980 pp.9-49 and 'William Blackmore: A 19th Century Englishman's contribution to American Indian Ethnology', in Christian F. Feest (ed.), *Indians and Europe. An Interdisciplinary Collection of Essays*, University of Nebraska, Lincoln, 1999 pp.321-336. See also *Colin Taylor: Ethnologist of the Plains Indians. A Memoir: 1937-2004; Recollections by his Friends. A Bibliography of his Work. Edited by Barry C. Johnson.*, Bartletts Press, Birmingham, 2006.

19 For instance, see Paula R. Fleming & Judith L. Luskey, *Grand Endeavors of American Indian Photography*, Smithsonian Institution Press, Washington D.C., 1993 and Paula Richardson Fleming *Native American Photography at the Smithsonian – The Schindler Catalogue*, Smithsonian Books, Washington and London, 2003. In 2008 Sandra Camarda was awarded a Ph.D. by University College London for her thesis entitled *Journeys into the materiality of photographs: the case of the Blackmore Collection.* This followed on from her MA dissertation at University College London *The Blackmore collection. Issues of Authenticity in the Construction of a Fictionalised Imagery of the 'Wild West' Through Native American Indian Photographs.* 2001.

complex photographic publications. Web resources of full text scans of literally millions of books – such as the Internet Archive and Google Books[20] – have enabled the author a level of detailed research in short timescales unthinkable to the likes of Herbert Brayer.

Aspects of Blackmore's role as a patron of the fine arts have also been examined by Philip McEvansoneya who highlighted Blackmore as an early Liverpool patron of Dante Gabriel Rossetti.[21] The Englishman's commission of a series of aquarelles of the Yellowstone region from Thomas Moran is referred to in a wide range of the literature on Moran.[22]

William Blackmore's interpersonal skills, his business acumen and personal scholarly interests were a powerful combination that he successfully configured (and repeatedly reconfigured) to achieve wide ranging aims and objectives. He was an expert social networker who was regularly considered a congenial companion. Blackmore was ready to muck-in with the rest on his long trips into the West and endeared himself to those he travelled with. Conversely he had the social skills to mix with the upper echelons of society. However, he was not without weaknesses in his character and these coupled to the frequently high-risk nature of doing business in the 'Wild West' resulted in him becoming a particularly prominent casualty of the hundreds of mining, cattle, railroad, and land companies that failed in the same period. In a comment that resonates with the credit crunch of 2008, Brayer wrote 'The West had gone through a period of over-expansion, over-development, and in large measure its enterprises were over-financed.'[23] Blackmore had inexhaustible energy, optimism and persistence. His vision – used many times in his prospectuses, pamphlets and other publications –

20 http://www.archive.org/details/texts and http://books.google.com/

21 Philip McEvansoneya, 'William Blackmore, Patron of Dante Gabriel Rossetti', *Review of the Pre-Raphaelite Society*, 9, Spring 2001 pp.9-17 and 'William Blackmore, Patron of Dante Gabriel Rossetti and Robert Moran, and ethnographer of the United States', *Journal of Pre-Raphaelite Studies*, (12), 2003 p.62-73.

22 Such as Anne Morand, Anne. *Thomas Moran, The Field Sketches, 1856-1923*, University of Oklahoma, Norman, 1996; Nancy K. Anderson, *Thomas Moran*, National Gallery of Art, Washington, D.C, 1997 and Thurman Wilkins, *Thomas Moran –Artist of the Mountains*, 2nd edition. University of Oklahoma Press, Norman, 1998.

23 Brayer, *op.cit.*, Volume I, p.338.

was that 'Westward the course of Empire wends its Way.'[24] While this was ultimately true, and the business opportunities of the opening up and settlement of the West were realised, Blackmore's role was lost. His business failure impacted on his legacy of the Blackmore Museum and his bankruptcy and suicide – a combination that mid Victorian society found unacceptable – put the seal on marginalising him into relative obscurity.

With photographs from his publications and wider collections now highly prized and the museum in Salisbury celebrating its one hundred and fiftieth anniversary of its foundation, it seems both timely and appropriate for a contribution towards a biography of William Blackmore.

24 This quotation is attributed to Bishop George Berkeley (1685-1753), the early 18th Century Anglo-Irish philosopher, who conceived the idea that in the 'New World' all the evils of European society could be left behind. In his *Verses on the Prospect of Planting Arts and Learning in America* published in 1826, the final stanza commences 'Westward the course of empire takes its way'.

2

Early Years in Salisbury

William Henry Blackmore was born in Crane Street, Salisbury on 2nd August 1827. His father, William Bennett Blackmore (1796-1859) was a woollen draper, cloth merchant, silk mercer and carpet warehouseman in partnership with Thomas Ogden Stevens (1799-1883) trading as the firm of Stevens & Blackmore. William Bennett was a prominent figure in Salisbury business and was mayor for 1841.[1] In 1842 the firm's premises was located in Oatmeal Row. In December 1851 the partnership was dissolved, probably as part of the hand over to the next generation of the family. The 1855 *Post Office Directory of Wiltshire* recorded Stevens & Blackmore as 'outfitters, linen & woollen drapers' with premises in Oatmeal Row, Minster Street and the Market Place.' This subsequent partnership ran until March 1871 when William noted in his diary, 'Partnership of Stevens & Blackmore dissolved today. Lasted for 80 years.'[2]

William Bennett had acquired some considerable wealth and his proven will gave the value of his estate and effects as under £10,000 – the equivalent of several million pounds in the early 21st century. Two of William Bennett's younger siblings – Henry and Humphrey – became owners of the Wilton carpet factory in 1835.[3] William Henry's mother Eliza (née Eliza Sharpe Shorto) (c.1803-1887) was the daughter of Henry Shorto (1778-1864), master cutler and proprietor of a lucrative cutlery, jewellery

1 This position as mayor was mentioned by Frank Stevens in his appreciation of Humphrey Purnell Blackmore following his uncle's death in 1929. See *Wiltshire Archaeological and Natural History Magazine*, Volume 44 (CL). June 1929 pp.377-378.

2 Blackmore Diary No. 2, Thursday 23rd March, 1871 p.2.

3 Yates and Company acquired the carpet factory in the late 1880s.

and silversmith business in the city. She also appears to have influenced the interests of her sons William and Humphrey in geology. The Blackmore family lived at a succession of residences in Salisbury though William Bennett ended his days in Milford House on the eastern outskirts of the city.

Henry Shorto, who was listed in 1855 as a resident of Rollestone Street, was also a Wiltshire pioneer in geology and influenced his grandson in the formation of William's scientific and archaeological pursuits. It is also likely that William and Humphrey Blackmore inherited some of their grandfather's collections. Shorto retired in around 1835 – possibly finding that he could not compete with the cheaper mass-produced cutlery products of Sheffield and Birmingham – and devoted himself to the study of botany, plant physiology and geology. A liberal with a keen appreciation of the fine arts, he had a lively interest in social reform and he may, around 1820, have founded a 'museum' in Salisbury to display his collection.[4] Indeed, William Blackmore's personal and professional interests – along with his brother Humphrey – were to be heavily influenced and supported by a wide range of members of his immediate family in Salisbury. Quite what books, prints, archaeological artefacts and fine and decorative art surrounded Blackmore in his childhood and adolescence have yet to be established.

Comparatively little is known of William Blackmore's childhood and early adult life in Salisbury. In 1830 there were some twenty-two private schools in Salisbury – twelve for boys and ten for girls. William might have attended the preparatory school 'for a limited number of young gentlemen' that was run in The Close by the Misses Sarah and Ann Noyes from about 1830 until at least 1846. Of more significance was the school set up by Henry Hatcher (1777–1846), the historian of Salisbury, in Fisherton in 1822, which moved to Endless Street in 1824 where it flourished until his death. There is no evidence that William attended Hatcher's school, though his brother in law Edward Stevens did,[5] and it would seem likely that if William had done so he would have

4 See Hugh S. Torrens, 'A Wiltshire Pioneer in Geology and his Legacy : Henry Shorto III (1778-1864), Cutler and Fossil Collector of Salisbury' *Wiltshire Archaeological and Natural History Magazine*, Volume 83, 1990 pp. 170-189.

5 R. W. H. Willoughby, 'The Salisbury and South Wilts Museum: Founded 1860',

subsequently mentioned this fact and the influence of Hatcher.[6]

William Blackmore clearly had an appetite for education from an early age. Some insights into William's desire not only to learn but also to promote learning in others come from comments made by his uncle, John Lambert (1815-1892), in a speech given at the formal opening of the Blackmore Museum. Lambert mentioned an incident connected with Blackmore's childhood and his 'desire to promote and diffuse knowledge'. 'After a long and laborious day of study, he had known Mr. Blackmore, when a mere boy, go into the neighbouring village of Harnham, [a southerly suburb of Salisbury located across the River Avon] regularly every night of the week for the purpose of giving instruction to the children of the agricultural labourers.'[7] Late in his life he was discussing his intention to found a college in Colorado. Blackmore also donated books to small, newly formed libraries. In 1877 the El Paso County Library Association acknowledged receipt of 'one hundred and sixty-four volumes of standard books from William Blackmore.'[8] On news of his death it was noted by the *Colorado Springs Gazette* that Blackmore 'had always manifested a great interest in this country, and contributed several hundred very valuable books to our county library.[9]

William's secondary education was at King's College, Bruton in Somerset, the school at which a number of his relatives were educated.[10] Subsequently, William was articled with his uncle John Lambert of the Salisbury firm of solicitors Lambert and Norton. In 1849, having

Wiltshire Archaeological and Natural History Magazine, Volume 57 Number CCVIII, Devizes, 1960 pp.314.

6 'Salisbury: Social life', *A History of the County of Wiltshire*, Volume 6 , Oxford University Press, London, 1962 pp. 141-144. See also John Britton, *Memoirs of the Life, Writings, and Character of Henry Hatcher*, Printed for J. Britton, to accompany his Auto-biography,1847. Britton gives few insights into Hatcher's activities in Salisbury.

7 *Account of the Blackmore Museum – Part I. The Opening Meeting*, H.F. & E. Bull, Devizes; Bell & Daldy, London ; J.R. Smith, London 1868 pp.82-83.

8 *Colorado Springs Gazette*, Saturday, 9th June, 1877 p.2.

9 *Colorado Springs Gazette*, Saturday, 8th June, 1878 p.7.

10 Thomas Augustus Strong, *Bruton Register. A Calendar of the Master and Pupils, &c., from 1826 to 1890*, Frowde, 1894 p.39.

qualified, William moved to Liverpool and joined firm of solicitors, Duncan, Squarey and Duncan.[11]

A comprehensive study of Victorian Salisbury has yet to be written.[12] Thus evaluation of the environment – business, cultural and social – in which William Blackmore grew up is somewhat constrained. Between 1831 and 1851 the population of Salisbury actually declined. In 1831 the population of the city, parishes and The Close was 9,876 which declined to 9,455 in 1851. The population of the city parishes, The Close together with the suburbs of Fisherton and Milford was 11,895 in 1831 and had declined to 11,657 by 1851.[13] While there was little major industrial manufacturing in Salisbury, this decline in population belies a fundamental and long lasting characteristic of the city. Salisbury has remained prosperous as a result of its wide catchment area and role as a market town. There was a striking variety of craft trades in Victorian Salisbury. There were seven watch- and clock-makers and ten cutlers listed in Pigot's trade directory of 1830. The 1841 census recorded twenty tanners and curriers in Salisbury.[14]

11 Blackmore was listed as having passed the exam during the Easter Term, 1849. *The Legal Observer, Digest, and Journal of Jurisprudence, Volume XXXVIII, May 1849 to October 1849*, Alexander Maxwell, London, 1849 p.49.

12 There are a range of titles that include coverage of mid 19th century Salisbury. They include T.J. Northy, *The Popular History of Old & New Sarum*, Wiltshire County Mirror & Express' Co., Salisbury, 1897; Elizabeth Crittal (ed.). *A History of the County of Wiltshire: Volume 6*, Victoria County History, London, 1962; John Chandler, *Endless Street*, Hobnob Press, Salisbury, 1983; Ruth Newman and Jane Howells, *Salisbury Past*, Phillimore & Co Ltd, Chichester, 2001; Bruce Purvis, *Salisbury: the changing city*, Breedon Books, 2003; D. Cross, *Salisbury: a history and celebration*, Frith Book Co for Ottakar's, Teffont, 2004. A number of articles on notable figures in mid Victorian Salisbury can be found in periodical and serial publications such as the *Wiltshire Archaeological and Natural History Magazine, The Hatcher Review* and *Sarum Chronicle*. Jane Howells has written a detailed study of the important role of women in Victorian Salisbury. Jane Howells, *Independent women in public life in Salisbury in the second half of the nineteenth century*. Ph.D., University of London, 2007.

13 Figures at http://www.wiltshire.gov.uk/community/getcensus.php?item=Salisbury accessed on 22nd July 2010. These figures do not account for boundary changes. I thank Jane Howells for explaining the intricacies of these figures.

14 See Jane Howells, *Independent women in public life in Salisbury in the second half of the nineteenth century.*, Ph.D., University of London, 2007.

During the 1840s there was a small number of stationers, booksellers and print sellers trading in Salisbury. These included Brodie & Co., Brown & Co. in The Canal, Clapperton in Catherine Street and, from 1848, Frederick A. Blake in the Market Place.[15] Whether William Blackmore first came across books and prints on 'Red Indians' at these establishments must be left to conjecture though the North American Indian had become a significant subject in the British imagination from the late eighteenth and early nineteenth centuries, especially in literature. The Romantic poets—William Wordsworth, Samuel Taylor Coleridge, Robert Southey, and Felicia Hemans—depicted fictional Indians as free spirits, noble savages endowed with a natural spirituality and living in harmony with their environment.[16] However, in October 1876 Blackmore wrote that 'during the last thirty years it has been my constant effort to collect and read all that has been written relative to these Aborigines' implying that by the late 1840s he was actively engaged in the study of North American Indians.[17]

Salisbury offered a few formal environments to satiate William Blackmore's appetite to acquire knowledge. There was no museum or public library. The Salisbury and Wiltshire Library and Reading Society was established in 1819, 'to promote literary and social intercourse', 'to establish a permanent reference library, circulate books among its subscribers', and provide a reading room for newspapers and 'ephemeral publications'. In the 1830s it had premises in the former Blue Boar Inn on the Market Place. In December 1820 the members resolved to open an apartment for the reception and arrangement of fossil specimens.[18]

15 Blake worked for Brodie and took over his business after Brodie went bankrupt. I thank Jane Howells for pointing this link out to me. By 1855 other listed booksellers included John Hearne and George Pittman, both of Silver Street, and T. A. Saunders and William Whereat, both of Winchester Street. See *Hodson's Booksellers, Publishers and Stationers' Directory*, W. H. Hodson, London, 1855 p.55.

16 See Robert M. Lewis, 'Wild American Savages and the Civilized English: Catlin's Indian Gallery and the shows of London', *European Journal of American Studies*, 1, 2008 at http://ejas.revues.org/2263 accessed on 27th August, 2010.

17 Blackmore writing in his Introduction to Richard Irving Dodge, *The Hunting Grounds of the Great West: A description of the plains, game, and Indians of the great North American Desert*, Chatto & Windus, London, 1877. p.xv.

18 See Hugh S. Torrens, *op.cit.*, p.184.

It is not clear whether this 'museum' ever materialised, or if it did whether it was transferred at the end of 1846 when the Library and Reading Society was re-opened under improved management 'at the Printing Office on the Canal'. This reading society certainly held scholarly works for in 1827 it was reported that Sir Richard Colt Hoare (1758-1838) had donated 'splendid works' as had the Rev. James Ingram (1774-1850), Anglo-Saxon scholar and President of Trinity College, Oxford, who had enriched the society with a copy of his *The Saxon Chronicle, with an English Translation, and Maps, Plates of coins . . . etc.* published in 1823.[19]

A Mechanics' Institute providing weekly lectures was opened in Salisbury in 1833. While it allegedly flourished for a number of years it had ceased to exist by the early 1840s. A Literary and Scientific Institution was founded in 1850, the year after William left for Liverpool. William's scholarly interests are therefore likely to have been primarily influenced by his grandfather Henry Shorto and his circle of local antiquarians and collectors. The likely role of Henry Hatcher (1777-1846), school master and local historian, and Dr. Richard Fowler (1765-1863), within this context is particularly relevant. The two were central figures in the circle of historians and antiquarians in Salisbury and had collaborated in examining the site of Clarendon Palace. Another significant local collector was the Reverend Edward Duke (1779-1852) of Lake House in the Avon valley north of Salisbury.[20] However, it is noticeable that while William Blackmore made but the slightest of references to Fowler in his address at the opening of his eponymous museum, he made no reference to Hatcher at all. This is a curious omission that has yet to be explained.[21]

19 *The New Monthly Magazine and Universal Register,* 1st May, 1827 p.222. For an account of libraries in Salisbury see B. M. Little, *A History of Libraries in Salisbury, 1850-1922,* M.Phil dissertation, Polytechnic of North London, 1980.

20 Duke was both a fellow of the Society of Antiquaries and the Linnean Society. His eldest son, Edward (1814-1895), also a clergyman, succeeded to his estates. The Duke collection was sold at auction by Sotheby, Wilkinson & Hodge on 10th July 1895. Augustus Wollaston Franks bought most of the objects for the British Museum.

21 'Mr. William Blackmore's Address', *Some Account of the Blackmore Museum – Part I. The Opening Meeting,* H.F. & E. Bull, Devizes; Bell & Daldy, London ; J.R. Smith, London, 1868 p.62.

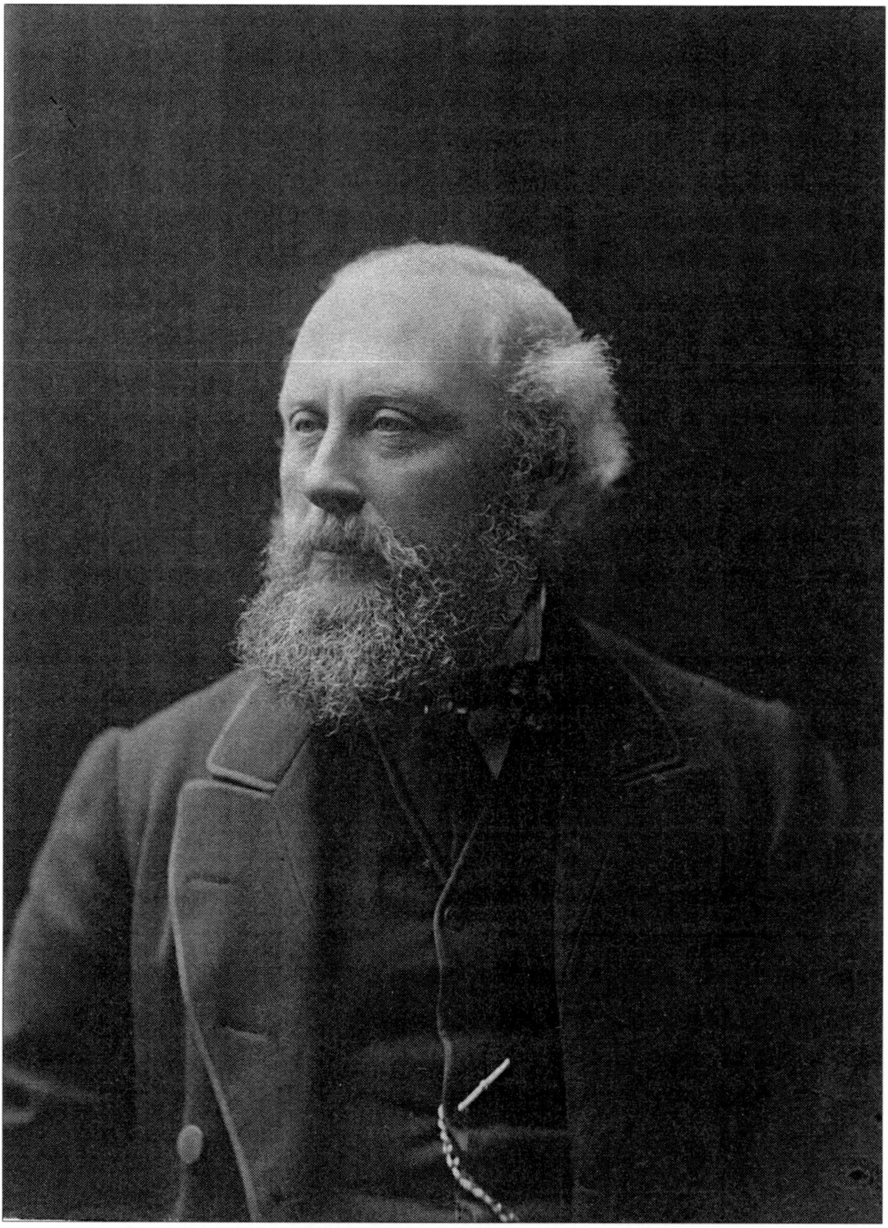

Edward Thomas Stevens (1828-1878)
Albumen print
Courtesy of Salisbury & South Wiltshire Museum

Hatcher, a considerable linguist, being fluent in French, Dutch, German, Spanish and Portuguese, frequently contributed to Salisbury and Devizes newspapers on matters of local interest, such as the article on Clarendon Palace that appeared in the Salisbury Journal in August 1844. In 1834 his *An Historical and Descriptive Account of Old and New Sarum* was published. In 1835 Sir Richard Colt Hoare (1758-1838) renewed an offer he had previously made to Hatcher that he should compile the Salisbury part of *The History of Modern Wiltshire* published between 1822 and 1844. Hatcher was given the material collected by Richard Benson, a barrister and the recorder of Salisbury. Benson and Hatcher were to fall out over the crediting of the volume on *Old and New Sarum, or Salisbury*, which was published in 1843, to their joint authorship.

Little has been established about how the historians and antiquarians in and around Salisbury met, exchanged views and examined each other's collections. How directly involved William and Humphrey Blackmore and their future brother in law Edward Stevens were with this circle during the 1840s must be left to conjecture, but the zeal they subsequently displayed for local geology indicates both real interest and commitment.

William was the eldest of seven children born to William and Eliza Blackmore; three sons and four daughters. Several of William's siblings were to become directly involved in his business activities in the USA as were his cousin George Lear Blackmore and his sister-in-law, Margaret Hamp. The Blackmore and Stevens families were also to play a central role in the creation of a museum in Salisbury and the management of William Blackmore's eponymous museum. It is therefore worthwhile documenting some basic facts about William's siblings and immediate family.

Henry (1828-1907)

Henry followed his father's profession and became a Salisbury draper in partnership with Edward Thomas Stevens (1828-1878) (*see ill. p. 17*). In 1855 he was resident in Minster Street but in 1867 was resident in

Crane Street, perhaps his father's former house, William Bennett having moved to Milford House in the eastern suburb of Salisbury. Henry, together with his brothers Humphrey and William, was instrumental in the founding of the Salisbury & South Wiltshire Museum in the early 1860s. He had a specific interest in ornithology and catalogued the new museum's collection of stuffed birds.[22] However, Henry was commercially relatively unsuccessful and around 1871 emigrated to America with his wife Charlotte Polhill (1832-1890), who had worked at the Godolphin School in Salisbury before marrying Henry in 1858. They spent a short time in New York, St. Louis and Denver and then moved to Colorado where they settled in the San Luis Valley on the tract of the Sangre de Cristo Grant owned by William Blackmore. Henry's ranch was near Monte Vista, Rio Grande County, Colorado and was named 'Cottonwood Cove Ranch'. He raised some nine children, seven of whom were born in Salisbury and two born in San Luis Culebra, Colorado. Henry became a successful rancher and farmer. He also acted as an agent and business partner for his brother William. Henry was reported to have returned to live in England for five years during the 1890s, probably after his wife's death, before returning to Colorado.[23]

Agnes (1830-1905)

Agnes, the eldest sister, married her second cousin John Senior (1820-1888), a noted solicitor of 2 New Inn (attached to Middle Temple in London), at St. Martin's Church, Salisbury in January 1858.[24] Senior was

22 Henry exhibited 'a large case of stuffed British birds, some of great rarity in this country' in the 'Temporary Museum' of the annual meeting of the Wiltshire Archaeological and Natural History Society held in Salisbury on 13th, 14th and 15th September, 1865. *Wiltshire Archaeological and Natural History Magazine*, Volume IX, 1866 p.38.

23 Obituary in *Monte Vista Journal*, Saturday, 26th January, 1907 as reproduced on http://www.findagrave.com/cgi-bin/fg.cgi?page=gr&GRid=42326157

24 *The Times*, Friday, 15th January, 1858 p.1. 'On the 13th inst., at St. Martin's Church, Salisbury, by the Reverend W.W. Tatum, rector, John Senior, of New Inn, London, solicitor, to Agnes, eldest daughter of William Blackmore, Esq., of Milford House, Salisbury.' Senior was the son of Lewis Gooden Senior (1786-1844) who took the surname Husey Hunt, which was a combination of the surnames of the previous owners of the estate of Compton Pauncefoot bequeathed to Lewis Gooden's wife Elizabeth Hussey.

a member of a noted Wiltshire family who lived in Compton Castle, Compton Pauncefoot near Castle Cary, Somerset. This had been built c.1825 for John Senior's father Lewis Gooden Senior (1786-1844) who changed his name to Hussey-Hunt. The 1881 census records John and Agnes living with their son and three daughters at 10 Park Road, Lambeth. Senior died in 1888 at 7 Court Road, West Dulwich, in South London. Agnes was recorded as living in The Hermitage, Crane Bridge Road in Salisbury at the time of her death.[25] Of all William Blackmore's siblings, Agnes seems to have had the least to do with his business dealings and related investment opportunities.

Ellen (1831-1884)

In September 1852, Ellen married a cousin, Edward Thomas Stevens (1828-1878), draper and partner of Henry Blackmore of the firm of Stevens and Blackmore (successor to Blackmore and Stevens until Henry moved to Colorado). Ellen and Edward had five children.[26]

Edward Stevens was educated in the private school of the Salisbury antiquarian Henry Hatcher in Endless Street. He became the first secretary and treasurer of the Salisbury Museum in 1860 and then honorary curator of the Blackmore Museum alongside his brother-in-law Humphrey Blackmore.

Stevens participated in excavations in and around Salisbury, at Grime's Grave in Norfolk and visited the Valley of the Somme, near Abbeville, France where Jacques Boucher de Crèvecœur de Perthes (1788-1868), more commonly referred to as Boucher de Perthes, had in around 1830 excavated flint instruments that led him to be the first to establish that Europe had been populated by early man. This theory was finally vindicated in 1859 when Charles Darwin published his *On the Origin of Species*.

25 See http://www.archerfamily.org.uk/family/senior.htm

26 The 1871 census found the Stevens family at 25 Cheesemarket, Salisbury. The Stevens children were listed as Edward (1853-1946), a student of law, aged seventeen; Alfred (1855-1921), aged sixteen; Ernest (1860-1913), aged ten; Owen (1865-?), aged four and two year old Frank (1868-1949).

During the 1860s and 1870s Stevens became a distinguished member of the scholarly establishment. In 1865 he became the Salisbury secretary of the Wiltshire Archaeological and Natural History Society and was a member of the committee of the International Congress of Prehistoric Archaeology held in Norwich and London in August 1868. He was elected a fellow of the Geological Society of London and became a member of the Anthropological Institute. Stevens developed an international reputation, in 1876, the year of his election as a Fellow of the Society of Antiquaries of London, he was elected a correspondent of the Academy of Natural Sciences of Philadelphia. He also became a Foreign Member of the Anthropological Institute of New York.

In 1872 John Henry Rivett-Carnac (1839-1923), an antiquary who had been a member of the Bengal Civil Service, visited Edward Stevens at his home above his family draper's shop in Minster Street. 'In the ten minutes during which we awaited our host, we had an opportunity of admiring his excellent library of antiquarian books and the signed photographs which adorned the walls, the gifts of many of the most distinguished scientific men of our own country and the Continent.'[27] Following his death on 18th August 1878, on the 14th to the 16th November the entire contents of Edward Stevens' home at 19 and 21 Minster Street, Salisbury were auctioned on site by Marsh, Dawes and Dear. Lot 635 refers to a 'set of photographs (framed), portraits of archaeologists.' It is unclear whether this house sale was necessitated by Stevens' debts related to William Blackmore's failed business ventures. Similarly, the possibility that Stevens died as a direct result of the stress brought about by his financial liabilities cannot be ruled out though obituaries did refer to his having had a long illness. His estate and effects were valued at probate as under £6,000, a considerable sum. However, what debts needed to be serviced from this sale of his estate remains unclear. After his death a memorial fund was established and

27 J. H. Rivett-Carnac, *Many Memories of Life in India at Home and Abroad*, William Blackwood, Edinburgh ; London, 1910 p.256. Rivett-Carnac had been a civil servant in India for much of his professional life. He had an interest in prehistoric archaeology. See his obituary in *The Times*, 14th May, 1923 p.7.

within matter of months had raised £500.[28]

Frank Stevens, was the youngest of Edward and Ellen Stevens' children. He was appointed the first professional 'Controller' (from July 1938 his title changed to Director) of the Salisbury & South Wiltshire Museum from 1913, and died in Salisbury on 9th November 1949, thus providing from the Stevens and Blackmore families almost a century of continuous involvement and management of the Salisbury and Blackmore museums.[29] As previously noted, in the early 1940s Frank Stevens provided biographical information for Herbert Oliver Brayer that was subsequently used in Brayer's monumental study *William Blackmore, a case study in the economic development of the West* published in 1949.

Frank Stevens played a pivotal role in the history of the Salisbury Museum and the fate of the collections of his uncle William. He became highly respected within museum circles, was elected Fellow of the Society of Antiquaries and was awarded an Order of the British Empire. On his death the *Museums Journal* stated that 'the Museum World has lost one of its elder statesmen.'[30]

Eliza ['Fanny'] (1831-1916)

Little is known about Eliza Blackmore, a maiden sister. She exhibited a number of paintings at the 1852 exhibition of 'Local Industry, Amateur Productions, Works of Art etc.'[31] Eliza was recorded in the 1881 census as living with her mother Eliza S. Blackmore at the home of her brother Humphrey. Eliza was still resident there at the time of the 1891 census but not at the time of the following census in 1901. In 1879 an Eliza Blackmore was a co-founder with her sister Ellen Stevens of the School of Art Needlework in Endless Street and in the same year Brayer noted

28 *The Hampshire Advertiser*, Saturday 1st February, 1879 p.7.

29 *The Times*, Saturday, 12th November,1949; p.1 'Deaths.' The probate record gives the date of death as 10th November 1949. Frank Stevens died in the Spero Nursing Home in Salisbury, leaving effects of some £7702 2s. 1d. Frank's elder brother Edward had also moved into the same nursing home.

30 *Museums Journal*, 1949 p.246.

31 Eliza exhibited four portraits, a study of 'Birds from Nature', a Sketch near Lewes, a watercolour and a portrait of an Old Woman.

she visited her brother William's Mexican adobe mansion on the lower Culebra in Colorado, though it is unclear exactly why.[32] It is probable that Eliza was acting on behalf of her brother Humphrey who was involved in finding a solution to the perilous state of their late brother's estate. Brayer reproduced Eliza's painting of the property in his biography of Blackmore. Eliza Blackmore died in Salisbury in 1916.

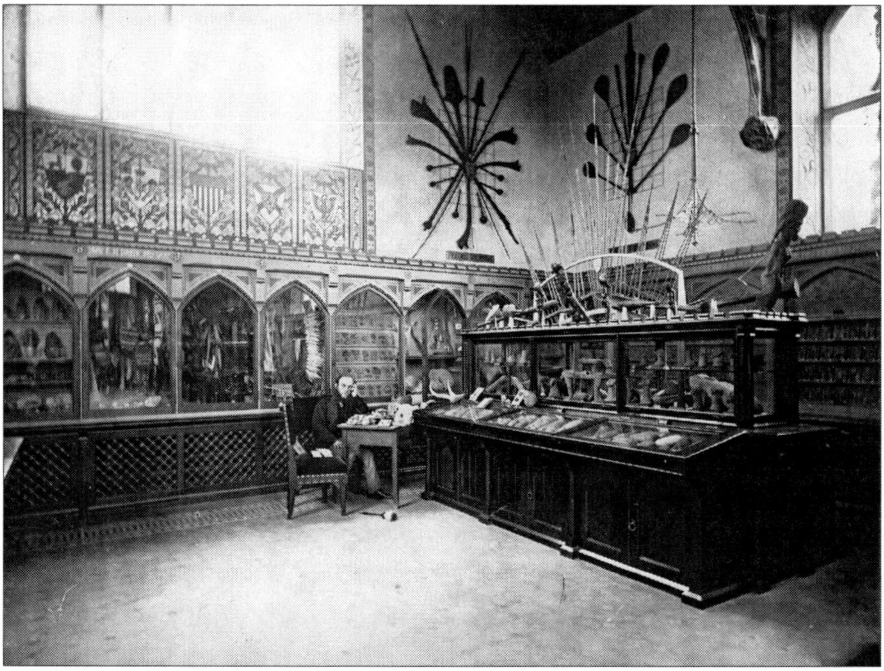

Humphrey Blackmore seated in the Blackmore Museum c.1870.
Albumen print
Courtesy of Salisbury & South Wiltshire Museum

Dr. Humphrey Purnell (1836-1929)

Humphrey Purnell Blackmore was a prominent Salisbury physician and surgeon who studied local geology and formed a significant collection

32 *Salisbury Journal*, 5th April 1879 p.5 announcing the opening of the school, and 10th May 1879 p.8 reporting on the event. Eliza's sister Ellen Stevens was one of the other co-founders. I thank Jane Howells for these references.

of artefacts and a notable collection of porcelain. His collections are exemplified by the items he exhibited in the 'Temporary Museum' in Salisbury in January 1862, an exhibition he had helped organise. These include flint implements, a brass tobacco box and a snuff-rasp. Humphrey was a founder, trustee and one of the two honorary curators of the Blackmore Museum – the other being his brother-in-law Edward Stevens. 1878 proved to be an *annus horribilis* for Humphrey for in that year his brother William committed suicide and his brother-in-law Edward died. Humphrey thus took over the sole responsibility for the Salisbury and Blackmore museums, a position that he held until 1913 and the appointment of his nephew Frank Stevens as the museum's first professional curator. Humphrey's interests also included natural history and he owned a copy of the first edition of Charles Darwin's *On the Origin of Species*. What influence Darwin's writings had on Humphrey's scholarly interests and whether it played any roles in the classification and typologies employed at the Blackmore Museum remains unclear.[33]

Humphrey Blackmore was educated at Queenwood College, a pioneering, liberal institution for science education, situated between Buckholt and East Tytherley near Stockbridge. It had been founded in 1847 by a Quaker George Edmundson (1798-1863) and burnt down in 1903.[34] In 1851 he was recorded as a pupil of William Martin Coates (1811-1885), an honorary surgeon at the Salisbury Infirmary, and was

33 A copy of this title, printed in an edition of 1250 and considered one of the most important single works in science, with Humphrey Blackmore's signature dated December 1859, was offered in 2008 by Bauman Rare Books for US$197,000. There is an uncorroborated claim from a member of the Blackmore family that William Blackmore acted as Darwin's solicitor. http://en.wikipedia.org/wiki/William_Henry_Blackmore.

34 D. Thompson, 'Queenwood College, Hampshire; A mid-19th century experiment in science teaching', *Annals of Science*, Volume 11, Number 3, Number 3/September 1955 , pp. 246-254. See also Colin A Russell ' *Edward Frankland: Chemistry, Controversy & Conspiracy in Victorian England*', Cambridge University Press, Cambridge, 1996, chapter 3. I thank Jane Howells for pointing this reference out to me. The 1851 census found Humphrey a fifteen year old student at Queenwood College. One of Humphrey's contemporaries was Henry Fawcett (1833- 1884), who had been blinded in a shooting accident in 1858. He was subsequently appointed Professor of Political Economy at Cambridge University in 1863 and became Member of Parliament for Brighton in 1865.

'permitted to attend the Infirmary in order that he may benefit by the practice of the house.'[35] Humphrey then studied medicine at St Andrew's University and then at St. Bartholomew's Hospital in London where he won first prize in Surgery, Medicine and Physiology. Having qualified in 1855 Humphrey returned to Salisbury in 1856 and became one of the doctors to the Salisbury Provident Club.[36] On 26th March 1857 was admitted a member of the Apothecaries' Hall and on the following 3rd April became a member of the Royal College of Surgeons. [37] In the same year he and became a partner of the surgeons' practice of Coates and Blackmore of Endless Street and in 1860 he applied to become surgeon to the Salisbury Infirmary.

Humphrey was to become one of the most notable general medical practitioners to have worked in Salisbury as well as acting as surgeon to a number of the medical clubs in and around the city. Another of his roles was as physician to the Fisherton Lunatic Asylum.[38] He became a Licentiate of the Society of Apothecaries in 1867. In 1868 he was appointed as representative of the Poor-Law Medical Service for the parishes of the City of Salisbury.[39] He was listed as a Physician at Salisbury Infirmary from 1874 until 1879, when he resigned.[40] On 26th June 1878 Humphrey was one of the members of the Southern Branch of the British Medical Association to host lunch for colleagues attending the fifth annual branch meeting in Salisbury and in the afternoon led a visit to the Blackmore Museum.[41] In 1908 Humphrey became a member of the Medico-Psychological Association of Great Britain and

35 Charles Haskins, *The History of Salisbury Infirmary*, Salisbury & District Infirmary & Hospital League, Salisbury, 1922 p.19.

36 A Salisbury Provident Dispensary had been founded in 1852 by Bishop Walter Kerr Hamilton (1808-1869). Dispensaries were often linked to medical clubs where subscribers were eligible for the benefits of medical care.

37 *The Times*, Thursday, 9th April, 1857 p.10.

38 P. M. S. Gillam, *A History of General Practice in and around Salisbury*, Salisbury Medical Bulletin, Supplement to Number 97, January 2000 p.15 which is an account of Humphrey Blackmore's career as a one of 'Two Notable Doctors.'

39 *Medical Times and Gazette*, December, 1868 p.686.

40 Charles Haskins, *op.cit.*, p.42.

41 *British Medical Journal*, 1878 p.909.

Ireland. The time available to Humphrey to dedicate to the Blackmore Museum should be seen within the context of his extensive professional commitments.

Vale House, 44 St Ann Street, next door to the Salisbury and Blackmore museums, was Humphrey's home and he left the property to the museum on his death. He was recorded as living there by at least 1867. He married Augusta Sophia (c.1847-1931) on 23rd October, 1877 at St. George's Church, Hanover Square, London but there were no children from the marriage.[42] In the 1881 census he was again recorded as resident at Vale House, where he was living with his mother and sister Eliza. His wife was not resident at the time of the census.

Humphrey was a member or honorary member of numerous scholarly societies such as the Wiltshire Archaeological and Natural History Society, the Geological Society (elected a fellow in 1890), the Zoological Society of London, the Palaeontographical Society and the Hampshire Field Club. He gave papers to a number of these and published articles up to the early 1920s.[43] Humphrey's geological researches in Wiltshire were used within the Geological Survey of the United Kingdom.

In Salisbury, Humphrey was an active and prominent member of the Elias de Derham chapter of the Freemasons. In 1873 he held the office of Excellent Z and was the Provincial Grand Registrar in 1876.[44]

William Blackmore's diaries indicate that he would travel the eighty-five miles from London to Salisbury to stay for little more than twenty-four hours. He appears to have stayed with his brother Humphrey while visiting Salisbury and was there in 1871 when that year's census

42 The marriage was noted in *The Medical Times and Gazette: A Journal of medical Science, Literature...*, London, 1877 p.479. This may have been Humphrey's second marriage since the Court for Divorce and Matrimonial Causes has a record of a Humphrey Purnell Blackmore as an appellant in an 1867 divorce case with a Annie Laurie Mills otherwise Annie Laurie Blackmore as the respondent. See The National Archives, Kew J 77/80/639. The register of Divorces and Matrimonial Causes refers to Annie Laurie Mills 'falsely calling herself Blackmore'.

43 A short note by Humphrey Blackmore on The Piltdown Flints was published in *MAN* , July, 1923 pp.98-99.

44 Frederick Hastings Goldney, *A History of Freemasonry in Wiltshire,* Virtue & Co., London 1880. p.197. The chapter was founded in 1867.

was being carried out. Humphrey Blackmore was closely linked with an unclear number of his brother's business activities and was the executor of William Blackmore's estate. He died in Vale House, Salisbury on Saturday 2nd February 1929 at the age of 93 and was buried in the London Road Cemetery.

Humphrey was sufficiently well known as a geologist for his obituary to appear in *The Times* that noted 'His researches covered practically every field of archaeology, and he had valuable collections in his house at Salisbury.' His nephew, Frank Stevens, gave a more accurate view when stating 'His private collections were extraordinarily varied.'[45] Following his death, parts of Humphrey's collections were sold at auctions held by Sotheby's in July 1929. Some of his collection of Sèvres porcelain was acquired by the British Museum in 1931. Blackmore also had a significant collection of Bristol porcelain.[46] The 'remainder' of the collections of Humphrey's estate were auctioned in Vale House by Woolley and Wallis in March 1932.

As previously mentioned, after his death, Humphrey's archive of his brother's material seems to have been largely acquired by the Historical Society of New Mexico through the intervention of the anthropologist Barbara Aitken. Robert Stirling Newall (died 1978), an archaeologist who assisted Colonel William Hawley (1851-1941) on his excavations of Stonehenge between 1919 and 1926 and who had a close connection with Salisbury Museum, may have been party to these negotiations and selection.[47] Edward Stevens (1853-1946) – Humphrey's nephew, the eldest son of Edward Thomas Stevens – acted as the executor

45 *The Times*, Wednesday 6th February, 1929 p.19. See *Wiltshire Archaeological and Natural History Magazine*, Volume CL. June 1929 pp.377-378. Probate of Humphrey's will was granted on 22nd February, 1929 to Edwards Stevens, his nephew, as sole executor. Humphrey's effects were listed as £1588 7s. 7d. but then resworn (on a date unknown) as £9806 4s. 6d., presumably as a result of the various sales of Humphrey's estate at Sotheby.

46 Blackmore contributed information to Hugh Owen for his *Two centuries of ceramic art in Bristol, a history of the manufacture of 'the true porcelain' by R. Champion, with a biography*. Bell and Daldy, London, 1873.

47 This was mentioned in a paper on 'Unsung Heroes of Archaeology in Salisbury Museum' given by Adrian Green on behalf of Peter Saunders at the conference celebrating 150 years of Salisbury Museum held on 2nd October 2010.

of Humphrey's estate. Significantly, Humphrey's will specifically named as a beneficiary William Polhill Blackmore (1860-1956), a nephew – son of Henry and Charlotte Blackmore – who lived in Baggs, Wyoming. Humphrey's household and practice papers covering the period 1853-1913 are now held at the Wiltshire & Swindon History Centre.

The evidence within Brayer's two volumes identifies several members of Blackmore's immediate family as being directly involved in his business dealings – forming part of his 'pool' of investors. These included his brothers Humphrey and Henry, his sister, Ellen, and his sister-in-law Margaret Hamp. Humphrey seems to have had the most substantial commercial interest related to William's business activities. Brayer gives a detailed account of how, after his brother's death, Humphrey Blackmore struggled to protect his own remaining business interests and itemised the level of some of Humphrey's investments. These included a single subscription of £1,000 for 10 shares in one land grant in 1872, and £9,500 in 1877 for the Mora-Cebolla-Los Luceros programme.[48] These very significant sums, possibly indicate that the 'skeletons' may well have been more those of Humphrey's than William's.

These amounts of personal investment point to Humphrey having relatively significant private wealth, probably built on the success of the family firm of Stevens & Blackmore and the family connection to the Wilton Carpet factory, owned since 1835 by Humphrey's uncles, Henry and Humphrey Blackmore. He was unlikely to have accrued as much as £1,000 per annum by working as a medical practitioner in a provincial city, even when adding together his income as a Poor-Law medical officer, hospital physician and dispenser of medicines in Salisbury.

Blanche (1839-1931)

Blanche married Arthur Boyle (1840-1910) in 1877, and in the same year went to live in Colorado and New Mexico, where her husband became the resident manager of William Blackmore's New Mexico land grants in Rio de Chama. Arthur Boyle later became a florist, though his original

48 Brayer, op.cit., volume I p.224 and p.249.

interests in England were cited as being in mining. He planned and developed the Clarendon Gardens in Santa Fe, the oldest gardens in the state, and planted orchards in the suburb of Buena Vista.[49] He became a prominent member of the Santa Fe community, was a founder and president of the New Mexico Horticultural Society and the secretary of the Santa Fe Tertio-Millennial Anniversary Association. He also served as the secretary of the Santa Fe Chamber of Commerce.

Arthur and Blanche's son, Robert Vanderveer (1885-after 1949), trained and worked as a surveyor for several years and was connected with the state land office. He then became proprietor of the family florist business at Clarendon Gardens and stood 'among the leaders in this business in Santa Fe.'[50] He was instrumental in keeping the memory of his uncle alive, working closely during the 1940s with Herbert Brayer, the biographer of his uncle William. Brayer appears to have written a large part of his book on William Blackmore at R. Veer Boyle's home in Santa Fe and noted in the introduction to his two-volume biography, 'The year spent in Mr Boyle's historic adobe *rancho* in Santa Fé while preparing the manuscript will long remain a cherished memory.'[51] One key consideration is how close Robert Vanderveer was to his cousin Frank Stevens since between them they supplied the majority of the personal details of William Blackmore's life.

One member of William Blackmore's immediate family to play a significant role in his business dealings was Sir John Lambert (1815-1892), K.C.B., who was married to William's aunt, Ellen– his mother's sister. A prominent Roman Catholic, educated at Downside School, Lambert was articled to a Salisbury solicitor in 1831 and he practised in Salisbury from 1836 to 1857. In 1854 he was elected mayor of Salisbury, the first Roman Catholic to be mayor of a cathedral city since the Reformation. Lambert

49 *The Southwestern Journals of Adolph F. Bandelier*, University of New Mexico Press, 1966 p.390 citing Ralph Emerson Twitchell, *The Leading Facts of New Mexican History*, The Torch Press, Cedar Rapids, 1911-1917 volume IV p.55.

50 Ralph Emerson Twitchell, *op. cit.*, p.55.

51 Brayer, *op.cit.*, volume I, p.2. Herbert Brayer's wife, Garnet M. Brayer, spent the best part of a year transcribing those of William Blackmore's diaries held in Santa Fe that were frequently written in shorthand. Husband and wife also calendared letters in the Blackmore archive in Santa Fe and the Boyle family.

funded the building of the Roman Catholic Church of St. Osmund in Exeter Street, built to the designs of Augustus Welby Northmore Pugin (1812-1852), and consecrated on the 2nd September 1848.

In 1857 Lambert was appointed a Poor-Law Inspector and in 1863 moved to London at the request of Charles Pelham Villiers (1802-1898), president of the Poor Law Board, to advise on the measures necessary to deal with the poverty caused by the American Civil War, and the Union Relief Acts and Public Works (Manufacturing Districts) Act of that year were prepared as a result of his recommendations. Lambert was a close colleague of Prime Minister William Gladstone (1809-1898) who in 1871 appointed him Permanent Secretary to the Local Government Board, a position he held until 1882. He became a Privy Councillor in 1885.

As a senior civil servant, Lambert was extremely well connected in government, diplomatic and business circles and was to advise Blackmore in many of his business enterprises. Lambert was particularly instrumental in encouraging his nephew to exploit the business opportunities afforded by the USA and link these to the newly emerging middle class investors in Great Britain. However, the relationship was symbiotic. In 1863, in preparation for William's first trip to the USA, Lambert had provided him with numerous introductions to congressmen, senators and the Secretary of the Treasury, Salmon P. Chase (1808-1873). Lambert request that Blackmore report in detail upon 'the feelings and opinions of the people in New York, and your judgement upon them, with respect to the [American Civil] War, so that I may get it shown to the Cabinet.'[52]

To return finally to William Blackmore; he married Mary Sidford (1822-1872)[53] on 14th May 1851 in the church of St. John the Baptist, Bishopstone near Salisbury. Mary's place of birth on the marriage certificate was given as 'Stoke, Wiltshire'. There were no children from the marriage. Mary was described as a 'kind' and friendly individual who

52 Letter from Lambert to Blackmore dated 4th December 1863. As cited by Brayer, *op.cit.*, Volume I, pp.36-37. Blackmore No.0025.

53 Mary was the daughter of John Sidford (1785-1842) a farmer in Broadchalke, and Mary Rich (1794-1856). She was the second eldest of eight children. I thank Ann Ferreira, a descendant of Mary Sidford, for this and other information about the Sidford family.

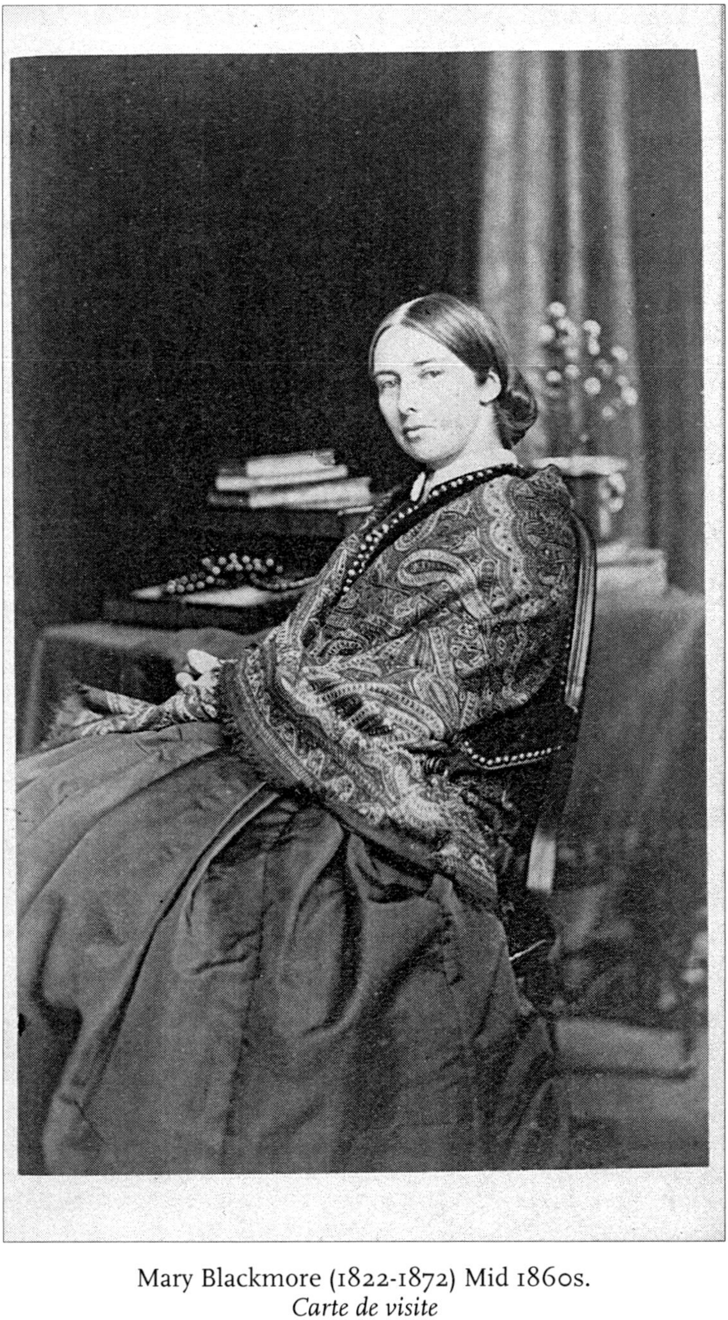

Mary Blackmore (1822-1872) Mid 1860s.
Carte de visite
Albumen print
Courtesy of Salisbury & South Wiltshire Museum

supported her husband's wide ranging endeavours. She would welcome visitors at the Blackmore homes in Hooton outside Liverpool and later at Shepley House in Carshalton south of London which was renowned for the hospitality shown by the Blackmores.[54] Whether the Sidford family had a deep rooted interest in archaeology is not clear though three of Mary's brothers donated flint chips discovered in a variety of locations around Salisbury.[55] William and Mary appear to have been animal lovers. William was photographed standing next to a large wolf hound outside Shepley House and the Blackmore papers contains two carte de visite photographs from the 'The Brighton Cats' series by Harry Pointer.[56]

Without children Mary was free to accompany William on his travels. Quite how extensive the couple's travels were during the 1850s and 1860s is unclear. A carte de visite format photographic portrait of Mary by the firm of Fratelli D'Alessandri, of the Via del Corso in Rome is amongst a small collection of portraits of Mary in the Salisbury & South Wiltshire Museum. This would indicate that the couple visited Rome, presumably on one of William's business trips, though nothing is known about his business dealings in Italy. In 1872 Mary accompanied her husband to the USA and was recorded as playing an active part in William's meetings with Native Americans. Mary's nephew, Sidford Hamp noted in his diary for Saturday 25th May, 1872, that he and his aunt had been at a meeting in Washington, D.C. between William and Red Cloud (1822-1902) a war leader of the Oglala Lakota (Sioux), and

54 Letter from the painter Dante Gabriel Rossetti to George Rae, who like Blackmore was an early patron of the Pre-Raphaelite artist. Letter 63.112 in William E. Fredeman, *The Correspondence of Dante Gabriel Rossetti – The Chelsea Years 1863-1872, Volume III 1863-1867*, D.S. Brewer, Cambridge, 2003 p.95.

55 George Sidford, of Bower Chalk. Flint found at Bower Chalk; Frederick Sidford, of Bishopstone. Flint found at Bishopstone; James Sidford, of South Newton. Heart shape flint found at South Newton in May 1868. See Stevens, *Flint Chips* (1870) pp.xxiv, 47, 70 and 71.

56 The Brighton photographer Harry Pointer (1822-1889) was well known for 'exerting a seemingly hypnotic spell on the cats who posed for him in every conceivable guise.' By 1872 more than one hundred images of cats had been published by Pointer. See Philippe Garner, *A Seaside Album – Photographs and Memory*, Philip Wilson Publishers, London, 2003 p.61.

'next saw two squaws to whom Aunt gave each a shawl, and some sham jewellery, they were very pleased and chattered in their own tongue like women!'[57]

However, Mary fell ill and died, probably of peritonitis, on 18th July 1872 in Bozeman, Montana, USA at the home of General Lester and Emma Willson while her husband was on a trip to the Yellowstone region, some fifty miles to the south. She was buried at the foot of a hill fifteen miles south of Bozeman on five acres of land specifically purchased by her husband to establish a cemetery, the Sunset Hills Cemetery. This hill was subsequently named Mount Blackmore in Mary's honour. The unique pyramid-shaped tombstone is inscribed 'Fide et Amore.' A mausoleum that William requested be built over his wife's grave – and for which he may have paid – was never constructed. A local newspaper, *The Avant Courier*, reported on Mary Blackmore's untimely demise; 'The deceased had by her amiability and peculiarly happy talent of gracefully adapting herself to the trying circumstances of a journey over our rugged mountains, endeared herself to the limited circle of acquaintances she had formed during her brief sojourn in our midst and her sudden demise caused an universal expression of sorrow at her loss and sympathy for him whose cup of happiness had so rudely been dashed to the ground.'[58]

57 Herbert Oliver Brayer, 'Exploring the Yellowstone with Hayden, 1872, Diary of Sidford Hamp', *Annals of Wyoming*, Volume 14, Number 4, October 1942 pp.253-298. Quotation from p.261.

58 *Avant Courier*, 25th July 1872. I thank Ann Ferreira for this reference.

3
Liverpool and Professional Life

WILLIAM BLACKMORE'S PROFESSIONAL life and business career would in itself have represented a remarkable achievement of the mid-Victorian era, a point underlined by Herbert Brayer's two volume biography that focussed on William's involvement in Spanish-Mexican land grants and subsequently his role in the financing of the Denver and Rio Grande Railway. Brayer's meticulous account remains the primary source covering these activities and this chapter is not intended to cover Blackmore's North American business activities in such detail.

However, consideration of Blackmore's wider business activities is relevant in obtaining a better understanding of the man, his short, medium and long term aims and ambitions, and how he mixed his social and business network to achieve success with both his commercial and his private interests.

BLACKMORE AND LIVERPOOL

Blackmore moved to Liverpool in 1849 probably as a result of his contact in the Salisbury area with the Squarey family, to whom he was related by marriage, and the opportunities – perhaps highlighted by his uncle John Lambert – offered in the thriving maritime city.[1]

Liverpool rapidly expanded as a commercial centre during the second quarter of the 19th century. Over one hundred and forty acres (0.57 km^2) of new docks, with ten miles (16 km) of quay space, were

1 Brayer refers to an 'invitation' to move to Liverpool. This was presumably from Andrew Squarey, though John Lambert may also have played a significant role. Brayer, *op.cit*, Volume I, p.31.

opened between 1824 and 1858.[2] In 1846 the Albert Dock, the first enclosed, non-combustible dock warehouse system in the world and the first structure in Britain to be built entirely of cast iron, brick and stone, was opened by the prince consort, Prince Albert (1819-1861). In 1857 the *Building News* observed that whereas in Manchester the warehouse was the most notable building type, and in London the club house predominated, in Liverpool 'piles of "offices", or commercial buildings, have, for some time past, given the largest scope to architectural display.'[3] Not all were pleased with this development, the architect and antiquarian James Allanson Picton (1805-1889), writing in 1873, bemoaned the 'hideous pile of brickwork' warehouses and that 'surely amongst the merchant princes who interest themselves in the structure, some might have been found to advocate the mere fraction of expense which would have converted the present incarnation of ugliness into something which would have dignified the commercial by allying it with the beautiful.'[4] While Liverpool was of a completely different size and style of built environment from the small medieval Cathedral city of his birth, William was to thrive in this burgeoning commercial port that was to a great degree a result of trading links with the USA and Liverpool's role as a gateway for American cotton to the Lancashire cotton mills.

Another rapidly increasing market was the trade in corn. The Corn Laws, introduced by the Importation Act 1815 and designed to protect corn prices in Great Britain and Ireland against competition from less expensive foreign imports, were repealed in 1849. The effect was that foreign producers, such as the prairie farms of North America, were then able to export vast quantities of cheap corn to Britain. In 1867 the Waterloo Dock in Liverpool was reconstructed, three sides forming purpose built vaulted corn warehouses in which mechanised systems raised the corn from the quayside, and stored, turned, ventilated and

2 For a general overview of these developments see John Belchem (ed.), *Liverpool 800: Culture, Character & History*, Liverpool University Press, 2006.

3 As quoted by Richard Pollard, Nikolaus Pevsner and Joseph Sharples, *Lancashire: Liverpool and the South West, Buildings of England*, Yale University Press,2006 p.68.

4 James Picton, *Memorials of Liverpool Historical and Topographical including A History of the Dock Estate*, Longmans, Green, and Co., London, 1873, Volume I pp.660-1.

discharged it to road, rail and water transport. In 1872 Sidford Hamp (1855-1919), William's nephew who was about to sail from Liverpool to join his uncle in America, wrote in his diary entry for the 6th May; 'If you want to see business, go to the Liverpool docks, and the adjacent railway stations, the heaps of cotton and corn are amazing.'[5] William Blackmore was thus surrounded by the daily evidence of tangible opportunities that America and its vast expanses of land offered to smart investors.

Liverpool trade directories of 1851 have no entry for William Blackmore but that year's census found him registered in Bebington in the Wirral, five miles south of Liverpool. By 1855 Blackmore was listed as an 'attorney' in Stanley Terrace, New Chester Road, New Ferry and he was resident in Hooton in Cheshire. William prospered and by 1857 he was listed as a partner in the law firm of Duncan, Squarey and Blackmore, and living in Sutton, near Chester.[6] He established his reputation through involvement with several significant maritime compensation cases and developed contacts with a number of important Americans who were 'getting rich quick' with land, mining and railway developments in the American West. Blackmore appears to have been an active partner in the firm until at least 1864 when the *Solicitors' Journal & Reporter* noted under its Notice of Admission of Attorneys that John Rice Roberts, MA had been articled to 'William Blackmore, Liverpool'. [7] In the same year Blackmore was listed as a

5 Herbert Oliver Brayer, 'Exploring the Yellowstone with Hayden, 1872. Diary of Sidford Hamp', *Annals of Wyoming*, Volume 14 Number 4, 1942 p.256. Hamp was on his way to the United States to join his uncle on the Hayden Geological Survey of Yelolowstone as an assistant cartographer.

6 I thank Margaret Daley of Liverpool Record Office for supplying listings for William Blackmore in Liverpool trade directories. The 'Squarey' of Duncan, Squarey and Blackmore was Andrew Tucker Squarey (1821-1900) who was born in Salisbury and was related to the Blackmore family by marriage. Squarey had been articled to his brother Coard William Squarey (1811-1893), of the firm of Squarey & Bickersmith, who in 1858 held the office of Mayor of Salisbury. Having passed his examinations in 1844, Andrew Squarey arrived in Liverpool in 1845 where he joined the solicitors firm of Duncan and Radcliffe. He became a partner by 1850 and then head of the firm. See 'The Late Mr.A. T. Squarey', *Liverpool Mercury*, 1st May 1900 p.8 and Lavinia M. Squarey, *Family Records and Pedigrees*, Bennett Brothers, Salisbury [1909].

7 *The Solicitor's Journal and Reporter*, 14th May, 1864 p.554. The same journal reported in 1870 that a Richard Middlemore had been articled to William Blackmore of

director of the Law Union Fire and Life Insurance Company, which had been established in 1854.

Blackmore remained a practicing solicitor in Liverpool until around 1869, having been instrumental some three years earlier in the setting up an office for Duncan, Squarey, Blackmore, Pearson and Hill in Founder's Court, Lothbury in London (opposite the northern façade of the Bank of England). In 1868 this office had amongst its client base the London, Chatham, and Dover Railway Company that was selling off surplus freehold land.[8] He kept his Liverpool office, which was still in existence in the early 1870s. Blackmore did this presumably to keep in good contact with his professional colleagues in Liverpool and thus the Americans arriving in England by the trans-Atlantic liners that used the port as a terminus.

It took William Blackmore around five years following his arrival in Liverpool to establish himself within the city's professional and social scenes. By the mid 1850s William there is evidence that he was in a position to actively exploit his professional and social networks there. In 1856 Blackmore became a member of the Liverpool Law Society, founded in 1827 and was elected a member of the Incorporated Law Society in February 1865.[9]

He joined the Historic Society of Lancashire and Cheshire (founded in 1848) on 20th September 1854 and was listed as being at 2 Exchange Street East and Sutton, Cheshire. His address then moved to 10, Water Street, Liverpool (the offices of Duncan, Squarey and Blackmore) and Hooton, Cheshire. One of the founding life members of the Society was William Brown (1784-1864), of the private bank of Brown, Shipley and Company with which Blackmore was to be closely connected.[10] Blackmore was an active member of the Society being an

'London and Liverpool.' *op.cit.*, 1870 p.285. However, A. Green & Co.'s 1870 *Directory for Liverpool and Birkenhead* p.228 lists Duncan, Squarey & Co. seemingly indicating that Blackmore was no longer a partner.

8 *Daily News*, Saturday 25th April, 1868 p.8.

9 See *The Legal Observer and Solicitors' Journal, May 1856 to December 1856*, Volume LII, London 1856 p.481.The certificate survives. Wiltshire & Swindon History Centre 776/579.

10 In 1860 Brown presented Liverpool with a public library and museum, the foundation

officer of the Archaeology Committee for the year 1856-1857, having become a committee member the previous year. He also exhibited a range of artefacts from his collection at meetings.[11]

Blackmore's interest in education and social reform is also evidenced by the fact that by 1858 he was listed as being a member of the Liverpool Local Committee of the National Society for the Promotion of Social Science.[12] This organization, also known as the Social Science Association, was the pre-eminent forum in mid-Victorian Britain for the discussion of social questions and the dissemination of knowledge about contemporary society. Founded in 1857 and active until 1884, it provided expert guidance to policy-makers and politicians in the era of Gladstone and Disraeli. The legal profession played a prominent role in

stone being laid on 15th April 1857. The scene was recorded by a photographer and a copy of the image is still held at the Liverpool Museum. Whether William Blackmore is captured in the scene has yet to be established.

11 *Transactions of the Historic Society of Lancashire and Cheshire*, Volume VIII, Session 1855-1856, 1856 p.242 noted that at a meeting of the society held on the 6th March 1856 a 'Mr Blackmore' exhibited four stone celts, two found near Galway, one at Backton, in Cumberland and one in New Zealand, and two bronze spears one of which was discovered in a bog in Leenane, Connemara. Blackmore had become a member of the archaeological Section Committee for the 1855-1856 session. At the meeting held on the 5th February 1857 Blackmore exhibited a medal of Sigismund, Emperor of Germany. At the 12th March Meeting Blackmore exhibited a crown piece of Mary Queen of Scots and a medal commemorative of the Restoration of Charles II, dated to 1675 and probably the work of the die sinker Thomas Symon. At meeting on 14th May he exhibited a medal of Dr. Priestley, dated 1783, with his bust on one side and a pneumatic trough and various pieces of chemical apparatus on the reverse. *op.cit.*, Volume IX, Session 1855-1857, 1857 p.279 and p.285 and p.290. See also, *op.cit.*, Volume XI, Session 1858-1859, Adam Holden, Liverpool, 1859 p.x. A 'Mr Blackmore' is cited as having exhibited 'A small figure of Hermaphroditus, in gold; probably Etruscan' at the 'Literary section' meeting on 13th January, 1859. *op.cit.*, p.251. On 14th November 1861 Blackmore exhibited at the meeting of the Literary Section one of the medals presented by Garibaldi to his companions in the conquest of Sicily, and a photograph of Sir Peter Lely's portrait of Oliver Cromwell in the Pitti Palace in Florence. See *Transactions of the Historic Society of Lancashire and Cheshire*, New Series, Volume II, Session 1861-1862, Liverpool, 1862 p.175.

12 *Transaction of the National Society for the Promotion of Social Science*, John W. Parker and Son, London, 1858 p.xviii. See http://napss.modhist.ox.ac.uk/Association.html Blackmore's business partner, A. T. Squarey was listed as being the local secretary for 'Jurisprudence and the amendment of the Law'. 'Local Intelligence', *Liverpool Mercury*, Saturday 14th August, 1858 p.4. Squarey may have delegated his role to Blackmore.

this society though Blackmore does not seem to have been prominent in its subsequent activities.

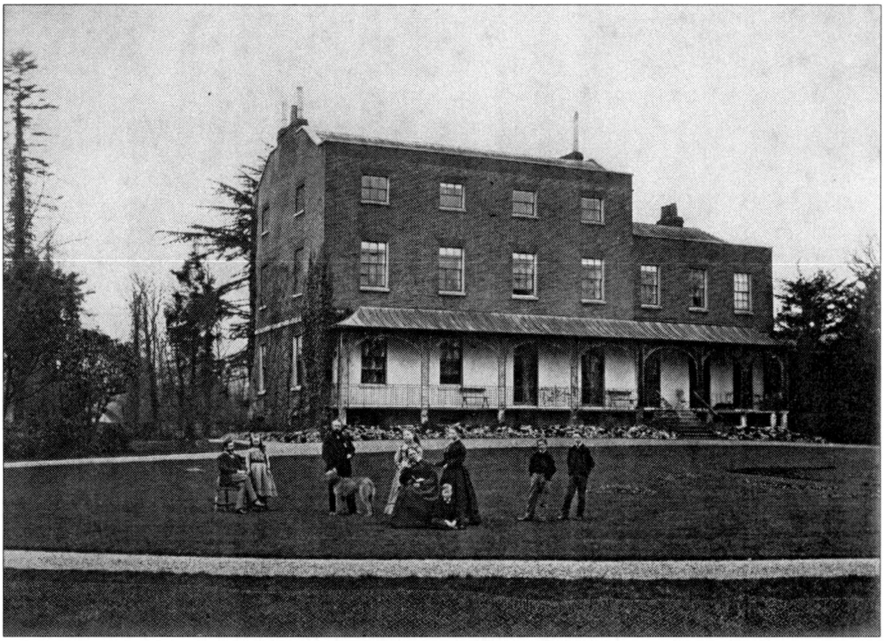

Shepley House – view of garden facade with William and Mary Blackmore and an unidentified family.
Possibly by William Drummond
Albumen print
Courtesy of Salisbury & South Wiltshire Museum

Having moved his principal business office to London, Blackmore established a residency in southern England. From 1865 Shepley House in Carshalton, south of London, was his and Mary, his wife's, home where he lavishly entertained an array of mid Victorian society. Brayer described Shepley House as a 'mecca' for English, American, French and German speculators and investors and that guests also included a diverse range of members of the science and arts communities including archaeologists, writers and painters. Brayer cites an instance of the US Senator James W. Nye (1815-1876) visiting Blackmore at Carshalton in June 1873 [which is presumably an incorrect date] and referred to other guests including Oliver Wendell Holmes, Sr.; Alfred, Lord Tennyson; Samuel Langhorne

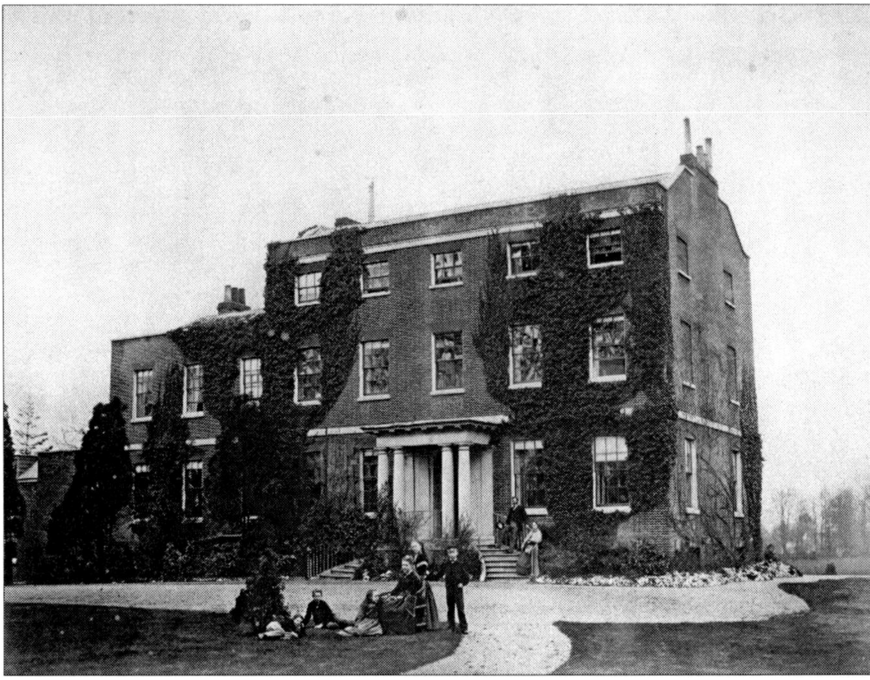

Shepley House – view of front facade with an unidentified group.
Possibly by William Drummond
Albumen print
Courtesy of Salisbury & South Wiltshire Museum

Clemens ('Mark Twain'); John Russell Bartlett, Secretary of State of Rhode Island; Sir John Evans, English archaeologist and geologist; Sir Arthur Church, Professor of Chemistry at the Royal Academy; Ernest Griset, French-born artist; Sir John Lubbock, English banker, politician, naturalist and archaeologist; the English archaeologist and evolutionary anthropologist Colonel Augustus Lane Fox, who from 1880 took the name Pitt Rivers, and Joseph W. Prestwich, English geologist.[13] There

13 Blackmore was first rated in this residence in July 1865 and last extant records for his being rated are April 1870. From July 1870 the house was taken over by Alfred Tylor (1824-1884), geologist and brass-founder who Blackmore knew. I thank Kath Shawcross, Borough Archivist & Local Studies Manager, London Borough of Sutton Local Studies Centre, for supplying this information. See Brayer, *op.cit,* Volume II p.42 See Brayer, *op.cit,* Volume I, p.32. Shepley House was located in the vicinity of the present Shepley Close, off Strawberry Lane, in Carshalton and survived until the mid-1930s when it was demolished.

are photographs held in Salisbury Museum of the house and grounds in which there was a distinctive, ornate wooden bridge. [14]

Around 1870 the Blackmores moved from Carshalton to an apartment in the fashionable Belgrave Mansions in Grosvenor Gardens, close to Victoria Station in central London. The building had been completed in 1868 and was considered somewhat experimental, resembling a 'hotel of the first class.' Accommodation was let unfurnished in suites of up to ten rooms or as single rooms. The cooking arrangements and general service of the establishment was kept distinct and under the control of a manager.[15] This move was probably a result of Blackmore's appreciation that he would be spending an increasing amount of time out of the country on business and did not want to incur the ongoing costs of running a substantial home such as Shepley House. Belgrave Mansions remained William's London home until his death in April 1878.

BLACKMORE – PROFESSIONAL AND BUSINESS CAREER

While Herbert Brayer's two volume biography of William Blackmore extensively documents his business ventures in the USA during the 1860s and 1870s, it is sparse in its coverage of William's professional and business career prior to his first visit to the USA in 1863. Brayer pointed out that Blackmore's descendants did not give him access to the speculators' papers and correspondence related to his business dealings in Britain and Europe during the 1850s – indeed stating that ledgers and business papers had been destroyed by the family. A summary created by Barbara Aitken before these documents were destroyed was supplied to Brayer, though this too has now been lost. Brayer also stated and

14 The photographs of Shepley House may have been taken by William Drummond. Three carte de visite views of the exterior of Shepley House with the imprint of 'Wm. Drummond, Late of Carshalton Surrey. Wellington Villa, Lind Road, Sutton New Town' are held at the S&SWM. Box 'Photographs of Wm Blackmore and Mary Blackmore Ref No 1732'.

15 Built to the designs of architect Thomas Cundy (1790-1867), surveyor of the Grosvenor estate from 1825 until 1866. Belgrave Mansions was described in *The Architect*, 13th February, 1869 p.90.

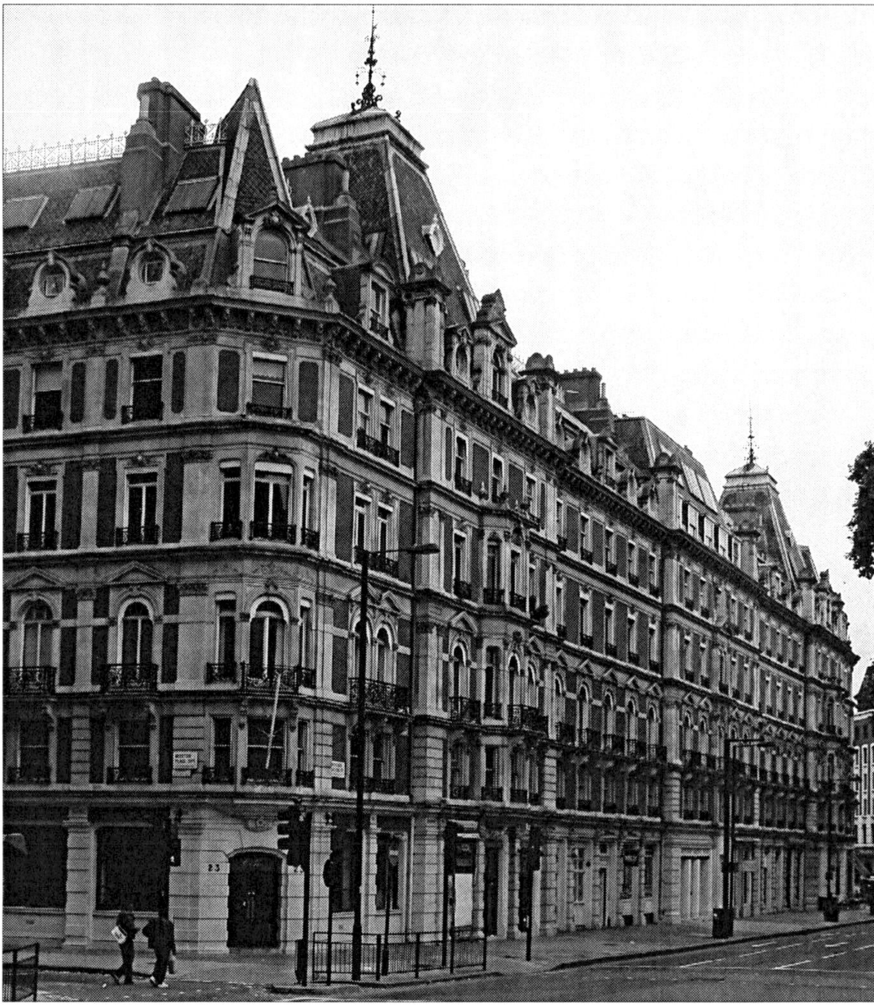

Belgrave Mansions, Grosvenor Gardens, London.
Photographed by the author in October 2010

that he was 'at the insistence of the family and its representatives . . .. reluctant to pursue this field of investigation.'[16]

What can be deduced is that by the early 1860s Blackmore had already become a significantly wealthy man who through his business contacts in Liverpool appreciated that America held the possibility of

16 Brayer, *op.cit*, Volume I p.32.

even greater opportunities and associated wealth connected to a new type of British private middle class investor. However, while Blackmore was engaged in promoting the Union Pacific Railway to European investors, his initial, somewhat audacious, business proposition outlined to the US Government during his 1863 trip to the USA was not successful. It was only in 1868 – and a significant increase in interest by the English investment market in American railroad, mining and land development securities – that he was to establish himself.[17] Brayer characterised the period of 1863 to 1869 'as one of apprenticeship for William Blackmore.'[18]

During the 1850s Blackmore's primary focus was as a practicing solicitor in Liverpool. His friend and partner Andrew Tucker Squarey had established himself as one of the leading solicitor's in Liverpool's business community. Squarey became an advisor to the American Chamber of Commerce in Liverpool (founded in 1801), the Steamship Owners' Association, the Exchange Buildings Company, the Thames and Mersey Marine Insurance Company, the British Shipowners' Company and the North and South Wales Bank. His obituary in the *Liverpoool Mercury* stated that in 1857 he abandoned private practice when he assumed the position of solicitor to the Mersey Dock and Harbour Board though in 1859 he was recorded as Secretary of the Steam Ship Owners' Association. Squarey's business contacts thus gave William Blackmore direct access to a wide variety of the business opportunities evolving across the Atlantic in America.

The firm of Duncan, Squarey and Blackmore expanded and by at least 1866 traded as Duncan, Squarey, Blackmore, Pearson and Hill. It advertised an office in Founders Court, Lothbury in London, the same address as the leading private bank of Brown, Shipley and Company from whom Blackmore may have arranged a sublet.[19]

17 The Union Pacific Railway was incorporated on 1st July, 1862 in the wake of the Pacific Railroad Act of 1862. It started in Omaha, Nebraska and ended at Ogden, Utah.

18 Brayer,*op.cit*, volume I p.57.

19 *The Standard*, Saturday, 9th June, 1866 p.1. Brown Shipley had paid some £22,000 for Founders Court, the former premises of the Central Telegraph Company. The office opened on 15th December, 1863. See Michael McCarthy, *The House that Built*

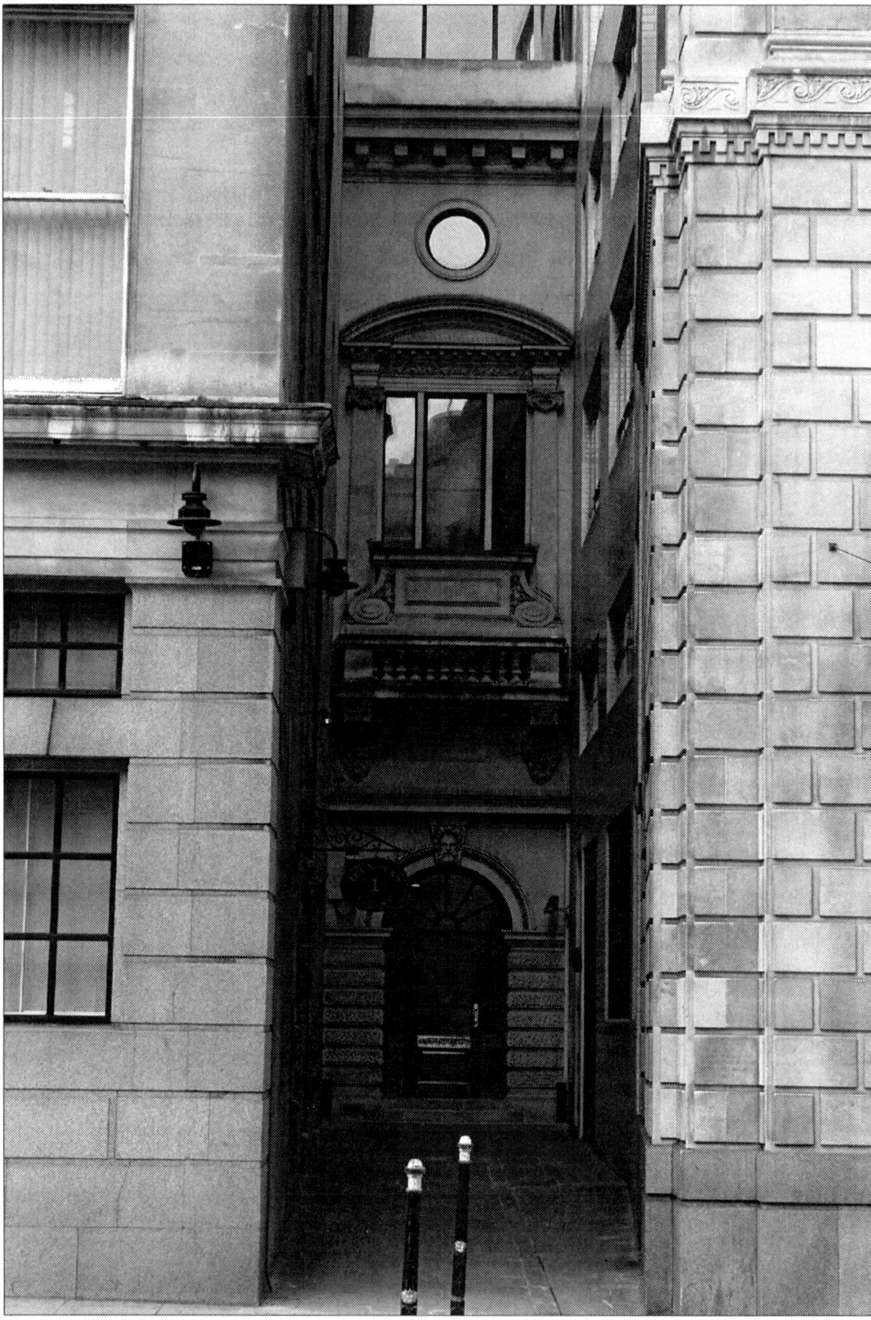

Founders Court, Lothbury, London.
Photographed by the author in October 2010

While William's focus from the late 1860s was on business interests in the USA he continued to provide legal advice in England well into the 1870s. In 1872 he acted on behalf of Sir Samuel Morton Peto and Edward Ladd Betts in their claim against the government of the Republic of Bolivia for breach of contracts entered into in June 1864 regarding railway construction, guano shipments and mining concessions.[20]

In 1873 he became a legal advisor to William Webster (1815-1897) in Webster's claim against the British government for alleged unlawful dispossession of his estates in New Zealand. Webster, an American citizen, had settled in North Island, New Zealand, in 1835 and set up as a general trader, timber merchant and shipbuilder. He quickly developed a prolific trade with the native Maoris, and by 1840 had purchased from them approximately 500,000 acres. In that year Great Britain proclaimed sovereignty over New Zealand and held that pre-1840 land purchases from natives would be considered invalid. This ruined Webster whose assets were destroyed and his credit collapsed. In the United States in 1858, he began to seek recompense for the injustices which he claimed he had suffered at the hands of the New Zealand government. In 1873 in England, he appealed to the Principal Secretary of State for the Colonies and was advised he had no grounds for further claims.[21]

Blackmore was also involved as agent and representative of Colonel Albert B. Steinberger (1840-1894), an American citizen, representative of President Ulysses Grant and self-styled 'Premier' of the Samoan Islands, in his claims against both the British and American governments for compensation for himself and the Samoan people following his arrest and deportation from the islands by Captain C.E. Stevens of *H.M.S. Barracouta* in 1876. Blackmore wrote a letter to *The Times* in August 1877, titling himself the 'representative in this country of the Samoan Government, and also of Colonel A. B. Steinberger, the

Trust – William Brown and the rise of Brown Shipley in 19th Century Liverpool, Brown Shipley, London, 2010 p.23.

20 Extensive documentation of this case is held at the Wiltshire & Swindon History Centre 776/644.

21 Documents held in Wiltshire & Swindon History Centre 776/646 dated to 1874.

present Premier of Samoa.'[22] A very extensive bundle of correspondence, notes, memoranda, printed papers and press cuttings relating to William Blackmore's involvement survives in the Wiltshire & Swindon History Centre.[23]

Quite when Blackmore had acquired sufficient disposable income to start significant personal investment in other business ventures remains to be firmly established. One clue may be the status he had achieved that enabled him to join the Historic Society of Lancashire and Cheshire in September 1854.

Blackmore was involved in a wide range of investments including land holdings, and several telegraph and railway enterprises in Great Britain and Ireland, France, Tunisia and possibly as far afield as Bolivia where as mentioned previously he had represented the railway contractors Messrs Peto and Betts, in its claim in 1864 against the Bolivian Republic.[24]

In 1857 William Blackmore was listed as a director of the Salisbury Railway Company (incorporated in 1856 as the Salisbury Railway and Market House Company). In 1866 he was a director of a number of other British and Irish railway companies; The Dublin and Meath Railway (established in 1858), The London, Worcester and South Wales Railway (established in 1865) and the Salisbury and Dorset Junction Railway (established in 1861).[25] By 1878 Blackmore was no longer a director of these railway companies – presumably having sold investments to service his mounting debts – but had become a director of the Sevenoaks, Maidstone and Tunbridge Railway Company (incorporated in 1859).[26] Other railway investments in Great Britain held by Blackmore included the Potteries, Shrewsbury and North Wales Railway Company (established in 1860), and the Mold and Denbigh Junction Railway Company (established in 1861). Related investments included the North

22 *The Times*, Saturday 25th August, 1877 p. 4.

23 Wiltshire & Swindon History Centre 776/648 dated to 1878.

24 Wiltshire & Swindon History Centre 776/664.

25 *Bradshaw's Railway Manual, Shareholders' Guide and Official Directory for 1867*, W. J. Adams, London 1867 p.83, 202, 286

26 *ibid.*, 1878 p.317-318.

Metropolitan Tramways Company, The Liverpool Tramways Company and some telegraph companies.[27]

William Blackmore's North American investments included the Santa Rita Company in New Mexico (1864), US$2,000 in Mississippi State Bonds (1871) and holdings in the Great Southern Railway Company (1875). He also held securities in the Chicago & Rock Island Railroad (US$10,500 in bonds), the West Shore Hudson Railroad (US$10,000 in bonds) and the Alabama Central Railroad (US$10,000 in bonds).[28]

The Wiltshire & Swindon History Centre hold three business, loans and investments account books belonging to William Blackmore covering the period 1856 to 1872.[29] From these one can establish that Blackmore's portfolio of business interests also included significant property. For instance, he owned the three hundred and fifty acre Banstead Park Estate south of London, earning income from renting land and property on the estate. He also sold shooting rights, and in Cash Statement No. 4 covering 1st to 30th June 1872 he noted that he had received from G. Hodgeman £50 for 'Shooting over Banstead Park.' Another property he owned was Coombe House near Croydon which in 1872 he had leased to a Mr. Collex.[30]

In January 1866 Blackmore appears to have drawn up an agreement with Richard Christopher Naylor (1814-1899), Victorian capitalist, builder of the Liverpool Cotton Exchange and the owner of Hurlingham House, Fulham – today the prestigious Hurlingham Club. Naylor was a neighbour of Blackmore's in the village of Hooton in the Wirral. The agreement was that Blackmore would purchase the Hurlingham House estate for £31,000 from Naylor. The intention was then to sell the house for a profit within the following year – unless there was a mutual agreement to hold on to it for longer to obtain a

27 Share certificates for; 400 shares in the Shrewsbury and Potteries Junction Railway dated 10th August 1866 survives; 440 shares for the Mold and Denbigh Junction Railway Company dated August 1866; the Liverpool Tramways Company and the North Metropolitan Tramways Company (both dated March 1871) survive. All can be found in the Wiltshire & Swindon History Centre 776/579.

28 Wiltshire & Swindon History Centre 776/579 and Brayer, *op.cit*, Volume II p.279.

29 Wiltshire & Swindon History Centre 776/623.

30 Wiltshire & Swindon History Centre 776/642.

better price. Profits were to be split between the two and Naylor was to receive at least £20,000. This venture does not seem to have reached fruition. In 1867 Frank Heathcote (1811-1879) obtained the permission of Mr Naylor to promote pigeon shooting matches on the Hurlingham estate and soon after formed the Hurlingham Club, originally for this purpose. The Hurlingham Club went on to lease the estate from Mr Naylor in 1869 and in 1874 acquired the freehold for £27,500.

There are also papers in the Wiltshire & Swindon History Centre dealing with the purchase and resale by Blackmore of Gwndwn Farm in the parish of Llanellyd, Merionethshire (dating from 1862-1869); and Pantglas Farm in the parish of Trawsfynydd, Merionethshire (dating from) 1862-1864.[31] Blackmore had an investment in the Wassel Grove colliery, near Stourbridge, Worcestershire and in 1872 he purchased the Trefonen Colliery in Wales, a financial interest that still remained in the family till at least 1890.[32]

From at least the early 1860s Blackmore was involved as a financial solicitor with one of the leading British banks, Messrs. Brown, Shipley and Company and counted them amongst his clients. This private bank had been founded in Liverpool in 1810 by William Brown (1784-1864), from 1846 to 1859 Liberal M.P. for South Lancashire, who was made a baronet in 1863. In 1825, William Brown was joined by a partner, Joseph Shipley (1795-1867), an American who was acting as an agent in Liverpool. The business financed merchants shipping goods between Britain, the United States and many other parts of Europe and the Americas. Establishing itself in the role of the 'Bank of the United States' as the leading negotiator of sterling and dollar bills of exchange, in 1859 Brown Shipley had exchange flows of US$45 million (UK£9.18 million) (against total American exports of US$133 million (UK£27.14 million).[33] The company worked in partnership with Brown Bros. &

31 Wiltshire & Swindon History Centre 776/625.

32 There are a number of letters from Emily M. France to Humphrey Blackmore regarding his financial interests in the Trefonen Colliery dating to 1889 and 1890. Wiltshire & Swindon History Centre 776/620.

33 The US Dollar to UK Pound exchange rate has been based on data from http://www.measuringworth.com.

Co. of New York, founded in 1818. The success of Brown, Shipley and Company enabled it to make very large advances to Liverpool merchants buying cotton for the Lancashire cotton mills or to British manufacturers exporting goods. Similarly the bank was well placed to negotiate bills of other merchants in Anglo-American trade. During the American Civil War, Messrs. Brown, Shipley and Company made a strategic decision and sided with the Unionist Northern States.

There are two Brown Shipley indexed loans ledgers in the Blackmore papers held in the Wiltshire & Swindon History Centre. These cover the period from April 1863 until 1871. One ledger records many loans by Brown Shipley & Co. related to railway companies with which Blackmore was involved, such as the Salisbury & Dorset Junction Railway Company and Dublin and Meath Railway Company. [34]

The reputation of Messrs. Brown, Shipley and Company for honesty, integrity and reliability was considered by contemporaries as second to none and this enabled the bank to pioneer payment through 'Letters of Credit,' a financial mechanism that William Blackmore was to repeatedly exploit. The company was also involved in investments in new communications technologies such as the Atlantic Telegraph Company, the first – but unsuccessful – attempt to create a transatlantic telegraph line. This Company was incorporated in December 1856 with £350,000 capital, raised principally in London, Liverpool, Manchester and Glasgow. On the 17th December, 1856, the Board of the Atlantic Telegraph Company appointed William Brown as Chairman. It has yet to be established whether William Blackmore was involved in raising capital for the Atlantic Telegraph Company though he subsequently had involvement in a number of communications technology investments. In 1867 he became associated with the Franco-American Direct Telegraph Company, subsequently incorporated as the Paris & New York Telegraph Company. Although he was unwell and in a perilous financial state, in January 1878 William became actively involved in selling of shares in the

34 Wiltshire & Swindon History Centre 776/627 and 776/628. The record loans made either by Brown Shipley itself or on behalf of named clients, and include the name of the borrower, amount, term, interest rate, security required and how and when loan repaid.

Electric Telephone Company in London, organising and paying for the printing of the prospectus.[35] These first commercial telephone services were set-up in 1878 and 1879 on both sides of the Atlantic.

The American Civil War may be considered to have been instrumental in enabling William Blackmore to reach the heights of his business success and the fortune accompanying it. In the years prior to the commencement of war in April 1861, Blackmore had established himself as a 'middleman' between promoters and investors on both sides of the Atlantic; that is American investors looking at opportunities in Europe and vice versa. With a commission ranging from 0.25% to 2.5%, Blackmore reinvested his profits in sizeable blocks of American securities and these he then marketed for a substantial profit in England.

The hostilities between the Unionist and Confederate states had a number of effects. It impacted on the American securities market in England, the value of the US Dollar dropped against foreign currencies and the cost of the war began to become a significant issue to all the stakeholders. More fundamentally, while Liverpool had closer business links with the Confederate South through the cotton trade, the banker William Brown and William Blackmore took a minority view and sided with the Unionist North – possibly as a result of their liberal principles, acquired on Blackmore's part by the influence of his grandfather Henry Shorto. This position was to greatly assist Blackmore in increasing his stature with his network of American contacts and with pro-Unionist sympathisers in the British government, financial and social circles.

Clearly by the mid 1870s Blackmore had established a very significant reputation within financial circles in the City of London. In a letter to Robert Hart (1835-1911), Inspector General of Chinese Maritime Customs from James Duncan Campbell (1833-1807) – his London agent and confidant and the non resident secretary of the Chinese Maritime Customs – dated 14th May, 1875, Campbell had mentioned that he had been told by Blackmore that he knew General Roswell Sabine Ripley (1823-1887), a former brigadier general in the Confederate Army who after the American Civil War became a businessman and resided in

35 The cheque signed by William made payable to the printer, Witherby & Co., is dated 26th March, 1878. Wiltshire & Swindon History Centre 776/579

England. In a response dated 2nd July, 1875 Hart asked 'Who is 'W. Blackmore'?' Campbell had already written on 26th February 1875 that Blackmore 'has means of obtaining information in the City such as very few men possess.' He stated that 'Everyone knows him and he knows everyone.'[36]

Blackmore's reputation has been largely founded on Brayer's two volume account of his role as a financier and entrepreneur who promoted British and Dutch investment in land in South West USA following the American Civil War. These business ventures of the 1860s and 1870s involved mining investments, Spanish and Mexican land grants and the building of railways. This matrix of cheap land, mineral and agricultural wealth and railways formed a potent mixture with which to entice financiers, speculators and investors. However it was also risky. A 'short-term-high return' concept was the guiding principle of a large portion of the English, Scottish, Dutch and German investors who purchased American securities following the Civil War. If one component failed to keep up to speed, then the model could, and frequently did, collapse.

Blackmore had been introduced to the North American business opportunities through the American lawyer Cyrus Martin Fisher of New York. Fisher was a promoter of American railroad and mining securities and he gave Blackmore insights into and advice about the rapidly emerging markets in the USA. He was also, according to Brayer, 'Counsellor to the United States Legation' in London and had been working in London on 'legal business' since around 1864.[37]

In the early months of the American Civil War, Jay Cooke (1821-1905), an American banker, promoter, entrepreneur and developer was

36 See *The I.[nspector] G.[eneral] in Peking. The Letters of Robert Hart – Chinese Maritime Customs 1868-1907*, Volume One, Belknap Press, Harvard, 1975 pp.197-198 and *Archives of China's Imperial Maritime Customs: confidential correspondence between Robert Hart and James Duncan Campbell, 1874-1907*, Foreign Languages Press, 1993 pp. 105, 106 and 108.

37 In July 1868 Fisher was called as a witness to a House of Commons Select Committee considering the Married Women's Property Bill. He stated that he had been in England for 'nearly four years' on legal business. See *Special Report from the Select Committee on Married Women's Property Bill*, House of Commons, [London] 17th July 1868 pp.26-33.

engaged by Salmon P. Chase (1808-1873), the Secretary to the Treasury, as special agent for the sale of the US$500million of so-called 'five-twenty' bonds—which were callable in five years and matured in twenty years. This bond aimed to help fund the costs to the Unionist North of the American Civil War and was authorized by Congress on 25th February, 1862. Though the Treasury department had previously failed in selling these bonds, Cooke was spectacularly successful and oversold the issue by some US$11million.

In late 1863 William Blackmore, encouraged by Cyrus Fisher, the banker Sir William Brown and his uncle John Lambert – who was now in London advising Charles Pelham Villiers (1802-1898), president of the Poor Law Board, on the measures necessary to deal with the poverty caused by the American Civil War – came up with an audacious proposal. Blackmore suggested exploiting the market in Great Britain with an issue of US$500million through the sale of gold bonds secured by a selection of lands in the public domain hypothecated for repayment of the loan. The loan for a thirty year period at an annual interest of 5% or less was suggested.

Lambert outlined three principles supporting the proposal that were to characterise William Blackmore's future land grant speculations in the USA. The proposal would appeal to the landless European industrial labour faced with unemployment and poverty; large and aggressive speculators were in search of more lucrative markets – and the fall in the value of the US Dollar made this even more attractive; and smaller British investors with a fixed income could also see benefits of investment. Blackmore also pointed out that while Great Britain and Ireland had a total land area of seventy million acres, public lands unsold and unappropriated in the USA measured some one hundred and thirty times greater; a staggering one billion acres. The Englishman also suggested in his published 'prospectus' that the aim was to induce 'the superior class of agriculturalist' with capital of US$20,000 to US$200,000.[38]

38 *Suggestions for a United States Government Loan: Made in January, 1864, To Salmon P. Chase, Esq., Secretary of the Treasury of the United States,* Witherby & Company, London [1863]. Brayer gives a detailed account. Brayer, *op.cit.*,Volume I, pp.34-46.

Armed with letters of introduction to congressmen, senators and Secretary Salmon P. Chase, Blackmore arrived in Washington in early December 1863. He aimed to get the introduction to Congress of a bill for the creation of the North American Land & Emigration Company

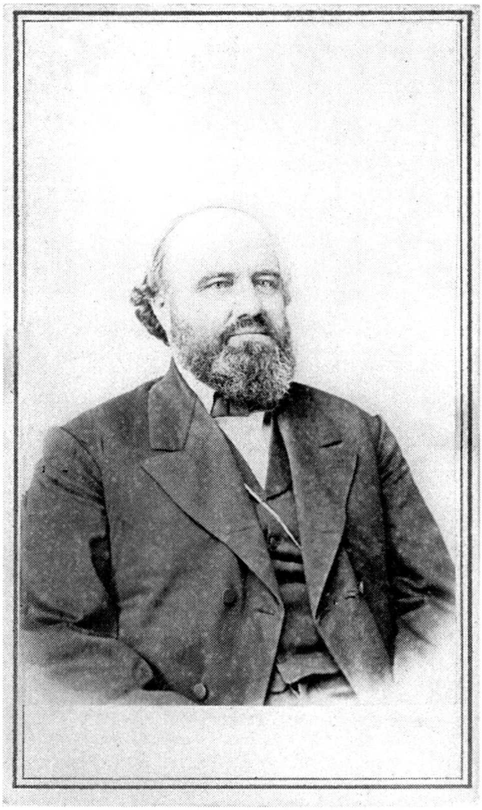

Samuel Clarke Pomeroy (1816-1891)
Published by E. & H. T. Anthony, 501 Broadway, New York from photographic negatives in Brady's National Portrait Gallery.
Carte de visite
Albumen print
Blackmore carte de visite album
Courtesy of Salisbury & South Wiltshire Museum Albumen print

in January 1864. Blackmore undertook a significant amount of initial lobbying and met Samuel Clarke Pomeroy (1816-1891), an influential member of the Senate from Kansas, who agreed to introduce the bill on 18th January 1864. Blackmore then left Washington and with the permission of the Secretary of War, Edwin McMasters Stanton (1814-1869) visited the Army of the Potomac, the major Union Army in the Eastern Theatre of the American Civil War. In the field, he met for the first time a number of Generals including William Tecumseh Sherman (1820-1891), George G. Meade (1815-1872), Philip Henry Sheridan (1831-1888), John Gibbons (1827-1896) and numerous other officers. These contacts and the friendships that developed were to play an important role in Blackmore's future business dealings. Blackmore exploited these military contacts to assist with his expeditions in the West, even at times requesting their protection as he explored tracts of lands he was considering purchasing. Their significance is reflected by a collection of over one hundred carte de visite portrait photographs of figures from the Unionist military found in one of Blackmore's surviving photograph albums now held by the Salisbury & South Wiltshire Museum. The significance of those officers depicted in Blackmore's own photograph albums and whether he met each and every one of them has yet to be established.

John Lambert's letters of introduction were not without an obligation for William Blackmore, though this too helped him to widen further his social and business contacts. Lambert asked that Blackmore report on 'the feelings and opinions of the people in New York, and your judgment upon them, with respect to the War, so that I may get it shown to the Cabinet.'[39]

Blackmore returned to Washington for Christmas 1863. He met with Secretary Chase in January 1864. Senator Pomeroy secured a first and second reading of the bill for the North American Land & Emigration Company and it was referred to the Senate Committee on Agriculture.[40] However, the bill was not taken forward and foundered and died in February 1864 as the Committee on Agriculture requested that the proposal be discharged from further consideration, primarily because of concerns about the private corporation that would 'necessarily look to their own [*sic*] pecuniary interests, and in the effort to advance these

39 Brayer, *op.cit.*, Vol. 1, p.37 citing a letter from Lambert to Blackmore dated 4th December 1863. It is unknown whether this report was ever shown or discussed by the Cabinet.

40 *Journal of the Senate of the United States of America*, 18th January 1864 p.95.

will neglect or sacrifice the interest of the immigrants.'[41] William had by then returned to England. In July Chase resigned his post as Secretary to the Treasury and Blackmore did not renew his proposition to the new Secretary William Pitt Fessenden (1806-1869).

William did not leave the USA entirely without some success or acquisitions. He returned to England having purchased the collections assembled by Edwin Hamilton Davis of Ohio antiquities, other artefacts found of his excavations in Peru and Central America, together with collections of Danish material. These were to subsequently housed in Blackmore's purpose built museum in Salisbury that quickly became well known in America, helping him to further enhance his credentials and reputation in the corridors of power in Washington, D.C.

Subsequently, Blackmore visited the USA on business trips several times between 1868 and the mid 1870s beginning his career as a representative of English mining interests in New Mexico after the American Civil War. These trips were often for a period of months – the 1872 trip being for no less than seven months, from March to October.

Blackmore made his first expedition to the American West in the autumn of 1868 on his second visit to North America. He travelled along the valley of the Platte River (a tributary of the Missouri River) on the Union Pacific Railroad. It was on this trip that the major business opportunities would come to the fore. An important consideration is that while on his extended expeditions into the American West Blackmore was able to combine both his professional and private interests. He spent time in New York and Washington discussing investment opportunities and lobbying politicians. He then headed West, to go hunting, to meet with Native Americans in their own habitat and to survey the great tracts of land that were central to his business interests.

A small set of general principles underpinned Blackmore's investments and business ventures in North America. Firstly, there was land, and the vast expanses of the West that were potentially available for acquisition and subsequent sale. The land had agricultural value primarily for cattle and sheep. It also had significant value for its mineral

41 As cited in Edith Abbott, *Historical Aspects of the Immigration Problem. Select Documents*, University of Chicago Press, Chicago, 1926 p.347.

deposits. Railroads acted as the catalyst to open up the vast tracts of land in the American West and thereby maximise the potential of the markets on the East Coast and then on to Euope. Blackmore invested both strategically and tactically in all these aspects of the commercial development of the 'Great West.'

William's investments in the USA were diverse and included the Minerva iron mine, Essex County, New York, the Emma silver mine and the Ophir silver mine,[42] both in Utah, the old Spanish silver and gold mine of the Tumacacori Mining and Land Company in Arizona, and a salt mine enterprise in Texas. Blackmore also owned other property in the USA, including real estate in Glen Falls, upper New York State, purchased for US$5,000 in September 1873. Not all these investments were successful. The Emma Silver Mining Company was a fraudulent sale of an exhausted mine near Little Cottonwood Canyon, Utah to British investors for several million dollars during the period 1871-1873. The US Ambassador to England Robert C. Schenck (1809-1890) was involved in this fraud. Whether Blackmore was involved as a financier for the Emma Silver Mining Company remains unclear.

Blackmore's over extension of his financial commitments and business interests coincided with a worldwide recession during the mid 1870s. Known as the Panic of 1873, it was caused primarily by economic problems in Europe, triggered by failures of financial markets in Vienna that spread. The stagnation that followed in Britain – the 'Long Depression' – was to last for two decades. This trouble ignited problems in the U.S., and brought about the failure of Jay Cooke & Company, which at that time was the largest bank in the United States of America. Credit dried up, foreclosures were common and banks failed. This was a poisonous cocktail for William Blackmore.

Another contributor to the Panic of 1873 was the Fourth Coinage Act, enacted by the United States Congress in the same year, which

42 Most of the ore taken out of Ophir was lead, silver, and zinc with copper impurities. There were no significant gold deposits. From 1870 to 1900 only $329,000 in gold was taken out compared with US$13,000,000 in silver and base metals. However, one shipment of silver bullion from the Pioneer Mill in April of 1874 was worth US$64,583. http://www.rootsweb.ancestry.com/~uttooele/ophirhistory.html

embraced the gold standard and demonetized silver. This depressed the price of silver and impacted on Blackmore since his investments included silver mining interests.

Brayer has provided a detailed account of William Blackmore's involvement with Spanish Land Grants and his role in financing of the Denver and Rio Grande Railroad. The Englishman appreciated the symbiotic interrelationship between land grants and the expansion of the railway network into the Territories of the West. What transpires is a complex web behind the financing of numerous investments, the relationship with a pool of investors and the re-estimation of the size of several land grants downwards from Blackmore's initial estimates. The resulting drop in value of these land holdings was coupled to William's inability to raise additional capital during the second half of the 1870s. This proved to be fatal to his North American investments. Its impact was long term and Humphrey Blackmore's involvement seems to have lasted into the early 1920s since there are papers dealing with his and William's financial investments in the Denver and Rio Grande Railroad Company and the Denver and Rio Grande Western Railway Company covering the half century between 1871 and 1921.[43]

Blackmore appreciated that his European investors might have a limited knowledge of the geography of the 'Great West' and the sheer scale of the opportunities he was outlining. He therefore had prepared maps of the southern Colorado and New Mexico region, coloured to accentuate the size of the land grants. Combined with a number of 'booster' publications – including a list of private land claims in New Mexico submitted to the US attorney general for confirmation – Blackmore aimed to provide tangible evidence to support his investment propositions.

The scale of Blackmore's ambitious enterprises is reflected in six land grants in New Mexico that he became jointly interested in exploiting with General Charles P. Clever (1830-1874), a German immigrant who became an adjutant general of New Mexico between 1861-1865 and in 1867 and 1868 and New Mexico Attorney General between 1862-1867.

43 Wiltshire & Swindon History Centre 776/641.

The grants totalled over 2,300,000 acres, the equivalent of some three times the size of Blackmore's home county of Wiltshire.[44]

Brayer's account of Blackmore's business ventures in land grants of the 1860s and 1870s remains the standard work for detailed analysis of this aspect of the Englishman's portfolio of investments. The synopsis below is aimed at highlighting a number of the key component elements, and the outputs and outcomes of these complex, high-risk activities.

SANGRE DE CRISTO GRANT

In 1863 William Gilpin (1813-1894) acquired the 1,038,196 acres of land of Charles Beaubien (1800-1864) known as the Sangre de Cristo Grant. The land was in the San Luis Valley along the Costilla, Culebra, and Trincheras Rivers in southern Colorado. In 1868 William Blackmore was brought in to promote the property in Europe. The grant was divided into the Trinchera and the Costilla estates. English investors were sceptical at first so Blackmore secured purchase of over a million dollars of stock by the Dutch private bank Wertheim & Gompertz that had been previously involved in a number of American railroad loans.

Blackmore and Gilpin distributed promotional pamphlets to investors and hired geologist Ferdinand Hayden to produce what ended up as a highly exaggerated survey to market the grant's mineral potential. In 1870 the United States Freehold Land and Emigration Company was incorporated with the aim of promoting emigration, particularly from Holland and Germany, to the 500,000 acre Costilla Estate.

Though not an entirely successful business venture, Blackmore made a net cash profit of UK£11,646 pounds on the Sangre De Cristo enterprise- that would have more than paid for his entire expenditure on founding the Blackmore Museum – and in addition had acquired 7,500 acres of promising land and US$450,000 in stock of the United States Freehold Land and Emigration Company. By 1877 he had been able to dispose of US$160,000 of the stock, probably making him a further US$16,000 in profit.[45]

44 See table on p.189 of Brayer, *op.cit.*,Volume I.

45 Brayer, *op.cit.*, Volume I, pp.122-123.

The land grants related to the Trinchera and the Costilla estates can be seen as the starting point and foundation of Blackmore's business dealings in some of the largest land grants in the Colorado and New Mexico region.

VIGIL AND ST. VRAIN GRANT

The placing of the Costilla Estate securities with the Amsterdam banking house Wertheim and Gompertz created a celebrity status for the Englishman amongst investment circles within both the USA and Britain. One of the next of Blackmore's business ventures was the Vigil and St. Vrain land grant, encompassing around ninety-seven thousand acres in the Arkansas Valley.

This business investment was bedevilled by arguments of ownership and Brayer estimated that Blackmore lost US$3,333.36 on the venture. A decade later in the 1880s the remarkable growth of southern Colorado would have enabled the English investor to have realised his original investment and made a substantial profit.[46]

Though a comparatively small business deal, Blackmore had been exposed to three critical dependencies in land grants. Firstly was the thorny issue of who exactly owned the land. Secondly, there was the legal verification of exactly how much land there was. Thirdly was the complexity surrounding founding a legally recognised company to exploit the tracts of land. All these were coalescing within a cocktail of the greed and sharp practices that characterised the 'Wild West.'

These considerations were to be amplified in Blackmore's largest land grant ventures, the New Mexico Trust Lands and the Chama Land Grant.

CHAMA LAND GRANTS

This investment consisted of 740,000 acres beside the Chama River, west of the Rio Grande, in northern New Mexico. It had been acquired from 1872 by Anthony Joseph who contacted Henry Blackmore, William's brother who had newly arrived in the San Luis Valley. William

46 Brayer, *op.cit.*, Volume I, pp.144-5.

Blackmore was subsequently tasked by Joseph to sell the land grant for not less than US$65,000.

This business venture proved to be a long and tortuous affair for William Blackmore. It involved the legal ratification of the actual grant; a continuously changing set of investors and the impact of the world wide economic recession. Blackmore's illness in the autumn of 1876 prevented him from travelling to America to address the issues and challenges and he compounded matters by not delegating matters in a timely fashion to a trusted associate such as his assistant Henry Johnson. When in August 1877 Blackmore finally came to an agreement with his brother-in-law Arthur Boyle to become his manager on the Chama estate time was running out. An additional consideration was around this time that the US government intended to undertake an official survey of the Chama estate. This highlighted the perennial problem with land grants; who owned exactly what size parcels of land; how much land was actually purchased under sales agreements; and what was the difference between the size of the land grant sold to investors compared to the officially agreed acreage.

By early 1878 Blackmore considered that if the contracted US government surveyor, S. C. McElroy, concluded that the Chama estate contained substantially less than the 710,000 acres on which his business model was based, he would find himself in a very serious predicament. At this point Blackmore was so desperate he went as far as to wire money to Arthur Boyle and instructed him to use it to bribe the official New Mexico surveyors, and thus protect the speculator's interests. Boyle failed in his attempt to bribe the surveyors or postpone the survey itself. A month after Blackmore's suicide, McElroy reported that the Chama land grant contained 472,736.95 acres – only two thirds of the area Blackmore and his partners believed to represent the grant – and that Blackmore and his business partner John Gerald Potter (1829-1908), an English wallpaper manufacturer, were to pay the US$1,645.20 for the survey. The arguments about the size of the Chama estate ran on for a quarter of a century and in 1905 the estate was estimated to cover a mere 1,422.62 acres. In 1880 Humphrey Blackmore finally handed over the management of the Chama grant to Potter in return for 15% of amount was realised in the property. In the same year he agreed that William's share in his New Mexico land trusts be given up to other shareholders in order to make up the acreage guaranteed by his late brother to them.

Blackmore was unfortunate in a number of his land grant dealings. The 'Wild West' was as much about sharp and unscrupulous business practices as it was with the shoot outs. The picture Brayer painted was that Blackmore may have not been sharp enough, earlier enough, to outwit his business opponents and only adopted underhand tactics (such as bribes) too late in the day. Whether, in Arthur Boyle, he delegated to someone who could successfully carry out such bribery is also a matter of conjecture. There was also growing concern in the USA about foreigners exploiting American assets, and not being on the ground, and the Englishman was probably unaware of the rising resentment and how this began to exert political pressure.

No single business failure in Blackmore's land grant ventures brought him down. However, cumulatively there were too many plates spinning. In addition, Blackmore's role as the principle financier of the Denver and Rio Grande Railroad was to put yet another nail in the coffin of his business ventures.

THE DENVER AND RIO GRANDE RAILROAD

The Denver and Rio Grande Railroad (D&RG) was founded in 1870 by General William Jackson Palmer (1836-1909), the American civil engineer, soldier, industrialist, and philanthropist, and his lifelong friend and partner Dr. William Abraham Bell (1840-1921), the Irish-born physician, photographer and businessman, as a narrow gauge railway system with the initial intention of connecting Denver with Mexico City. After a tumultuous first decade peppered with financial crises, the railroad came under the control of the financier Jason 'Jay' Gould (1836-1892) in 1880 and it took on a new set of business objectives. The line would eventually only be extended as far south as Santa Fe, New Mexico in the South and Salt Lake City in the West.

The narrow gauge was initially adopted for the D&RG on account of its relative cheapness and the main source of revenue was considered to be mineral traffic. The laying of track started in 1871 and the line headed South from Denver reaching Pueblo by the end of 1872.

Palmer and Bell met William Blackmore in late December 1871 and again in early January 1872 at his London residence at Belgrave Mansions. Blackmore became the principal financier of the Denver & Rio Grande Railroad and negotiated significant funding from Wertheim & Gompertz of Amsterdam.

Initially the D&RG's bonds were swiftly taken up in Amsterdam. However, the railroad was plagued with financial problems. An overarching consideration was the worldwide economic recession that started in 1873. This had reduced the number of immigrants to the 'Great West' and dented the confidence of investors; finding funding for extending the line to protect its chosen markets was proving difficult; securing trade for the railroad was posing a significant challenge as was the rival Santa Fe railroad; the D&RG was unable to meet its payroll commitments and on the 30th April 1877 it defaulted on the payment of the interest on its bonds due the following day.

The interrelationship between land grants and railroad development also proved to be a disastrous combination for William Blackmore and his involvement with the D&RG. Palmer had set up the National Land & Improvement Company to buy land alongside the route of the D&RG for speculation. Blackmore's business interests also included ownership of bonds in a variety of interrelated land grants, including those owned by the National Land & Improvement Company. Blackmore was particularly susceptible to the failure of the D&RG since he was the middleman to numerous British shareholders who depended on the dividends from their investments as their income. These shareholders could not sit and wait for their investments to come good. The National Land & Improvement Company also defaulted on its payment of dividends and Brayer calculated this resulted in Blackmore losing some US$2887.50 combined income from dividends. This forced Blackmore to use his financial reserves, and even to extend his borrowing, to meet his contractual commitments. This became a vicious and unsustainable circle.

The losses Blackmore incurred in his involvement with the D&RG and National Land & Improvement Company were not enormous.

However, they formed part of the catalogue of business failures and losses that cumulatively brought Blackmore's business empire crashing down. The interrelationship within Blackmore's business model – land, agricultural and mineral value and railroads – was in essence a sound one. In hindsight Blackmore could have saved his business empire by ceasing an expansionist policy, consolidating what he already held and managing his investments more cautiously. The fact that during the last few years of his life he was not on site in America to direct operations and address issues and challenges in an effective and timely fashion proved to be a major contributory factor to the collapse of his portfolio of investments. Finally, though many aspects of character and interpersonal skills had brought him great success, some traits were instrumental in his ultimate downfall. Blackmore appears to have been reluctant to delegate perhaps because he felt he was the only person who had a full grasp of all his business investments and their interrelationships. This indecision was to cost him dear.

4
The Blackmore Museum

William Blackmore was a considerable philanthropist and his financial sponsorship covered a range of activities distributed across England, Europe and the USA. He donated objects to the British Museum, the Smithsonian Institution and the Peabody Museum, funded geographic and geological surveys in North America and archaeological excavations in and around Salisbury and in France. He covered the cost and actively supported book and other publications as well as conferences.[1] He donated books to newly formed libraries in Colorado. These projects often combined his business and his private interests.

The zenith of Blackmore's philanthropic achievement was his eponymous museum located in his home town of Salisbury. While as late as 1875 Blackmore continued to plan and discuss founding a college and associated museum dedicated to the Physical Sciences and Practical Geology in Colorado, this was never realised.[2] Thus the Blackmore Museum and the diverse collections he assembled for it remained his primary legacy until the 1930s.

The founding of the Blackmore Museum coincided with William Blackmore's acquisition of the Squier and Davis collection in 1864.

1 In 1866 *The Gentleman's Magazine* noted in its 'Notes of the Month' that Blackmore had 'undertaken to defray the cost of the explorations' by his brother Humphrey and Mr. Adlam of the prehistoric so-called Highfield Pit Dwellings in Fisherton, a westerly suburb of Salisbury. *The Gentleman's Magazine,* July, 1866 p.43.

2 A copy of Blackmore's programme for establishing English Settlements and Grand Educational Institute in the 'Great West' dated 1872 survives in the Blackmore Collection – Museum of New Mexico. Fray Angélico Chávez History Library, Santa Fe.

While he stated that this 'forms but a small portion of the contents of this Museum'[3] it was probably the catalyst for Blackmore's decision to create a purpose built building to house his extensive collections.

By the mid 1860s Blackmore was financing a range of archaeological excavations and related activities. He funded Dr. Felix Garrigou (1835-1920) of Tarascon in his excavations of the prehistoric caves in the Pyrenees, some of the resulting specimens being deposited in Blackmore's museum.[4] In 1866 it was reported that Blackmore had 'undertaken to defray the cost of the explorations' by his brother Humphrey and Mr. A. T. Adlam, a local market gardener, of the prehistoric so-called Highfield Pit Dwellings in Fisherton, a westerly suburb of Salisbury.[5] Two years later he donated £4. 9s. 6d. to help cover the costs of the International Congress of Prehistoric Archaeology held in Norwich in August of that year.[6]

William Blackmore's philanthropy in the USA was an order of magnitude greater. He formed a close working relationship with the Smithsonian Institution, donating a wide variety of items and arranging for the loan of his collection of photographs of North American Indians. Blackmore significantly sponsored the 1872 United States Geological Survey of the Territories expedition of the Yellowstone region

3 'Mr. William Blackmore's Address', *Some Account of the Blackmore Museum – Part I. The opening Meeting*, H.F. & E. Bull, Devizes; Bell & Daldy, London; J.R. Smith, London, 1868 p.60.

4 *Annual Report of the Regents of the Smithsonian Institution.. for the Year 1868*, Washington, 1869 p.410

5 'Notes of the Month', *The Gentleman's Magazine*, July, 1866 p.43. It has yet to be established whether William was involved in Humphrey's excavations in Bemerton in September 1863 or Milford Hill in April 1864 when, together with James Brown, a local tobacconist, discovered flint implements. These finds were displayed at a meeting of the Archaeological Institute on 1st July 1864 and paper by Humphrey Blackmore was communicated by Edward Stevens. See *The Gentleman's Magazine*, August 1864 p.196.

6 International *Congress of Prehistoric Archaeology: Transactions of the Third Session..*,Longmans, Green, and Co., London, 1869 p.xxx. Blackmore also invited the Congress to visit the Blackmore Museum. See *International Congress of Prehistoric Archæology: Transactions of the Third Session which opened at Norwich on the 20th August and closed in London on the 28th August, 1868*, Longmans, Green, and Co., London,1869 p.418.

led by Ferdinand Vanderveer Hayden (1829-1887)[7], also helping to fund equipment for the photographer William Henry Jackson (1843-1942) and the English-born painter Thomas Moran (1837-1926). This expedition was Hayden's most ambitious and he had raised some US$75,000 (UK£13,761) in funding. The party consisted of eighty-three men and included Blackmore and his wife Mary. Hayden later related how Blackmore amused himself on the south-western shore of the Yellowstone Lake by catching trout from the lake and then cooking them in boiling water 'without removing the fish from the hook.'[8] However, while Blackmore's objectives were to explore and document the vast tracts of land he wished to sell to European investors, it also gave him an opportunity to observe Native Americans in their natural habitat and collect objects representing their material culture. These, and in addition the photographs taken by Jackson and the paintings by Moran, were intended for inclusion in the Blackmore Museum.

At the end of his first visit to the USA in late 1863, Blackmore decided to seek out and examine the Native American archaeological artefacts excavated between from 1845 to 1847 from the mounds in Chillicothe, Ohio in the Mississippi valley, the largest collection of which was that of Ephraim George Squier (1821-1888) and Edwin Hamilton Davis (1811-1888).[9] After a number of fruitless attempts to locate either Davis or Squier, Blackmore was on the point of leaving for England when he met Davis in New York. Davis had been unsuccessful in his efforts to sell the 1,300-piece Mound City group collection to either

7 Hayden was a physician, surgeon, Professor of Mineralogy and Geology at the University of Pennsylvania, participant in Western expeditions beginning in 1853, and leader of the widely acclaimed 'Hayden Survey', the United States Geological and Geographical Survey of the Territories, 1867-1879. He acquired an international reputation as a geologist.

8 *Annual Report of the United States Geological and Geographical Survey of the Territories, . . .*, Volume 9; Washington,1873 p.52.

9 Chillicothe was the centre of the ancient Hopewell tradition, which flourished from 200 BC until 500 AD. This Native American culture had trade routes extending to the Rocky Mountains. They built mounds for ceremonial and burial purposes throughout the Scioto and Ohio River valleys. Squier and Davis excavated some 200 pre-historic Indian mounds and surveyed some 100 earthen enclosures. They estimated that there were some 10,000 mounds and 1,500 earthworks extant in the State of Ohio.

the Smithsonian Institution or the New York Historical Society. He therefore prepared a catalogue featuring his cumulative collections and placed them for sale on the open market. The catalogue included not only Ohio antiquities, but also those from Davis' excavations in Peru, Central America, and Denmark. His preference was for the collection to remain in the United States. Blackmore was sensitive to its significance as a collection of national importance. The American scholar John Russell Bartlett stated that;

> Mr. Blackmore told me that he felt very reluctant to remove the Collection from the United States, where he thought it should remain, and it was not until he had been assured that the Societies to which it had been offered had declined buying it, that he concluded to take it.[10]

Blackmore purchased the collection from Davis for US$10,000 (the contemporary equivalent of UK£1,004) perhaps taking the advice of his brother in law Edward Stevens. It is also worth noting that the US Dollar had plummeted against the UK Pound in 1864 making the acquisition of the Squier and Davis collection relatively cheap. Davis had allegedly spent some US$5,000 of his own funds on the excavations of the mounds and a further US$5,000 caring for it.[11]

Having acquired the Squier and Davis collection Blackmore then established the Blackmore Museum as a legal entity, bought a site in the garden of the Salisbury & South Wiltshire Museum in St. Ann Street and set about the design and build of the museum bearing his name.

There were fewer than one hundred museums in Great Britain in the early 1860s so the creation of any new one was significant. The fact that two museums were founded in Salisbury in the first half of

10 Statement made in Bartlett's 'Preface to the American Edition' in Edward Stevens, *Flint Chips; a guide to pre-historic archaeology, as illustrated by the collection in the Blackmore Museum*, Salisbury, Brown and Co.,and F. A. Blake; Bell and Daldy, Salisbury, London,, 1870 p.xx.

11 Terry A. Barnhart, 'The Hamilton Davis collection of American Antiquities', *Journal of the History of Collections*, Volume 16, Number 2, 2004 pp.59-87. The sum for excavation is referred on page 64. Davis mentioned the total sum of $10,000 in a letter to Joseph Henry date 14th December, 1863 cited in Barnhart's endnote 55 on page 85.

the 1860s was particularly noteworthy. In addition, while the Salisbury Museum founded in 1860 represented the norm – the adaption of an existing building to house a collection – the Blackmore Museum was purpose built to a unique design that encompassed a unity of purpose.

The Blackmore Museum consisted of one large room seventy feet long and thirty-five feet wide together with a library and an office at the rear. The *Salisbury and Winchester Journal* gave an extensive two-page description of the opening. 'The building has been erected from designs by Mr. John Harding [a local architect], Mr. R. Futcher of Fisherton Works being the contractor, and Mr. P. Bentlif having the superintendence of the work.' The floor was 'laid with Minton's encaustic tiles, of suitable patterns' including the inlaid arms and initials of its founder while 'the walls and roof are most chastely decorated with polychromy by Messrs. Harland and Fisher, the well-known decorators, of Southampton-street, Strand, [London].' The building was 'heated by a hot-water apparatus supplied by Messrs. Wilton and Sons, . . . lighted with gas . . . fitted by Mr. Neale.'[12] The total cost of Blackmore's bequest to his native city was estimated to have been at least £10,000.[13]

The architectural form of the Blackmore Museum followed a conventional design of a number of libraries. A rectangular shape with windows set up above unbroken wall space on which display cabinets could be integrated. The architectural style adopted for the Blackmore Museum was the Gothic Revival and it is likely that the Oxford University Museum of Natural History that opened in 1860 had been influential. The Oxford building was a striking example of the Victorian neo-Gothic style of the Dublin-based architects Thomas Newenham Deane (1828-1899) and Benjamin Woodward (1816-1861). Its style was strongly influenced by the ideas – and contemporary input – of the art critic John Ruskin.[14] The first occupants of the building were the Oxford University

12 *Salisbury and Winchester Journal*, 7th September, 1867 pp. 6-7. I thank Bruce Purvis for supplying this information. John Harding was active in Salisbury as an architect up to around 1900. He held the office of Diocesan Surveyor and his office was in the Canal, Salisbury. Futcher is listed as having a brickworks in Fisherton from at least 1855.

13 *The Morning Post*, Friday 6th September, 1867 p.5.

14 Frederick O'Dwyer, *The Architecture of Deane and Woodward*, Cork University Press, Cork, 1997.

science departments; Astronomy, Geometry, Experimental Philosophy, Mineralogy, Chemistry, Geology, Zoology, Anatomy, Physiology and Medicine. These were aligned to Blackmore's collections as a 'science' rather than a fine arts collection. Some sixty years after its opening it was stated of the Blackmore Museum 'No finer example of the marriage of Prehistory to the Gothic Revival can be quoted.'[15] Whether Blackmore visited many anthropological, ethnographic or archaeological museums during his business trips to France, Germany and the Netherlands remains unclear and the loss of his diaries and papers covering his European ventures of the 1850s and 1860s means that an answer may never be forthcoming.

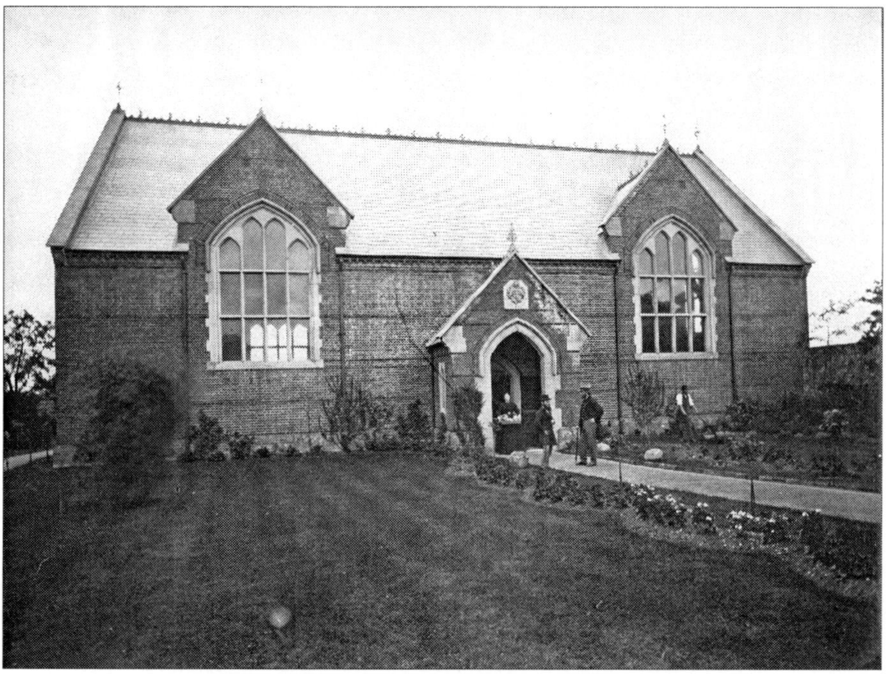

Blackmore Museum - Exterior view c.1867.
Albumen print
Courtesy of Salisbury & South Wiltshire Museum

15 *Antiquity*, Volume 11, 1937 p.38.

The formal opening of the Blackmore Museum took place with an evening conversazione on Wednesday 4th September 1867 when a number of papers were read followed by a reception attended by some four hundred guests who were entertained to a concert directed by Charles John Read, a local musician and composer. Read, together with Edward Stevens and Humphrey Blackmore, had been one of the organisers of the 'Temporary Museum' of pictures and works of art held in January 1862 at the Council Chamber in Salisbury.[16] The following day a procession led by the Mayor and other dignitaries including the Bishop of Salisbury left the Council House and walked to the new Blackmore Museum. Such was the significance of this grand opening that the event was reported in *The Times* and a half page illustration appeared on the cover of the following week's issue of the *Illustrated London News*.[17] Prominent Americans were also present, Benjamin Moran (1820-1886), Secretary of the American Legation in London and John Russell Bartlett (1805–1886), the Secretary of Rhode Island and former secretary of the American Ethnological Society.[18] Previously, on 21st August, The *Daily News* had published a report that included reference to 'an interesting programme [that] has been published' for the opening of the museum. This included reference to 'E. George. Squier' presenting a paper on 'The Ruins of Tiahuanaco, Bolivia, the henge of the New World.'[19] This was none other than American archaeologist Ephraim George Squier, the colleague of Edwin Hamilton Davis, from whom Blackmore had purchased the bulk of the collections now populating his museum in

16 See *Catalogue of the Temporary Museum, Pictures, Works of Art, &c., exhibited at The Council Chamber Salisbury, At the Conversazione given by the Salisbury Literary & Scientific Institution and Salisbury and South Wiltshire Museum, on Thursday, 23rd January, 1862, and following days.*, Bennett, Salisbury [1862].

17 'Opening of the Blackmore Museum', *The Times*, Saturday 7th September, 1867 p.6. *Illustrated London News*, Saturday 14th September, 1867.

18 'The Opening of the Blackmore Museum, Salisbury', *The Daily News*, Saturday 7th September, 1867 p.5. There is a typographical error in this text, Moran being referred to as 'Mr. Morant'.

19 'The Blackmore Museum at Salisbury', *The Daily News*, Wednesday 21st August, 1867 p.6. In early August 1871 Blackmore accompanied Squier on a visit to the mounds of Ohio, from where so many of the artefacts in his museum had originated. *Blackmore Diary No. 2* p.5.

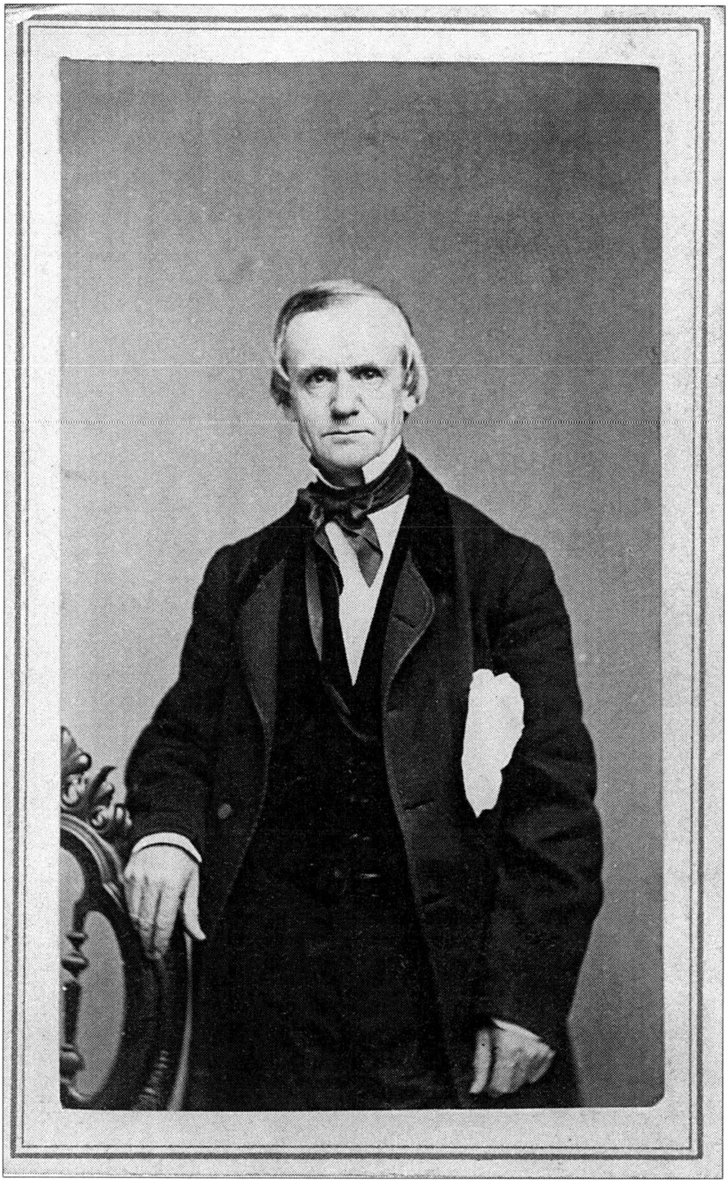

John Russell Bartlett (1805–1886)
Photographed by Wayland & McMillan, No.25 Westminster Street [London?]
Carte de visite
Albumen print
Blackmore carte de visite album
Courtesy of Salisbury & South Wiltshire Museum

Salisbury. There is no evidence that this lecture took place. However, lectures were given by some of the leading contemporary scholars; John Evans (1823-1908), the archaeologist, geologist, and numismatist; Joseph Prestwich (1812-1896), the geologist and pioneering archaeologist; John Thurnam (1810-1873), the psychiatrist, archaeologist, and ethnologist and William Boyd Dawkins (1837-1929), the geologist and archaeologist.

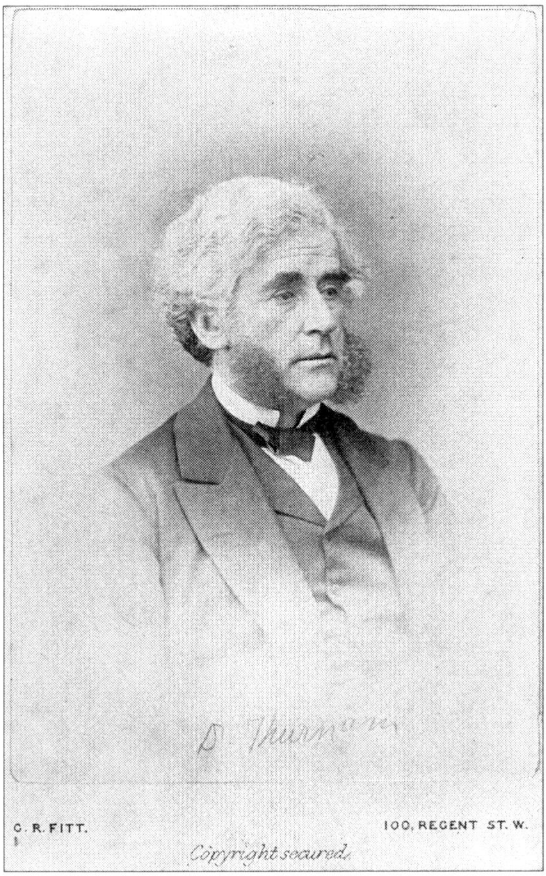

John Thurnam (1810-1873)
Photographed by G. R. Fitt, 100 Regent Street, London.
Carte de visite
Albumen print
Blackmore carte de visite album
Courtesy of Salisbury & South Wiltshire Museum

The Wiltshire Archaeological and Natural History Society 'under a deep sense of the great liberality of Mr Blackmore in founding the Magnificent Museum in Salisbury . . . thought it fit . . . to publish a general account of the Museum, as well as the proceedings which accompanied its inauguration, and the papers read thereat.'[20] The first part – The Opening Meeting – was published in 1868. The second part – Report of the Blackmore Museum – was probably published in late 1870. The editors were Humphrey Blackmore and Edward Stevens. The second part is problematic in that while its date of publication has been frequently cited as 1869, the text contains page references to Steven' *Flint Chips* publication on the Blackmore Museum of 1870 and pages of the issue of the *Geological Magazine* for 1st June, 1870. However, Stevens' preface to *Flint Chips* is dated March 1870. Thus it would appear that Stevens was writing – in parallel and between around 1868 and 1870 – two descriptive catalogues to the Blackmore Museum collections.

Why the Blackmore Museum came to be built in Salisbury was referred to by Blackmore in his opening address. He stated that while some of his Liverpool friends had proposed to purchase his collection and install it in the new museum given to the city by Sir William Brown 'the natural desire of benefiting my native city, encouraged by my brothers, and my brother-in-law, Mr. Edward T. Stevens, prevailed over the rival claims of the British Museum and Liverpool, and I finally decided to place the collection at Salisbury.'[21] One consideration that may have significantly influenced Blackmore was the fact that the Liverpool collector Joseph Mayer (1803-1886) had already established his museum in the City. In 1852, inspired by the British Museum's Egyptian collections, Mayer opened a museum in Colquitt Street. By the mid 1860s Mayer had titled his collection the 'Museum of British and Foreign Antiquities' and in 1867, he donated it to the city of Liverpool. Given the diversity and quality of its contents, this new

20 Published in two parts. *Some Account of the Blackmore Museum, Part I. The Opening Meeting* and *Part II. Report of the Blackmore Museum*, H. F. & E. Bull, Devizes: Bell & Daldy; J. R. Smith, London. Quotation from the Preface on p.iii in Part I.

21 *Some Account of the Blackmore Museum, Part I.* p.60.

municipal collection housed in the Liverpool Museum became Britain's most important public museum after the British and South Kensington Museums.[22] These facts had somewhat stolen Blackmore's thunder and the attached kudos.

Blackmore also alluded to another influence on the decision of the museum's location in statements made by the naturalist and geologist Professor Edward Forbes (1815-1854) in a lecture entitled 'On the Educational Uses of Museums' he had given in 1853. Forbes had written 'it is to the provincial museums that I believe that we must look in future for the extension of intellectual pursuits throughout the land.'[23] Thus the combination of existing museums and collections in London and Liverpool left Salisbury as the logical location for the Blackmore Museum. Another contributory factor was William Blackmore's family. He must have considered the kindred spirits of his brother Humphrey and brother in law Edward Stevens as trustworthy and industrious associates in whose hands he could leave much of the practical day to day running of his museum.

The Blackmore Museum quickly established a reputation as a place worth visiting and Murray's 1869 *Handbook for Travellers in Wiltshire, Dorsetshire and Somersetshire* stated that, 'Few collections are calculated to throw more light upon the habits of prehistoric man than that in the Blackmore Museum'.[24]

22 See Margaret Gibson and Susan M. Wright. (eds.), *Joseph Mayer of Liverpool, 1803-1886.*, Society of Antiquaries of London in association with the National Museums and Galleries on Merseyside, London, 1988. Drawings by Henry Summers of the interior of the Mummy Room and Jewellery Room in Mayer's Egyptian Museum dating to 1852 are held in the Liverpool City Record Office.

23 *Some Account of the Blackmore Museum, Part I.* p.61. The lecture formed the Introductory Lecture at the Metropolitan School of Science. Blackmore may also have been influenced by a paper 'On the Importance of Public Museums for Historic Collections' by the amateur archaeologist and numismatist Charles Roach Smith (1806-1890) read at the meeting of the Historic Society of Lancashire and Cheshire on 19th January, 1859. See *Transactions of the Historic Society of Lancashire and Cheshire, Volume XII, Session 1859-60*, London, 1860 pp.117-126. Roach Smith had established a Museum of London Antiquities that was acquired for £2,000 by the British Museum in 1856.

24 John Murray, *A Handbook for Travellers in Wiltshire, Dorsetshire and Somersetshire*, London, 1869 p.10

The first museum in Salisbury, the Salisbury & South Wiltshire Museum, had been founded in 1860 and was based upon the largely medieval collection of about 1,350 items discovered during the drainage of the water channels in the city centre during the 1850s. It is one of the finest early collections of knives, shears, spoons, padlocks, keys, buckles, arrow and spear heads, rings, spurs, horse trappings and pilgrim badges.

A number of convergent strands emerging during the 1840s and 1850s were behind the founding of the Salisbury Museum in 1860. Firstly was the general rise in appreciation of the benefits of education to a wider section of society, a fact clearly close to William Blackmore's heart. This was characterised by the founding across Great Britain of mechanic's institutes, literary and philosophical institutes, literary and scientific societies, and similar organisations. Legislation such as the 1845 Museums Act also provided a catalyst. New museums represented civic identity, civic pride and civic health. The impetus of the Great Exhibition of 1851 had a wide ranging effect as did more specifically the rise of scholarly antiquarian societies – particularly county archaeological, architectural, history and natural history societies which peaked in the 1840s and 1850s and included annual general meetings held in different provincial cities accompanied by 'temporary museums.'[25] Finally there was a variety of local archaeological excavations in and around Salisbury itself – some by Salisbury locals, others from noted antiquaries from further afield.

In June 1852 a letter in the *Salisbury and Winchester Journal* signed 'C.V.G' – probably Charles Vaughan Grinfield – stated that 'we may almost ask with surprise, why has not Sarum a permanent Antiquarian Museum?'[26] This observation was compounded by the loss to the city

25 See A. Hume, *The Learned Societies and Printing Clubs of the United Kingdom*, G. Willis, London, 1853 and Philippa Levine, *The Amateur and The professional; Antiquarians, Historians and Archaeologists in Victorian England, 1838-1886*, Cambridge University Press, 1986.

26 *Salisbury and Winchester Journal*, 19th June 1852. Jane Howells has suggested to me that this was Charles Vaughan Grinfield, MD, one of the exhibition's committee members. In February 1852 it had been noted that Henry Danby Seymour (1820-1877), Member of Parliament for Poole, had 'recently presented to a gentleman of this city, a cabinet of entomological specimens, in order to form the nucleus of a Public Museum in Salisbury.' *Hampshire Advertiser & Salisbury Guardian*, Saturday, 28th February, 1852 p.5.

of artefacts being discovered in local excavations. In 1853 John Yonge Akerman (1806-1873), the Secretary of the Society of Antiquaries and a himself a Wiltshire man, had excavated an Anglo-Saxon cemetery at Harnham and the following year he excavated a field opposite Old Sarum, finding a burial accompanied by a pewter chalice and paten.[27] The artefacts from these excavations had been deposited in the British Museum.

A temporary exhibition of 'local industry, amateur productions, works of art, antiquities, objects of taste, articles of vertu, etc.' was formed and opened on the 12th October 1852.

The 1852 exhibition had been organised by two secretaries; James Smith (1820-1910), the editor of the *Salisbury and Winchester Journal*, and Walter Francis Tiffin (1817-1890), a prominent local artist and collector of prints and of porcelain. The two had collaborated the previous year on Smith's book *Wilton and its Associations*, for which Tiffin had created a number of illustrations that were engraved by Josiah Wood Whimper [also known as Whymper] (1813-1903).[28]

Snapshots of Salisbury collectors and antiquaries can be found in those who lent objects to the 1852 exhibition[29] and the contents of the temporary museum formed in Salisbury in 1854 as part of the Second Annual Meeting of the Wiltshire Archaeological and Natural History Society. The picture painted is the diversity of local private collections, spanning Old Master paintings and prints, through decorative arts, photographs, geological artefacts to curiosities – such as a lock of Admiral Nelson's hair.

Edward Walter Brodie (1830-1911), a wine and spirit merchant

27 The Harnham excavations were described in Akerman's *Remains of Pagan Saxondom*, published in 20 parts, 1852-1855 in London by John Russell Smith.

28 James Smith, *Wilton and Its Associations*, George Brown, Salisbury and J. B Nichols & Son, London, 1851. This book had been published by subscription. One of the subscribers was 'W. Blackmore' of Sarum, though this was probably William Bennett Blackmore, William Henry's father. James Smith emigrated to Australia in 1854. See Jane Howells, 'Salisbury's 1852 "Great Exhibition"', *Sarum Chronicle*, 2, 2002 pp. 25-34.

29 *Catalogue of the Salisbury Exhibition of Local Industry, Amateur Productions, Works of Art, Antiquities, Objects of taste, Articles of Vertu, etc.,Opened on the Twelfth of October 1852*, James Bennett,[Salisbury] [1852].

who was related to the family that had been owners of the *Salisbury and Winchester Journal* until 1848, had formed a significant collection of artefacts from the drainage work undertaken in Salisbury. In May 1854 John Yonge Akerman exhibited a selection of artefacts from Brodie's collection at a meeting of the Society of Antiquaries in London.[30] The following September the Wiltshire Archaeological and Natural History Society held its annual general meeting in Salisbury and Brodie exhibited his collection in the Council Chamber at the Town Hall. He offered to present his collection to the city as the nucleus of a museum though he continued to exhibit it. On the 7th May, 1857 Brodie exhibited some of his drainage collection and other items found at Wilton at the Society of Antiquaries.[31] In August 1858 Brodie exhibited items from his collections, including part of his 'Drainage' collection, at the fifteenth annual meeting of the meeting British Archaeological Association held in Salisbury.[32] However, it remains unclear as to why in 1859 a group of subscribers led by the bookseller William Brown[33] formed a 'Relic Fund', purchased the Brodie collection at auction for £32 10s. and in April 1860 established a new museum governed by trustees, formed a 'Provisional Committee' and appointed Edward Thomas Stevens as 'provisional' secretary and treasurer.[34]

30 This was published as 'Note on a Variety of Objects discovered during the progress of Excavations for Sewerage in Salisbury', *Archaeologia* London, 1855 pp.71-73 and included a full page illustration of 'Heads of Missile Weapons found at Salisbury.'

31 *The Gentleman's Magazine*, June 1857 p.712.

32 *The Journal of the British Archaeological Association*, 1859 p.21. He had been elected an associate in 1858.

33 This may be William Brown who died on 15th February 1867 aged 35 years of age. See *The Bookseller*, 30th March, 1867 p.204.

34 A letter in the collections of the Salisbury & South Wiltshire Museum, dated 19th September 1859 from Job Edwards, an antiquary from Amesbury, to Edward Kite (1832-1930) an antiquary from Devizes, records the amount paid and noted that the collection 'will most likely lead to the formation of a Museum'. As cited in Peter R. Saunders, *Channels to the past: the Salisbury drainage collection*, Salisbury & South Wiltshire Museum, Salisbury, 1986 p.2. See also R. W. H. Willoughby, 'The Salisbury and South Wilts Museum: Founded 1860.' *Wiltshire Archaeological and Natural History Magazine*, Volume 57 Number CCVIII, Devizes, 1960 pp.307. Frank Stevens stated that the Brodie collection was purchased after Brodie's death. See 'Salisbury Museum. The Story of its Growth. The Latest Addition of a Gallery.'

Edward Stevens' son Frank listed a number of members of the 'Provisional Committee' in his history of the Salisbury Museum published in 1948. This included William, Humphrey and Henry Blackmore, though there is little corroborating evidence that William was significantly involved in the venture.[35] Another curious fact is that having sold his collection, Edward Brodie played no significant subsequent role in the Salisbury Museum.[36]

The founding of the Salisbury Museum was not without its challenges. Andrew Bogle Middleton (1819-1879), a surgeon who lived in The Close and who in 1864 was to write an important statistical study on the sanitary conditions in Salisbury before and after the drainage of the canals in the early 1850s, felt aggrieved that while he considered that he had first proposed a museum he had subsequently been excluded from the 'Provisional Committee.'[37] In July 1860 Middelton began a correspondence with Edward Stevens through the columns of the *Salisbury and Winchester Journal.* Stevens took either a magnanimous or a strategic approach and resigned from the committee in order that his personal conflict with Middleton might not jeopardise the venture. This appears to have had little significant effect since Stevens continued to be actively involved in the new museum while Middleton did not play any further role.

Salisbury's first museum was initially housed at No.1 Castle Street next door to the recently opened market house. It opened in June 1861 for four hours a week. Dr. Richard Fowler, FRS, FSA (1765-1863),

originally published in the Wiltshire Gazette on 26th October, 1933 and reprinted in edited form in the *Wiltshire Archaeological and Natural History Magazine*, clx. June, 1934 p.541.

35 Frank Stevens, *The Salisbury Museums 1861-1947*, Bennett Brothers, Salisbury [1948] p. 3. The other committee members listed by Stevens included James Nightingale, James Hussey and Walter Kerr Hamilton, the Bishop of Salisbury.

36 Little is known about Brodie. He was still listed as a wine and spirit merchant in the Kelly's 1875 directory for Salisbury and was recorded as living in Fugglestone St. Peter, near Wilton in the 1881 census. Brodie then moved to London.

37 A. B. Middleton, *The Benefits of Sanitary Reform as shown at Salisbury, as shown at Salisbury in nine years' experience therof: a paper read before the British Association for the Advancement of Science, at Bath, September 17th, 1864*. Simpkin & Co., London, 1864. This paper was also published in the *Journal of the Statistical Society of London*, December, 1864 pp.553-557.

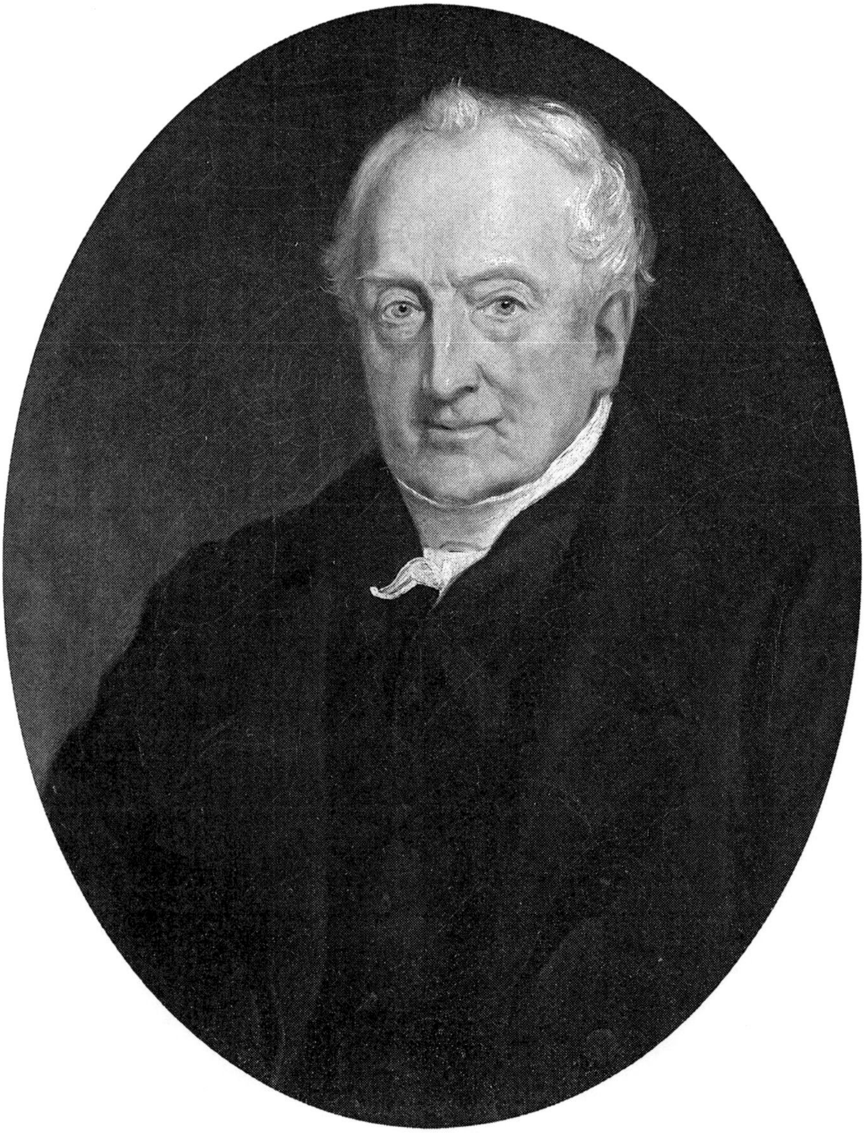

Dr Richard Fowler (1765-1863)
Oil on canvas
Courtesy of Salisbury & South Wiltshire Museum

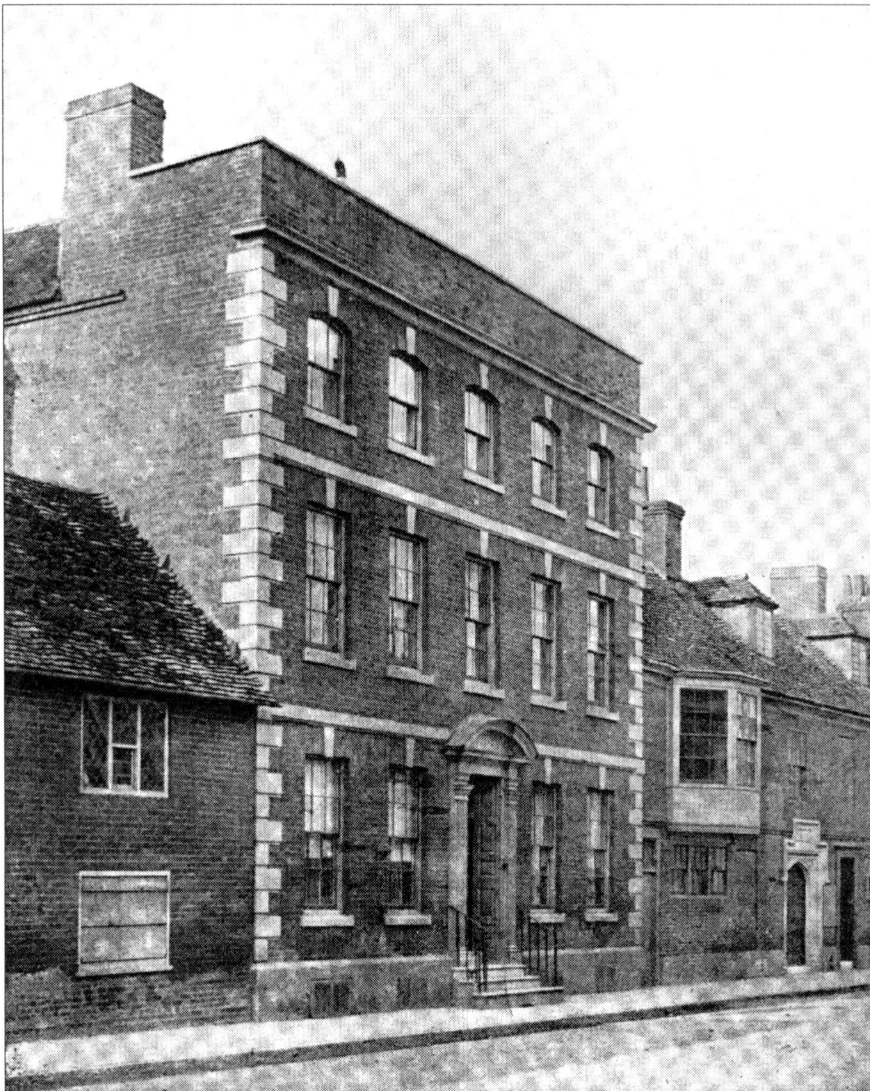

View of Colonel Baker's House, St. Ann Street c.1862.
Frontispiece to Frank Stevens, *The Salisbury Museums 1861-1947: A Record of Eighty-Six Years of Progress* Bennett Brothers, Salisbury [1948]
Courtesy of Salisbury & South Wiltshire Museum

considered Salisbury's leading physician, a prominent local antiquary, and close friend of Henry Shorto, William and Humphrey Blackmore's grandfather, then pro-actively moved to put the museum on a sounder footing. Fowler, who had accompanied Henry Hatcher in his exploration of the site of Clarendon Palace and had founded and built the Working Men's Club in St Ann Street, then purchased Numbers 40 and 42 St Ann Street – the house of the late Colonel Baker – and endowed them to the museum's Trustees for the site of a permanent museum which opened in January 1864. In 1862 Fowler gave the Salisbury Museum a large part of his library and collections and it was estimated that the total cost of this investment by Fowler was to have been some £700.[38]

A sixty-page catalogue to the collections of the Salisbury & South Wiltshire Museum was published in 1864. This was edited by Edward Stevens, who had also catalogued the Stone, Bronze, and early Iron objects. Humphrey Blackmore documented the Mammalian remains belonging to the pleistocene period while Henry Blackmore arranged and catalogued the collection of British birds. William Osmond jnr. (1821-1890), of the Salisbury firm of architectural masons, had catalogued the Mediaeval seals, while the local antiquary James Edward Nightingale (c.1817-1892) documented the Mediaeval series and the pottery. The *Journal of the British Archaeological Association*, referred to the Rev. Charles Henry Tomlinson as being in charge of the arrangement of the minerals but he was not credited in the published catalogue.[39] A significant number of the objects on display had been 'deposited' by Humphrey Blackmore and Edward Stevens. William Blackmore was noticeable by his absence.

The Salisbury Museum was considered a success by contemporaries;

> It should be distinctly understood that this is not a mere bare enumeration of the objects deposited in the museum, but that popular and intelligible

38 'Antiquarian Intelligence. Salisbury & South Wilts Museum', Journal *of the British Archaeological Association*, Volume XX, London, 1864 pp.93-95. It is significant that Edward Thomas Stevens was executor of Fowler's will. *The Hampshire Advertiser, Saturday, 18th April, 1863 p.4.*

39 *ibid.* See also *Catalogue of the Salisbury & South Wilts Museum*, Bennet, Salisbury, 1864.

> explanations of the uses, objects, purposes, and nature of the objects registered, are freely and fully appended. Too much praise cannot be given to those who have thus striven to make the Salisbury Museum instructive to visitors of all denominations and degrees of education and intelligence.[40]

It is worth noting that while Humphrey and Henry Blackmore helped catalogue the newly formed collections of the Salisbury & South Wiltshire Museum neither they nor their brother-in-law Edward Stevens were listed amongst the list of officials of the museum. The Trustees of the museum were the Town Council of the City of New Sarum. The President was the Bishop of Salisbury, supported by thirteen vice-presidents made up of the Mayor of Salisbury and local members of the nobility and members of parliament. This was very typical of committees formed to do anything in Salisbury at the time. The name of Andrew Bogle Middleton did not appear though the Rev. Edward Duke (1814-1895), son of one of the leading antiquaries of the Salisbury area, was included. While James Clench and James Wilton – both of The Canal – were Honorary Secretaries, there were no 'curators' listed. Given the comparatively impressive list of officers it is worth pointing out that at the time of its opening the Salisbury & South Wiltshire Museum still consisted of objects displayed in only two rooms.

In 1867 Stevens was named as the 'General Curator' of the Salisbury & South Wiltshire Museum, Humphrey and Henry Blackmore being Honorary Curators of the Natural History collections. This situation regarding Stevens' role at the Salisbury & South Wiltshire Museum changed in around 1870 when he became 'Director' of the Museum, a role that was in addition to his position as Honorary Curator of the Blackmore Museum. The formality of this appointment was called into question by G. Sidney Read, the Honorary Curator of the Numismatic Department who considered Stevens' appointment was 'informal.' In a printed letter to the President, vice-president, honorary officers and

40 *The Geologist. A Popular Illustrated Monthly Magazine of Geology*, London [June] 1864 p.239. A review of *Descriptive Catalogue of the Salisbury and South Wilts Museum, Bennett*, Salisbury: Bennett. 1864 and *Proceedings of the Inauguration of the Salisbury and South Wilts Museum*, Bennett, Salisbury, 1864.

members of the museum, Stevens tendered his resignation. However, the annual report for that year notes that Stevens had retained the position.[41]

Both Edward Stevens and Humphrey Blackmore were subsequently instrumental in the organising of another significant exhibition in Salisbury. In January 1862, together with Charles John Read, a local musician and composer,[42] they organised a 'Temporary Museum' of pictures and works of art held at the Council Chamber in Salisbury. This exhibition was held as part of the 'conversazione' given by the Salisbury Literary & Scientific Institution and the Salisbury & South Wiltshire Museum. As with the 1852 exhibition and the 'Temporary Museum' of the 1854 Annual Meeting of the Wiltshire Archaeological and Natural History Society it gives another insight into the collections formed by leading members of the Salisbury community.

While Salisbury might not have been considered an appropriate geographic location for an ethnographic collection of such international significance there was local awareness of the importance of the Blackmore Museum. The 1866 edition of *Brown's Strangers' Handbook to Salisbury* predicted that 'There is little doubt that the Blackmore Museum will rank as a National rather than a merely Local Museum.'[43] At the Blackmore Museum's opening ceremony, Horatio Bolton Nelson, 3rd Earl Nelson (1823-1913) pointed to Salisbury's emerging position as a transport hub, stating that the city was 'so generally connected by railways with almost every other place in England' that the establishment of the Blackmore Museum 'might really be called a boon to the nation at large.'[44] The London & South Western line from Salisbury (actually Milford, an

41 I thank Adrian Green for pointing this document out to me, a copy of which is held in the S&SWM.

42 Probably Charles John Read (born c. 1821), organist and composer, organist of St. Thomas' Church, Salisbury and 'professor of music' – as listed in *Kelly's Directory of Wiltshire*, 1867 p.335. In the 1881 census Read was resident in The Close in the house of his brother Raphael W. Read.

43 Brown's *Series of Strangers' Handbooks. No.2. The Illustrated Guide to the City of Salisbury*, Brown and Co., Salisbury 1866 p.56.

44 *Some Account of the Blackmore Museum – Part I. The opening Meeting*, H.F. & E. Bull, Devizes; Bell & Daldy, London ; J.R. Smith, London 1868 p.35

eastern suburb) to Southampton had opened in 1847; Great Western services first appeared in Salisbury in 1856 and the direct line to London in 1857. The line to Exeter was completed in 1859. In 1866 the Salisbury and Dorset Junction Railway opened a more direct railway route from Salisbury to Bournemouth and Poole via Downton and Fordingbridge to join the Ringwood/Wimborne line at West Moors. This, as Horatio Nelson highlighted, made Salisbury a significant crossroads on the rapidly expanding railway network. William Blackmore was involved in this evolving railway network. In 1857 he was a director of the Salisbury Railway Company and later a director of the Salisbury and Dorset Junction Railway, established in 1861.[45]

The collections destined for display in the Blackmore Museum had been exhibited prior to the Museum's opening. The first showing of the Davis collection after its arrival in England was at a meeting of the South of England Literary and Philosophical Society held at the Hartley Institution in Southampton in January 1865.[46] No other reference has been found to other formal or public displays of the collection but it is likely that – as the *de facto* curator – Edward Stevens gave access privately.

Acquisitions and donations to the Blackmore Museum began before its opening. In 1866 the *American Phrenological Journal* reported that ' we have had the pleasure of sending to Mr. Blackmore specimens of Indian – Sioux – skulls to the Salisbury Museum.'[47] Another part of Blackmore's collection were objects from the lake villages of Switzerland that had been formed for Blackmore by Admiral the Honourable E. A. J. Harris, who was for a period in the early 1860s Her Majesty's Minister in Berne. Harris had been assisted by a number of Swiss archaeologists including Dr. Ferdinand Keller, Dr. Johann Uhlmann, Dr. Carl Ludwig

45 As cited in *Bradshaw's railway manual, shareholders' guide and official directory* for 1857 and 1867.

46 A report of the meeting appeared in *The Hampshire Advertiser County Newspaper*, 28th January, 1865 p.2.

47 *The [American] Phrenological Journal and Life Illustrated*, September, 1866 p.96. These skulls were deposited with the Royal College of Surgeons in 1934.

Rütimeyer and Frédéric Troyon.[48] Blackmore may have used other 'scouts' to acquire objects for his collections though it would appear that unlike some of his contemporaries, he did not extensively purchase items from dealers.

Not all of the Squier and Davis collection was to be displayed in Salisbury since Blackmore donated fifty-seven of the artefacts to the British Museum. Some in 1866, another set in 1868 and in 1872 items from the Santa Cruz islands and Pacific were donated. These may have been considered duplicates or surplus to requirements. Conversely, similar discussions were held with the Smithsonian Institution in 1870 when Assistant Secretary Spencer Fullerton Baird wrote to Blackmore on 11th June;

> Our duplicates are, now, somewhat numerous and no one has a better right to the first choice from among them than yourself. If we could only look forward to a speedy visit from you and have you make the selection for yourself it would be a source of the highest gratification to us.[49]

These examples underline the commonplace practice of exchanging objects between individual collectors and collections that was prevalent during the mid 19th century. It evidenced a degree of international collaboration supporting a common goal. Blackmore's ability to build an international network of contacts to meet his aims and objectives again underlines his interpersonal skills.

Whether William Blackmore was involved in the detail design of either the architecture or the fixtures and fittings of his museum remains unknown. Similarly, the issue of the display and classification of the wide ranging objects from his collections has yet to receive a detailed analysis. At this point it is worth considering the possible influence on Blackmore by his contemporaries.

48 See *Some Account of the Blackmore Museum – Part II* p.171 and Annual *Report of the Board of Regents of the Smithsonian Institution . . . for the year 1868*, Washington, D.C., 1869 p.411.

49 As cited in Michael Petraglia and Richard Potts, *The Old World Paleolithic and the Development of a National Collection*, Smithsonian Contributions and Studies Series, Washington, D.C., 2004 pp.67.

In his address at the opening of his Museum in 1867 Blackmore listed a wide variety of 'friends' who were prominent members of the scholarly societies pushing forward the boundaries of the study of a number of newly emerging disciplines including anthropology, ethnography, geology and archaeology. Some such as Augustus

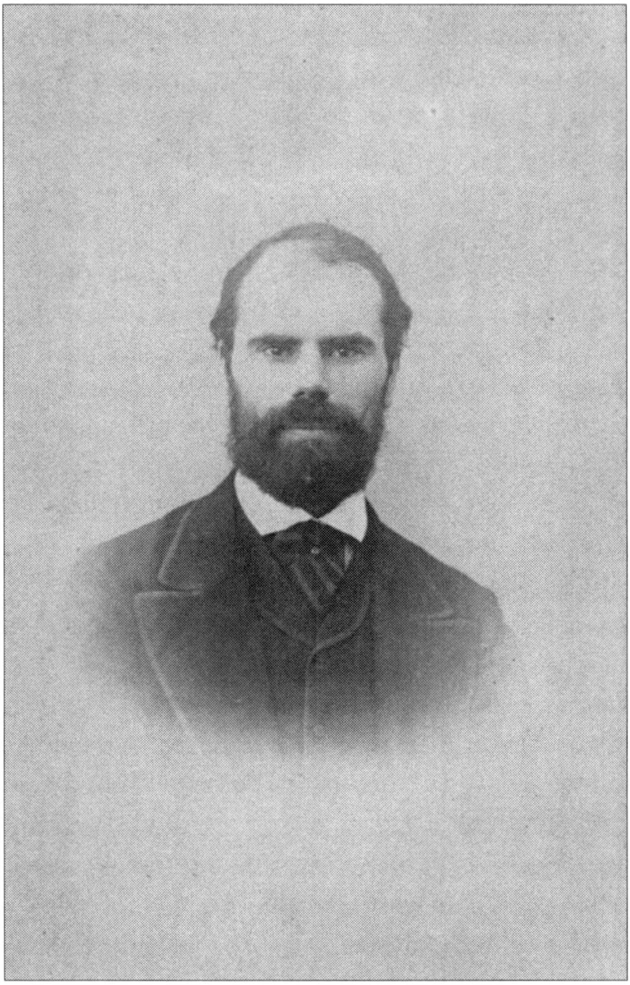

Augustus Wollaston Franks (1826-1897)
Carte de visite
Albumen print
Courtesy of Salisbury & South Wiltshire Museum

Wollaston Franks (1826-1897) and Joseph Henry (1797-1878) were part of the small band of museum professionals. Others like him, had 'days jobs', and their scholarly pursuits were 'hobbies'. Two contemporaries of Blackmore are particularly relevant since they were private collectors, their interests overlapped with William's and their collections became

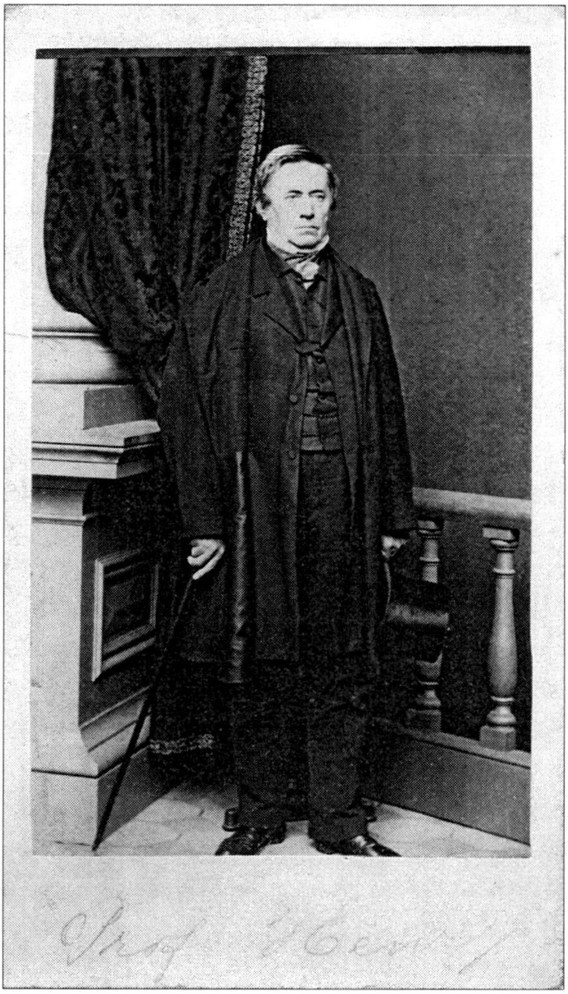

Joseph Henry (1797-1878)
Photographed by James W. Queen & Co., 924 Chestnut Street Philadelphia
published by E. Anthony, 501 Broadway
Carte de visite
Albumen print
Courtesy of Salisbury & South Wiltshire Museum

housed in public collections around the time of the opening of the Blackmore Museum; these are Henry Christy and Augustus Henry Lane Fox Pitt Rivers.

HENRY CHRISTY

Henry Christy (1810-1865) was a man of private means as a result of the success of his father's London firm of hatters for which he worked for a short period. He had begun collecting around the time of the Great Exhibition of 1851 and travelled widely in North Africa, Asia, Mexico and British Columbia during the 1850s as well as in Norway, Sweden, Denmark and France. As a result he had formed a significant ethnographic collection housed in his home in Victoria Street in London.

Christy visited Copenhagen in 1852 where he was impressed and influenced by the Danish museums. He met Christian Jurgensen Thomsen (1788-1865), the archaeologist responsible for the first practical application of the Three Age system of periodisation of human prehistory and curator of what became the National Museum of Denmark.

In 1858 Christy confirmed the discoveries made in the Somme valley in Northern France around 1830 by the French archaeologist Jacques Boucher de Crèvecœur de Perthes (1788-1868). These flint implements clearly proved the great antiquity of man in Europe. Christy joined the Geological Society, and in company with his friend Edouard Lartet (1801-1871) explored the caves in the valley of the Vézère river, a tributary of the Dordogne River in south-western France. Some of the finds were acquired by the Blackmore Museum as were casts of other objects in the Christy collection. These appear to have been donated by the Trustees of the Christy Collection after Henry Christy's death. Edward Stevens clearly had a detailed knowledge of the Christy Collection and made numerous references to objects in it in his *Flint Chips* of 1870.

On his 1852 trip to Denmark Christy had met Carl Ludwig Steinhauer (1816-1897), who had become an assistant to Christian Thomsen in 1846 when the ethnography collections were separated from the rest of what were then the Royal Danish collections. Steinhauer is credited with stimulating Christy to broaden his collections and in

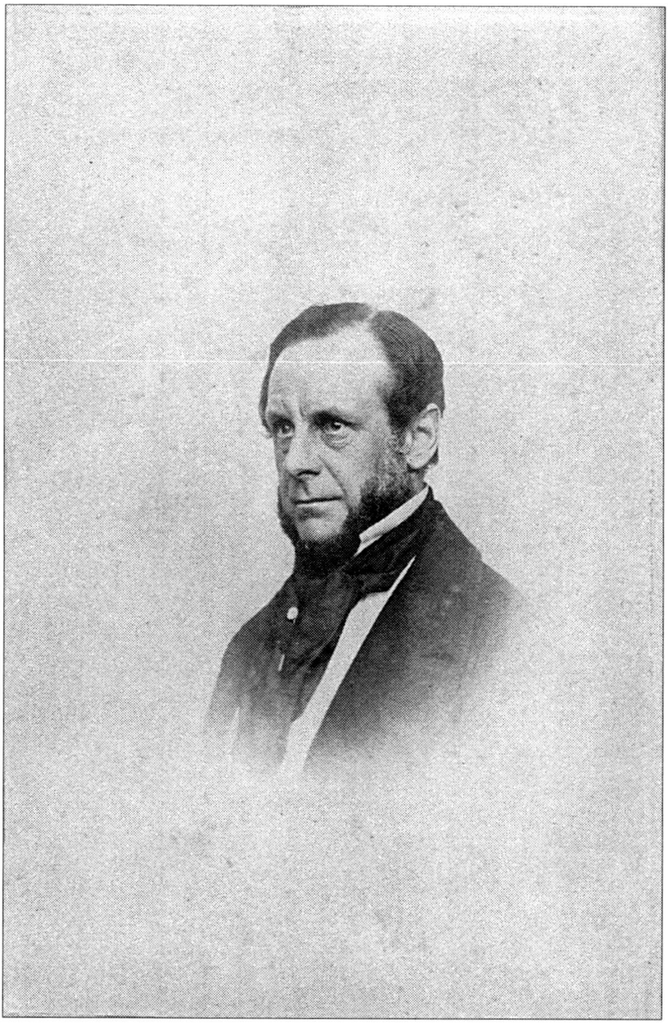

Henry Christy (1810-1865)
Carte de visite
Albumen print
Courtesy of Salisbury & South Wiltshire Museum

1861 the Dane was asked to catalogue Christy's collection.[50] *Catalogue of a collection of ancient and modern stone implements, and of other weapons, tools, and utensils of the aborigines of various countries, in the possession of*

50 David Mackenzie Wilson, *The British Museum; A History.*, British Museum Press, London, 2002 p.159.

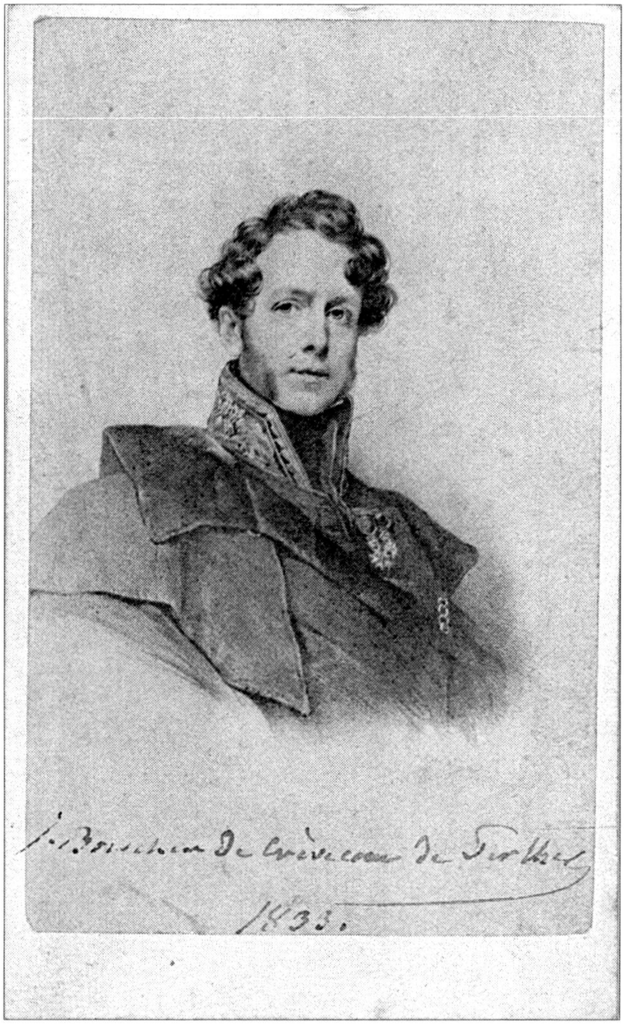

Jacques Boucher de Crèvecœur de Perthes (1788-1868) Photograph by Dubosq, 44 Rue St. Gilles, Abbeville "d'aprés un portrait 1833"
Carte de visite
Albumen print
Courtesy of Salisbury & South Wiltshire Museum

Henry Christy was published by Taylor and Francis the following year. This seventy-six page privately distributed publication provided an artefact-by-artefact catalogue within a scheme for looking at both Old World prehistory and ethnographic materials from outside Europe.

However, it recorded only those items from Christy's collection that were put on display in the single room in his home in Victoria Street that had been made available as his 'museum.' The title is not listed in the *Catalogue of the Library of the Blackmore Museum* and it is unknown whether Blackmore ever visited it, though this seems highly probable.

In 1864 Christy concluded his excavations in the Périgord district with the French palaeontologist Edouard Lartet (1801-1871) – the expenses for which he paid – and in June of that year gave a paper 'On the Prehistoric Cave-Dwellers of Southern France' to the Ethnological Society.[51]

After his death in 1865 Christy's ethnographic collection – probably consisting of around one thousand items – came to the British Museum under a section of his will dated 5th February 1863. Four rooms, the hall and a corridor in Christy's former apartment at 103 Victoria Street were converted into a temporary display space and Augustus Wollaston Franks developed and arranged the Christy Collection using display cases Christy had acquired from the 1862 London International Exhibition.[52] Room I contained ancient stone implements from Europe, Asia, and Africa, and more recent objects from the 'Esquimaux' of America and Aisa. Room II contained objects from Asia and Africa. Room III held items from Polynesia, New Zealand and Melanesia. Australia and part of North America were displayed in the Corridor while Room IV contained the remainder of the American collections.[53] Edward Stevens wrote in 1870 that 'The foundation of a National Ethnological Museum exists in the Christy Collection, already the property of the nation' and noted that 'the development and arrangement of this very instructive museum is

51 Henry Christy, 'On the Prehistoric Cave-Dwellers of Southern France', *Transactions of the Ethnological Society of London*, Vol. 3, 1865 pp. 362-372.

52 Although Franks notebooks for the 1860s and 1870s include drawings of display cases, it is not clear whether he had influence on, or was influenced by, the design of the display cases at the Blackmore Museum.

53 *Guide to the Christy collection of Prehistoric Antiquities and Ethnography. Temporarily placed at 103, Victoria Street, Westminster.*, Trustees of the British Museum, [London], 1868 pp.4-5. Humphrey Blackmore's copy is held at the S&SWM. The Christy Collection was only open between 10am and 4pm on Fridays, tickets were issued at the main hall of the British Museum.

being most admirably carried out by Mr. Franks, and it is hoped that the public will second his efforts, by assisting him to fill up the gaps which must necessarily exist, for some time to come, in the continuity of the series in such a collection.'[54]

Lane Fox, a contemporary of Christy's, differentiated his collection from that of Christy thus; 'in the Christy collection the arrangement [is] geographical, whereas I have from the first collected and arranged by forms.' In 1862 the Christy collection was divided into 'early', 'later' and post stone age 'Antiquities' and an 'Ethnography' section divided by geographical region – Greenland, the 'Caribes', the ancient Peruvians, the ancient Mexicans, the modern Mexicans, the Eskimo, the North American Indian.[55] How aware William Blackmore was of the debates in the early to mid 1860s around classification and display of ethnographic objects within the Christy collection is not clear though it is likely that Edward Stevens was.

No evidence has been found that Henry Christy either formed a significant photograph collection or considered photography as a key tool to achieve his aims and objectives. In 1872 Part I of *British Museum Collections. Photographed by Stephen Thompson* was published. This was the Pre-Historic and Ethnographical Series and was composed of one hundred and fifty-seven plates selected and catalogued by A.W. Franks. The photographs cost 2s. 6d. each mounted – more than a copy of the Guide to the Christy Collection published in 1868 – or £9. 12s. 6d. complete in two portfolios. The majority of the objects in this series were from the Christy Collection.[56] The finance for this venture came from the wealthy solicitor Charles Harrison (1835-1897) whose offices were in Bedford Row, Bloomsbury, near the British Museum. Harrison had

54 Edward Stevens, *Flint Chips; a guide to pre-historic archaeology, as illustrated by the collection in the Blackmore Museum, Salisbury, Brown and Co.,and F. A. Blake; Bell and Daldy*, Salisbury, London,, 1870 pp.xv-xvi.

55 William Ryan Chapman ,'Arranging Ethnology: Pitt Rivers and the Typological Tradition' in George W. Stocking (ed.), *Objects and others: essays on museums and material culture. History of Anthropology Volume 3*, University of Wisconsin Press, Madison, 1985 pp.15-48 – references on pp.25-26.

56 For a detailed discussion of these photographs see Elizabeth Edwards, *Raw Histories: Photographs, Anthropology and Museums.*, Berg Publishers, London, 2001, pp.70-3.

made his fortune as a solicitor for railway companies such as the London Chatham and Dover Railway and a number of insurance companies. Blackmore knew him professionally. Harrison was elected a member of the Ethnological Society in 1869. It has not been established whether Blackmore owned a copy of this series of photographs, but given that in 1874 he donated to the Smithsonian another Part – Part III [Plates 350-595] of the Assyrian Series, selected and catalogued by Samuel Birch and George Smith – it would seem almost inconceivable that he didn't.

It seems likely that William Blackmore knew Henry Christy, but how well remains unclear. Christy's name does not appear in the list of friends, colleagues and contacts that Blackmore cited in his address at the opening of the Blackmore Museum, though it would appear that good contacts with the Trustees of the Christy Collection were formed in the immediate years after Henry Christy's death. Both Blackmore and Stevens were listed as donating items to the Christy Collection between July 1866 and July 1868, that is after Christy's death. Blackmore donated four stone pipes from the Ohio mounds.[57] Therefore the primary link between the Blackmore Museum and the Christy Collection is likely to have been through Augustus Wollaston Franks.

The Christy Collection finally moved to the British Museum in 1883-1884 on the departure of the natural history collections to South Kensington.

AUGUSTUS HENRY LANE FOX PITT RIVERS

Augustus Henry Lane Fox Pitt Rivers (1827-1900) is considered to be the 'father of scientific archaeology' and a generation ahead of his time. He was particularly interested in typology and evolution and he is recognised as having 'scientifically' organised his extensive collections. Pitt Rivers is connected with Salisbury both through links with William Blackmore, Edwards Stevens and the Blackmore Museum in the 1860s, and over a century later when the Salisbury & South Wiltshire Museum was gifted

57 *Guide to the Christy Collection of Prehistoric Antiquities and Ethnography. Temporarily placed at 103, Victoria Street, Westminster,* The Trustees of the British Museum, [London] 1868 pp.23-24 and 18-19.

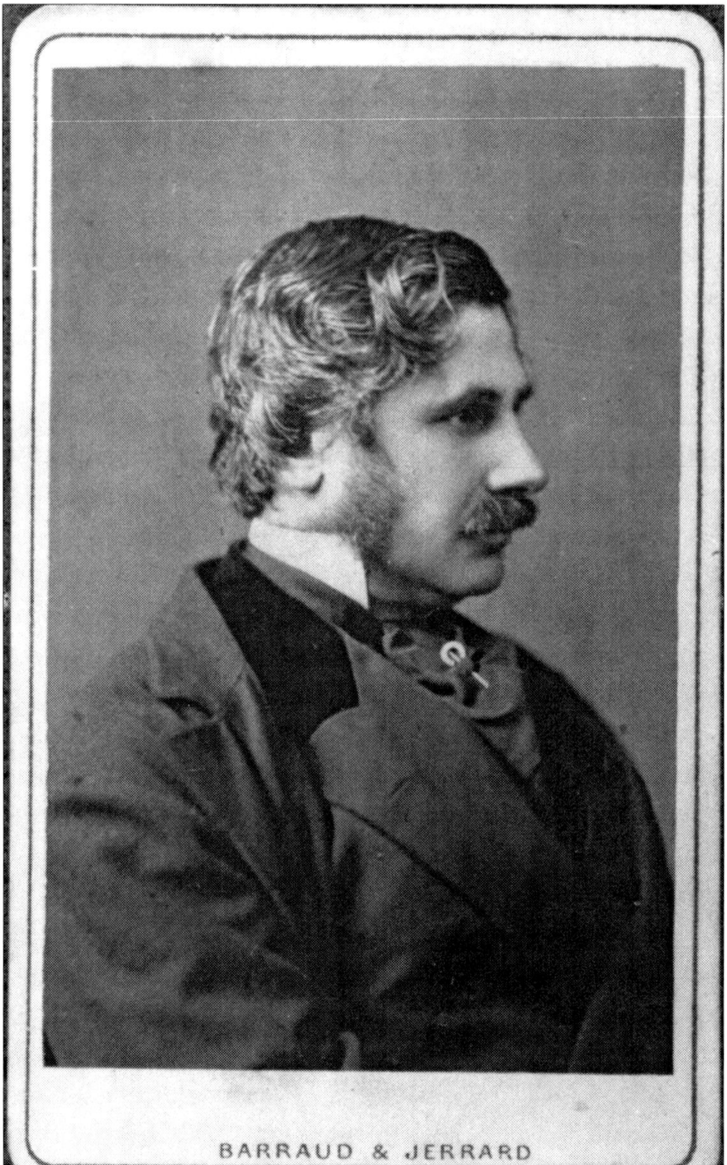

Augustus Henry LaneFox (1827-1900)
Photographed by Barraud & Jerrard, 96 Gloucester Place, St Marylebone, London c.1875
Carte de visite
Albumen print
Courtesy of Anthony Pitt-Rivers

the Wessex collections of Pitt Rivers by HM Treasury.[58] Lane Fox is better known as Augustus Pitt Rivers following his inheritance in 1880 of the Rushmore Estate in Cranborne Chase, Dorset from a great uncle, Horace Pitt Rivers, 6th Baron Rivers (1814–1880), and consequently the remainder of the fortune of the English civil servant and politician Richard Rigby (1722-1788) accumulated in wheeler-dealing within the political circles of the 18th century British parliament. Lane Fox did not assume his great uncle's title but thereafter adopted the surname Pitt Rivers in honour of his benefactor.[59] The following account will use the convention of referring to Lane Fox for his activities prior to 1880. After this date the name Pitt Rivers will be used.

Commissioned into the Grenadier Guards in 1845, Augustus Henry Lane Fox (1827-1900) served in the Crimea War (1853-1856). He started accumulating primitive weapons in 1851, while a professional soldier. While he was an inveterate collector, the majority of objects in his extensive holdings were sourced from dealers and auction houses. Lane Fox spent up to £300 per year – around a third of his income – amassing a significant collection housed in his London home and scholarly reputation to match. However, though already substantial and significant, little is known about Fox Lane's 'first' collection, that is the one formed prior to 1880.[60]

Although at the time of William Blackmore's untimely death Lane Fox was an already established and prominent individual within the scholarly circles, he continued to acquire new roles that consolidated

58 For an account of the acquisition see Peter R. Saunders, 'What happened to the Pitt Rivers Wessex Collection?', *Museums Journal*, Volume 75, No.4, March 1976 pp.156-8. For the life of Pitt Rivers see Mark Bowden, *Pitt Rivers: The Life and Archaeological work of Lieutenant-General Augustus Henry Lane Fox Pitt Rivers*, Cambridge University Press, Cambridge, 1991. See also David K. van Keuren, 'Museums and Ideology: Augustus Pitt Rivers, Anthropological Museums, and Social Change in Later Victorian Britain', *Victorian Studies*, Vol. 28, No. 1 (Autumn, 1984), pp. 171-189. Van Keuren mentions neither the Blackmore Museum nor Edward Stevens.

59 The Rushmore Estate consisted of some 27,000 acres and had an average annual income of around £20,000.

60 Pitt Rivers, *Address delivered at the Opening of the Dorset County Museum, Dorchester January 7 1884* p.8. See also Alison Petch, 'Chance and Certitude: Pitt Rivers and his first collection', *Journal of the History of Collecting*, 2006 pp.249-256.

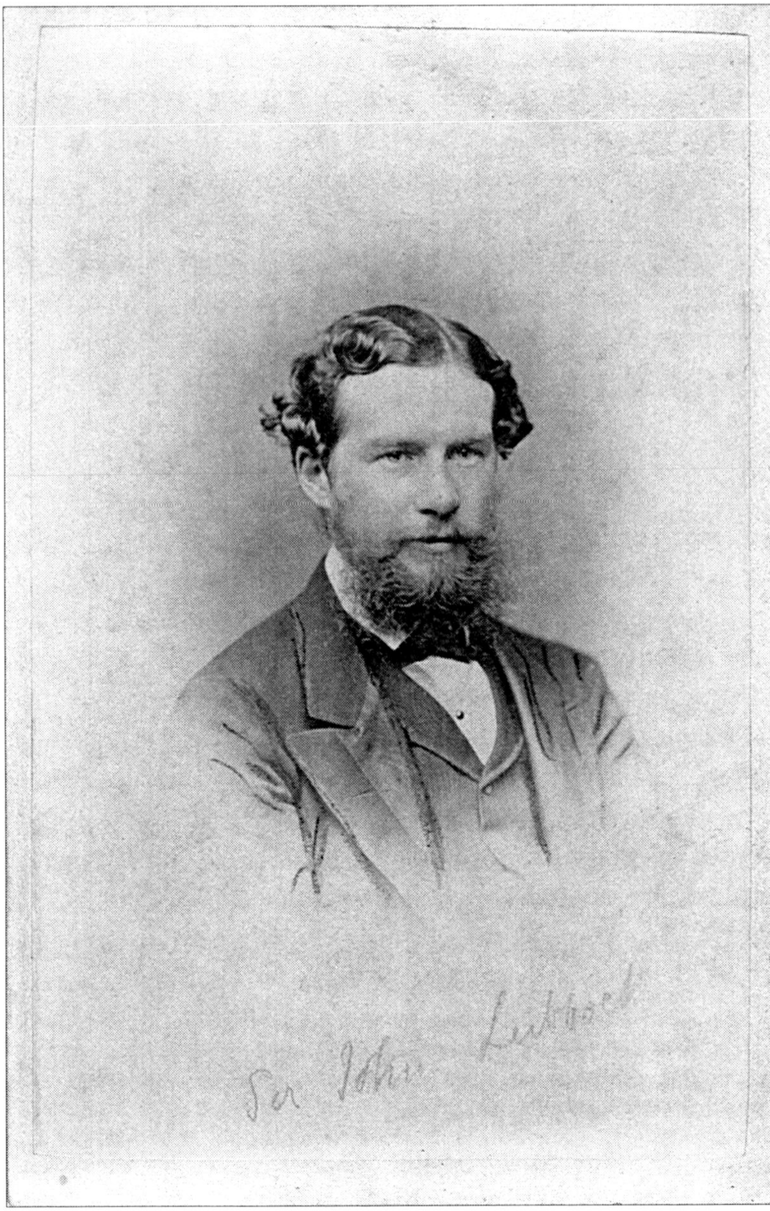

Sir John Lubbock (1834-1913)
Photographed by H. J. Whitlock, 11 New Street, Birmingham
Albumen print
Blackmore carte de visite album
Courtesy of Salisbury & South Wiltshire Museum

and enhanced his reputation and legacy. In 1882, now known as Pitt Rivers, he was made the first Inspector of Ancient Monuments, largely due to Sir John Lubbock (1834-1913), the banker, biologist, archaeologist, entomologist and Liberal politician, whose enactment of the Ancient Monuments Act in that year introduced the role. Pitt Rivers' excavations on his Rushmore Estate created a set of artefacts that together with some of the thousands of objects he bought between 1880 and 1900 he housed in a museum in Farnham, Dorset.

Lane Fox undertook his earliest archaeological fieldwork in Ireland, after being posted there as Assistant Quartermaster General in 1862. His first excavation was upon an earthwork at Roovesmore Fort in Aglish, County Cork in 1865, an undertaking soon succeeded by similar work in both Ireland and England. By this point in his career he had already become part of the scholarly establishment. Lane Fox was elected to the Ethnological Society of London (1861), the Society of Antiquaries of London (1864) and the Anthropological Society of London (1865).

In September 1867 Lane Fox discovered flint implements in some pits in Cissbury Camp near Worthing, Sussex, referred to in *Some Account of the Blackmore Museum* (1868).[61] This excavation, undertaken under the auspices of the Anthropological Institute, was a significant turning point in Lane Fox's interests and from then on his chief professional activity was centred on excavations rather than acquiring artefacts through dealers and auction houses. In 1867 Lane Fox went on half-pay and devoted the rest of his life to the study of cultural anthropology and British archaeology.

It is not clear whether Lane Fox displayed his collections at Park Hill House, Brompton Crescent in Clapham, South London where he lived from 1858 to 1862 or during the period from 1863 to 1865 when he lived in his mother's house at 1 Chesham Street. His ever expanding collection was probably first exhibited at 10 Upper Phillimore Gardens, Kensington, where he lived from 1866 until 1878 and which was the first house he considered his own London home. However, the material soon outgrew this accommodation and in 1874 it went on loan to the

61 *Some Account of the Blackmore Museum*, 1868 p.204.

Bethnal Green Branch of the South Kensington Museum.[62] Five years later the collection moved to larger rooms in the West Galleries of the South Kensington Museum. It was subsequently offered to Oxford University in 1883, moving to its new quarters, the Pitt Rivers Museum, in 1885.

Lane Fox knew and had met William Blackmore both professionally and socially during the 1860s. Both were members of the Ethnological Society that Blackmore had joined in 1866. In 1868 they both sat on the organising committee of the International Congress of Prehistoric Archaeology – Lane Fox as Honorary Secretary and Blackmore as an honorary member. Both were officers of the Anthropological Institute – the two being on the first Council formed in 1871. Lane Fox was president and Blackmore a council member in 1872 and then 1874-1877. Brayer noted that Lane Fox had been a guest at Shepley House – presumably in the late 1860s – but failed to give the source of this piece of information.[63]

The certificate for Lane Fox to be elected a fellow of the Royal Society was hung in the Members Room on the 4th February 1875. This was signed from personal knowledge by the mineralogist, metallurgist and chemist David Forbes (1828-1876); the zoologist and palaeontologist George Busk (1807-1887); the anthropologist and eugenicist Francis Galton (1822-1911) and three others, all of whom William Blackmore knew well – John Lubbock, Augustus Wollaston Franks and Edward Burnett Tylor. None other than Charles Darwin signed the certificate from 'General Knowledge' of Lane Fox.[64] These sponsors reflected Lane Fox's high ranking contacts within the scientific establishment. They also formed part of the circle that William Blackmore inhabited.

62 See Alison Petch, *Pitt Rivers and his connections to London* http://england.prm.ox.ac.uk/englishness-Pitt Rivers-and-London.html See also 'On the Principles of Classification Adopted in the Arrangement of His Anthropological Collection, Now Exhibited in the Bethnal Green Museum.' *The Journal of the Anthropological Institute of Great Britain and Ireland*, Volume 4, 1875 pp.293-308.

63 Brayer,*op.cit.*, Volume I p.32 It is probable that this information was supplied by Frank Stevens.

64 Journal Book of The Royal Society, Volume L, 1860-1881. Lane Fox was formally recommended for election as a fellow at the meeting of the Royal Society held on the 4th May, 1876 and elected at the meeting on 30th November, 1876.

Lane Fox also knew Edward Stevens well, having acted as the secretary to the organising committee of the International Congress of Prehistoric Archaeology held in Norwich and London in August 1868 while Stevens was a member of the Special Committee. In 1869 Lane Fox exhibited some of the worked flints he had excavated at the meeting of the Ethnological Society on 9th November of that year. At this meeting Lane Fox proposed an exploration of Stonehenge by a committee of the British Association mentioning that he had discussed this with Edward Stevens and recommended that Stevens form part of this committee.[65] Stevens clearly respected Lane Fox and cited two published articles by Lane Fox in his *Flint Chips.*[66]

In 1870 Stevens was accompanied by Lane Fox, Canon William Greenwell (1820-1918) and others in searching for flint implements at Grime's Graves in Norfolk, the only Neolithic flint mine in Britain. Later that year a paper on these excavations was read by Greenwell at the Blackmore Museum as part of the Seventeenth Annual Meeting of the Wiltshire Archaeological and Natural History Society. Greenwell was also a donor to the Blackmore Museum. Humphrey Blackmore and Edward Stevens hosted a lunch for members of the Society at the Museum and Stevens read a paper on 'The Stone Period'.[67]

Pitt Rivers gave the inaugural address of the Annual Meeting of the Royal Archaeological Institute in Salisbury in 1887. He stated of the Blackmore Museum that 'the munificence of Mr. W. Blackmore, the

65 *The Journal of the Ethnological Society of London (1869-1870)*, Vol. 2, No. 1, 1870 pp. 1-5. A series of photographs of Stonehenge by Stephen Thompson was exhibited at this meeting though it is not clear who commissioned these. A model based on Stevens' reconstruction of Stonehenge was created in collaboration with Humphrey Blackmore.

66 'Primitive Warfare', *Journal of the Royal United Services Institute*, December 1867 [NB This may be an error by Stevens. The citation is *Journal of the Royal United Services Institute*, Volume 11, Issue 47 1868 , pages 612 – 645 . A second part published *Journal of the Royal United Services Institute*, Volume 12, Issue 51 1869 , pages 399 – 439] The other publication cited was 'Examination of the Hill Forts of Sussex, with an account of excavations at Cissbury and Highdown', *Archaeologia*, vol. xlii, 1869.

67 W. Greenwell, *'Grimes Graves': A Paper read at the Blackmore Museum at the Seventeenth Annual Meeting of the Wiltshire Archaeological and Natural History Society*, Frederick A. Blake, Salisbury [1870]. *Wiltshire Archaeological and Natural History Magazine*, Volume XIII, 1872 p.12.

Museum, which bears his name, has made Salisbury a place of reference for information on the antiquities of the [Palaeolithic] period.'[68] Pitt Rivers was to lecture again at the Blackmore Museum in the 1890s and correspondence with Humphrey Blackmore survives.[69]

The influence of Lane Fox on the Blackmore Museum primarily centres on his approach to organising artefacts. By the early 1860s Lane Fox did not have the kind of wealth that William Blackmore had already acquired and which enabled Blackmore to commission a purpose built museum and fund two published, detailed accounts of its collections. The Blackmore Museum had already been open for seven years by the time Lane Fox's collections were put on display in Bethnal Green when in 1875 Lane Fox described his principles of classification thus:

> The collection is divided into four parts. The first has reference to physical anthropology, and consists of a small collection of typical skulls and hair of races. This part of the collection, as it relates to a subject that has received a large amount of attention from anthropologists, and has been frequently treated by abler hands than mine, I do not propose to enter. The remainder of the collection is devoted to objects illustrating the development of prehistoric and savage culture, and consists of – Part II. The weapons of existing savages. Part III. Miscellaneous arts of modern savages, including pottery and substitutes for pottery; modes of navigation, clothing, textile fabrics and weaving; personal ornament; realistic art; conventionalised art; ornamentation; tools; household furniture; musical instruments; idols and religious emblems; specimens of the written character of races; horse furniture; money and substitutes for money; fire-arms; sundry smaller classes of objects, such as mirrors, spoons, combs, games, and a collection of implements of modern savages, arranged to illustrate the mode of hafting stone implements; Part IV refers to the prehistoric series, and consists of specimens of natural forms simulating artificial forms, for comparison with artificial forms; a collection of modern forgeries for comparison with genuine

68 *Wiltshire Archaeological and Natural History Magazine*, 1889, p.19.

69 M. W. Thompson, *Catalogue of the correspondence and papers of Augustus Henry Lane Fox Pitt Rivers,,, in the Salisbury & South Wiltshire Museum*, Royal Commission on Historical Manuscripts, 1976. Letters 978; 983; 1,106; 1,112.

prehistoric implements; Palaeolithic implements; Neolithic implements; implements of bronze, iron and bone.

The collection does not contain any considerable number of unique specimens, and has been collected during upwards of twenty years, not for the purpose of surprising any one, either by the beauty or value of the objects exhibited, but solely with a view to instruction.[70]

In this paper Lane Fox stated that 'Many ethnological museums exist in this country and elsewhere' and he explained that his collection 'performs some function that that is not performed by the majority of other museums.' He characterised his approach as 'the arrangement which I have adopted, the development of specific ideas and their transmission from one people to another, or from one locality to another, is made more apparent, and it is therefore of greater sociological value.' Lane Fox also pointed out that in some museums 'arrangement has been made to suit the form of the room, or of the screens.'[71] Curiously Lane Fox made no specific mention of any of the 'many ethnological museums' referred to. This seems odd since the Blackmore Museum represented a paradigm that Lane Fox already knew.

Further research may unearth more insights into the professional relationship between Blackmore and Lane Fox and quite who influenced whom. The fact remains that the Blackmore Museum was up and running seven years before Lane Fox's collections went on display at the Bethnal Green Museum and two decades before they were put on display in Oxford. Lane Fox was undoubtedly influential, though the effect on the Blackmore Museum of his collections has yet to be acknowledged. Conversely, the influence of Blackmore, Edward Stevens and the Blackmore Museum on Lane Fox has yet to be established.

Having discussed two contemporaries who may have influenced the Blackmore Museum, a closer analysis of various aspects of the Museum now follows.

70 'On the Principles of Classification Adopted in the Arrangement of His Anthropological Collection, Now Exhibited in the Bethnal Green Museum.' *The Journal of the Anthropological Institute of Great Britain and Ireland*, Vol. 4, 1875 pp.293-294.

71 *Ibid.*, pp.294-295.

While the physical layout of the display cases in the Blackmore Museum containing the objects and their classification may be considered innovatory, as yet it is unclear who was behind this modernism. The display cases were built by the firm of Futcher at its Fisherton works and cost £100.[72] Custom built cases covered the interior walls of the museum and a series of free standing ones were distributed across the open floor of the building. There are some similarities with the style of the fifty-six shallow wall cases distributed in three horse shoe shaped galleries in the Museum of Practical Geology, opened in Jermyn Street in London in 1851.[73] A photograph of the display cases under construction in the Blackmore Museum survives in the Salisbury & South Wiltshire Museum. The unidentified photographer – probably from Salisbury – took this view on a specially built platform looking down across the interior of the museum. The photograph may well have been used as a contractual document indicating the state of the works and was sent to Blackmore to show progress.

Where the design for the free standing cases originated has yet to be established. These had a central vertical glazed case section which enabled objects to be closely viewed from both sides. Other items were placed – fully exposed – on the top of this central glazed section. Below this, along each long side of the rectangular display case, were two hip-height, glazed cases slopping upwards towards the central section of the case. The plinth was split between a series of shallow and deep storage drawers which could be slid out for viewing. The very centre of the base plinth contained a fully enclosed space for storage accessed through doors at either end of the cases. This last point

72 A Receipt for £100 for the display cases from Futcher dated 25th September 1865 survives amongst the Humphrey Blackmore Papers at the S&SWM. Robert Futcher was given an initial advance of £200 on the 6th December 1864. Another receipt from Futcher dated 28th January 1865 for £200 for the Blackmore Museum contract and on 24th May 1865 a receipt for £250. The bundle of documents is numbered '11'.

73 The architect of The Museum of Practical Geology and the Government School of Mines Applied to the Arts was James Pennethorne (1801-1871). The building was demolished in 1936. Blackmore knew William Boyd Dawkins (1837-1929) who was connected to the Museum as a member of the Geological Survey of Great Britain between 1861 and 1869. Dawkins became a junior colleague of T. H. Huxley (1825-1895) at the Royal School of Mines, also housed in Jermyn Street.

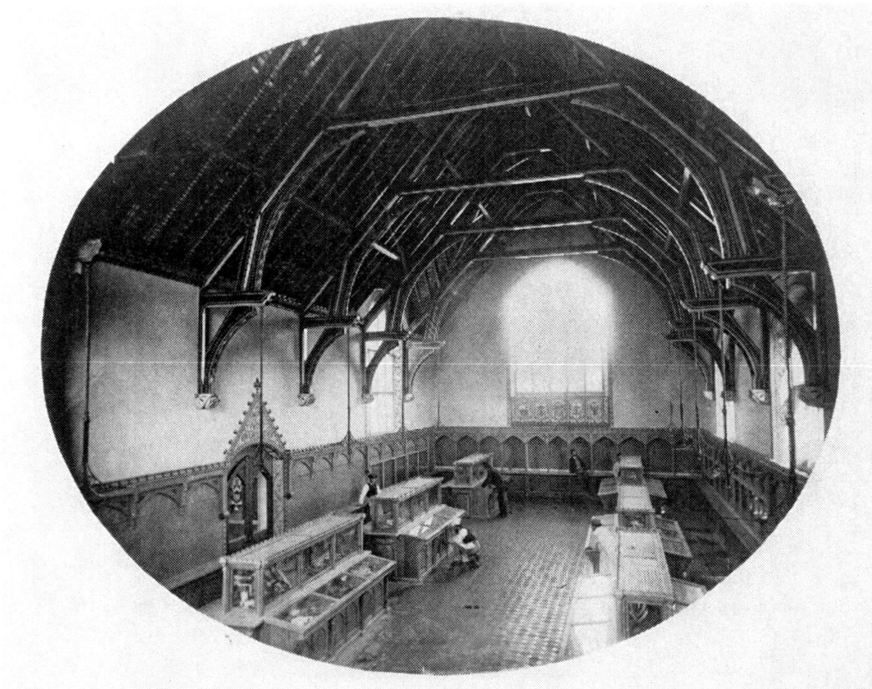

Interior View of the Blackmore Museum with display cases under construction in 1867.
Albumen print
Courtesy of Salisbury & South Wiltshire Museum

is worth underlining since the Blackmore Museum had no basement or other storage area.

Another consideration was the ergonomics of the display cases. Clearly some thought had gone into this since as it was pointed out at the time of the museum's opening 'every specimen is so close to the glass of the case that it can be examined most minutely: fortunately also there is a total absence of that painful reflection and glare from the glass, which is not unfrequently experienced in Museums.'[74] After his death, Stevens was considered to be behind the 'perfect arrangement' of the collections.[75]

74 *Some Account of the Blackmore Museum – Part I. The opening Meeting*, H.F. & E. Bull, Devizes; Bell & Daldy, London ; J.R. Smith, London 1868 p.2.

75 *The Hampshire Advertiser*, Saturday, 9th November, 1878 p.7 reprinting a report from the *Salisbury Guardian*.

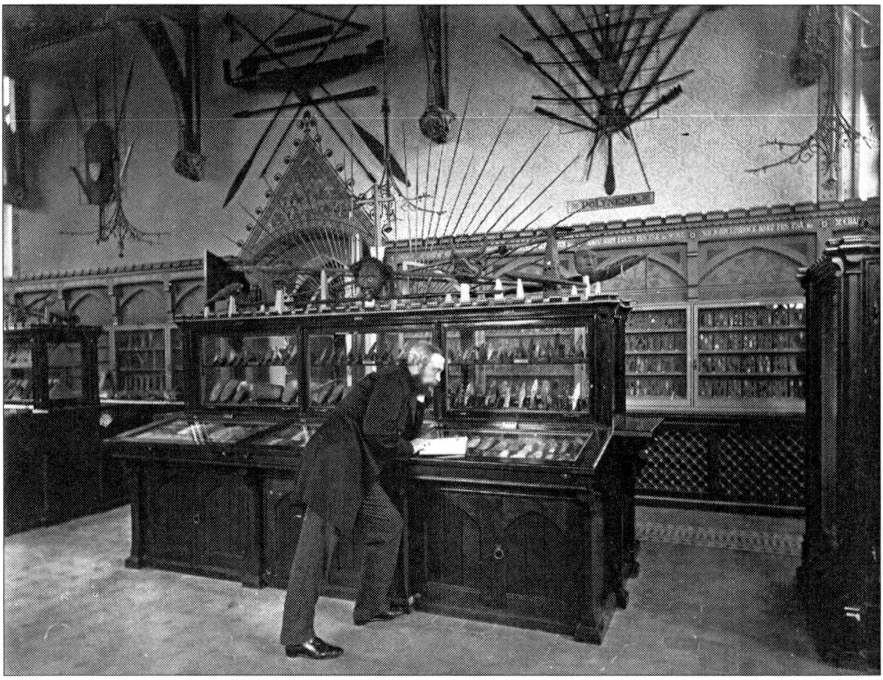

Edward Stevens leaning against cases C26 and C27 containing Danish Neolithic specimens in the Blackmore Museum c.1870.
Albumen print
Courtesy of Salisbury & South Wiltshire Museum

The classification of the objects and their display in the Blackmore Museum is key to its contemporary significance. Davis had supplied Blackmore with a manuscript *Catalogue of American Antiquities Collected by Edwin Hamilton Davis* that arranged the collection into five divisions; articles of stone, animal substances, articles of metal, articles of burnt clay and human remains. This manuscript gave details of the localities in which each piece had been found by Squier and Davis during their excavations in the mid 1840s, cross-referenced to the plate and page number in the archaeologists' *Ancient Monuments of the Mississippi Valley* published in 1848 as the first volume of the Smithsonian Institution's Contributions to Knowledge series, and the Institution's first publication. Davis' *Catalogue of American Antiquities* formed a fundamental building block for the Blackmore Museum's own cataloguing and was to be extensively used by Edward Stevens for his *Flint Chips* publication of 1870.

Two hundred and fourteen cases were needed in the Blackmore Museum to arrange the objects by the Four-Age System of Palaeolithic, Neolithic, Bronze and Iron introduced by John Lubbock in his 1865 publication *Pre-historic Times, as illustrated by ancient remains, and the manners and customs of modern savages*, possibly the most influential archaeological text book of the 19th century. Lubbock had been invited to attend the opening of the museum but had sent his apologies since he was attending the annual meeting of the British Association for the Advancement of Science in Dundee. In his letter of apology Lubbock wrote:

> Your Museum will be an honor to Salisbury, and will add additional interest even to a county so rich as yours in archaeological treasures. Mr. Blackmore deserves the hearty thanks of all scientific men for the zeal with which he has brought together so rich a collection. I must add that the arrangement you have adopted also seems to me excellent.[76]

A hierarchy of contemporary scholarship was formed through the inscribed names of men of science and archaeology on the walls above the cases. This evidenced the context in which the objects should be viewed.[77] A paradigm of the pseudo-medieval display methodology evidencing technological progress.

The innovatory nature of the display and classification system at the Blackmore Museum was further underlined in the 1868 catalogue that had as a category, 'Implements, Weapons, and Ornaments of Modern Savages, which serve to throw light upon the use of similar objects belonging to prehistoric times.' This has been considered as

76 *Some Account of the Blackmore Museum – Part I.* , H.F. & E. Bull, Devizes; Bell & Daldy, London ; J.R. Smith, London 1868 p.78. Lubbock is known to have acted 'as a lecturer' to a visit he made to the museum in March 1872 with the Scottish politician, statesman, and author Sir Mountstuart E. Grant Duff (1829-1906). Sir Mountstuart E. Grant Duff, *Notes from a Diary 1851-1872*, Volume 2, John Murray, London 1897 p.229.

77 For a general overview of Victorian museum design and display see Carla Yanni, *Nature's Museums: Victorian science and the architecture of display*, Princeton Architectural Press, New York, 2005. The Blackmore Museum has received little attention by architectural historians or scholars of the various components of museum studies.

an element contributing to the start of ethno-archaeological museum narrative. Despite the fact that foreign objects did not represent the local or County history, the purpose of these objects was for the comparative analysis of ethnography.[78]

So what were William Blackmore's aims and objectives for his museum? The Rules of the Blackmore Museum are worth listing since they succinctly encapsulate the core principles of William Blackmore's foundation and set the basis of the symbiotic relationship between the Museum and the Salisbury & South Wiltshire Museum.

RULES OF THE BLACKMORE MUSEUM

RULE I.

THIS Museum shall be called the 'BLACKMORE MUSEUM,' having been established by Mr. WILLIAM BLACKMORE, of Liverpool and London, at whose expense solely it will be maintained.

RULE II.

The property of the Blackmore Museum shall be deposited at Salisbury, and shall be vested in Trustees for the purposes of the Museum.

RULE III.

The Blackmore Museum shall be under the management of the Committee of the Salisbury and South Wilts Museum, subject to the consent of the Blackmore Museum Trustees, to be given at each Annual Meeting of the Members of the Salisbury and South Wilts Museum.

RULE IV.

The Trustees shall have power to close the Blackmore Museum for any special purpose, upon giving twenty-four hours' notice in writing to either of the Secretaries of the Salisbury and South Wilts Museum.

RULE V.

The Committee of the Salisbury and South Wilts Museum shall not be

78 *Some Account of the Blackmore Museum – Part II.* , H.F. & E. Bull, Devizes; Bell & Daldy, London ; J.R. Smith, London 1868 p.309; Yun Shun Susie Chung, 'Prehistoric Narratives in County Archaeological Museums in Mid-Nineteenth Century England', *Stanford Journal of Archaeology*, 2002, at www.stanford.edu/dept/archaeology/journal/newdraft/chung/paper.pdf.

held responsible for any claims or charges in respect of the Blackmore Museum.

RULE VI.

It shall not be competent for the Trustees to make any dividend, gift, division, or bonus in money or otherwise unto or between any of the members of the Blackmore Museum.

RULE VII.

Honorary Curators shall be appointed by the Trustees, and the arrangement of specimens shall be left in their hands.

RULE VIII.

The Trustees shall have power to remove any objects from the Blackmore Museum, for exhibition or scientific examination, at their discretion.

RULE IX.

An Honorary Secretary (who shall also act as Librarian) shall be appointed by the Trustees, and all books, drawings, manuscripts, and communications shall be under his charge.

RULE X.

No alteration shall be made in the Rules of the Blackmore Museum except with the unanimous consent of the Trustees, and no such alteration shall be binding upon the Committee of the Salisbury and South Wilts Museum except after a month's notice given to either of the Secretaries of the same.

RULE XI

The Blackmore Museum shall be open to the public free of charge from 10 A.M. until 4 P.M., at least three days in each week, such days to be appointed by the Committee of the Salisbury and South Wilts Museum.*

RULE XII.

The attendants are strictly prohibited from accepting any gratuity from visitors to the Museum.

* The Blackmore Museum may be seen daily, Sundays and Saturday excepted.

The most detailed account of William's personal motivation is to be found in the address he gave at the formal opening of his museum;

> And now for the objects of this Museum. The chief object I have in view is the increase of knowledge. Increased knowledge will bring greater happiness, a high state of civilisation, a firmer and deeper faith in the truths of religion.

Other standard Victorian principles of 'progress' through education were underlined by Blackmore;

> A third, and not less weighty motive in the establishment of this Museum, had been the benefit of my native city, more particularly by giving increased means of study to the young men of Salisbury . . . [and] That the free use of the Museum will be a benefit to the inhabitants of my native city.

Blackmore also pointed to the formation of the 'special relationship' between England and the USA;

> And I now most sincerely trust that the care taken in England, in the preservation and free exhibition to the public, of some of the earliest and most interesting of antiquities of the United States, will be an additional link and bond of union between the two great families of the Anglo-Saxon race, whose destiny it appears to be to dominate and civilise the whole earth.

Edward Stevens added to objectives of the Museum in a paper presented to delegates attending the Seventeenth Annual Meeting of the Wiltshire Archaeological and Natural History Society in September 1870. In this he was specific in stating that the chief objective of the Blackmore Museum was 'to illustrate the simple arts of the Stone Period, and to enable students to study them as test of human culture.'[79] Yet the museum was significantly more than this.

Blackmore continued to acquire items for his museum after it opened. In 1868 he was in Paris and purchased a number of bronzes. Items from America, Italy, Ireland and Australia were also added.[80]

79 *Wiltshire Archaeological and Natural History Magazine*, Volume XIII, 1872 p.28.
80 *The Athenæum*,No.2122, 27th June, 1868 p.897 'Our Weekly Gossip'.

However, these were comparatively small scale additions to the Blackmore Museum's collections. A practical consideration that at the time of its opening in 1867 the space available for the display of artefacts had been all but filled. The building contained no basement where additional items could be stored. No additional gallery space was to be added to the Blackmore Museum and thus its collections remained comparatively static from the time of its opening.

If one takes the metrics by which a Museum's success may be measured as visitor numbers, public lectures, publications, exhibitions and collections development then how successful might the Blackmore Museum be considered to have been?

In terms of visitor numbers, a full set of statistics for the period from 1864 until William Blackmore's death has yet to be established. During the year ending June 1870 it was reported that 40,000 had visited the Salisbury & South Wiltshire and Blackmore Museums, an increase of over 5000. The report also noted that since the opening of the Salisbury & South Wiltshire Museum in 1864 it had received 126,000 visitors.[81] By 1878 it was noted that 379,000 had visited the Museum since its opening.[82] However, in the following year there had been only 22,718 visitors to the museum in the previous twelve months and that while the annual income of the Salisbury & South Wiltshire Museum had been augmented by £157 2. 6d. in order to keep the Blackmore Museum 'in Salisbury' – perhaps suggesting that following William's death it might be broken up and dispersed – 'it is yet not known whether this amount will provide sufficient for the purpose.'[83] By 1899 visitor numbers to the Salisbury & South Wiltshire and Blackmore Museums had fallen to 9,321.[84]

81 *The Hampshire Advertiser,* Saturday, 23rd July, 1870 p.7 mentioning 'the report of the committee.' This figure should been seen within the context that the 1871 census gave the population of the City of Salisbury as 13,839.

82 *The Hampshire Advertiser,* Saturday, 9th November, 1878 p.7 reprinting a report from the Salisbury Guardian. This represents an average of over 27,000 visitors per annum. It is worth noting that the Annual Report for the Museum for 1933-1934 reported that there had been some 12,970 visitors that year.

83 *The Hampshire Advertiser,* Wednesday 18th June, 1879 p.4.

84 *Wiltshire Archaeological and Natural History Magazine,* Volume XXX, 1899 p.359.

The period from the opening of the museum until 1870 was one of dynamism and output. In 1868 the Wiltshire Archaeological and Natural History Society had;

> under a deep sense of the great liberality of Mr. Blackmore in the founding the Magnificent Museum at Salisbury, which is called after his name; and profoundly sensible of the immense benefit to the Archaeologists of Wiltshire, which the possession of this Museum within their county confers, have thought it fit to mark their sense of obligation and gratitude to the munificent founder and his coadjutors, by offering in the name of the Society to publish a general account of the Museum, as well as the proceedings which accompanied its inauguration, and the papers read thereat.[85]

This two part publication included the first published catalogue the Blackmore Museum. In 1870 it was supplemented by *Flint Chips; a guide to pre-historic archaeology, as illustrated by the collection in the Blackmore Museum, Salisbury* the most important of the Blackmore Museum's publications that was published by Bell & Daldy of London and two Salisbury booksellers Brown and Co and F.A. Blake. This five hundred and ninety-three page publication included an inserted 'Preface to the American Edition' by John Russell Bartlett (1805–1886), the co-founder of the American Ethnological Society and who had been present at the Museum's opening. In this he stated that the Blackmore Museum was 'one of the best in Europe.'[86] Bartlett later stated that 'it is doubtful whether one of equal extent and so rich in the works of primitive men in America can again be made.'[87] The combination of the museum's display and *Flint Chips* formed a valuable index of the state of knowledge

85 'Preface', *Some Account of the Blackmore Museum – Part I.* , H.F. &E. Bull, Devizes; Bell & Daldy, London ; J.R. Smith, London 1868 p.iv.

86 Edward T. Stevens, *Flint Chips: A Guide to Historic Archaeology, as illustrated by the collection in the Blackmore Museum, Salisbury.*, Bell and Daldy; Brown and Co., and F.A. Blake, London and Salisbury, 1870 p. xx. Bartlett had attended the museum's opening in 1867 during a trip to Europe to attend the International Archaeological Congress in Antwerp.

87 From a report by Barlett to the American Antiquarian Society cited in *Colorado Springs Gazette*, Saturday, 8th June, 1878 p.7.

within the various branches of prehistoric archaeology in the period just before 1870. It also evidenced Stevens' close connections with the leading contemporary experts in the fields of archaeology, ethnography and anthropology. William Blackmore was also part of this circle. While the boundaries between archaeology and ethnology and between the amateur and the professional were somewhat murky at this time, the Blackmore Museum together with *Flint Chips* and its author Edward Stevens were instrumental in sorting this out. A new breed of curator was establishing the foundations for the classification and comparative study of well documented and well displayed collections with the museum setting.[88]

The print run of *Flint Chips* was probably a substantial one. The hand of William Blackmore may be sensed behind this publication, not just in the covering of production costs but also the associated marketing campaign. Numerous copies can be found on Web second hand book sites and there are various references to this title being donated to a range of foreign museums soon after its publication.[89] For instance Blackmore sent more than twenty copies to the Smithsonian Institution.

Almost thirty years after its publication *Flint Chips* remained a significant work. 'Only in the Blackmore Museum is the entire collection catalogued, and this catalogue is almost a text-book of archaeology, although it now needs revision.'[90]

Another form of dissemination of the Blackmore Museum's collections was through plaster casts. In 1876 the Peabody Museum recorded that it had paid US$300 for casts of objects in the Blackmore Museum.[91] The Blackmore Museum itself displayed a significant

88 Terry A. Barnhart, 'The Hamilton Davis collection of American Antiquities', *Journal of the History of Collections*, Volume 16, Number 2, 2004 pp.59-87 (on pp 78-9).

89 A copy offered by Peter L. Stern & Co., Inc. (USA) in 2009 was inscribed at the top of the title page by the recipient, 'J. Wyman from the Trustees of the Blackmore Museum.' Jeffries Wyman (1814-1874), a correspondent of Darwin, was Hersey Professor of Anatomy and later, the curator of the Peabody Museum of Archaeology and Ethnology at Harvard. With Louis Agassiz and Asa Gray he made Harvard America's foremost centre for the study of natural history.

90 George A. Dorsey, 'Notes on the Anthropological Museums of Central Europe', *American Anthropologist*, New Series, Vol. 1, No. 3, July 1899 pp. 462-474.

91 *Report on the Peabody Museum of Archaeology and Ethnology, Harvard University*, 1876 p.35.

number of casts of objects from foreign collections, such as the Dolmens (or Cromlechs) of France; two stone hatchets from Djelfa, Algeria; flint arrowheads from Moosseedorf in Switzerland (the originals in the collection of Dr. Uhlmann); and a variety of stone hatchets and implements found in Italy;

In the year of the opening of the Blackmore Museum a report in the *Proceedings of the American Antiquarian Society* stated that 'The city of Salisbury can now boast of possessing, in the Blackmore Museum, the finest collection of stone implements and other objects of art of our aborigines in the world.'[92] Some one hundred and thirty-three donors to the Blackmore Museum – mostly individuals – were listed in Stevens' 1870 *Flint Chips* catalogue including Ephraim George Squire, Ferdinand Hayden, and August Wollaston Franks (Curator of British and medieval antiquities and ethnographical collections at The British Museum). Foreign donations were received from Abbeville, Paris, The Hague, Basel, Zürich, Gibraltar, Natal, Boston, San Francisco, New York, Washington, D.C., Ontario in Canada and India. The thirteen institutional donors included the Smithsonian, the Trustees of the Christy Museum, the New York Historical Society, the Royal Archaeological Institute of Great Britain and Ireland, the Society of Antiquaries of Scotland and the Société Polymathique of Morbihan in Brittany.

Donations continued to the Blackmore Museum. In August 1871 George Finlay (1799-1875), the Athens-based historian, sent twelve stone implements found in Greece to Edward Stevens enabled by 'the kindness of my friend Mr Frank Noel.' Stevens replied – somewhat tardily – in July 1872 stating that he believed the specimens to be the 'best series shown in England' and that Augustus Franks from the British Museum – who had been spending a day or two at the Blackmore Museum – was 'much pleased with them, he has some [in the collection at the British Museum], certainly not a better series.'[93]

92 In a report by John R. Bartlett '*Proceedings of the American Antiquarian Society*, Cambridge, MA, 1867 p.55.

93 Letters dated 31st August, 1871 and 3rd July, 1872 , numbered '7' in Humphrey Blackmore Papers, S&SWM.

Over the next couple of decades the Blackmore Museum continued to gain a significant reputation. A number of distinguished visitors toured the museum and made complimentary remarks. Augustus Franks, who had sent a paper to be read at the museum's opening, visited the museum in 1866 and 1872 and made notes.[94] Similarly, the museum received good comment in guidebooks, newspapers and other publications. In 1884 *The Times*, while reporting on 'The New Collections at The British Museum' stated that 'The Blackmore Museum at Salisbury is a nearer approach to a public ethnographical museum' than the national museum in London.[95] In 1887 it was noted that Baron Anatole von Hügel (1854-1928), who in 1883 became the first curator of the University of Cambridge Museum of Archaeology and Anthropology, had been 'struck by finding in the Blackmore Museum a somewhat similar [stag horn] tool, made of bone, and still used in Cornwall, for barking oak trees.'[96] In August 1890 Thomas Henry Huxley (1825-1895), the biologist known as 'Darwin's Bulldog' for his advocacy of Charles Darwin's theory of evolution, visited the Blackmore Museum and was 'very much struck by it.'[97]

Not all visitors to the museum were as welcome as the likes of Franks, von Hügel and Huxley. In 1896 national and international reports noted that a number of objects including six rare and valuable New Zealand jade-stone curious had been stolen and replaced with

94 Marjorie Caygill and John Cherry (eds.), *A.W. Franks – Nineteenth-century Collecting and The British Museum*, British Museum Press, London, 1997 Appendix 4 pp.350, 353 and 354. In June and July 1866 Franks visited Salisbury had while negotiating an exchange of material with items from the Christy Collection recently acquired by the British Museum. He sketched items from Blackmore's collection and in the Salisbury Museum at this time. The sketches are in Book A of Franks' drawings in the Department of Prehistoric and Romano-British Antiquities of the British Museum.

95 *The Times*, Wednesday 28th April, 1886 p.8.

96 *Cambridge Antiquarian Communications, Volume VI, 1884-1888*, London, 1891 p.450.

97 *Life and Letters of Thomas Henry Huxley*, Volume 3, Macmillan, London, 1903 p.169. A carte de visite photographic portrait of Huxley is to be found in one of Blackmore's photograph albums held in the Salisbury & South Wiltshire Museum. Huxley gave the opening address at the meeting of the Ethnological Society of London on Tuesday 19th April at which Blackmore presented his paper on 'Notes on some of the Principle Tribes of the Indians of the United States.'

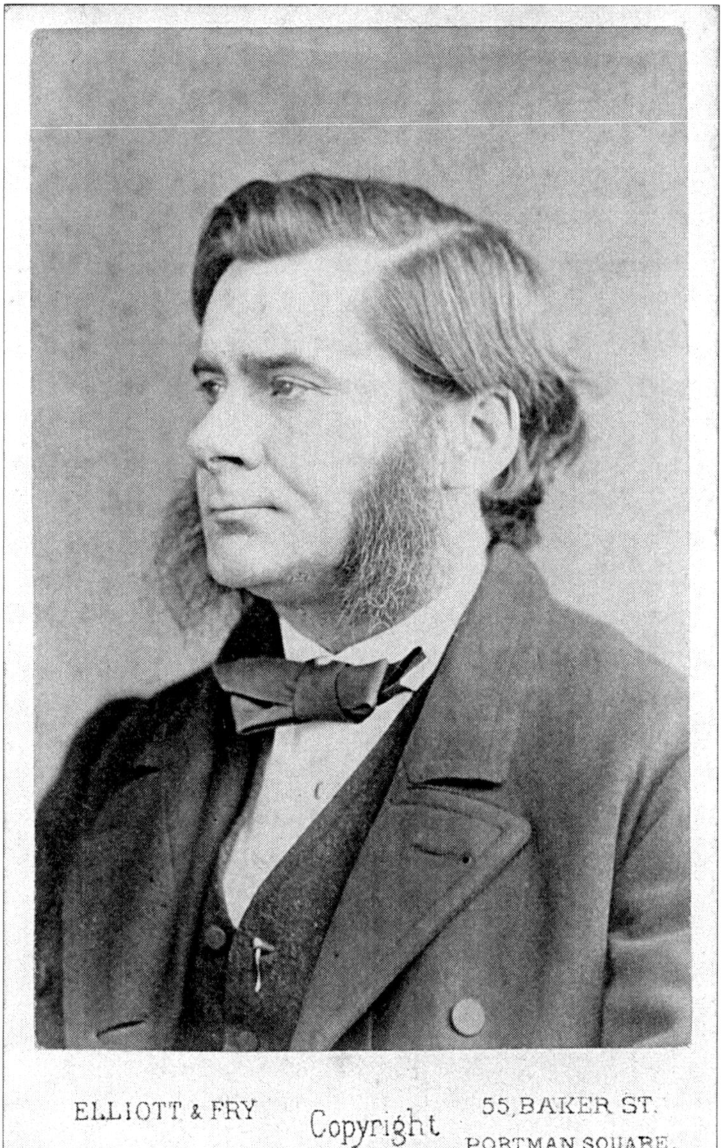

Thomas Henry Huxley (1825-1895)
Photographed by Elliot & Fry, 55 Baker Street, London
Carte de visite
Albumen print
Blackmore carte de visite album
Courtesy of Salisbury & South Wiltshire Museum

imitations made of plaster.[98] In 1914 in was reported that 'expert thieves' had made 'a raid on the Neolithic section of the Blackmore Museum'.[99]

In a review of the contemporary state of anthropology in Europe in 1892, the *Popular Science Monthly* noted that while the 'little Blackmore Museum . . . at present cuts no great figure in anthropological work' the building contained 'a great series of photographs of American Indians and a wonderful library of Americana.'[100] The museum's importance was mirrored in that year's edition of *Murray's Handbook for England and Wales* that stated 'the Blackmore Museum, one of the best arranged and most instructive collections of pre-historio remains of man from all parts of the world . . .'[101] In 1899 the *Transactions of the Glasgow Archaeological Society* stated that the museum was 'equal to any archaeological museum in the country.'[102] The 1907 edition of the *Encylopaedia Britannica* described the museum as 'one of the finest collections of prehistoric antiquities in England.'

The museum also formed a place of pilgrimage for American archaeologists, largely due to the Squier and Davis collection. In 1899 the eminent early U.S. ethnographer George Amos Dorsey (1868-1931) wrote; 'The Blackmore Museum of Salisbury contains one of the best selected and arranged collections of man's prehistoric relics that I have ever seen.'[103] The following year, Roeliff Brinkerhoff (1828-1911), the founder in 1875 of the Ohio State Archaeological and Historical Society – that could have held a rightful claim to the David and Squier collections – considered the Blackmore Museum possessed 'the largest collection of American antiquities in all Europe.'[104] More general tourist

98 *Journal of the British Archaeological Association*, 1896 p.77

99 *The Antiquary: a Magazine Devoted to the Past*, 1914 p.3.

100 Prof. Frederick Starr, 'Anthropological Work in Europe', *The Popular Science Monthly*, Volume XLI, May to October 1892 p.71.

101 *Handbook for England and Wales*, (2nd edition) John Murray, 1890 p.357.

102 *Transactions of the Glasgow Archaeological Society*, Glasgow, 1899 p.58.

103 George A. Dorsey, 'Notes on the Anthropological Museums of Central Europe', *American Anthropologist*, New Series, Vol. 1, No. 3, July 1899 pp. 462-474.

104 Roeliff Brinkerhoff, *Recollections of a Lifetime*, The Robert Clarke Company,1900 p.385. Brinkerhoff referred to the Blackmore Museum as being fire-proof. Brinkerhoff made this statement in an address to the Ohio State Archaeological

guides also made mention of the Blackmore Museum. Numerous editions of *Appleton's European Guide Book for English speaking travellers* consistently refer to the Blackmore Museum as 'of especial interest to Americans'.

It is unclear whether the Blackmore Museum had a formalised education policy or strategy. The Museum appears to have made collaborative links with the Salisbury Literary and Scientific Institution. In March 1868 Edward Stevens invited the Institution to a conversazione for up to one hundred and fifty attendees. The event included musical entertainment and refreshments supplied by the Trustees of the Museum. Edward Stevens gave a lecture on the collections of the Museum.[105] Whether such meetings were a regular occurrence remains to be established. After the deaths of William Blackmore and Edward Stevens in 1878, Humphrey Blackmore continued taking groups of visitors around the museum. The *Wiltshire Archaeological and Natural History Magazine* cites regular lectures at the Blackmore Museum during the 1880s and 1890s. However, Frank Stevens noted that while between 1886 and 1915 seventy-eight free and popular lectures were delivered by well known men, the collections taken from attendees barely covered the costs of hosting them in the first place.[106]

However, the Blackmore Museum did have a one 'educational' display. Cases D 2 and D 3 included forgeries of implements of drift type, some from Abbeville and others made locally by Yorkshireman Edward Simpson, alias 'Flint Jack', an itinerant knapper and creator of a wide range of forgeries including Roman and British urns, fibulae, coins, flint arrow heads, stone hammers and flint hatchets. Such forgeries were commonplace across Britain and mainland Europe during the mid

Society in March 1898. See *Ohio History*, Volume 6, April-July 1898 p.431.

105 For a notice of the invitation and a short report see *The Hampshire Advertiser, Saturday, 14th March, 1868 p.4 and Saturday, 4th April, 1868 p.4.*

106 Frank Stevens, *The Salisbury Museums, 1861-1947: A Record of Eighty-Six Years of Progress*, 2nd edition, Salisbury, 1954 p.5. One well known lecturer was The Rev. Robert Hawley Clutterbuck (1837-1896). See his obituary in *Wiltshire Archaeological and Natural History Magazine, Volume XXIX*, 1897 p.72. Curiously, Stevens noted that the lectures were discontinued during the First World War because the Defence of the Realm Act (1914, amended 1915) – known as 'DORA' – made them impossible.

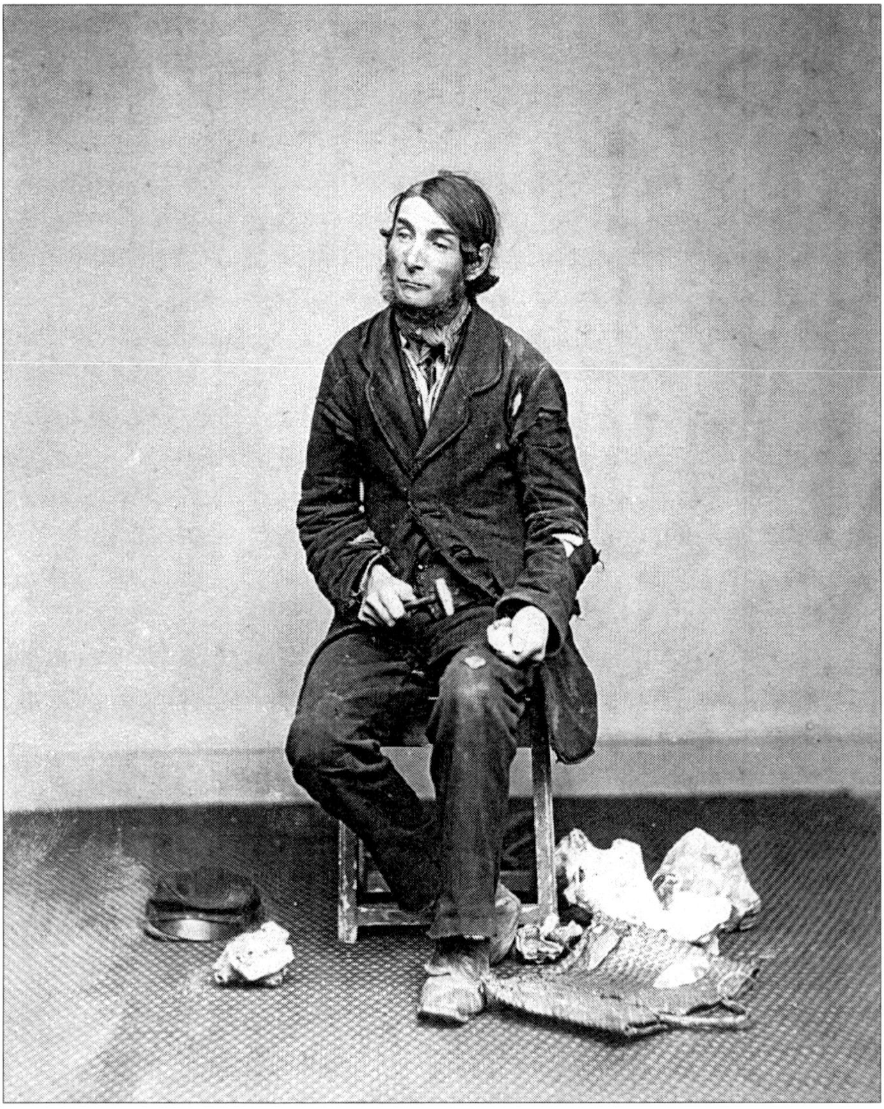

"Flint Jack" working on a flint. 1863.
Photographed by Frederick Treble.
Albumen print
Courtesy of Salisbury & South Wiltshire Museum

19th century and it is significant that the Blackmore Museum took a distinctive stance to highlight this trade. 'A glance at the specimens in Cases D 2 and 3 will suffice to convince the visitor that he is looking at forgeries, not at counterfeits, for there is scarcely a single example which is a good imitation of a genuine original.'[107]

Clearly 'Flint Jack' had ruffled a few feathers in Salisbury and was a marked man. Case D 2 included a photographic portrait of this individual, taken when he was in Salisbury, in 1863. The story behind Case D 2 and 3 is not without interest. It was reported that 'Flint Jack' had visited the museum and attempted to sell some flints to Edward Stevens. Stevens quickly determined that the flints were forgeries. However, he took a somewhat liberal perspective and interesting associated next steps. He paid for 'Flint Jack' to be photographed by the Salisbury photographer Frederick Treble and rather than call in the police, 'gave him ['Flint Jack'] employment by ordering him to make him a complete set of flints for exhibition.'[108]

In 1865 Treble's photograph of 'Flint Jack' was shown as one of the items from Blackmore's collection at a meeting of the South of England Literary and Philosophical Society held at the Hartley Institution in Southampton.[109] 'Flint Jack' had a thirty year career producing forgeries and Stevens' lesson of 1863 went unheeded. In March 1867 *The Times* reported that the 'notorious Yorkshireman – one of the greatest imposters of our times – was last week sentenced to 12 months imprisonment for felony at Bedford.'[110] This sentence was for theft rather than forgery. Undeterred, and at least one further prison sentence later, 'Flint Jack' was back in Salisbury and reported to have visited the museums and

107 Stevens, *Flint Chips* p.591.

108 *The Reliquary, Quarterly Archaeological Journal and Review*, October, 1867 p.74. This formed an article (pp.65-76) 'Flint Jack; A memoir and An Appeal.' by Llewellynn Jewitt F.S.A., who wrote that 'The man possesses more real practical antiquarian knowledge than many of the leading antiquarian writers of the day; and he is a good geologist and palaeontologist.' Jewitt wished to create a fund to support 'Flint Jack' after he was released from his recent custodial sentence in Bedford jail. The article was illustrated with an engraving after the photograph taken of 'Flint Jack' in Salisbury in 1863.

109 *The Hampshire Advertiser*, Saturday 28th January, 1865 p.2.

110 *The Times*, Tuesday 19th March, 1867 p.11.

met with some of 'gentlemen connected with them' in 1872, the year of his possible death.[111]

In terms of museum publications, after the publication of Edward Stevens' *Flint Chips* there were no significant contributions documenting the collections, exhibitions or educational activities of the Blackmore Museum. Humphrey Blackmore did publish a number of articles, though these were primarily on geological rather than ethnographic or anthropological subjects.

The development of the Blackmore Museum's collections was comparatively limited, though the Museum was considered a suitable resting place for some collections. Stevens gave some indication on the acquisitions policy when he wrote in 1870:

> It is our desire to improve the 'general collection' rather than to extend it; we seek to render it more illustrative, and more generally representative of the industry of the Stone Age of various countries. But we do not propose to limit the extension of the American and the local groups, for we wish these to become the leading features of the Collection.[112]

In 1875 it was noted in the *Athenaeum* that the collection of bronze and stone implements, celts, arrow-heads, vases, pottery , etc. formed by the Rev. William Collings Lukis (1817-1892), of Wath, Ripon was to be disposed of and it suggested that it 'may find a resting place either in the Blackmore Museum, at Salisbury, or in the national collection in the British Museum.'[113]

The demise of William Blackmore was to have a profound effect on his museum and its collections since he had been the sole source of funding and no endowment was in place. The exact details of how from the mid 1870s the state of William's finances was impacting on both the Salisbury and Blackmore museums may never be clearly ascertained. However, it appears that the reductions of Blackmore's disposable

111 *ibid.*, Wednesday 21st August, 1872 p.4. 'Flint Jack' may have died about this time. See *Aberdeen Weekly Journal*, Monday 13th December, 1880 p.2.

112 Stevens, *Flint Chips*, p.xvi.

113 This proposal was reprinted in *The York Herald, Tuesday, 5th January, 1875 p.8. The collection was eventually purchased by the British Museum.*

income that funded the museum had been noted by contemporaries. Frank Stevens stated that prior to William's death 'difficult times were approaching, and as the first enthusiasm died down, questions of finance began to arise, and an adverse balance began to appear in the [museum] Treasurer's Report.'[114] The Trustees of the Blackmore Museum acted quickly following William's death and it was reported in September 1878 that they had requested a meeting 'to take into consideration the subject of raising an annual sum for the purpose of meeting the expenses of carrying on that Museum'. An appeal was made to the public, and the report hopefully suggested that 'The sum required is very small, and we have no doubt that the amount will be readily obtained.'[115] Subsequent reports indicated the sum to be £80 per annum.[116] It was clear that Humphrey Blackmore considered himself in no position to cover these running costs of his late brother's Museum.

However, there are a number of other relevant considerations that influenced the direction taken by the Blackmore Museum after William's untimely death. Firstly, while William's interest in the 'noble Red Man' was shared by his brother in law Edward Stevens, Humphrey Blackmore was not a kindred spirit.[117] William's interests in ethnology and anthropology were not continued by any other colleague connected with the Salisbury & South Wiltshire Museum. Thus with his passing the expansion and exploitation of the North American collections was abruptly terminated.

114 Frank Stevens, *The Salisbury Museums 1861-1947*, Bennett Brothers, Salisbury [1948] p.5

115 The report appeared in the *Salisbury Guardian* and was reprinted in *The Hampshire Advertiser,* Wednesday, 4th September, 1878 p,4.

116 *The Hampshire Advertiser,* Saturday, 9th November, 1878 p.7 reprinting a report from the *Salisbury Guardian.*

117 Following Edward Stevens' death in 1878 the entire contents of his house – 18 & 21 Minster Street – were sold in a three day auction by Marsh, Dawes and Dear on 14th, 15th and 16th November 1879. Amongst the lots were the contents of his library which included a copies of Catlin's *North American Indians* (lot 545), four of the six volumes of Schoolcraft's monumental *Historical and Statistical Information Respecting the History, Condition, and Prospects of the Indian Tribes of the United States,* (lot 548) and the *Ancient Monuments of the Mississippi Valley* (lot 551). A copy of this house sale catalogue is held in Salisbury Public Library. R SAL014.

A second factor is the change in interests and focus on the development and management of the existing collections. Quite whether significant numbers of scholars came to the Blackmore Museum in the last quarter of the 19th century to study the library of Americana or the extensive photographic collection of Native Americans has yet to be established. Frank Stevens noted that during the 1880s many of the important founders of the Salisbury Museum passing away and it was difficult to find replacements.[118] After Humphrey's death the Salisbury Museum refocused on collections relating to its locality. Thus the North American and other non-local material became peripheral to the Salisbury Museum's core aims and ambitions.

Thirdly, the history of the Salisbury & South Wiltshire Museum and Blackmore Museum is, like many museums, riddled with financial crises. Humphrey Blackmore deserves credit for keeping the Blackmore Museum in existence after his brother's death. The wide ranging financial issues and challenges facing Humphrey could have led him to discard the museum, or at least rationalise it with the Salisbury & South Wiltshire Museum. He did neither opting to provided funding for the Blackmore Museum to continue in something like tick-over mode.

Nevertheless, the museum continued to receive donations. In January 1883 it was noted that a collection of flint implements discovered in India had been presented to the museum. These were donated by John Henry Rivett-Carnac (1839-1923) who had visited Edward Stevens in Salisbury in 1872. The items were formally presented by Coleridge John Kennard (1828-1890), elected Member of Parliament for Salisbury in November 1882 'in commemoration of the triumph of Constitutional principles on the occasion of the recent election.'[119]

By 1902 the two museums had been amalgamated and Humphrey Blackmore remained the Honorary Curator. Frank Stevens, William Blackmore's nephew and the son of Edward Stevens, became the museum's first professional curator in 1913. Evidence suggests that he

118 Frank Stevens, *The Salisbury Museums, 1861-1947: A Record of Eighty-Six Years of Progress*, 2nd edition, Salisbury, 1954 p.5.

119 *The Times*, 31st January, 1883 p.9 and *The Hampshire Advertiser*, Saturday, 3rd February, 1883 p.7.

began a collections rationalisation and de-accessioning campaign while his uncle Humphrey was still alive. Perhaps Frank Stevens' greatest achievement was putting the finances of the Salisbury & South Wiltshire and Blackmore museums on a sounder footing, though his uncle Humphrey deserves credit for their being any footings on which to build.

While during the first half of the 20th century the Salisbury & South Wiltshire Museum gained additional collections, primarily through donations, and newly built galleries to display them, the Blackmore Museum fared less well. It was not even freely open to the public and Karl Baedecker' 1927 *Guide to Great Britain* noted that the Blackmore Museum was 'Shown on application.'[120]

Around 1919 the first of a significant number of items from the Salisbury & South Wiltshire and Blackmore Museum were acquired by the Bournemouth Natural Science Society (BNSS). This was largely as a result of the professional contacts between Frank Stevens and Heywood Sumner (1853-1940) a leading illustrator of the Arts and Crafts movement, local archaeologist and a member of the BNSS. Sumner had provided the illustrations for Stevens' *Stonehenge today & yesterday . . . With plans and illustrations by Heywood Sumner* published by Sampson Low & Co of London in 1916. Over some sixteen years a variety of artefacts were moved from Salisbury to Bournemouth though the archives of the two institutions provide comparatively little detailed information. In the c.1919 deaccession the BNSS received two large collections (200 and 187 specimens respectively) of Ancient Egyptian artefacts. In 1928 and 1930, the BNSS received forty-eight and six cases, respectively, of stuffed birds from Salisbury – these probably being formed in part from Henry Blackmore's original collection. In 1931, the BNSS received another two dozen Ancient Egyptian items. A further nine items were acquired in 1939[121]

The death of Humphrey Blackmore in 1929 heralded the ultimate watershed of the fate of the Blackmore Museum. The de-accessioning

120 Karl Baedecker, *Great Britain: Handbook for Travellers*, Baedeker; Allen & Unwin, Leipzig ; London,1927 p.104.

121 I thank John Cresswell, Curator of the Bournemouth Natural Sciences Society for this information. Email 15th June 2009.

of the core of the Blackmore collections began in earnest, the foreign collections being largely dispersed to other museums in the 1930s, 1950s, 1960s and mid 1970s.[122] How much of this activity reflected the compelling need to raise funds to balance the finances of the museum remains unclear. However, in retrospect the policy behind this process stands as an exemplar of how to handle the problematic nature of the breaking up and redistribution of a collection. Major British institutions were contacted and acquired the bulk of William Blackmore's collections. A substantial portion of William Blackmore's papers found its way to New Mexico where it was mined by Herbert Brayer for his two volume biography of the Englishman.

The Blackmore Museum collections were not the only parts of the Salisbury & South Wiltshire and Blackmore Museum that were sold. A point worth noting is John Musty' comment on the prices realised for the sale of books from the Salisbury Museum Library and the Blackmore Library in the 1930s. Simply put, 'there was little demand for books of this type in the 1930s.'[123] Whether there was similarly little demand for the Blackmore Museum's artefacts and photographs is less clear but it can be safely stated that neither were highly valued at the time. The option to sell Blackmore Museum artefacts on the open market was largely resisted.

The first and major dispersal of the contents of the Blackmore Museum and William's papers began in the early 1930s through a variety of agreements, donations, sales and auctions. Which party initiated these sales remains to be established and the minutes of the meetings of the museum's Trustees sheds little light. The sales seem to have been part of something of a co-ordinated approach from a number of interested parties to acquire artefacts from the Blackmore Museum. The 'Mound City Group', or 'Davis' collection as it was called, together with the bulk of Blackmore's albums of photographs were acquired by the British Museum, the photographs are now held in The Centre For

122 See *Acquisition and Disposal Policy of The Salisbury & South Wiltshire Museum*, Policy approved by the Board of the Salisbury & South Wiltshire Museum, 29 April 2004.

123 John Musty, 'The Catlin affair: the dispersal of the Blackmore Museum library, Salisbury', *Hatcher Review*, Volume 3, Number 26, Autumn 1988 pp.309.

Anthropology, Dept. of Africa, Oceania and the Americas (AOA). The Blackmore Peruvian and Central American artefacts went to Cambridge University and the Denmark specimens remained at the Salisbury & South Wiltshire Museum.

Lucie Carreau has located a letter in the archives of the Cambridge Museum of Archaeology and Anthropology that gives some insights about the manner in which institutions collaborated in acquiring significant parts of the Blackmore collections. It begs the question as to whether the Salisbury & South Wiltshire Museum had a financial imperative to sell some of its artefacts and what parameters were used to inform that decision. The minutes of the museum's trustees reveals little about the decision making process or the imperatives behind it. The letter dated 30th May 1930 was sent by Thomas Athol Joyce (1878-1942), deputy keeper of Ethnography, Department of Oriental Antiquities and Ethnography at the British Museum, to Louis Clarke (1881-1960), curator of the Cambridge University Museum of Archaeology and Ethnology from 1922 until 1937. It reads:

> Dear Louis,
>
> I heard this morning that the Blackmore Museum have accepted my offer for their archaeological and ethnographical specimens. The matter has to go before the Charity Commissioners but I do not anticipate any difficulty there. I have a four figure grant from the Reserve, & Beasley will put up an immediate cheque to cover the purchase. He is taking the purely 'ethnographical' stuff, with a certain amount of exchange. But definitely we have the pick. There will be quite a lot to handle, so if you want a few representative pipes for Cambridge, I think we can easily make a deal.[124]

124 Email from Lucie Carreau 17th October 2008. I thank Lucie Carreau for sharing her PhD. research material on the *Harry Beasley Collection of Pacific Artefacts* with me. For biographical information on the eccentric yet respected Clarke who was Director of the Fitzwilliam Museum from 1937 until 1946, see Graham Clark, *Prehistory at Cambridge and Beyond*, Cambridge University Press, Cambridge,1989 p.40. See also Clarke's obituary in *The Times*, Thursday 15th December, 1960 p.13.

In 1931 the British Museum acquired significant parts of Blackmore's collections including sixteen oil paintings of North American Natives by Zeno Shindler and forty-two Ledger Drawings in the so-called Tall Bear series.[125] It remains unclear whether these paintings by Shindler were displayed in the Blackmore Museum and indeed whether they formed part of the museum's holdings or Blackmore's private estate.

Another person who played a significant role in the dissemination of Blackmore Museum artefacts was the British brewer and private collector, Harry Geoffrey Beasley (1882-1939). In February 1931 he acquired part of the Blackmore Museum's ethnographic collections for his Cranmore Ethnographical Museum in Chislehurst in Kent that had opened in 1928. This included two hundred and sixty Oceanic objects, and over one hundred and sixty-five objects from North America (Inuit, Plains, North West Coast). From his death in 1939 until 1955, Beasley's collections were dispersed to six museums; The British Museum, Pitt Rivers Museum in Oxford, Cambridge Museum of Archaeology and Anthropology, National Museum of Scotland in Edinburgh, World Museum in Liverpool and Red House Museum in Christchurch (the latter transferred its ethnographic collections to Leeds in the 1980s). Each of them would have included artefacts from the Blackmore Museum. Irene Beasley, Harry's widow, also kept items for herself after her husband's death. She sold some to British and American dealers in the 1950s and 1960s. After her death in 1974, her daughters sold the rest of the collection (those items their mother had kept) at an auction by Graves Son and Pilcher of Hove on 3rd March 1975. As a result there therefore remain some artefacts from the Blackmore Museum on the market to this day.[126]

The bulk of the material from the Blackmore Museum now held by the British Museum was confirmed in early 1932. The Salisbury &

125 Drawings 1-16 were drawn by Mah-to-han-ski (Tall Bear (1825-1892)), one of three head Warriors of the Fox Band of the Kiyuksa band of the Oglala Lakota; also known as the Cut Off Band of Oglala Dakotas.; drawings 17-42 were probably drawn by a Lakota artist, Pretty or Good Bear (Mah-tow-wash-ta (1820-1888)).

126 Email from Lucie Carreau 17th October 2008.

South Wiltshire Museum's disposal book for 24th February 1932 records the transfer to the 'British Museum (Dept of Ceramics & Ethnology)' 'Photographs of North American Indians and miscellaneous. Notes, newspaper cuttings & pamphlets, ethnographical material & various North American objects. Bundle of spears etc. (Blackmore Museum) 1 paddle & small N. American implements'.[127]

William Blackmore's papers also posed a number of issues for the Salisbury Museum and the executors of his estate. In 1932 Barbara Aitken (1879-1967), a prominent anthropologist who had worked with the innovative educator and passionate amateur archaeologist Edgar Lee Hewett (1865-1946), secured for the Historical Society of New Mexico a substantial set of these papers relating to Blackmore's activities in New Mexico. Little is currently known of the professional relationship between Barbara Aitken, Humphrey Blackmore and Frank Stevens though this must have played a key role in how part of William's archives were to be acquired by the Historical Society of New Mexico.

The material transferred to New Mexico included diaries, letters, pamphlets, newspaper clippings and some one hundred and twelve photographs in carte de visite, stereoscopic, Cabinet and other photographic formats though it is unclear why only these photographs were selected for the Historical Society of New Mexico.[128] It remains to be ascertained from whom Aitken acquired the papers but it would seem that following the death in February 1929 of Dr. Humphrey Purnell Blackmore, William's brother and his executor, a number of members of the family were involved. Edward Stevens of Hollymount, Tanners Hill, Hythe – Humphrey's nephew, the eldest son of Edward Thomas Stevens – was appointed sole executor. Two of Blackmore's nephews were also instrumental. Frank Stevens, Curator of the Salisbury & South Wiltshire Museum assisted and secondly R. Veer Boyle of Santa Fe, son of Arthur Boyle and Blackmore's sister Blanche.

127 I thank Peter Saunders for supplying this information.

128 I thank Tomas Jaehn, Curator, Fray Angelico Chavez History Library, Palace of the Governors, Santa Fe for supplying a list of the photographs in the Blackmore Collection. A number of these photographs can be viewed online at the 'Digital Collections' page of the Palace of the Governors web site http://www.palaceofthegovernors.org/

In the 1930s the Historical Society of New Mexico stopped collecting New Mexicana materials and in the early 1960s transferred its holdings to the Chavez Library and the New Mexico State Records Center and Archives (which received much of the land grant material) both located in Santa Fe. Material was split and some of the Blackmore papers may have been mislaid.

Prior to Humphrey Blackmore's death there had been attempts to repatriate the Squier and Davis collection to the USA. During August and September 1925 Professor James Stewart Hine (1866-1930), Curator of the Division of Natural History of the Ohio State Archaeological and Historical Museum, was visiting London where he studied at the British Museum. He made a trip to Salisbury to inspect the Blackmore Museum, reportedly took tea with the 'Director of the Blackmore Museum' and talked over the possibility of the eventual return to Ohio of the Ohio material held in Salisbury.[129]

On 9th June 1930 the Board of Trustees of the Ohio State Archaeological and Historical Society met to consider the purchase of the Squier and Davis collection from the Blackmore Museum. General Edward Orton Jr. (1868-1932), the prominent Columbus philanthropist and businessman, was travelling in Europe and had sent a communication stating that the collection could be purchased for the approximate sum of US$7,500. The Board agreed a motion to authorise Orton to expend up to US$8,000 for the collection and the Society had to authorize this sum to be borrowed. However, Orton was not able to negotiate the purchase of the Squier and Davis collection from the Blackmore Museum, presumably since the offer from Thomas Joyce of the British Museum had already been accepted.[130]

The sale of Humphrey Blackmore's estate continued on the 2nd, 3rd and 4th March 1932 when Woolley and Wallis of Salisbury auctioned 'Property of the Estate of the late Dr. H. P. Blackmore. This was in essence the house sale of Humphrey's residence, Vale House. This included pictures, engravings, books, silver, ivories, bronzes, intaglios

129 *Ohio History*, Volume 35, January, 1926 p.246. It is not clear whether the 'Director' referred to was Frank Stevens or Humphrey Blackmore.

130 *Ohio History*, Volume 40, July, 1931 p.535.

and cameos, objet d'art and 'articles of Interest and Rarity' described as 'the remainder of the collection.'[131] It is unclear whether the funds raised may have benefitted Edward Stevens as 'the executor' of Humphrey's estate rather than the Trustees of William's eponymous museum.

The variety of channels through which the Blackmore Museum collections were broken up widened. On Wednesday 14th September 1932 Stevens' Auction Rooms in London's Covent Garden held an auction of 'Native Curios & Weapons etc., Pictures and Books, Jewellery and Plate etc.' Lots 175 to 202 were artefacts from the Blackmore Museum.[132]

On the 9th October 1934 a set of thirty-eight skulls and casts were dispatched from the Blackmore Museum to the Royal College of Surgeons.[133] Other parts of the Blackmore collection were sold to or acquired by the Pitt Rivers Museum in Oxford during the 1930s. In 1941 the Salisbury Museum donated a small collection – presumably of Blackmore material – to the Ethnology Department of the County Museum in Liverpool. [134]

While Franks Stevens had overseen the passing of much of his uncle's collections to other institutions, there were some remnants. In 1950, soon after his death, a first 'great clearance of surplus material' was made from the museum, though it has yet to be established exactly how much was from William Blackmore's original collection.[135] In 1951 a Maori piece from the Blackmore Museum was acquired by the museum in Otago, New Zealand.[136] Whether this formed a sale, was a gift or an exchange is unclear. On 9th March 1953 an 'unspecified number of

131 Frank Stevens' copy of this auction catalogue is held in the S&SWM.

132 An annotated copy of the catalogue can be found in the S&SWM. The items are primarily African, though there are Pacific region items such as four Australian spears (lot 201), a Thibetan [sic] prayer wheel (lot 194) and Two Fiji clubs (lot 183).

133 A typescript list is in the S&SWM.

134 S&SWM letter from Andrew West, Assistant Keeper of Ethnology to Peter Saunders of the S&SWM dated 24th November, 1981.

135 Frank Stevens, *The Salisbury Museums, 1861-1947: A Record of Eighty-Six Years of Progress*, 2nd edition, Salisbury, 1954 p.19.

136 Henry Devenish Skinner, *Comparatively Speaking: Studies in Pacific Material Culture, 1921-1972*, University of Otago Press, 1974 p.197.

photographs of North American Indians' were sold to the Newberry Library in Chicago.[137]

By 1960 William Blackmore's museum was a pale shadow of its former glories. 'It is a little saddening to visit the Blackmore Museum today. There is no money to heat it and in the winter footfalls echo in the empty room and it is cold like stone.'[138] By 1964 *The Times* reported that 'unless substantial grants are made to help it continue' the Salisbury Museum was threatened with closure.[139]

The sale of Blackmore Museum artefacts continued well after Frank Stevens' death and in 1975 a small selection of miscellaneous Merovingian antiquities was sold to the Ashmolean Museum in Oxford.[140] This was part of 'Remaining Blackmore Material' offered to a variety of museums' including the Dumfries Burgh Museum; City of Birmingham Museum and Art Gallery; Smith Art Gallery, Stirling; Morwellham Quay Centre for Recreation and Education, Tavistock; South African National Museum of Military History; P. Runeeckles, Helston, Cornwall; Pembrokshire Museums, Haverfordwest; The Bowes Museum, Barnard Castle, Co. Durham; and Brighton and Hove Museum. Leeds Museum also bought some pieces. The prices ranged from £25 to a mere 50p.[141]

137 Letter from Hugh Shortt, Director of the Salisbury Museum to Walter L. Fertig dated 3rd April 1973. S&SWM Blackmore file 2. In 1911, Edward E. Ayer (1841-1927), a Chicago businessman, donated more that 17,000 pieces on the early contacts between American Indians and Europeans. A number of the photographs of American Indians published by the Trustees of the Blackmore Museum form part of the Ayer collection. These may have been acquired through the Ayer endowment fund.

138 R. W. H. Willoughby, 'The Blackmore Museum', *Wiltshire Archaeological and Natural History Magazine*, Volume 57 Number CCVIII, Devizes, 1960 p.320. The Museum's committee had agreed in a meeting on the 31st January 1929 to the gas supply to the museum being cut off. S&SWM Reports and Minutes Agenda 1917-1929.

139 *The Times*, Tuesday 29th September, 1964 p.13

140 Arthur MacGregor, *A Summary Catalogue of the Continental Archaeological Collections in the Ashmolean Museum: Roman Iron Age, Migration Period, Early Medieval*, British Archaeological Reports International Series 674, Archaeopress, Oxford, 1997 p.13 citing Frank Stevens, *The Salisbury Museums 1861-1947: a record of eighty-six years' progress*, 2nd edition, Salisbury, 1954. Clearly, given the date of this second edition, another author added text to this edition, possibly Hugh de Saumarez Shortt, who succeeded Frank Stevens as the museum's curator.

141 Typescript list dated 7th May 1975 in S&SWM.

THE BLACKMORE MUSEUM LIBRARY

Another, less well discussed dimension of William Blackmore's eponymous museum was its library. Blackmore formed an extensive and significant library of books, particularly on Americana, and this formed an integral part of his museum and its objectives. It appears that the Blackmore Museum library also contained graphic material – such as prints, drawings and photographs though how they were catalogued and stored has yet to be established.

During his lifetime his collection of books would appear to have been divided between his home – specifically Shepley House – and 'the wonderful library of Americana' in the Blackmore Museum in Salisbury. Presumably, following his death, William's collection of books was consolidated in the library of his museum, though it is possible that some found their way into the possession of his brother Humphrey.

Quite what books Blackmore had available to him while he travelled in the USA remains unclear. The privately printed catalogue of this library published in or shortly after 1871 lists around one thousand books, including early and rare editions on North American Indians.[142] A hand written description of the 'Monograms for Books for Blackmore Museum' states that there should be two catalogues; one alphabetical and the other a catalogue in ten subject sections. 'When a book relates to two or more subjects, to be marked with each monogram and catalogued in second catalogue under each section.'[143] However, the chronology of Blackmore's acquisition of books is not known. He clearly continued to acquire both contemporary works and older items as the 'Addenda to the New World' section of the 1871 catalogue indicates.

142 *Catalogue of the Library of the Blackmore Museum, Salisbury.*, Published by W. Wells, printer, 'Times Office, Salisbury, pp.72. This includes a wide range of subjects including local history, mythology, and 'voyages and travels'. It presumably dates to 1871 or after since a number of titles are listed as having this date of publication. A rare publication, there are copies in University of California at Los Angeles (ID 4016932) and UC Santa Barbara (Southern Regional Library Z921 .B43) The Salisbury Museum has a 20 page 'issue' of this title. No other catalogue to the library is known, though the number of volumes is likely to have been increasing given Blackmore's disposable income during the first half of the 1870s.

143 List numbered '39' in Humphrey Blackmore Papers, S&SWM.

No register of the visitors to the library of the Blackmore Museum has been located and there are sparse references to those who did use the library for scholarly purposes. One of the most significant users was Augustus Wollaston Franks from the British Museum who visited the Blackmore Museum and made himself familiar with the library's up to date American publications.[144] The wider role of the library of the Blackmore Museum in developing ethnological and anthropological studies in Great Britain awaits evaluation.

The catalogue of the library of the Blackmore Museum has some curious anomalies. For instance, there were no copies listed of *The People of India*, a seminal photographic publication published by W.H. Allen and Co. of London in 8 volumes between 1868 and 1875.[145] This has been regularly cited as prompting Blackmore to suggest to the Smithsonian that a similar publication on Native Americans should be produced, though it is relevant to point out that Blackmore had already published photographs of Native Americans under the imprint of the Trustees of the Blackmore Museum in 1865. That Blackmore did not own a copy of *The People of India* while in 1870 he donated a copy of each of the first four volumes of this title to the Smithsonian seems unlikely.[146]

Until 1920 the Salisbury & South Wiltshire Museum and the Blackmore Museum retained their separate libraries, and there was some duplication and overlap. Given that there was no resident specialist

144 See J. C. H. King 'Franks and Ethnography' in Marjorie Caygill and John Cherry (eds.), *A.W. Franks – Nineteenth-century Collecting and The British Museum*, British Museum Press, London, 1997 p.151. Franks visited the collection in June and July 1866 while negotiating an exchange of material with items from the Christy Collection and again in 1872. Franks also collected book plates and the collection he donated to the British Museum included one for the Blackmore Museum. No. 33975 in *Franks Bequest. Catalogue of British and American Book Plates Bequeathed to the Trustees of the British Museum*, Volume III, Trustees of the British Museum London, 1904 p.297.

145 J. Watson Forbes and John William Kaye, *The People of India. A Series of photographic Illustrations with Descriptive Letterpress, of the Races and Tribes of Hindustan*, William H. Allen and Co., London, 1868; 1869.

146 *Annual Report of the Board of Regents of the Smithsonian Institution*, 1871 p.27 See Paula Richardson Fleming, *Grand Endeavors of American Indian Photography*, Smithsonian Institution, Washington, 1993 p.22.

in Americana it would seem that the Blackmore Museum library was infrequently used. Humphrey Blackmore did little to encourage the use of the Americana and it remains unclear how much material was in fact stored, perhaps in his neighbouring home, and thus inaccessible.

In 1920 the Salisbury Museum Library was transferred to the Salisbury Public Library where it was held as a separate and distinct collection. In 1932 some of the books from the Salisbury Museum Library were sold at auction or gifted to other institutions – including Salisbury Public Library – others were retained by the Museum. However, the sub-committee appointed to make the selections was able to extend its terms of reference to include the Blackmore Library.[147] The remaining books from the Salisbury Museum Library not selected by the sub-committee together with the entire Blackmore Museum Library were valued by the auctioneer (presumably Sotheby's) at £200-£250 and the recommendation was to send them all to auction. An estimated three tons of books were then shipped to London on the 21st August 1934 and the dispersal of books continued until March 1935, through a number of Sotheby's auctions.[148]

In November 1934 a tranche of books from the Blackmore Museum were sold at auction at Sotheby's by order of the Trustees.[149] Two of the lots were works by Blackmore's friend George Catlin and were withdrawn from the sale following an offer from an unidentified American who was willing to pay £20 (rather than the estimate of £8-£9) if the lots were withdrawn. Sotheby's had in fact incorrectly catalogued

147 The archaeologist John Musty (1923-2000) was tasked in the 1960s by the then director of the museum Hugh de Saumarez Shortt (1913-1975) to compile a card catalogue of the Frank Stevens Memorial Library. John Musty, 'The Catlin affair: the dispersal of the Blackmore Museum library, Salisbury', *Hatcher Review*, Volume 3, Number 26, Autumn 1988 pp.303-310.

148 Musty *op.cit.*, p.306. Musty states that the books were insured for £400 and the shipper, a Mr Harfit, estimated that there were three tons of books to transport.

149 *Catalogue of Printed Books and a Few Manuscripts Comprising the Property of Dr. G.E. Friend; the Property of Mrs. M.B. Kerin; the Property of Mrs. H.W. Walmisley, A Large Collection of Books on Travel and Exploration; Ethnology; and History; chiefly relating to North America; The Property of the Salisbury, South Wilts. and Blackmore Museum [Sold by Order of the Trustees]etc.*, November 5th -7th , 1934, Sotheby and Co., London 1934. Lots 770-904.

the items as three hundred and twenty-five lithograph facsimile plates by Catlin, whereas in fact they were original pen and ink drawings. Suspicious of this offer, the lots were withdrawn and, the following month, offered as two lots of a Sotheby's auction in London. They were described as 'a large collection of drawings, by George Catlin (1796-1872), of the Indians of North and South America' and formed part of an auction of books, manuscripts and autograph letters.[150] These two volumes containing were sold for £440. In 1964 they were sold again in a Sotheby's auction for £4,000.[151]

The breaking up of Blackmore's extensive library continued. On 4th and 5th March 1935 Sotheby's held an auction of printed books, manuscripts and letters including 'Books of Travel and Ethnology, sold by order of the Trustees of the Salisbury, South Wilts and Blackmore Museum.'[152] A number of these books were acquired by Francis Edwards

150 *The Times*, Monday, 26th November, 1934 p.3. *Catalogue of Valuable Printed Books and a Few Manuscripts, Autographs Letters and Historical Documents... A Large and Important Collection of Drawings by George Catlin, of the Indians of North and South America (Sold by Order of the Trustees of the Salisbury, S. Wilts. and Blackmore Musuem)...*, Sotheby & Co, London , Tuesday 18th and Wednesday 19th December 1935 Lots 321 and 322. Lot 321 was formed of two volumes; 72 original pen and ink drawings of North American Indians comprising over 200 portraits of costume, headdress and arms titled *The North Americans in the Middle of the Nineteenth Century, A Numerous and Noble Race of Human Beings fast passing to Oblivion, & Leaving no Monuments of their Own, behind them.* The second part of the lot was *The South Americans, 130 Portraits, full length, copied from his original oil paintings, same size, with great care, by Geo. Catlin,* together with a similar collection of 31 large drawings each containing several portraits. Lot 323 was made up of 'eight original watercolours by Catlin illustrating an annual religious ceremony practised by the Mandan Tribe of North American Indians', bound with 13 coloured lithographs 'Oikee-Pa: a religious Ceremony, and other customs of the Mandans' and George Catlin., *An Account of an Annual Religious Ceremony practised by the Mandan Tribe of North American Indians,* privately printed, n.d..

151 *The Times*, Tuesday, 14th April, 1964 p.14.

152 *Catalogue of valuable printed books, illuminated and other manuscripts, autograph letters and historical documents, &c.: comprising books of travel and ethnology, sold by order of the trustees of the Salisbury, South Wilts. and Blackmore Museum . . . . . . on Monday and Tuesday, the 4th and 5th of March, 1935.* Sotheby & Co., London, 1935. *The Times*, Tuesday, 19th February, 1935 p.27. There were 25 lots that realised £108 11s. The Museum's annual report for 1934-1935 reported that the total amount realised through the various auctions was £900 pounds, of which £440 had been achieved by the Catlin drawings.

who issued his *Books on the North American Indians and The Far West Including Many From the Blackmore Museum, Salisbury; Catalogue No. 587.* However, this catalogue does not identify which items came from the Blackmore Museum. Thus by the mid 1930s William Blackmore's extensive library of Americana was no more.

CONCLUSION

The Blackmore Museum thus acts as a paradigm of mid-Victorian philanthropy and William Blackmore's wide ranging interests. In many respects it set a new template for the display, study and publication of 'pre-historic' artefacts. Its demise also reflects the perennial issue of a museum solely funded through the largesse of a wealthy individual who failed to ensure ongoing funding to provide a lasting legacy. The fact that no kindred spirit could be found to promote the anthropological and North American collections of the Blackmore Museum was another contributory factor. However, this may also reflect the lack of appetite in the late 19th and early 20th centuries to study these areas. The relative financial value of many of the Blackmore Museum's holdings also indicates fluctuations in taste. While 'flint chips' were highly prized in the mid 19th century, this was not sustained. The value of William Blackmore's photographs of North American Indians have gone full circle. Highly prized by the Smithsonian Institution in the 1860s they were considered of academic value and suitable only for donation to the British Museum in the 1930s. However, by the late 20th century they commanded high prices in auction house sales and by specialist antiquarian book dealers.

Had William Blackmore's business ventures prospered and he had been able to continue to support his museum his legacy would have been significantly different. His bankruptcy and suicide blighted his long term contribution to a variety of aspects of anthropology, ethnology, and archaeology.

5
Blackmore as an Art Patron and Collector

As with many wealthy mid Victorians, William Blackmore was a collector and became a comparatively small scale but significant art patron. Examination of this facet of his life and interests sheds further light on his personality, character and the context of his collecting habits. The evidence that follows points to a man with many interests who was keen to exhibit parts of his wide ranging collections within the meetings of a number of scholarly institutions to which he belonged. These covered institutions and organisations in Liverpool, London and his native Wiltshire. It also points to a shrewd exploiter of the politics of patronage and its interrelationship with social networking.

The context of collecting shifted during the middle of the 19th century as industrialists and new professional classes acquired great wealth and became collectors, patrons and philanthropists. Liverpool presents a paradigm of this shift. Sugar refiner Henry Tate (1819-1899), whose wealth derived from his Liverpool factory, is a well known example as a result of the public gallery bearing his name on London's Millbank and the Tate public libraries distributed across South London. Other prominent Liverpool collectors included a coal mine proprietor, a variety of merchants including a jeweller and silversmith, ship owners, insurance underwriters, a chain and anchor manufacturer, and a number of bankers. One major patron of the arts in Liverpool was the merchant and banker Sir William Brown (1784-1864), who was a professional associate of William Blackmore. In the second half of the 1850s Brown – who was not a major collector himself – was to donate some £40,000 for the building of a museum and library in the city. Six photographs of the commemorative laying ceremony of the foundation stone of the Free Library were made.[1]

Blackmore was not unusual in terms of the diversity of his collecting habits. His 'Cabinet of Curiosities' included prehistoric implements, the material culture of a wide range of peoples – including Europeans, South and North American Indians and natives of the Pacific – coins and medals and manuscripts. However, a hierarchy of collecting had appeared over a number of centuries, and painting has been considered the pinnacle, maintaining a kudos still apparent today. In parallel, historians of collecting have tended to focus on individual aspects of the collections of prominent collectors. This has the effect of losing the wider significance of the entirety of a collector's interests. If one can tell much about an individual from the books in their home – and the 1871 privately printed catalogue of the Blackmore Library gives a number of insights into a library that contained more than one thousand titles – one can tell even more from their collecting habits. Nevertheless, William Blackmore does pass muster with the apogee of collecting taste through his patronage of the Pre-Raphaelite artist Dante Gabriel Rossetti.

William Blackmore's interests are reflected in those diverse learned and scholarly societies, both in the Great Britain and the USA, which he joined or was elected a member. Being elected a member is a key differentiator since it bestows a mantle of having achieved a sufficient level of measured acceptability on the elected; that an individual has passed the test and is thereby deemed worthy of inclusion into the ranks of an elite peer group. An overview of Blackmore's connection with learned and scholarly societies now follows.

Curiously, Blackmore was not a founding member of the Wiltshire Archaeological and Natural History Society founded in 1853 and played no significant role in the Society, though the Society was later to accolade him in an unprecedented manner following the opening of his eponymous museum. Five years after arriving in Liverpool as a newly qualified solicitor Blackmore's social status had risen sufficiently for him

1 Six photographs were donated by a Mr. Keith. *Transactions of the Historic Society of Lancashire and Cheshire*, Volume IX. Session 1856-57, London, 1857 p.291.

to join the ranks of the Historic Society of Lancashire and Cheshire. On 20th September 1854 he was elected a member and played a prominent role in the Society. Who his sponsors were remains unclear, though William Brown is likely to have played a role. Blackmore's partner Andrew Squarey became a member only in March 1863.

William was elected a member of the Ethnological Society of London in 1866 and became a member of the Council in the same year. He also sat on the committee led by Sir John Lubbock investigating the prehistoric monuments of the great Tolmaen at Constantine in Cornwall, an alleged ancient place of Druid worship.

Blackmore was elected a member of the American Philosophical Society in January 1869, a year in which he also became a correspondent of the Academy of Natural Sciences in Philadelphia.[2] In 1870 he was elected a member of the British Association for the Advancement of Science and in the following year he became a correspondent of the Numismatic and Antiquarian Society of Philadelphia. In 1872 he joined the Council of the newly formed Anthropological Institute of Great Britain as a representative of the Ethnological Society and became a Vice-President. He left the Council, rejoining it in 1874 and remained on it until 1877. While he did not make any further contributions to the proceedings of the Anthropological Institute 'his assistance and advice at the Council, and his presence at our evening meetings, were highly valued by his colleagues.'[3] These facts point to the prominent position Blackmore had secured for himself amongst a wide range of scholarly societies. While he achieved this position on merit rather than benefaction, Blackmore's social networking skills played a significant role.

Blackmore's position within the scholarly establishment is

2 *Transactions of the American Philosophical Society*, Volume 13, Part 3, 1869 p.vii. His membership number was 1635. See *Proceedings of the American Philosophical Society*, Volume 26, 1889 p.172. At the Society's meeting held on 18th December 1868 it was noted 'A donation for the Cabinet, was received through Dr. Hayden, from Mr. Blackmore: 32 Russian medals electrotyped and distributed by the British Museum.' *Proceedings of the American Philosophical Society*, Vol. 10, No. 80 July, 1868 pp. 540-541.

3 See Blackmore's obituary in the Report of Council in the *Journal of the Anthropological Institute*, Volume VIII, London, 1879 pp.400-1.

represented by a paper he gave to the Ethnological Society of London in April 1869 on the North American Indians. This paper was an impassioned appeal stating that 'old Indians are left to die of starvation upon the plains' and 'the various tribes existing in the western parts of the United States are being rapidly decimated, and before many years pass away the noble Red Man of the original Six Nations will be a creature of the past.'[4] The Ethnological Society had a number of reasons to place Blackmore on their top table and elect him a member of the Society's council. Blackmore had already established his reputation through the founding of his eponymous museum predominantly populated by the Squier and Davis collection. He had a detailed knowledge of the North American Indian and had firsthand experience of visiting them in their native habitat. He was also well connected with the leading political circles in both Britain and America.

The *Transactions of the Historic Society of Lancashire and Cheshire* give a number of insights into the Society and Blackmore's personal collections during the 1850s and early 1860s. There were around four to five hundred members of the Historic Society during the period William was an active member including such luminaries as Joseph Mayer and William Brown. The Society had a museum and a library housed in a single room at 57 Ranelagh Street.

Blackmore had become a member of the Archaeological Section Committee for the 1855-1856 session. The *Transactions* for this period noted that at a meeting of the society held on the 6th March 1856 Blackmore exhibited four stone celts, two found near Galway, one at Backton, in Cumberland and one in New Zealand, and two bronze spears, one of which was discovered in a bog in Leenane, Connemara.

Blackmore formed a collection of coins and medals and exhibited some items in meetings of the Historic Society of Lancashire and Cheshire in Liverpool in 1857. At the meeting held on the 5th February

4 William Blackmore, 'The North-American Indians: A Sketch of Some of the Hostile Tribes, Together with a Brief Account of General Sheridan's Campaign of 1868 against the Sioux, Cheyenne, Arapahoe, Kiowa, and Comanche Indians'. The text was printed in *The Journal of the Ethnological Society of London (1869-1870)*, Vol. 1, No. 3, 1869 pp. 287-320.

Blackmore exhibited a medal of Sigismund (1368-1437), Holy Roman Emperor of Germany. At the 12th March meeting he exhibited a crown piece of Mary Queen of Scots and a medal commemorative of the Restoration of Charles II, dated to 1675 and probably the work of the die sinker Thomas Simon (1618-1665). At the meeting on 14th May he exhibited a medal of Dr. Joseph Priestley (1733-1804), dated 1783, with Priestley's bust on one side and a pneumatic trough and various pieces of chemical apparatus on the reverse. Blackmore may have added items to his collection at the auction in 1859 and 1860 of the collection formerly owned by John Rushout, 2nd Baron Northwick (1770-1859). A copy of the auction catalogue for the Greek series of the Northwick Collection is listed in the 1871 catalogue to the Blackmore Library.[5] On 7th March 1861 he exhibited at a meeting of the Archaeological Section a reduced bronze copy of the Venus de Medici. On the 14th November 1861 he exhibited at the meeting of the Literary Section one of the medals presented by the Italian military and political figure Giuseppe Garibaldi (1807-1882) to his companions in the conquest of Sicily, and a photograph of a portrait of Oliver Cromwell by Sir Peter Lely in the Pitti Palace in Florence.[6] Blackmore is cited as having exhibited 'A small figure of Hermaphroditus, in gold; probably Etruscan' at the Literary Section meeting on the 13th January, 1859.[7]

5 Blackmore also owned a copy of *Northwick's Specimens of Ancient Coins of Magna Graecia and Sicily, engraved by H. Moses; the text by Dr. H. Noehden* (1826). The 1871 privately printed catalogue of the Blackmore Library lists a wide variety of books on coins including H. N. Humphrey's *Coin Collectors Manual* of 1853. Blackmore had a scholarly interest in this element of his collection. There were five books on coins by John Yonge Akerman; an early work, Evelyn's *Numismata, a Discourse on Medals, Antient and Modern* of 1697; de Bie's *Imperatorum Romanorum Numismata Aurea* of 1738; Cooke's *Medallic History of Imperial Rome* published in 1781 and more contemporary works such as his friend John Evans' *Coins of the Ancient Britons* of 1864. One title of local interest is *Numismata Antiqua, in tres partes divisa collegit olim et aeri incidi vivens curavit Thomas Pembrochiae et Montis Gomerica comes* of 1746. This covered the collection of the Earl of Pembroke at Wilton House, near Salisbury.

6 Another Liverpool collector, Peter Stuart (1814-1888), a merchant, owned a significant collection of memorabilia documenting Garibaldi's struggle for Italian independence.

7 *Transactions of the Historic Society of Lancashire and Cheshire*, Volume VIII, Session 1855-1856, 1856 p.242 *op.cit.*, Volume IX, Session 1855-1857, 1857 p.279 and p.285 and p.290.. See also, *op.cit.*, Volume XI, Session 1858-1859, Adam Holden, Liverpool,

Blackmore's collecting habits were also influenced by a range of family members, colleagues and associates. The role of his grandfather Henry Shorto in forming William's interest in geology and archaeology has been mentioned previously. The influence of the Salisbury circle of Dr. Richard Fowler, Henry Hatcher and The Rev. Edward Duke and their collections is unclear but relevant. In Liverpool Blackmore came into the sphere of Joseph Mayer (1803-1886), a Liverpool jeweller and goldsmith, who formed a wide ranging collection of antiquities including pre-historic metalwork, ivories, medieval European manuscripts, Egyptian artefacts, gems, arms and armour, Wedgwood and Oriental ceramics and ethnographical items. In 1852 Mayer opened a museum housing his collection in Colquitt Street – near the Liverpool Royal Institution Museum – and this was given to the City of Liverpool in 1867. Its value was estimated at a phenomenal £80,000.[8]

The range of Mayer's collections is indicated by sale of part of his collection in February 1859. In May 1854 Mayer had purchased the majority of the collection of the connoisseur, jeweller and diamond merchant Bram Hertz (1794-1865) at a three day auction held by S. Leigh Sotheby and John Wilkinson. Mayer stripped this collection of what he needed for his own collection and on 7th February 1859 sold the remainder. This included Assyrian, Babylonian, Egyptian, Greek, Etruscan, Roman, Indian, Peruvian, Mexican and Chinese antiquities as 3,138 lots in an auction held over fifteen days, again by S. Leigh Sotheby and John Wilkinson.[9] Blackmore owned a copy of the catalogue to this sale and was to refer to Mayer as one of his friends who had been instrumental in helping to establish his museum in Salisbury. Mayer did become a

1859 p.x. *op.cit.*, p.251 and *op.cit.*, *New Series Volume I, Session 1860-61*, Liverpool, 1861 p.334 and New Series, Volume II, Session 1861-1862, Liverpool, 1862 p.175.

8 Thomas Greenwood, *Public Libraries: a history of the movement and a manual for the organisation and management of rate-supported libraries*, Cassell & Co., London, 1891 p.447.

9 *Catalogue of the celebrated and well-known collection of Assyrian, Babylonian, Egyptian, Greek, Etruscan, Roman, Indian, Peruvian, Mexican and Chinese antiquities, formed by B. Hertz, corresponding member of the Archaeological Institute at Rome, now the Property of Joseph Mayer, Esq. F.S.A. &c. &c. Of Liverpool*, S. Leigh Sotheby & John Wilkins, London, 1859. The copy of this catalogue in the University of California Berkley library is annotated with the prices realised. The sale totalled £640 4s. 6d.

donor to the Blackmore Museum.[10] Whether Mayer attempted to convince Blackmore to establish his museum in Liverpool – or perhaps donate his collections to the newly formed Liverpool Museum is unknown.

Another prominent member of the Liverpool community was the banker William Brown (1784-1864). Blackmore had a professional contact with Brown through Duncan, Squarey and Blackmore. Both were members of the Historic Society of Lancashire and Cheshire, Brown having been a founder and vice-president. By the 1850s Brown had become a pillar of Liverpool society and a significant philanthropist. He spent some £40,000 on the building of a museum and library completed and given to the city in 1860. The street on which it was located, Shaw's Brow, was renamed William Brown Street. The museum and library was built to the designs of the architect Thomas Allom (1804-1872) in the Neo-Classical style. While Blackmore followed Brown in building a museum it was not on the same scale and the Gothic Revival style was employed for the museum in Salisbury. While Brown funded the museum and library he did not donate any collection of fine or decorative arts. The Gallery of Science and Inventions represented his particular contribution to the displays. However, Brown also had a photographic collection and this may have influenced Blackmore. At a meeting of the Archaeological Section of the Historic Society of Lancashire and Cheshire held on the 6th January 1859, Brown exhibited 'A collection of Photographic Views, principally taken in Italy and Honduras.'[11]

Blackmore focussed his attentions on Liverpool during the late 1850s and early 1860s. He did not exhibit at the 1862 *Temporary Museum of Pictures, Works of Art, &c.*, exhibited at the Council Chamber in Salisbury. However, following the founding of the Blackmore Museum in 1864 Blackmore began to play a more active and prominent role in his home town. In September 1865 Blackmore exhibited items from his collections at the 'Temporary Museum' held in the Council House in Salisbury as part of the Wiltshire Archaeological and Natural History

10 *Some Account of the Blackmore Museum – Part I. The opening Meeting*, H.F. &E. Bull, Devizes; Bell & Daldy, London ; J.R. Smith, London 1868 p.66.

11 *Transactions of the Historic Society of Lancashire and Cheshire*, Volume XI, Session 1858-59, Liverpool 1859 p.250.

Society's eleventh annual general meeting. His exhibits included a model of the unique finger pillory preserved in the church of Ashby de la Zouche, Leicestershire together with several gold objects found in the graves at Chiriqui in Panama, Central America – one of these objects, made in gold and in the form of a frog, had loose balls in the eye sockets, which rattled when shaken![12]

By the middle of the 1850s William Blackmore had established himself within the influential professional and social circles in Liverpool. As McEvansoneya has written 'the middle classes progressively sought the cultural, intellectual, and social distinction believed to be the corollaries of the political and economic power they had already achieved.'[13] However, Blackmore was often more strategic and tactical in his approach to commissioning works of art and his collecting habits. In the early 1860s, with significant disposable income, Blackmore was faced with the question of what a successful member of the Liverpool business community should spend his money on. One part of the answer was that Blackmore began to collect significant works of contemporary art.

Liverpool was the only provincial British town to have its own school of Pre-Raphaelite artists, whose members formed part of the Liverpool Academy of Arts, a private society of artists founded in 1812. The Academy taught students, elected artists as associates and full members to govern its working, and organised exhibitions. From 1845 until about 1860 it played a significant part in wider Pre-Raphaelite history. For several consecutive years from 1851 the Liverpool Academy awarded its annual £50 prize to a Pre-Raphaelite painter. This caused a division between factions in the Academy and a split, outraging traditionalists who thought prize winners such as *Valentine Rescuing Sylvia from Proteus* by William Holman Hunt (1827-1910) – the winner in 1852 – and *The Blind Girl* by John Millais (1829-1896) – winner in 1857

12 *Wiltshire Archaeological and Natural History Magazine*, No.XXVII, Volume X, July 1866 p.35. The frog was subsequently exhibited in the Blackmore Museum though its provenance was not documented in Stevens' *Flint Chips*.

13 Philip McEvansoneya, 'William Blackmore, Patron of Dante Gabriel Rossetti and Robert Moran, and ethnographer of the United States', *Journal of Pre-Raphaelite Studies*, (12), 2003 p.62-73. Quoted on page 62 to 63.

– to be scandalous.[14] The Academy fell apart and into debt. It ceased to be an active, significant or influential entity by the late 1850s, when the rival Liverpool Society of Fine Arts was formed, and its last exhibition took place in 1867.[15]

Works by Dante Gabriel Rossetti (1828-1882) were exhibited at the Liverpool Academy exhibitions in 1858, 1861, 1862 and 1864.[16] In 1859 Rossetti made a fundamental change to his painting subject matter, style and materials. In July 1859 he persuaded one of his patrons, the artist George Price Boyce (1826-1897), to commission a portrait of Fanny Cornforth (c. 1835- c. 1906) – Rossetti's model and mistress – which became the famous picture *Bocca Baciata*.[17] Rossetti adopted the Venetian Cinquecento style replacing his earlier preference for the Florentine and Sienese Quattrocento. This form of half length female portrait depicted with luxurious costumes and in vibrant colours was to become one of Rossetti's staples during the 1860s. Rossetti also chose painting in oils rather than the watercolours he had used to establish his reputation during the 1850s. William Blackmore was to become one of Rossetti's earliest patrons of this form of work.

Blackmore could have been introduced to Rossetti in London though there were a number of collectors in Liverpool who acquired works by the artist. These included the sugar refiner Henry Tate (1819-1899), ship owner Frederick Richards Leyland (1831-1892), insurance underwriter Philip Rathbone (1828-1895) and the chain and anchor manufacturer Albert Salisbury Wood (1838-1911).[18] However, Blackmore

14 Both paintings are now in the Birmingham City Museum and Art Gallery. The Holman Hunt painting was purchased in 1887 by the Corporation of Birmingham for 1,000 guineas. The Millais was presented by Rt Hon William Kendrick in 1892.

15 See Edward Morris and Emma Roberts, *Liverpool Academy and Other exhibitions of Contemporary Art in Liverpool, 1774-1867: A History and Index of Artists and Works Exhibited.*, Liverpool University Press, Liverpool, 1999.

16 *op.cit.*, pp.526-527.

17 Boyce was a British watercolour painter of landscapes and vernacular architecture in the Pre-Raphaelite style. Rossetti charged £40 for the work. The painting is now in the Museum of Fine Arts, Boston.

18 For an overview see Pat Starkey (ed.), *Riches into Art – Liverpool Collectors 1770-1880. Essays in honour of Margaret T. Gibson.*, Liverpool University Press, Liverpool, 1993. See particularly Dianne Sachko Macleod, *Art and the Victorian middle class – Money*

was one of the early collectors of Rossetti. He began collecting oil paintings by Rossetti before George Rae (1817–1902), a banker of Birkenhead and one of Rossetti's most important patrons.[19] In a letter to Rae dated 13th December 1863 Rossetti wrote; 'A picture of mine which you might like to see went lately to Mr Blackmore (of the firm of Duncan, Squarey & Blackmore) at Hooton. Do you know him at all? He is just now gone to America, but if you were that way, Mrs Blackmore is so kind that I feel sure she would show you the picture.'[20] Rae acquired his first Rossettis – two watercolours – in 1862 and built a large collection of over two hundred paintings including nineteen paintings and drawings by this artist alone. He housed his collection of Rossettis in a specially designed room. Blackmore was part of the circle that included Rae.

In 1863 Blackmore was recorded as having paid £60 for the portrait of *Helen of Troy* by Rossetti.[21] This painting, bequeathed to the Kunsthalle in Hamburg in 1921, may have left the possession of the Blackmore family (probably Humphrey) in the mid 1890s and been sold

and the making of cultural identity, Cambridge University Press, Cambridge, 1996. Macleod references some nineteen significant painting collectors in Victorian Liverpool though curiously not Blackmore's partner A. T. Squarey. One significant collector was John Gray Hill (1839-1914). Having qualified as a solicitor in London in 1863, Hill joined the firm of Duncan, Squarey and Blackmore in Liverpool. He became a partner in around 1866. In 1867 Hill became secretary to the American Chamber of Commerce in Liverpool and also of the Liverpool Steamship Owners' Company. While Hill was a collector of works by Rossetti – amongst other artists of the Aesthetic movement – these were largely acquired after William Blackmore's death.

19 For an overview of Rae's professional life see Francis E. Steele, *Present-Day Banking: Its Methods, Tendencies and Characteristics.*, Butterworth, London, 1909 pp.195-8. See also Julian Treuherz, 'Aesthetes in Business: The Raes and D. G. Rossetti', *The Burlington Magazine*, Vol. 146, No. 1210, January, 2004 pp. 13-19.

20 Letter 63.112 in William E. Fredeman, *The Correspondence of Dante Gabriel Rossetti – The Chelsea Years 1863-1872, Volume III 1863-1867*, D.S. Brewer, Cambridge, 2003 p.95.

21 William Michael Rossetti, *Dante Gabriel Rossetti as Designer and Writer*, Cassell & Company Limited, London, 1889 p.41. W.M. Rossetti stated that painting might have been removed to the Blackmore Museum in Salisbury following Blackmore's death though no clear proof supports this conjecture. In 1899 it was reported that the painting was either in Germany or America. See Henry Currie Marillier. *Dante Gabriel Rossetti, An Illustrated Memorial of His Art and Life*,. George Bell & Sons, London, 1899 p.129.

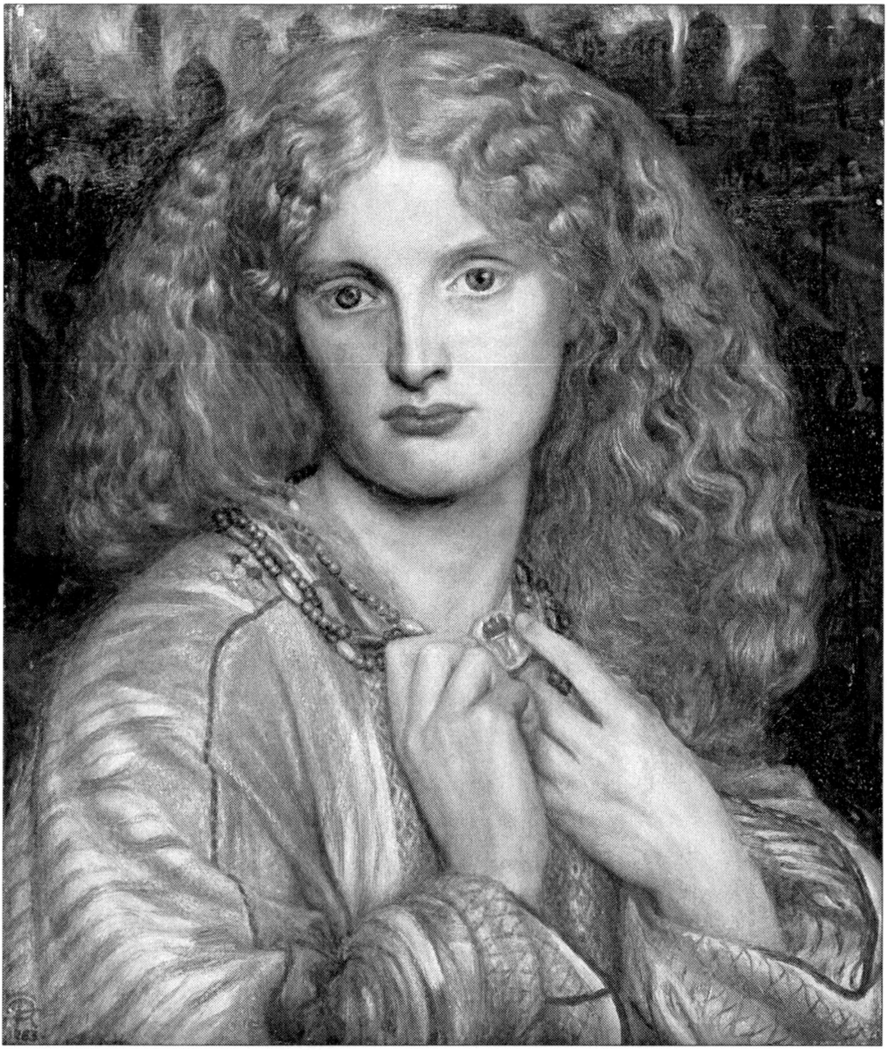

Daniel Gabriel Rossetti (1828-1882)
Helen of Troy. 1863.
Oil on canvas
Hamburger Kunsthalle, Hamburg, Germany/ The Bridgeman Art Library

via P. & D. Colnaghi to Edwin Amsinck (1826-1897) at the suggestion of Emil Heilbut (1861-1921), an art critic and consultant.[22]

Philip McEvansoneya has published on Blackmore's ownership of two other paintings by Rossetti – *Fazio's Mistress* and *Monna Vanna*.[23] All three paintings owned by Blackmore were half-length female portraits, typical of Rossetti's works of the 1860s. However, while Blackmore was to own these paintings by Rossetti during the mid 1860s, this may have been something of a whim rather than a personal conviction to form a collection of the artist's works. *Fazio's Mistress* – painted in the Titianesque style – was commissioned by William Blackmore sometime in early or mid-1863, was on Rossetti's easel in October, and was completed and sent to Blackmore on 19th November 1863. Rossetti had initially sent a preliminary sketch to Blackmore in order to initiate the commission. This was sent with the painting to Blackmore in November 1863. The whereabouts of the preliminary sketch is not known. Blackmore lent the finished oil painting to the exhibition held at the Liverpool Academy in 1864 and subsequently sold it to George Rae who had described it as 'the gem' of the Academy exhibition.[24] It was repainted for Rae in 1873 when the artist renamed it *Aurelia*. In 1916 the Tate Gallery purchased this painting with assistance from Sir Arthur Du Cros (1871-1955) and Sir Otto Beit (1865-1930) through the Art Fund from the Trustees of the Estate of George Rae.

Blackmore was also the first owner of *Monna Vanna*, finished by Rossetti at the end of October 1866, and retouched by the artist at Kelmscott in 1873 when it was re-named *Belcolore*. Rossetti had originally offered the painting to the tobacco, cotton and timber merchant, and

22 I thank Dr. Alexander Bastek, Kulturstiftung Hansestadt Lübeck for this information. Email to author 21st May, 2010.

23 See Philip McEvansoneya, 'William Blackmore, Patron of Dante Gabriel Rossetti', *Review of the Pre-Raphaelite Society*, 9, Spring 2001 pp.9-17 and 'William Blackmore, Patron of Dante Gabriel Rossetti and Robert Moran, and ethnographer of the United States', *Journal of Pre-Raphaelite Studies*, (12), 2003 p.62-73.

24 See Mary Bennett, 'A Check List of Pre-Raphaelite Pictures Exhibited at Liverpool 1846-67, and Some of Their Northern Collectors,' *The Burlington Magazine*, Volume 105, No. 728, Victorian Art. Painting, Furniture, Sculpture November, 1963 pp.486-495.

ship owner John Mitchell (1798-1876) of Everton. Rossetti again followed the manner of Titian, Veronese, and the other Venetian Old Masters and called it 'probably the most effective . . . room decoration which I have ever painted.'[25] However, Blackmore did not keep this painting in his collection for long and in the summer of 1869 the painting passed into the hands of George Rae. In July 1869 Blackmore wrote to George Rae stating that the sale of *Monna Vanna* and *Fazio's Mistress* to him would thus form 'an almost unique and perfect series of works by our friend.'[26] The background to this sale begs a number of questions. Did Blackmore wish to sell the paintings or did he need to? Did he sell the paintings to Rae as a favour or because he needed to raise funds? Or, as McEvansoneya has suggested, was Blackmore severing his connections with Liverpool.[27]

The Liverpool connection with Rossetti also included Blackmore's friend and colleague from Salisbury, Andrew Tucker Squarey (1821-1900). On 17th November 1863 Squarey and Blackmore visited Rossetti at 16 Cheyne Walk in London, presumably to view progress on *Fazio's Mistress.*[28] In 1865 Squarey commissioned the water-colour *Hamlet and*

25 Oswald Doughty and John Robert Wahl (eds.), *Letters of Dante Gabriel Rossetti, Volume II: 1861-1870*, Oxford University Press, Oxford, 1965 p.606. This may be the painting Rossetti offered to Blackmore for 500 Guineas in a letter dated 1st December 1865. Letter 65.169 in William E. Fredeman, *The Correspondence of Dante Gabriel Rossetti – The Chelsea Years 1863-1872, Volume III 1863-1867*, D.S. Brewer, Cambridge, 2003 p.352. In September 1866 Rossetti wrote to Blackmore thanking his for a cheque for £200 'on account of the price of the picture.' Rossetti had also been invited to visit the Blackmore residence and consult on the hanging of the picture.' Letter 66.159 Fredeman (2003) pp.472-473.

26 Letters regarding this sale survive in the National Museums Liverpool. Letters from Rossetti to Blackmore dated 14th, 24th and 27th July 1869 and 9th and 16th August 1869. Also Blackmore to Rae, 24th July 1869. See Julian Treuherz, 'Aesthetes in business: the Raes and D. G. Rossetti', *The Burlington Magazine*, Volume 146, No. 1210, January, 2004 pp.13-19. This work was also purchased in 1916 by in the Tate Gallery with assistance from Sir Arthur Du Cros and Sir Otto Beit through the Art Fund.

27 McEvansoneya (2003) p.66.

28 Letters from Rossetti to Blackmore dated 16th November and 19th November 1863. See Letters 63.100 and 63.101 in William E. Fredeman, *The Correspondence of Dante Gabriel Rossetti – The Chelsea Years 1863-1872, Volume III 1863-1867*, D.S. Brewer, Cambridge, 2003 pp.87-88.

Ophelia by Rossetti, painted in 1866. It was still owned by the Squarey family in 1899. Squarey's substantial collection of paintings – including a significant number of works by contemporary British artists – was sold in auctions in 1900 and 1912.[29]

Records of sales of works of art from the annual exhibitions held by the Liverpool Academy survive for the years 1854 to 1862 and 1865. Blackmore's name is not listed as a purchaser of any works. However many more exhibited pictures were sold privately and thus do not appear in the Academy's official manuscript lists.[30]

Blackmore purchased no further works by Rossetti or any other major contemporary British artist and there are few clues as to other paintings he may have owned. Although active in the first half of the 1860s, Blackmore did not subsequently form a large collection of paintings. It is likely that on William's death Humphrey Blackmore inherited those paintings that were still in his brother's possession.

Little is known of Blackmore's collection of watercolours, prints and drawings and there is little evidence that he formed a substantial one. The local historian James Edward Nightingale (1817-1892) of Wilton gave an insight to the diversity of Blackmore's graphic collections. He noted that 'The earliest drawing I have met with of Wilton House in its original state, is contained in an early manuscript copy of the Pembroke Terrier, in possession of the late Mr. W. Blackmore, It is merely a pen and ink sketch, and is date 1563 . . .'[31] A reduced copy of this drawing was used to illustrate Nightingale's article. The manuscript was still in the Blackmore Museum in 1906 (No. 1484) though its whereabouts is currently unkown.[32]

29 H. C. Marillier, *Dante Gabriel Rossetti, An Illustrated Memorial of His Art and Life*, George Bell and Sons, London 1899 p.96. See Philip McEvansoneya, 'Dante Gabriel Rossetti's 'Hamlet and Ophelia' and its patron.', *The Burlington Magazine*, Number 1273, Volume CLI, April 2009 pp.219-23.

30 The lists have been transcribed in Edward Morris and Emma Roberts, *Liverpool Academy*, 1999 pp.677-705.

31 J. E. Nightingale, 'Some Notice of William Herbert, first Earl of Pembroke of the Present Creation', *Wiltshire Archaeological and Natural History Magazine*, Volume XVIII, 1879 pp.81-131. Cited on p.89.

32 *Wiltshire Archaeological and Natural History Magazine*, Volume XXXV, 1908 p.312 The original is in Wiltshire & Swindon History Centre WSA 2057/S3.

That Blackmore made an effort to increase his watercolour collection is recorded. In the memorandum of understanding between Blackmore and Davis dated 26th January 1864 is a reference to a portfolio of Davis's watercolours on which Blackmore had first option. Blackmore subsequently offered Davis US$1,000 for the watercolours but the American declined it.[33]

Blackmore did own a collection of engravings related to William Penn (1644-1718), the English real estate entrepreneur, philosopher, and founder of Pennsylvania. One of Blackmore's chief business associates, Morton Coates Fisher (1835-1889), was a descendant of William Penn. A collection of correspondence, notes, portraits, and pamphlets of William Blackmore is now held by the Historical Society of Pennsylvania in Philadelphia. It is believed that part of this material was intended for a sketch of Penn by Blackmore. Given Penn's role in developing land grants this project seems to point to Blackmore strategically aligning his collecting habits with his business interests. Perversely, Blackmore was to suffer a similar fate to Penn, who died penniless in 1718.

Blackmore's primary residence between 1865 and 1870 was Shepley House in Carshalton, south of London, where he lavishly entertained an array of mid Victorian high society.[34] There are photographs held in Salisbury Museum of the exterior of the house, grounds and an ornate wooden bridge over the River Wandle that ran through the grounds. Quite what collections furnished such a substantial property remains a matter of conjecture but evidence suggests that these matched his prominent stature with the business communities in Liverpool and London. A draft

33 Terry A. Barnhart, 'The Hamilton Davis collection of American Antiquities', *Journal of the History of Collections*, Volume 16, Number 2, 2004 pp.59-87. See pages 73-4.

34 Blackmore was first rated in this residence in July 1865 and last extant records for his being rated are April 1870. From July 1870 the house was taken over by Alfred Tylor (1824-1884), geologist and brass-founder. Presumably Blackmore moved in 1870 from Shepley House to his apartment in Belgrave Mansions, near Victoria Station in London. I thank Kath Shawcross, Borough Archivist & Local Studies Manager, London Borough of Sutton Local Studies Centre, for supplying this information. Brayer *op.cit.*, Volume I, p.193 cites an instance of the US Senator James W. Nye (1815-1876) visiting Blackmore at Carshalton in June 1873. Shepley House was located in the vicinity of the present Shepley Close, off Strawberry Lane, in Carshalton and survived until the mid-1930s when it was demolished.

will written in January 1866 specifically refers to furniture, plate books, pictures, prints, bronzes and other works of art, china, glass, linen, wines and liquors.'[35] One can reasonably presume that the luxurious house contained appropriate furniture and decorations but little has been firmly established. For instance while he did own some bronzes which he was forced to sell in November 1877 to raise capital, did Blackmore own other pieces of sculpture.?[36] Did he have significant collections of silver and porcelain? That Blackmore owned pieces of furniture of some value is known. Brayer refers to Humphrey Blackmore estimating that the sale of his late brother's furniture from his apartment in Belgrave Mansions and in and his office in Founders Court would pay his debts in those places.[37]

Other than the commission to Rossetti, Blackmore was, however, involved in another fine art commission of significance. In May 1872 Blackmore commissioned for US$800 (UK£147) a series of aquarelles of the Yellowstone region from the English-born American artist Thomas Moran (1837-1926) whose works today are amongst the most prized.[38] The background to this commission is significant since it can be seen as another piece of Blackmore's strategic approach to link himself to the American establishment.

Moran had accompanied Ferdinand Hayden's 1871 expedition to Yellowstone during July and August of that year. Blackmore had seen a set of Moran's field sketches in Washington, D.C. in the winter of 1871.[39] Together with photographs by the Hayden expeditions' photographer William Henry Jackson – who became a lifelong friend

35 Wiltshire & Swindon History Centre 776/579. However, these are the standard terms used in contemporary Inland Revenue forms for Residuary Accounts.

36 See endnote 58.

37 Brayer, *op.cit.*, Volume I, p.319

38 The auction of American Art at Christie's in New York on 21st May 2008 set a new record for a 19th-century American painting with the sale of Thomas Moran's landscape *Green River of Wyoming* (dated 1878) to Pennsylvania's Avery Galleries for US$17.7 million against a pre-sale estimate of US$3–5 million. This price more than doubled the previous record for a 19th century American painting.

39 Ruth B. Moran's notes for biography of her father now in the Gilcrease Institute. As cited by Carol Clark, *Thomas Moran – Watercolours of the American West*, University of Texas Press, Austin, 1980 p. 41 footnote 14.

of Blackmore's – Moran's watercolours were used as exhibits brought before the US Congress and they were instrumental in the decision to make Yellowstone a National Park just seven months after Moran's work on the Hayden Survey ended. Yellowstone National Park was signed into law by President Ulysses S. Grant on 1st March, 1872.

On 2nd May, 1872 Moran's seven by twelve foot panoramic *Grand Canyon of the Yellowstone* was at put on display at the Leavitt's auction rooms in Clinton Hall on Astor Place in New York. Blackmore was in the USA on a business trip at the time and if he did not attend this event he would certainly have known about it. Moran's painting caused a sensation, filling the insatiable interest in Yellowstone that had had been stoked since the late 1860s and that had been further fuelled by the excitement generated by Jay Cooke (1821-1905), the Philadelphia banker and principle financier of the Northern Pacific Railroad, in order to instil in the public imagination the proximity of the newly created national park to the Northern Pacific line. The line would pass through southern Montana, just above Yellowstone's North Entrance.

The painting transformed Moran's reputation and his fortunes. Three months after the creation of the Yellowstone National Park, the US Congress purchased the painting for US$10,000 – half the amount Moran had originally asked for the painting – and displayed it in the Senate lobby. The influential contemporary art critic Clarence Cook was later to call it 'the only good picture to be found in the Capitol.'[40] Moran was now in the top league of American painters alongside Albert Bierstadt (1830-1902).

Blackmore was aware of Moran's rising star, the artist's professional relationship with Ferdinand Hayden and may also have got wind that Jay Cooke wished to commission Moran to create a series of watercolours of the Yellowstone region. In 1871 Cooke had loaned Moran US$500 to secure a place on Hayden's team. Blackmore pre-empted Cooke with his commission to Moran in May 1872 and the aquarelles were delivered to

40 'Art in the Capitol', *Scribner's Monthly*, 5, No.4, February, 1873 p.499 as cited in Thurman Wilkins and Caroline Lawson Hinkley *Thomas Moran: Artist of the Mountains*, 2nd edition, University of Oklahoma Press, Norman, 1998 endnote 16 p.316.

Blackmore several months before the set painted for Cooke. Blackmore then consolidated his position by successfully requesting that he accompany Ferdinand Hayden on his 1872 survey of Yellowstone. Cooke went bankrupt in the Panic of 1873, a fate that Blackmore was lucky to have avoided. Through the results of a successful investment in the Horn Silver Mine in Utah Cooke had paid off his debts by 1880 and again become wealthy. His set of sixteen of Moran's aquarelles were subsequently broken up, unlike those of Blackmore, and fourteen have disappeared.

The sixteen images of Yellowstone created by Moran in his studio from his broadly painted field studies made during Hayden's 1872 survey were significant, being some of the first colour images of Yellowstone to be seen on the East Coast of the USA. While today these aquarelles are seen as works of art, to contemporaries they were seen as documentary records. They received ecstatic reviews in the autumn of that year when they were exhibited at the Goupil Gallery in New York prior to being shipped to Blackmore in England. The review that appeared in *Scribner's* described them as the 'most brilliant and poetic pictures that have been done in America thus far.'[41] Hayden wrote that Blackmore considered these images were a fitting memorial to his wife who had unexpectedly died in Bozeman during the Yellowstone expedition.[42] A rumour spread that Blackmore intended to present the aquarelles to Queen Victoria.[43]

Moran's aquarelles were sent to Salisbury and may have been put on open display in the Blackmore Museum. The 'scientific' credentials of these aquarelles were enhanced when William exhibited them at the *conversazione* of the Royal Society, held on the 26th April, 1873.[44]

41 'Thomas Moran's Water-Color Drawings,' *Scribner's Monthly* 5, no. 3, January 1873 p.394.

42 A letter from Hayden to Moran dated 29th August 1872 he wrote 'Now he [Blackmore] wishes to have [the pictures] as a sort of monument to her memory.' Transcript in the Moran papers in the Gilcrease Institute, as cited by Thurman Wilkins, *Thomas Moran –Artist of the Mountains,* 2nd edition. University of Oklahoma Press, Norman, 1998 endnote 129 p. 339.

43 Thurman Wilkins, *op.cit.,* p.103. Wilkins gives no source for this claim.

44 The four page checklist of this *conversazione* held in the library of the Royal Society

These Royal Society *conversazioni* were prestigious, select events with comparatively few exhibitors and around five hundred to six hundred visitors, primarily Fellows of the Society. How Blackmore was able to secure the display of his aquarelles in such an august setting is unclear, though a significant number of contacts within his social network were Fellows of the Royal Society.

Thereafter, little information has been unearthed about the fate of Moran's aquarelles. On William's death they came into the possession of Humphrey Blackmore and were reported as on display in the Blackmore Museum in 1882. This was confirmed again in 1889.[45] Little used, following Humphrey's death in February 1929 his executor put them up for auction at Sotheby & Co. on Monday 22nd July 1929. However, they were withdrawn, though why has yet to be established.[46] The Moran watercolours then appeared almost three years later as part of lot 347 in the Woolley and Wallis sale of the remainder of Humphrey Blackmore's estate at the house sale of Vale House.[47] The catalogue entry noted that the watercolours 'were exhibited at the Royal Society, London, in 1873, Dr. Blackmore [sic] receiving the thanks of the President and Council for the loan.'

notes that in 'Room II. Drawings in Water-colour. Scenes in the Valley of the Yellowstone. Lent by Mr. W. Blackmore.'

45 See Nancy Anderson, *Thomas Moran*, National Gallery of Art; Yale University Press, Washington; New Haven, 1997 p.74 and *Magazine of Western History*, November 1889 p.6 'where these famous water-colors may now be seen.'

46 *Catalogue of Old Engravings...... Engraved Portraits. The Property of the Late Dr. H. P. Blackmore, of Salisbury, (Sold by Order of the Executors)... and a series of portraits of American Indians, The Property of the Late Dr. H. P. Blackmore, of Salisbury, (Sold by Order of the Executors)* Sotheby & co., London, Monday 22nd and Tuesday 23rd July, 1929 lot 155. The S&SWM holds a notebook containing cuttings from the catalogues of auctions held between 19th and 26th July, 1929 listing the lots from Humphrey Blackmore's collection. The lots have been annotated with prices realised. The Moran watercolours have been annotated '(withdrawn)' though why has not been recorded. Humphrey owned a number of paintings attributed to significant artists. Lot 150 was a described as a painting by Sir Joshua Reynolds titled *The Snake in the Grass* that made £80. This may be a copy of the original work also known as *A Nymph and Cupid: 'The Snake in the Grass'* purchased for the National Gallery in 1871 and now in the Tate Gallery in London.

47 The sale took place on the 2nd, 3rd and 4th March 1932 in Vale House in Salisbury.

Their provenance from then until they were acquired by the Thomas Gilcrease Foundation in 1947 is reasonably complete.[48] In 1937 this 'group of watercolours, from collections now in the Southwest, which came to this country a few years ago from the Blackmore family in England' was being exhibited in the USA.[49] They were acquired for the Gilcrease Institute in 1955 and are now in the Thomas Gilcrease Museum in Tulsa, Oklahoma.[50]

As was the case of his association with Rossetti, Blackmore purchased no further works by Moran nor did he form a collection of graphic views of the 'Great West.' Photography was to remain his preference.

Another artist whom Blackmore engaged for a number of projects was Antonio Zeno Shindler. While Shindler's most significant work for the Englishman was as a photographer, copying Blackmore's photographs of North American Indians or printing from the negatives Blackmore had acquired from the McClees Gallery, he was also commissioned to produce sixteen paintings of North American Indians. These were all based on photographs. The portrait of Keokuk has been copied from Thomas Easterley's Daguerreotype of 1847, that of Red Plume the head and shoulders of a Daguerreotype seated portrait by John H. Fitzgibbon of 1851-1852, that of Yellow Hawk (Se-tan-si-tan)is after one of Shindler's own photographs taken in 1867 and the portrait of Red Dog (Shun-Ka-Lu-Ta or Shon-Kan-Lou-Tah), chief of the Lakota Oglala is after the

48 The full provenance of these watercolours between the 1932 Woolley & Wallis sale of Humphrey Blackmore's estate and their appearance at the Newhouse Gallery, New York, in 1937 has yet to be established. The Newhouse Gallery purchased the watercolours from the dealer Paul Larsen whose address was in Duke Street, St. James', London. They were then sold to Jay Catherwood Hormel (1892-1954), head of the Hormel food company, then passed to his son George A. Hormel (1928-2006) in Los Angeles, and then passing through the Los Angeles dealer C. B. Jamison to M. Knoedler and Co. Inc, in New York to Thomas Gilcrease.' Carol Clark, *Thomas Moran – Watercolours of the American West*, University of Texas Press, Austin, 1980 p.128 No.37.

49 *The Connoisseur*, Volume 99, 1937 p.38.

50 *Catalogue of water-colour drawings of the Yellowstone region, great national park of the United States, painted by J [i.e. T.] Moran, for William Blackmore; and list of photographs by W.H. Jackson.* [n.p., n.d.]. Worldcat locates only one copy, in the Ayer Collection of the Newberry Library, Chicago. Call Number Ayer 290.B5875.

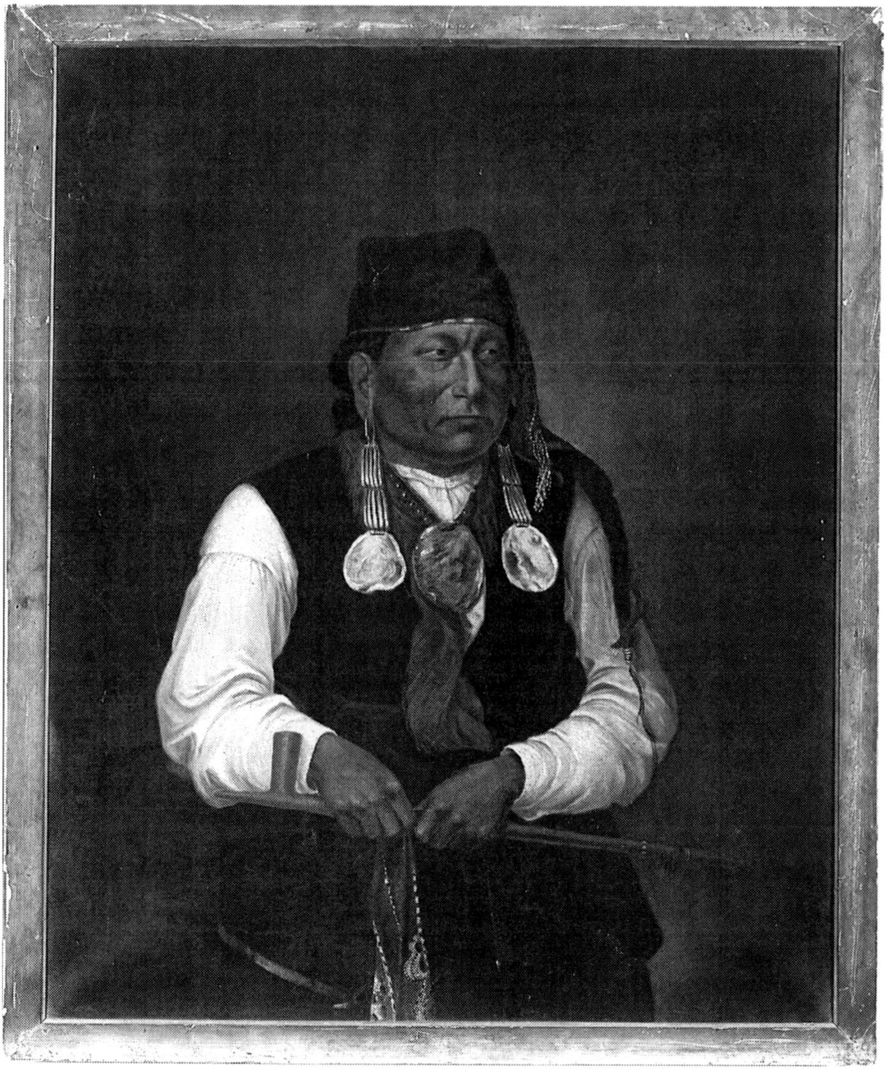

Red Dog (Shun-Ka-Lu-Ta or Shon-Kan-Lou-Tah), chief of the Lakota Oglala. Painting dated to 1872-1874 by Antonio Zeno Shindler based on a photograph taken by Alexander Gardner in May 1872.
Oil on canvas
Courtesy of The Trustees of the British Museum

photograph taken by Alexander Gardner in May 1872. These paintings were intended to hang in the Blackmore Museum, perhaps mimicking Catlin's *Indian Gallery*, or the gallery of paintings by King and Stanley in the Smithsonian. These paintings by Shindler were completed between around 1870 and 1874 and taken to England soon after, where they formed part of the collections of the Blackmore Museum that were acquired by the British Museum in 1931.[51]

In 1872 Blackmore commissioned one other painting of significance. This was to document a cruise on River Potomac taken by Blackmore on 29th May 1872 on the steamer the *Lady of the Lake*. Blackmore was accompanied by over sixty guests including Joseph Henry of the Smithsonian Institution, Red Cloud and other Indians delegates. Blackmore's nephew, Sidford Hamp, described the excursion at some length in his diary:

> Today at 10/30 AM we all went down to the dock, to go on an excursion down the river. (The Indians were to come, and some friends of Uncle's) At about a qua[r]ter to Eleven they came, and off we started. Nothing happened till after lunch, when 4 of the Red Gentry sang us a song, and then 'Red Dog' made a speech, saying that 'they had been treated very friendly in Washington, and he would treat any one kindly who might come to his country.' Two negroes on board sang us some songs and then we went down to dinner. It was such a lark to see the Injuns eat. One mixed strawberries and olives together another plumbcake and pickled oisters. Some ate holding the things in their hands, and some ate ice cream, pineapple, and fowl all at once, with a knife and fork. Altogether they managed very well. During desert Uncle made a speech and proposed health of the President, the Queen, and the Chiefs, and their squaws &c. The Indians answered but I could not here the interpreter. Afterwards 'Red Cloud" made a very good speech and said that 'he, and the others were very much pleased with their treat, and that he should tell his people at home.' In a little while we got back, and

51 Shindler's paintings may not have been the first such copies of portrait photographs acquired by Blackmore. A diary entry for 30th October 1868 notes the Englishman had paid US$200 for 'Pictures of Indian Warrior from photographs' from the Fitzgibbon Gallery in St. Louis. Blackmore Diary 17 p. 21.

> all the Indians shook hands with Uncle and Aunt, and one gave Uncle a beautiful tobacco-pouch. Every one, I think, enjoyed themselves very much. In the evening Uncle told me to get 2 copies of each City paper, but it was so late that nearly all were sold, so I had to walk right to the other end of Pen[n]sylvania Avenue and go into 10 shops before I could get them. Very fine. I forgot one anecdote of the Indians, one of the ladies had some gold in her teeth, and one Indian put his finger right into her mouth, to point it out to his companions.[52]

The painting by Antonio Zeno Shindler is titled *Red Cloud with William Blackmore*. It depicts Blackmore and Red Cloud standing on deck shaking hands with a figure – probably Joseph Henry – beside them. In November 1872 Shindler wrote to Joseph Henry from New York City asking for a photograph of the Smithsonian's director so that his portrait could be included in this painting.[53] Where the painting was intended to be displayed has yet to be established. It was acquired by Denver Public Library in 1934 though its provenance remains unclear and no reference of the painting being sent to England or exhibited there has been located.[54] Shindler is also recorded as having painted in 1870 the portrait of a Sioux Woman from the Yankton tribe, South Dakota, for the Blackmore Museum.[55] Again, what subsequently happened to this painting remains to be established.

There is some evidence that Blackmore acquired other painted portraits of North American Indians. In the entry in his diary for 19th September 1868 he refers to purchasing a 'portrait of an Indian Chief taken in 1867 – 'Big Ribs'' for US$50.00 from a Chicago artist C. S. Stobie. Big Ribs, was an Oglala Sioux second in rank to Red Cloud. The artist was Charles Stewart Stobie (1845-1931), an Indian scout, artist

52 Herbert Oliver Brayer, 'Exploring the Yellowstone with Hayden, 1872, Diary of Sidford Hamp', *Annals of Wyoming*, Volume 14, Number 4, October 1942 p.262.

53 Fleming, *Shindler Catalogue*, (2003) p.7 citing letter dated 28th November, 1872, Smithsonian Institution Archives Record Unit 26, volume 126 p.73.

54 I thank Dr. J. Wendel Cox, Senior Special Collection Librarian, Denver Public Library for this information. Email 8th June 2009.

55 *Annual Report of the Board of Regents of the Smithsonian Institution for 1921*,Part 1., Washington, 1922 p.627.

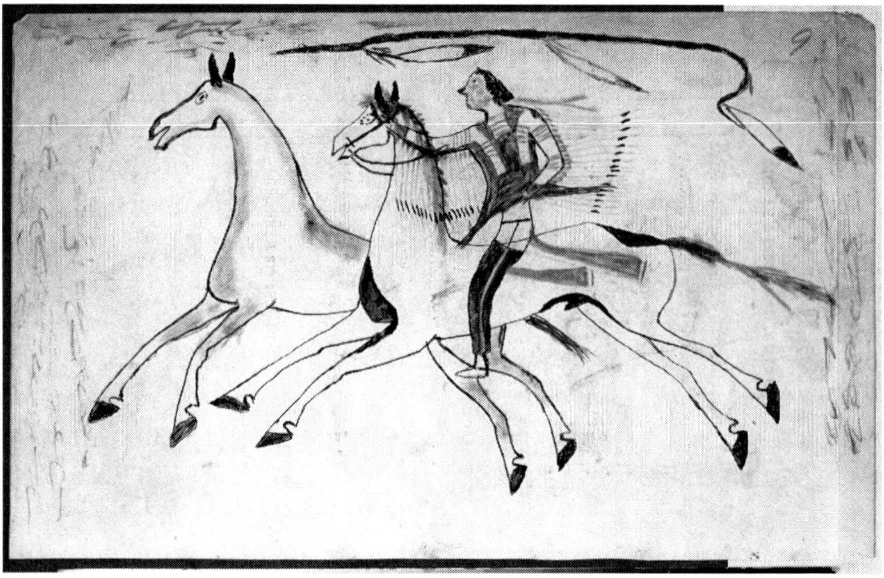

Mounted Native North American warriors.
Drawing by Tall Bear (Mah-to-han-ski) (1825-1892)
Pictograph, 1874.
Courtesy of The Trustees of the British Museum

and early photographer.[56] Stobie had ventured West from Chicago in 1865. He lived with Utes in Colorado and had been a member of a war party that took seven scalps in a skirmish with a band of Cheyenne and Arapaho near Grand Lake. What happened to this painting is unknown.

Blackmore actively acquired a wide variety of items for his collections while on his extensive journeys around the 'Great West.' In October 1874 he visited an encampment of around 1,500 of 'Two Lances' band (formerly Whistlers) of the Oglala Sioux beside the River Platte, some thirty miles south of Sidney Barracks, Nebraska Territory. He acquired at least forty-two coloured pictographs, sixteen drawn by Tall Bear (Mah-to-han-ski) (1825-1892) while the remainder were probably drawn by a Lakota artist, Pretty or Good Bear (Mah-tow-wash-ta). Called 'the autobiography of Tall Bear,' who is further identified as a member

56 Blackmore Diary 16 p.58. The entry also refers to 'Series of sketches taken in the West .Now in Denver' and gives Stobie's address '71 Hanover Street (N. Archer Road) Chicago' suggesting that Blackmore may have visited the artist's studio.

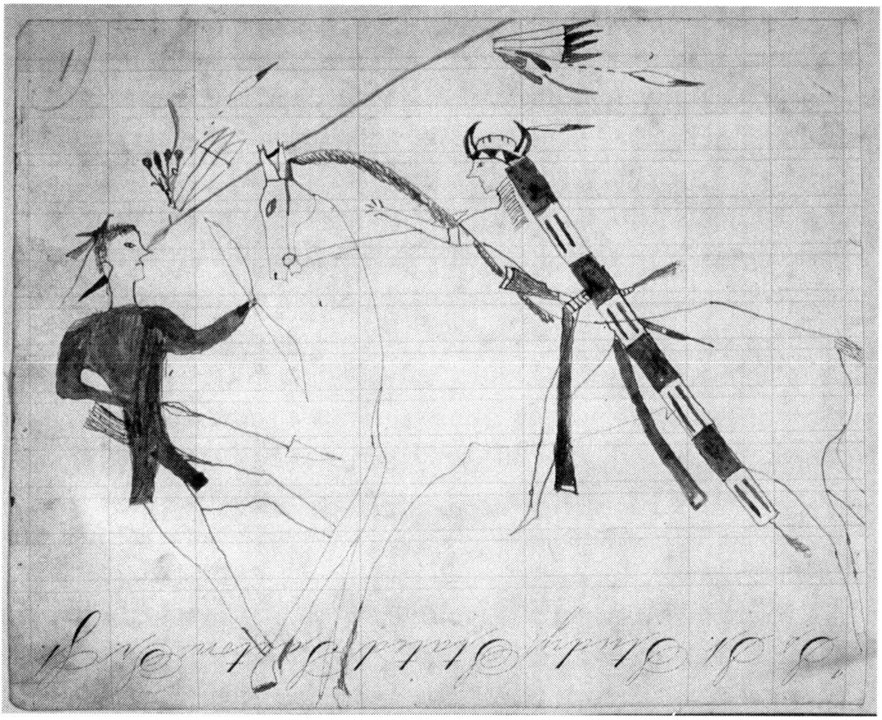

Mounted Native North American warrior, possibly White Horse, throwing a lance through the head of a Pawnee warrior.
Drawing by Tall Bear (Mah-to-han-ski) (1825-1892)
Pictograph, 1874.
Courtesy of The Trustees of the British Museum

of the Whistler band of the Oglala Sioux.[57] These images were held in the Blackmore Museum but as with much of Blackmore's collection of Americana were little used and no significant references to them made. Blackmore did not add further pictographs to his collection. This points once more to a tactical approach to his collecting habits. Following Humphrey Blackmore's death, in 1931 they were transferred to the British Museum from the Blackmore Museum .

As discussed above, there is very sporadic evidence of Blackmore's fine and decorative art collections and, to date, a comprehensive, accurate

57 Colin F. Taylor 'The 'Tall Bear' Drawings in the William Blackmore collection at the British Museum', *European Review of Native American Studies*, Volume 18, No,2, 2004 pp.1-12.

and detailed description has yet to be assembled. No evidence has been found for a major sale of any of William Blackmore's collections following his untimely death. In a letter to Humphrey in November 1877 William noted he was selling bronzes, some watercolours and furniture to service the loan his brother had made to him and he may well have sold other items privately during the last few years of his life in order to raise funds.[58] Another possibility is that Humphrey Blackmore, as executor of his brother's estate, oversaw a number of private sales to help offset his debts. Similarly, Humphrey probably managed the division of his brother's collections and came to possess a number of items – such as the Moran watercolours of Yellowstone and a portrait of the explorer Humboldt by George Catlin that had been given by the artist to William Blackmore in 1871.[59]

William Blackmore's relationship with George Catlin is covered in detail in Chapter 7.

Though he was not a major mid Victorian patron and collector, Blackmore both commissioned and owned some noteworthy works of fine and decorative art. Nevertheless, his eponymous museum was one of the most significant pieces of British provincial philanthropy of the 1860s. One may leave open to conjecture how William's patronage and collecting habits would have evolved had his business ventures succeeded and he had continued to accumulate great wealth.

58 Wiltshire & Swindon History Centre 776/579.

59 Brian W. Dippie, *Catlin and His Contemporaries: The Politics of Patronage*, University of Nebraska, 1990 p.422.

6
Blackmore and Photography

PHOTOGRAPHY PLAYED A role in linking together a number of aspects of William Blackmore's interests, aims and objectives. These spanned both his professional and personal activities. The medium fundamentally assisted his interest in documenting the geographical, agricultural, mineral and commercial opportunities of the 'Great West', the material culture of the Indians of North America and Blackmore's ambitious plans to become a photographic publisher.

There are a number of aspects of Blackmore's interaction with photography. Firstly, where and when did Blackmore encounter photography? What was the scale and scope of the collection of photographs he formed, both before and after his first trip to the USA in 1863? How was photography used within the Blackmore Museum? There is also the evaluation of the photographic publications of the imprint of the Trustees of the Blackmore Museum, and there was Blackmore's use of photography to support his business ventures. Finally there is the consideration of the contemporary reception of his photographs and their medium to long term influence.

BLACKMORE AND HIS EXPOSURE TO PHOTOGRAPHY

Quite when Blackmore first encountered photography is not known. He was a twelve year old living in a provincial English city when photography was announced in 1839. However, while during his teenage years photography was becoming more widely known, it is unlikely that there were significant numbers of photographs available in Salisbury by 1849, the year Blackmore was to leave for Liverpool.

Liverpool was one of the earliest provincial cities to have had an active photographer and to have a professional Daguerreotype portrait studio. In late October 1839 three Liverpool newspapers carried advertisements of a demonstration of the Daguerreotype process organised by the optician and mathematical instrument maker Abraham Abraham (born between 1799 and 1803 – died after 1858). John Benjamin Dancer (1812-1887), a scientific and optical instrument maker, experimented with Daguerreotype views of buildings in Liverpool in 1839, possibly after he had seen Abraham's demonstration. During June and July 1840 a large exhibition was held at the Liverpool Mechanics Institution at which Abraham Abraham exhibited a Daguerreotype camera and apparatus, along with eight Daguerreotypes, all views of Paris.[1] At the end of September 1841 the photographic studio of Mr Spencer located on Mount Gardens opened, perhaps only the fourth of its kind in Britain.[2] The establishment advertised in the *Liverpool Mercury*.[3]

It is possible that a small number of American photographs would have been available in Great Britain during the 1840s. The Great Exhibition of 1851 probably acted as a significant catalyst for an increase in numbers. Fourteen American photographers exhibited Daguerreotypes at the Crystal Palace though none were of ethnographic subject matter or depicted North American Indians.[4] It is probable that Blackmore was

1 These were the *Liverpool Courier, Liverpool Mercury* and *Liverpool Chronicle.* Abraham formed a partnership with John Benjamin Dancer in Manchester where from 1841 they ran a photographic studio at 13 Cross Street. See R. Derek Wood, *The Daguerreotype in Liverpool in 1839: Ste Croix, A. Abraham and J. B. Dancer.* at http://www.midley.co.uk/sourcetexts/liverpool_dag1839_wood.htm accessed on 20th August, 2010.

It is probable that Dancer and Abraham photographed George Catlin's visiting troop of Ojibwa Indians at this Manchester studio in November 1843. This is discussed in more detail in Chapter 7.

2 See Michael Hallett, 'The Manchester-Liverpool Circle', *The PhotoResearcher*, Number One, October 1990 pp.7-13 and Audrey Linkman, *Professional Photographers in Liverpool 1851-1900*, The PhotoHistorian Supplement No.98, 1992.

3 *Liverpool Mercury*, Friday 14th June, 1844 p.1.

4 The official catalogue lists Matthew B. Brady, C. H. Brainard, O. B. Evans, Fontain & Porter, David E. Gavit, C. C. Harrison, Martin M. Lawrence, J. J. E. Mayall, Mead & Brothers, W. A. Pratt & Co., Marcus A. Root, John A. Whipple, Jesse H. Whitehurst

the holder of one of the 6,063,986 recorded tickets given to visitors to the Crystal Palace in London's Hyde Park, and like many other visitors found its sheer scale and scope somewhat overwhelming.

After the Great Exhibition commercial photography increased significantly throughout Great Britain. When J.B. Edwards, an operative chemist of 42 Berry Street, Liverpool was advertising photographic materials and examples of photography at his premises by October 1853 there were a handful of photographers in the city. In March of 1853 the Liverpool Photographic Society was formed.[5] Photographs from America were exhibited at the Society in August 1854 when photographs of the tomb of George Washington, views of the White House and a portrait of President Franklin Pierce (1804-1869) by Whipple and Black were exhibited together with several Daguerreotypes of the Niagara Falls by a photographer named as 'Bobbit', in fact Platt D. Babbitt (1822-1872).[6] By 1855 there were in the region of forty commercial photographers in Liverpool, each displaying specimens.[7] It has yet to be established whether William Blackmore was a member of the Liverpool Photographic Society or visited its exhibitions in the 1850s.

Photography was also probably exhibited and displayed at meetings held in Liverpool at the Royal Institution – where the Liverpool Photographic Society was initially based and where the Society's exhibitions were held –and the Literary and Philosophical Society of Liverpool, where on 13th December 1852 John Hartnup (1806-1885), Assistant Secretary to the Royal Astronomical Society, appointed in 1843 as the first Director of Liverpool Observatory, exhibited a 'very beautiful and life-like Daguerreotype portrait of General Pierce, the President of the United States.' The following 2nd May Dr. J. B. Edwards exhibited at a meeting 'photographs of microscopic objects taken by the electric

and J. H. Whitehurst. *Official Descriptive and Illustrated Catalogue of the Great Exhibition of the works of Industry of All Nations, Part V. Foreign States – Division II, and Index*, London, 1851 p.lii

5 *Liverpool Mercury*, Friday 14th October, 1853 p.16.

6 *ibid.*, Friday 4th August, 1854 p.9.

7 See Bernard & Pauline Heathcote, *A Faithful Likeness. The First Photographic Studios in the British Isles 1841-1855*, Lowdham, 2002 pp.164-5.

light.'[8] In April 1854 J.P.G. Smith exhibited photographs of specimens of snow crystals.[9]

Which of William Blackmore's circle in Liverpool were early adopters of photography has yet to be established. The Liverpool collector Joseph Mayer was a member of many of the scholarly organisations in the City and a founder of the Historic Society of Lancashire and Cheshire. It is unclear whether he had any role in the Liverpool Photographic Society or had a photographic collection of any significance.

Blackmore's first significant exposure to photography possibly came through the Historic Society of Lancashire and Cheshire that had been founded in the year of Blackmore's arrival in Liverpool and which he had joined in September 1854.[10] By 1854-1855 the society's 'museum' included a collection of photographs.[11] The society soon became aware of the Liverpool Photographic Society through the donation of the first issue of the Photographic Society's journal to the Historic Society's library.[12]

At a Special General Meeting of the Historic Society of Lancashire and Cheshire held on 4th March 1858 a motion, proposed by Rev. Dr.

8 *Proceedings of the Literary and Philosophical Society of Liverpool.. 1851-1853, No. VII,* 1851 p.152 and p.205. In 1855 the large equatorial telescope of Hartnup was used when taking photographs of the moon. These were exhibited at the Royal Astronomical Society and a meeting of the British Association for the Advancement of Science at St George's Hall, Liverpool as well as several photographic exhibitions. The photographs were projected to show the moon with a diameter of 50 feet, to much acclaim. A Dallas process 'Photolectric Engraving' illustration of the Moon 'from a photograph taken at the Liverpool Observatory in Sept. 1854 by Messrs. John Hartnup and J. A. Forrest' was used to illustrate the paper given by Forrest on 14th May, 1863. See *Transactions of the Historic Society of Lancashire and Cheshire, New Series, Volume III Session 1862-63,* Liverpool, 1863 opposite p.257.

9 *Proceedings of the Literary and Philosophical Society of Liverpool.. 1853-1854, No. VIII,* 1855 p.158.

10 Curiously, Blackmore appears not to have been a member of the Literary and Philosophical Society of Liverpool, founded in 1812. The published proceedings of this society record numerous meetings from the early 1850s at which photographs were exhibited.

11 H. J. Cauty donated a photograph of St. George's Hall and another of the Liverpool Observatory in April 1855. *Transactions of the Historic Society of Lancashire and Cheshire, Volume VII Session 1854-55,* London, 1855 p.50*.

12 *The Liverpool Mercury and Double Supplement,* Friday 10th February, 1854 p.14.

Abraham Hume (1814-1884), a founding member and Secretary to the Society, and seconded by Thomas Sansom, a clerk at HM Customs in Liverpool and Honorary Secretary to the Society, to join the Liverpool Photographic Society with the Historic Society was unanimously passed. This included 'that communications on Photography be admissible at all the ordinary meetings.'[13] By the mid 1860s there was a Photographic Committee of the Historic Society though other committees were also to take an interest in the medium to further the Society's aims and objectives.[14] Significantly the Society had already held photographic periodicals such as the *Photographic Journal* and the *Bulletin de la Société Française de Photographie* from their first issues in the early 1850s. From 1858, as a member of the Historic Society of Lancashire and Cheshire, Blackmore would have had a significant opportunity to become acquainted with the new photographic section or the display of photographs at the meetings of other of the Society's sections. There was also knowledge of scholarly activities in the USA for as early as 1853 it was noted that a substantial number of publications had been donated by the Smithsonian Institution and the State Historical Society of Wisconsin.[15] The international coverage of the Historical Society was

13 *Transactions of the Historic Society of Lancashire and Cheshire, Volume X, Session 1857-58*, London, 1858 p.355.

14 At the meeting of the Scientific Section held on the 16th November, 1865 Henry Greenwood 'called attention to the rapid disappearance of many interesting buildings in Liverpool, owing to the numerous improvements in progress, and pointed out the desirableness of making a systematic attempt to preserve, by means of photography, representations of parts of the town presenting features of interest. It was moved by the Rev. Dr. Hume, V.P., seconded by Mr. Greenwood, and resolved – That the Photographic Committee of the Society be requested to enquire and report as to the best means of carrying this purpose to effect.' *Transactions of the Historic Society of Lancashire and Cheshire*, New Series, Volume VI, Session 1865-66, Liverpool, 1866 p.288. It does not appear that the Photographic Committee reported back since no account is to be found in the Society's *Transactions*. The Rev. Hume exhibited on the 9th January 1868 'various Photographs of the Compagnia Church at Santiago, Chili [sic], after its destruction by Fire'. *Transactions of the Historic Society of Lancashire and Cheshire*, New Series, Volume VII, Session 1866-67, Liverpool, 1867 p.350.

15 *Transactions of the Historic Society of Lancashire and Cheshire*, Volume XI, Session 1858-59, Liverpool, 1859 p.243. The Proceedings and Papers, Session VI. 1853-54, Liverpool, 1854 p.1 records a significant donation of publications by the Smithsonian Institution in 1853 including E. Squier's *Description of the Antient Works in Ohio* and

also reflected by a display of photographs at the meeting of the Scientific Section on 17th November 1859 when W. G. Helsby exhibited twenty-five Daguerreotype views of Chile.[16]

The Historic Society's published transactions indicate that Blackmore's active involvement with the Society diminished significantly in the early 1860s, probably as a result of his new found business interests in the USA. He remained a member but from 1865 no address is attached to his name, indicating that he had by this date moved from Liverpool to London and was resident at Shepley House in Carshalton.

Blackmore may well have been aware of the documentary use to which photography could put from activities of his partners in his own office. In 1862 an architectural competition to rebuild and enlarge the Liverpool Exchange was underway. An advertisement in the *Building News* read;

> £1,000 for the best design, and £259 for the next two best designs, to rebuild and enlarge the Liverpool Exchange. Copies of the instructions and conditions, with plans and sections of the site, and photographic views of the present Exchange, and the adjacent buildings, for which a charge of one guinea will be made, may be had on and after the 16th inst., on application to Mr. A. T. Squarey, 10, Water Street, Liverpool. All designs must be sent on or before the 31st March 1863.[17]

It is known that during the 1850s Blackmore had extensive European business interests connected to railway and telegraph companies. It can be assumed that this necessitated regular travel to London and to the Continent. These would again have given him an opportunity to have seen and perhaps collected photographs though it

Stanley's *Portraits of North American Indians, with Sketches of Scenery.*

16 *Transactions of the Historic Society of Lancashire and Cheshire*, Volume XII, Session 1859-60, Liverpool, 1860 p.220. William Glaskell Helsby and his brother ran a photographic studio in Valparaíso, Chile. This is probably the same as T.C. Helsby, reported to be a Daguerreian artist in Buenos Aires, Argentina, in 1846. He was also reported in Tahiti. See http://www.worthpoint.com/worthopedia/daguerreotype-rare-chile-south-america-w-g accessed on 6th August 2010.

17 *The Building News*, 16th December 1862 p.502.

is unlikely that there would have been significant numbers of images of North American Indians.

BLACKMORE'S PHOTOGRAPHIC COLLECTIONS

By 1862, and a year before Blackmore's first visit to the USA, there were at least fifty photographers operating in Liverpool and each is likely to have had a range of commercially available images.[18] In addition, photographs would have been commercially available through a number of standard outlets including print dealers, bookshops and stationers. Whether the strong links with the USA enabled these Liverpool outlets to offer photographs of North American Indians is unknown but would seem unlikely. Thus prior to his first trip to the USA, Blackmore's photographic collection was probably modest and consisted primarily of family portraits.

The Salisbury & South Wiltshire Museum holds one photographic portrait of William Blackmore taken by an anonymous photographer probably during the late 1850s or early 1860s. The Museum also holds a number of views of Shepley House near Carshalton (above pages 39, 40) – Blackmore's residence during the second half of the 1860s.

By 1861 Blackmore certainly owned photographs of works of art since he exhibited a photograph of the portrait of Oliver Cromwell (1599-1658) by Sir Peter Lely (1618-1680) in the Pitti Palace in Florence at the meeting of the Literary Section of the Historic Society of Lancashire and Cheshire held on 14th November 1861.[19]

There are no other records that provide insights into the scale and scope of Blackmore's collection of photographs during the 1850s and early 1860s. As a result the full extent of William's photographic holdings – including subject areas outside that of the Native American – may never be known.

18 *Liverpool Gores Directory for 1862*. See http://freepages.genealogy.rootsweb.ancestry.com/~liverpoolphotographers/1862_Gores_Directory.html accessed on 6th August 2010. See also, J. B. Dancer, 'Early Photography in Liverpool and Manchester', *Manchester City News*, 22nd May 1886, p.2f, reprinted shortly after in *British Journal of Photography*, 11th June 1886, vol.33, pp.372-373.

19 *Transactions of the Historic Society of Lancashire and Cheshire*, New Series, Volume II, Liverpool, 1862 p.175.

The second half of the 1860s was to see a radical transformation of Blackmore's photographic collection. He rapidly acquired one of the leading collections of photographs of North American Indians.

BLACKMORE AND PHOTOGRAPHY OF NATIVE AMERICANS

When Blackmore became interested in the graphic depiction of the American 'Great West' and its indigenous natives remains unclear. In the early years of his professional career in Liverpool there might have been stimuli such as the exhibition of a portion of the mammoth panorama of the Upper Mississippi by Henry Lewis (1809-1904) that was exhibited in Liverpool from late 1851 and early 1852 at the Panorama Hall at 65, Bold Street.[20] The upper river half of the panorama, when completed in May, 1849, covered a canvas of 45,000 square feet with the height of twelve feet and length of 3,750 feet, or three-quarters of a mile. The painting also portrayed the settlements and the life of the people along the river. There were views of the Indian tribes – their huts, villages, encampments, and 'highly interesting pictures of Indian country.'[21]

Blackmore probably began his library of Americana in the late 1840s though no evidence has been found to indicate that he had formed any photographic collection of North American natives during the period up to his first visit to the USA in 1863.

William Blackmore's exploitation of photography to underpin his interest in North American Indians was far reaching in its scale, scope and significance. He assiduously collected commercially available photographs – whether loose prints or in carte de viste, stereoscopic or Cabinet format – and commissioned photography, both in the studio and in the field. Another significant strategic approach taken by Blackmore was to purchase original photographic negatives. This gave him both the ability to print – rather than purchase – multiple copies

20 *Liverpool Mercury*, Tuesday 6th December, 1851 p.1. The advertisement referred to the 'Third week' of the 'largest painting in the world' being on display. Lewis exhibited the panorama as part of a European tour and it was put on show in the Netherlands and Germany in 1852 and 1853.

21 Joseph Earl Arrington, ' Henry Lewis' Moving Panorama of the Mississippi River', *Louisiana History: The Journal of the Louisiana Historical Association*, Vol. 6, No. 3, Summer, 1965 pp. 239-272.

for his publications and also removed the issue of copyright. Blackmore presumably either negotiated the sale of the copyright at the time of the purchase of the photographic negatives or considered as the owner of the negatives, he also owned the copyright and reproduction rights.

The number of photographs of Native North Americans available in England during the 1840s and 1850s was minimal at best. While it has yet to be established which British photographer took the first photograph of a North American Indian it is known that in the early 1840s the Ioway Indians that formed part of George Catlin's travelling show were photographed on a number of occasions. In November 1843 they were photographed in Manchester, probably at the studio of John Dancer (1812-1887) and Abraham Abraham. Perhaps the most significant set of photographs created took place in 1844 when Antoine Claudet (1797-1867) photographed the Ojibwa Indians brought to England by the American showman Arthur Rankin (1816-1893) in his studio on the roof of the Adelaide Gallery, behind St. Martin's in the Fields church. This group also toured as part of George Catlin's show. Claudet's Daguerreotypes were copied by Vizetelly Brothers and turned into engraved illustrations in Charles Stuart, *A Short History and Description of the Ojibbeway Indians now on a visit to England with correct likenesses, engraved from daguerreotype plates, taken by M. Claudet* published in the same year.[22] Copies of this title are rare and it is not listed in the printed catalogue of the library of the Blackmore Museum. It is unknown whether Blackmore was aware of the Claudet Daguerreotypes.

In Edinburgh on 4th August 1845 David Octavius Hill (1802-1870) and Robert Adamson (1821-1848) had taken photographs of the Rev. Peter Jones (1802-1856) (known as Kahkewaquonaby – The Waving Plume) an Ojibwa Methodist minister, the son of Augustus Jones (c. 1757-1836), a Welsh land surveyor, and Tuhbenahneequay (1780-1873),

22 Charles Stuart *A Short History and Description of the Ojibbeway Indians now on a visit to England with correct likenesses, engraved from daguerreotype plates, taken by M. Claudet*, London, 1844. This was a comparatively cheap publication costing sixpence. What happened to Claudet's Daguerreotypes is unknown, though they would have been considered commercially valuable.

daughter of Mississauga Chief Waubanasay. Jones was on his third visit to Great Britain and attempting to raise money for Indian schools in Canada that would promote civilisation and Christianity. He was photographed in both Indian attire and western clothes and copies of these Calotypes are to be found in the National Galleries of Scotland. It remains unclear how well known these images were to contemporaries either in Great Britain or North America and Blackmore seemed to have made no attempt to acquire copies for his collection.

Increasing numbers of Daguerreotypes of North American Indians began to be taken during the second half of the 1840s. Thomas Martin Easterly (1809-1882) photographed a number of North American Indians in his studio in St. Louis, Missouri, including Chief Ke-o-kuk (Watchful Fox), the leader of the Sac and Fox tribe, who sat for the photographer in March 1847.[23] Another significant St. Louis photographer of this period was John H. Fitzgibbon (1816?-1882) who also began taking portraits of Native Americans in the spring of 1847. By January 1852 Fitzgibbon was advertising that he had over one thousand Daguerreotypes on display in his gallery.[24] How many were of North American Indians is unclear but Fitzgibbon subsequently exhibited photographs of Indians at the 1853 Exhibition of Works of Industry at the New York Crystal Palace. A contemporary reviewer stated, 'His collection of Indian Warriors is a very fine one, which we understand is to be forwarded to the Ethnological Society of London, to have copies and busts made from them.'[25] This does not seem to have taken place.

In October 1868, on his first trip to the 'Great West', William Blackmore sought out and acquired Daguerreotypes from both Easterly

23 The Missouri Historical Society holds six hundred and thirty six Daguerreotypes by Easterly dating from 1847 to 1872. Easterly was unusual in that he refused to adopt the Albumen and Collodion negative processes that had become the norm for professional photographers by the 1860s.

24 See Peter E. Palmquist and Thomas R. Kailbourn, *Pioneer Photographers from the Mississippi to the Continental Divide: A Biographical Dictionary, 1839-1865*, Stanford University Press, 2005 p.255.

25 Horace Greeley, *Art and Industry as Represented in the Exhibition at the Crystal Palace New York —1853–4*, Redfield, New York, 1853 pp.171–7. As accessed via http://daguerreotypearchive.org/texts/B8530001_GREELEY_ART_INDUSTRY_1853.pdf on 4th August 2010.

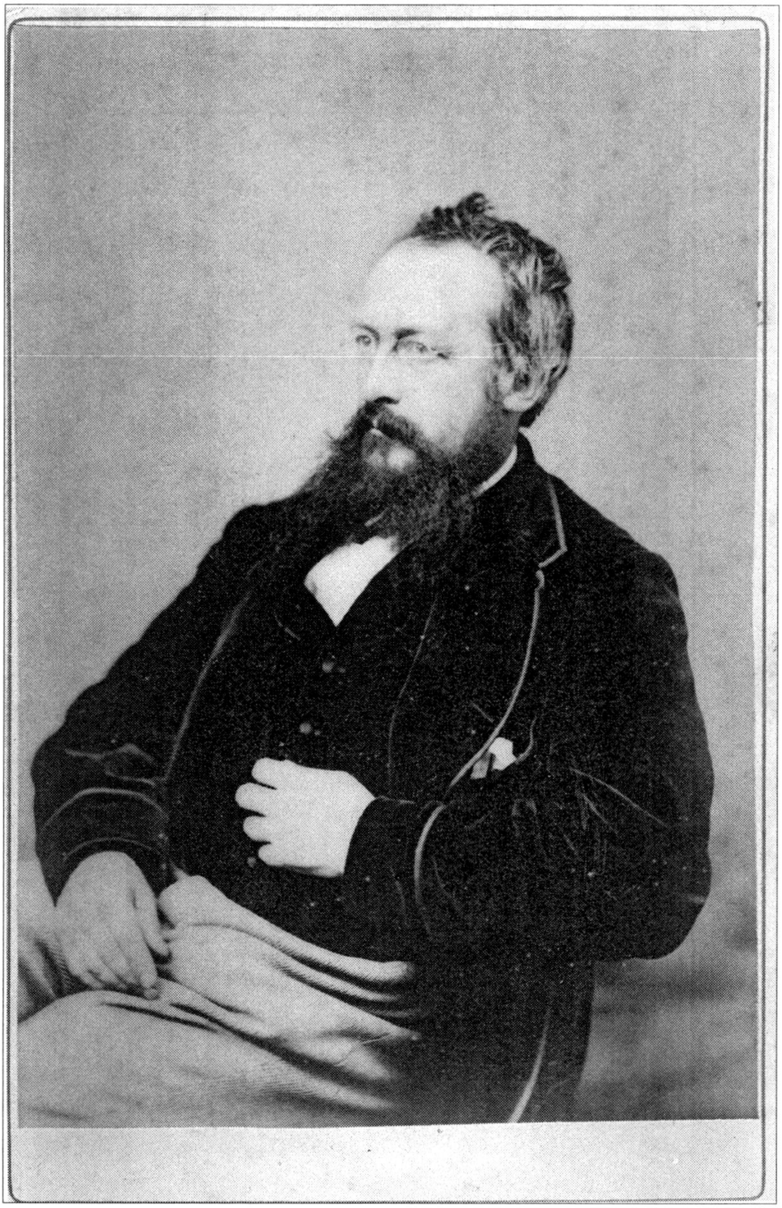

William Blackmore
In October 1868. Mezzo-Tint Photograph by Fitzgibbon, 116 South 4th Street, St. Louis, Mo. Meinerth's Patent, July 16th, 1867.
Albumen print
Courtesy of Salisbury & South Wiltshire Museum

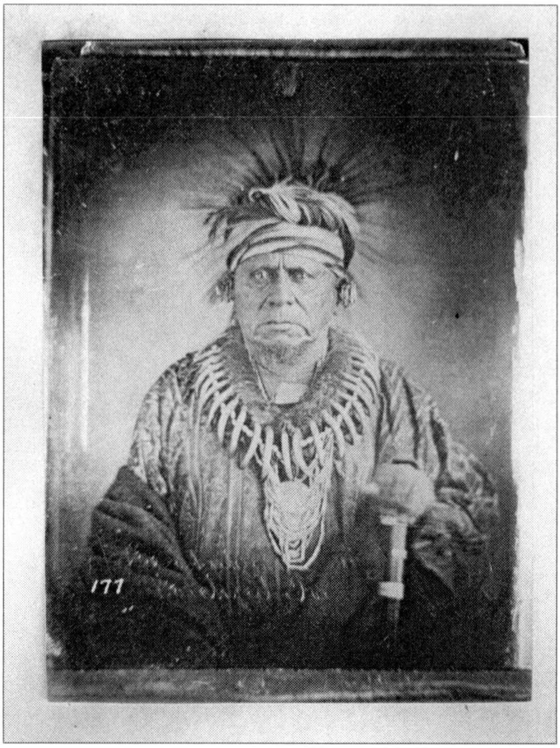

Kiyo'kaga or One Who Moves About Alert (1780 or 1783-1848). Known as Ke-o-kuk.
1868 copy by Antonio Zeno Shindler of a Daguerreotype by Thomas Martin Easterly dated 1847.
Albumen print
Blackmore Collection Album 21
Courtesy of The Trustees of the British Museum

and Fitzgibbon – taken by the latter primarily between 1851-1852 – and also had his portrait taken in the Fitzgibbon Gallery in St. Louis.[26] Blackmore's photographic collection also includes photographic prints made from re-photographing some of Easterly's 1840s Daguerreotype portraits including Ke-o-kuk and Longhorn. Paula Fleming has referred to the calibre of the Fitzgibbon Daguerreotypes as reflecting 'Blackmore's curatorial eye and perceptive historical sense' since 'they represent not

26 Blackmore Diary No.17 p.21. He paid US$58 in cash and US$300 in a draft drawn on a Brown Brothers account.

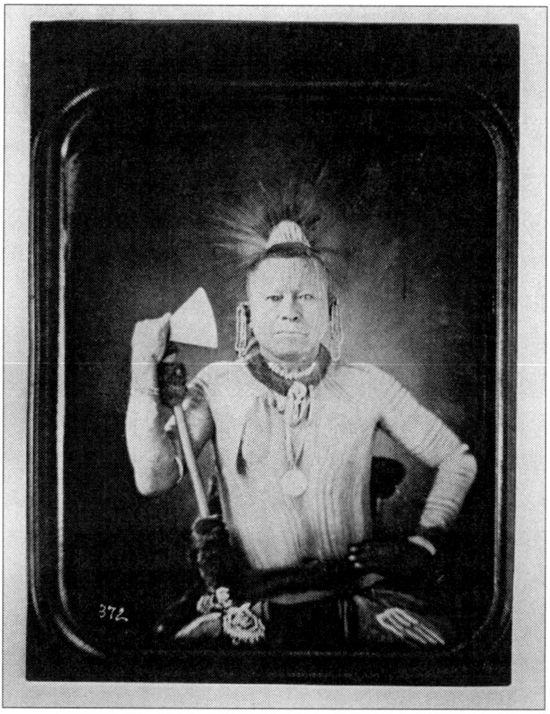

Longhorn, a Sauk and Fox Chief, sitting on a chair.
1868 copy by Antonio Zeno Shindler of a Daguerreotype by
Thomas Martin Easterly dated 1847.
Albumen print
Blackmore Collection Album 21
Courtesy of The Trustees of the British Museum

only the earliest photographic studio images of Native Americans but also the very best of artistic daguerreotype portraiture.'[27]

Given the appetite for photographic portraits of celebrities, it is curious that other leading London photographers during the 1840s – such as the studios of Richard Beard (1801-1885), who had set up as early as 1841, and of William Kilburn (1819-1891) that opened in 1846 – did not take the opportunity to record some of the touring ethnographical exhibitions that abounded during the 1840s and 1850s. These included 'Hottentots', 'Kaffirs', Chinese, Maoris, South Sea Islanders, 'Aztec

27 Fleming, *Shindler Catalogue*, (2003) p.26.

Lilliputian' and North American Natives.[28] George Catlin's Indian Gallery ran in London from 1840 until 1845 and six Objiwa Indians formed part of his touring show in the mid 1840s. A Daguerreotype by an anonymous photographer in the Chicago History Museum allegedly depicts the six Objiwa and while the museum's online catalogue states that it is possible the image was taken c.1846 by an English photographer it may also have been taken in North America in around 1851, some five years after their return.[29]

In 1847 John Jabez Edwin Mayall (1810-1901) exhibited a Daguerreotype of a North American Indian at his American Daguerreotype Institution at 433 West Strand, London.[30] The identity of the sitter has yet to be established, though it was presumably taken in Mayall's studio.

The first delegation of North American Indians to be photographed in Washington, D.C. was a group of nineteen from the Arapaho, Cheyenne, Sioux, Oto and Iowa tribes who visited Washington, D.C. between 1st November 1851 and 11th January 1852. During this period the Cheyenne warrior Alights on a Cloud (d.1852) had his Daguerreotype portrait taken with the famous Irish-born actress and Spanish dancer Lola Montez (1821-1861). This photograph has been attributed to the Boston photographer Josiah Hawes (1808-1901) of the firm of Southworth & Hawes.[31] Other Daguerreotype portraits were taken of visiting Native

28 See Richard Altick, *The Shows of London: A panorama history of exhibitions, 1600–1862*, The Belknap Press of Harvard University Press, Cambridge, Mass. and London, 1978, particularly Chapter 20, 'The Noble Savage Reconsidered'and also J.C.H. King, 'A Century of Indian Shows: Canadian and United States Exhibitions in London 1825-1925,' *European Review of Native American Studies* 5,1991 pp.35-42. See also, Robert M. Lewis, 'Wild American Savages and the Civilized English: Catlin's Indian Gallery and the Shows of London', *European Journal of American Studies*, 2008, document 6, Online URL : http://ejas.revues.org/index2263.html

29 The Daguerreotype by an anonymous photographer is now in the collection of the Chicago Historical Society. ICHi-08800.

30 *Catalogue of Daguerreotype Panoramas, Falls of Niagara, Shakespere's Birth-Place, Tomb, Relics, Photographic Pictures, Portraits of Eminent Persons, &c., in the Gallery of the Daguerreotype Institution*. Catalogue number 30. See Photographic Exhibitions in Britain 1839-1865 at http://peib.dmu.ac.uk.

31 Paula Richardson Fleming and Judith Luskey, *The North American Indians in Early Photographs*, Dorset Press, New York, 1986 p.28.

American Indian chiefs during this period and are to be found in the National Anthropological Archives of the Smithsonian Institution.

The opening of the American West to settlers resulted in an increasing number of delegations to Washington, D.C. In the winter of 1857-1858 there were in the region of ninety delegates from thirteen tribes visiting. This significant number acted as the catalyst for the first systematic effort to make a comprehensive photographic record of the visiting North American Indians. In the winter of 1857 James E. McClees (1821-1887), a successful Philadelphia photographer, opened a lavish photographic studio at 308 Pennsylvania Avenue, Washington, D.C. Two of McClees' photographic operators, Julian Vannerson (1827-1875) and Samuel A. Cohner (1826-1869), took at least sixty portraits of the visiting Indian delegates during the winter of 1857-1858.[32]

In the 16th December 1857 issue of the Washington newspaper the *Daily National Intelligencer*, McClees announced his 'Indian Gallery', which listed some fifty-five photographic portraits, measuring 6 ½ by 8 ½ inches. This 'gallery' was split into twelve tribes; Mdewanton Sioux (nine photographs), Yankton Sioux (six), Sisiton and Wahpeton Sioux (eight), Pawnees (seven), Sacs and Foxes (three), Poncahs (two), Pottawotamies (five), Chippewa (one), Delawares (seven), Shawnees (two), Choctaws (three) and Seminoles (two).[33] The entire set was

32 There had been previous attempts to document prominent Indians who visited Washington. Thomas Loraine McKenney (1785-1859), United States superintendent of Indian trade in Georgetown, then port of entry for the District of Columbia, conceived the idea of forming an official government collection of portraits of prominent Indians who visited the capital. Charles Bird King (1785-1862) a prominent Washington portrait painter was commissioned and his depictions of the leaders of at least twenty tribes were reproduced as hand coloured lithographs in Thomas McKenney and James Hall's three-volume classic, *History of the Indian Tribes of North America*, published in 1837, 1842 and 1844 respectively. Further editions continued to be printed until 1870. Blackmore owned a copy of the 1844 edition.

33 See James R. Glenn, 'The 'Curious Gallery': The Indian Photographs of the McClees Studio in Washington, 1857-1858, *History of Photography*, Volume 5, No.3, July 1981 pp.249-262. A copy of the two page prospectus and the list of the Indian Gallery itself are to be found in the papers of William Wadden Turner (c.1810-1859), librarian at the United States Patent Office and an expert on American Indian languages, who may have assisted in the documenting of the Indian names. Smithsonian Institution National Anthropological Archives Ms. 76-112. Glenn states that 'One

available bound in one volume 'at a reasonable price' or the photographs could be had individually. Hand coloured photographs were available from the studio's artists Messrs. Aubert and Kerchove.

The volume was ready in late 1858 though it was not extensively reviewed and complete copies have yet to be located.[34] While it is unclear how successful McClees' 'Indian Gallery' was at the time of its publication it became highly significant for Blackmore, though it is unclear exactly when he became aware of it. Firstly, it set a template for the structure of recording Native American Indians by their tribes, albeit studio portraits of delegates to Washington, D.C. Secondly, Blackmore was to purchase the original negatives of the McClees studio and created a set of thirty of these images which he subsequently reused to form the first photographic publication under the imprint of The Trustees of the Blackmore Museum, Salisbury.

In 1859, perhaps spurred on by McClees' 'Indian Gallery', Joseph Henry (1797-1878), the Secretary of the Smithsonian Institution, proposed to James Denver (1817-1892), the Commissioner of Indian Affairs, that 'the idea has been suggested that photographic likenesses of the individuals of the different Indian deputations which from time to time visit Washington, would form a valuable addition to the interesting collection of portraits already in the possessed by the Government and deposited in the Smithsonian Institution.'[35] It has yet to be established whether Blackmore was at this time either interested in Native Americans or aware of Henry's proposal since he had yet to visit the United States.

Blackmore appears to have started collecting photographs of North American Indians in earnest during his first trip to the USA in

of Turner's favourite schemes had been to publish Indian linguistic data illustrated with photographs of men who spoke the languages' and that Hayden adopted and then realised the dream (p.253).

34 Fleming and Luskey *op.cit.* identified a review, which appears to be of the photographs rather than the album itself, in the *Photographic and Fine Art Journal*, 5th April 1858 p.98-99.

35 Letter dated 21st February, 1859 from Joseph Henry to James Denver, Commissioner of Indian Affairs. Office of Indian Affairs, Record Group, Letters Received, National Archives and Records Administration, Washington, D.C., As cited in Fleming and Luskey *op.cit.* p.246.

1863. His purchase of the Squire and Davis collection at the end of this visit would have given him an additional catalyst to document the fast vanishing cultural link between the mounds in Chillicothe, Ohio in the Mississippi valley and those of the indigenous natives of the 'Great West.'

He was not unique amongst his contemporaries in his interest in exploiting photography to document North American Indians. One such kindred spirit was Ferdinand Vanderveer Hayden (1829-1887) who was to become a close friend of the English investor and to whom he supplied a number of professional services as Blackmore travelled around the 'Great West' looking for land-grants to purchase, establishing the agricultural and mineral wealth of these lands and acquiring photographs.

In 1856 Hayden had been engaged by the United States government, and commenced a series of investigations of the one hundred and nine Western Territories. By 1862 Hayden was utilizing photography in his reports. In that year his book *Contributions to the Ethnography and Philology of the Indian Tribes of the Missouri Valley* was published by C. Sherman and Son of Philadelphia. It was illustrated with seven lithographs by Thomas Sinclair (c.1805-1881) of Philadelphia after photographs by James Dempsey Hutton (c.1828-1868), Topographical Assistant to Captain William F. Raynolds, T.E. The title page of this book noted that it had been 'prepared under the Direction of Capt. William F. Raynolds, T.E. U.S.A., and published by permission of the War Department.' Hutton had been appointed in April 1859 to this post to assist in the exploration of the territory between Fort Pierre, Dakota Territory and the headwaters of the Yellowstone River. He took the photographs in the field during the period 1859 to 1860.[36] A copy of this title is recorded in the Catalogue of the Library of the Blackmore Museum though it is listed as the '1869' edition. This would appear to be a typographical error since no 1869 edition is known.

36 See Peter E. Palmquist and Thomas R. Kailbourn, *Pioneer Photographers of the Far West: A Biographical Dictionary, 1840-1865*, Stanford University Press, 2002 pp.316-318. The Sinclair firm produced many lithographs for various government publications throughout the century. It had a further association with Hayden in printing the 65 lithographs to illustrate his *Report of the United States Geological Survey of the Territories.*, Government Printing Office, Washington,1878.

Blackmore and Hayden met for the first time in the autumn of 1868 though whether they had been in correspondence prior to that remains unknown. During this trip, in September 1868, Blackmore visited Leavenworth in Kansas and purchased the negatives – and perhaps some prints – of Hutton's photographs including some of those used to illustrate Hayden's 1862 book. Two photographic prints after Hutton's from this series survive in the British Museum, including one depicting four Arapaho men, including Chief Friday (Warshinun) on the right, sitting outdoors in front of a wagon without its cover. This image formed the basis for Thomas Sinclair's lithograph for Plate 2 Figure 7 of *Contributions to the Ethnography and Philology of the Indian Tribes of the Missouri Valley*.[37] However, it is significant that Blackmore did not follow the same model of reproducing photographs by engraving or lithography for his own publications.

In 1865 Ferdinand Hayden – some six years after Joseph Henry's initial proposal – made a suggestion to the American Philosophical Society and American Academy of Natural Sciences that photography be more strategically used to document the North American Indian tribes.[38] This was in the same year as Blackmore's first photographic publication under the imprint of the Trustees of the Blackmore Museum, though it is not clear whether there was any connection between the two. However, Hayden's proposal underlines the issues and challenges facing the geologist and his colleague Joseph Henry in acquiring both the support and financial backing of government departments and agencies in Washington, D.C.

After an interlude caused by the American Civil War Hayden was appointed in 1867 as geologist-in-charge of the United States Geological and Geographical Survey of the territories. He subsequently was to take both photographers and artists on his various survey expeditions, in some instances finding a sponsor to cover the costs. However, it was not until 1879, the year after William Blackmore's death, that the Bureau of Ethnology (later the Bureau of American Ethnology) was founded by

37 British Museum AN618145001.

38 Mike Foster, *Strange Genius: The Life of Ferdinand Vanderveer Hayden*, Roberts Rinehart Publishers, Niwot, 1994 p.138.

Act of Congress. The primary purpose of the Act was to transfer the archives, records and materials relating to the Indians of North America from the Interior Department to the Smithsonian Institution. The German-born John Karl Hillers (1843-1925) became the Bureau's first photographer, though he had been a photographer for the US Geological Survey since 1871. The Bureau issued instructions to photographers on the photographic procedures for portrait and genre studies though it remains unclear what photographic conventions were adhered to before this point. No evidence that Blackmore established his own views on the style of the portraits he had commissioned has been located, though it seems likely that he would have given some instructions when commissioning photography.

Blackmore formed a close and multifaceted relationship with the Smithsonian Institution in Washington D.C. In 1868, a mere five years after his first trip to America, Blackmore loaned his ever expanding personal collection of photographs to Joseph Henry, the Secretary of the Smithsonian Institution. This gesture followed the fire in the Smithsonian in January 1865 that had destroyed the picture gallery of portraits of American Indians by John Mix Stanley (1814-1872) and Charles Bird King (1785-1862).[39] This will be discussed in more detail in the chapter on Blackmore, the Smithsonian Institution, Richard Dodge and George Catlin, though it is worth underlining that by 1868 Blackmore's photographic collection was acknowledged as being so pre-eminent.

Blackmore believed that photography was the best medium for recording the rapidly vanishing Native American communities and his collection represents his major contribution to Native American studies. He set about creating a comprehensive archive of such images and was strategic and dynamic in fulfilling his objectives. His 'passion for photographs, not paintings, set his priorities'[40] and Blackmore built an extensive collection totalling some two thousand images that dated from

39 Two photographic stereoscopic views of the picture gallery taken in 1858 by the American Stereoscopic Co., Langenheim, Lloyd & Co. are in the Smithsonian Institution collections. See http://www.si.edu/ahhp/stereoviews/stereo%20views%20of%20the%20castle.htm

40 Brian W. Dippie, *Catlin and His Contemporaries: The Politics of Patronage*, University of Nebraska Press, Lincoln, 1990 p.421.

the late 1840s up to at least 1875, and possibly the subsequent three years before his untimely death.

Some of these photographs Blackmore purchased from commercial outlets such as photographers and book or print dealers. He had other photographs copied. However, a significant number were the result of his own commissions or contractual negotiations. He collected records of North American Indians both in studio settings while on their delegation visits to Washington D. C. and New York as well as documentary views in their native habitats.

Blackmore formed a close professional relationship between Alexander Gardner in Washington, D.C. In New York Jeremiah Gurney was commissioned to take a set of studio portraits of a visiting delegation of Cheyenne, Arapaho, and Wichita Indians. However, the documentation to prove conclusively that Blackmore commissioned either or both of them has yet to be located.

By the late 1860s Blackmore had formed a wide ranging photographic collection that included ten Daguerreotypes as well as paper photographs and over four hundred glass plate negatives. Blackmore actively sought out additions to his photographic collections. While in St. Louis he noted in his diary for 30th October 1868 that he had purchased Daguerreotypes from the Fitzgibbon Gallery, having his own portrait taken at the same time.[41] Eight are Daguerreotype portraits by John H. Fitzgibbon (1816?-1882), of St. Louis, dating from 1851-1852. It is significant that Blackmore acquired these images that represent the earliest photographic studio portraits of Native Americans. It is also curious that Fitzgibbon still had these Daguerreotypes in his possession, almost two decades after they were taken, and that if he valued them so much that he was willing to sell them to Blackmore. The two other Daguerreotypes are by Thomas Martin Easterly (1809-1882), also of St. Louis, and are copies of paintings; a copy of an 1847 painting by Seth Eastman (1808-1875) of a Mdewakanton Dakota scene of Sioux Indian disposing of their Dead and a Charles Deas (1818-1867) painting, also dated to 1847, depicting an 'Indian Seated on the edge of a

41 Blackmore Diary No.17 p.21. On page 23 is reference to 'Two daguerreotypes' and '5 Daguerreotypes.'

Bold Precipice.'[42] For unknown reasons these Daguerreotypes were not returned by the Smithsonian to Blackmore after they had been copied by Shindler.

Blackmore's personal photographic collections of Native Americans are today primarily distributed between the Salisbury & South Wiltshire Museum, The British Museum, the Smithsonian Institution, the Pitt Rivers Museum, the Fray Angelico Chavez History Library in Palace of the Governors in Santa Fe, the Newberry Library in Chicago and the Western History Research Centre, University of Wyoming. Members of the extended Blackmore family may still hold some images that are known only through reproductions – such as illustrations in Brayer's biography of Blackmore that refers to a family album, probably then in the possession of the Boyle family in Santa Fe, the whereabouts of which is currently unknown. Public and university libraries such as the Beinecke Library of Yale University hold sets of the photographic publications of the Trustees of the Blackmore Museum that may have originated from the Blackmore Museum in Salisbury or William's personal collections or been gifts to individuals or institutions.

As with many of his generation, William Blackmore collected carte de visite portrait photographs of contemporary celebrities. The Salisbury & South Wiltshire Museum also holds four carte de visite albums with a de luxe binding and the embossed emblem of the Blackmore Museum. One of these contains no photographs, and it is unclear whether it ever contained any. The three other albums – that have had some of the original photographs removed from them – hold carte de visite portraits; one of American politicians and military figures (plus four topographical views of Niagara Falls); another of British politicians, celebrities etc. including Huxley, Humboldt and Faraday; and a mixed album with a few portraits of British painters and some American celebrities. Significantly, in the albums of American celebrities each photographic portrait has been numbered in pencil above the window for the carte de visite card. This

42 Fleming, *Shindler Catalogue*, (2003) pp.12-13 and 27. The Deas painting is now in the Autry Museum of Western Heritage in Los Angeles and the Eastman painting in the Thomas Gilcrease Museum in Tulsa, Oklahoma.

suggests that there was a separate index of the sitters, which has yet to be located. The most significant remnant of the Blackmore Museum's collection is an album of portraits of Native North and South Americans Natives in the Salisbury & South Wiltshire Museum – titled on the spine as 'Ethnology'.

It remains unknown when Blackmore first met with Alexander Gardner, the Scottish-born photographer who had come to work in the Washington, D.C. photographic studio of Matthew Brady (1822-1896) in 1856 before opening his own studio, 'Gardner's Gallery', in May 1863 on 7th and D Streets. Gardner also acted as an official Union army photographer from 1862. At this point, he appears not to have photographed any visiting Indian delegations and whether Blackmore visited this studio on his visits to Washington, D.C. during his 1863 trip to the USA is unknown.

In April 1867 Antonio Zeno Shindler (1823-1899), who was operating the former McClees studio now owned by Robert W. Addis, was commissioned by the US Government to produce three sets of photographs of the visiting Dakota Indians for the use of the delegates though their use and impact has yet to be confirmed.[43] At the same time Gardner began photographing some of the Indian delegates visiting Washington, D.C.

Probably on his second visit to the USA Blackmore acquired photographs taken by Alexander Gardner at Fort Laramie in May 1868 at the signing of the Peace Commission treaty negotiations with the Cheyenne and Arapaho tribes, just months before the Englishman's first trip to the 'Great West.' Gardner had been made official photographer for this meeting and took a number of photographs of tribes in their habitat on the Northern Plains. He later published a number of the images as bound portfolios entitled *Scenes in the Indian Country*. There are nine photographs by Gardner taken at Fort Laramie in the Blackmore Collection at the British Museum, and some have the same decorated frame on the photograph mount that match those

43 Fleming, *Shindler Catalogue*, (2003) p.20 citing U.S National Archives and Record Administration, Set of Congressional Documents, Serial no.1332, 40th Congress, 2nd Session 1867-1868, volume 9, doc 71 p.21

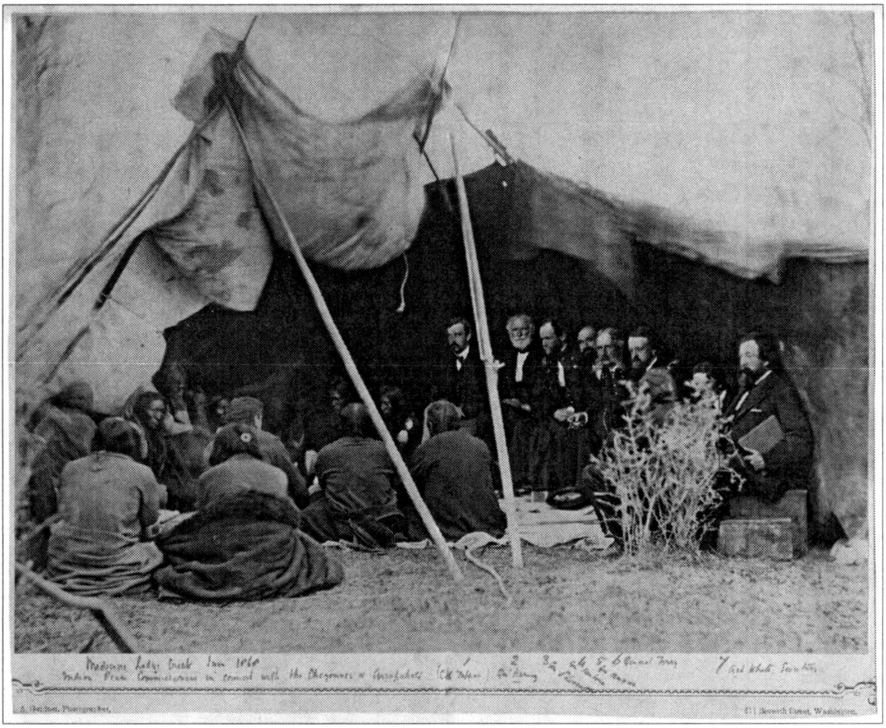

Alexander Gardner.
General William T. Sherman, and other military personnel and Indian Peace Commissioners negotiating with Cheyenne and Arapahoe leaders, Medicine Lodge Creek, June 1868.
Albumen print
Blackmore Collection
Courtesy Palace of the Governors Photo Archives , Santa Fe (NMHM/DCA), 058659

used in *Scenes in the Indian Country*.[44]

Interest in North American Indians in their natural habitat is reflected in other images in the Blackmore collection such as a

44 Gardner returned from Fort Laramie with some two hundred negatives, around half being 10 x 8 inch format and the remainder in the stereoscopic format. Gardner published the large plate negatives. Ninety-eight prints from the now lost stereoscopic views form part of the papers of General Christopher Colon Augur (1821-1898), who had attended the negotiations at Fort Laramie in 1868, held in the Ayer collection, Newbery Library, Chicago. See Raymond DeMaillie, ''Scenes in the Indian Country': A Portfolio of Alexander Gardner's Stereographic Views of the 1868 Fort Laramie 'Treaty Council'', *Montana, The Magazine of Western History*, 31, 1981 pp.42-59.

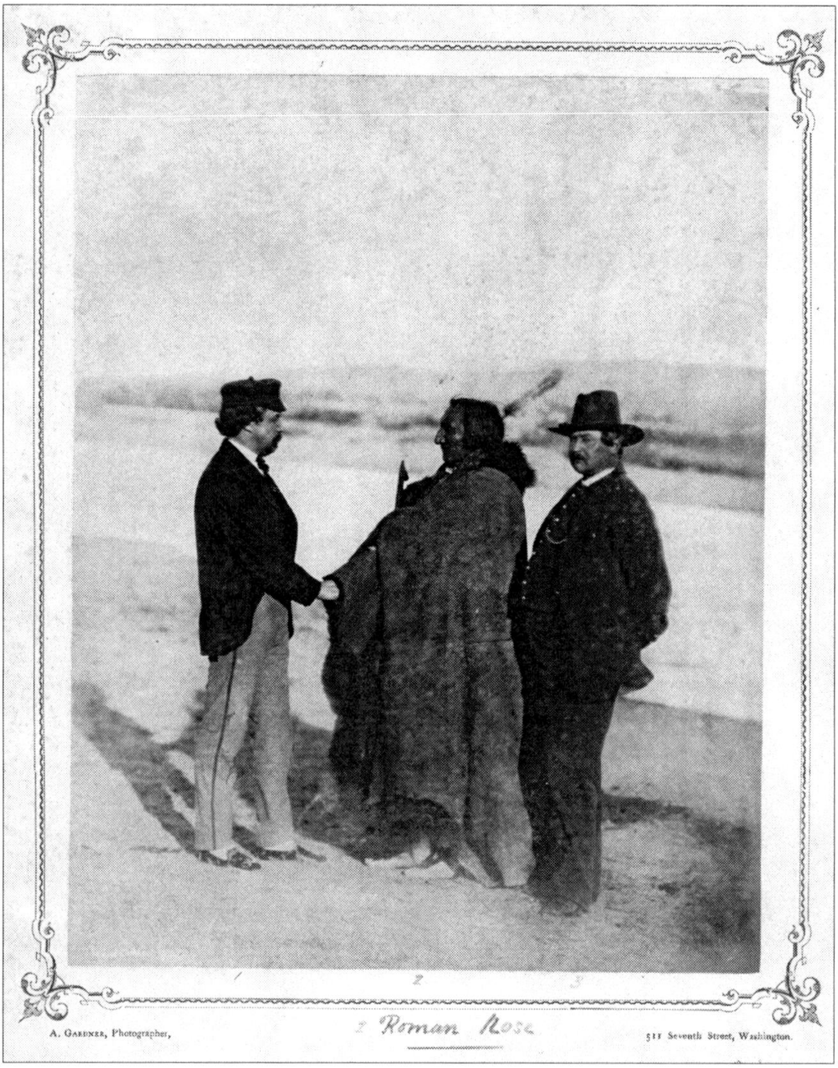

Alexander Gardner.
Samuel F. Tappan (1831-1913), journalist, military officer, abolitionist and a Native American rights activist standing on the left, shaking hands with Roman Nose (Woo-ka-nay or Woqini) (c. 1835 – 1868), leader from the Cheyenne tribe. With Major Edward B. Grimes standing on right.
Fort Laramie, April or May 1868.
Possibly a plate from the series *Scenes in the Indian Country*.
Albumen print
Blackmore Collection Album 40
Courtesy of The Trustees of the British Museum

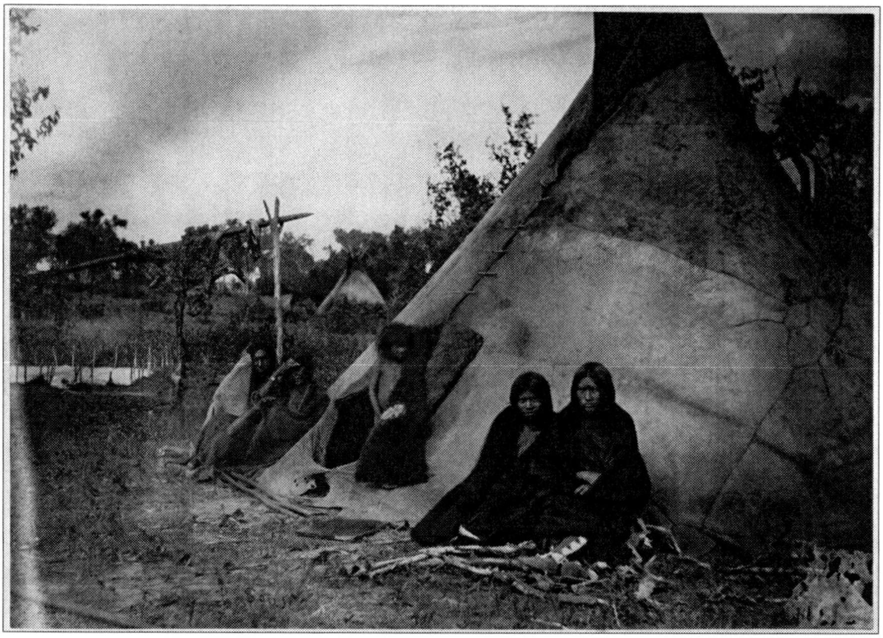

William S. Soule.
Women and children outside tipi in Cheyenne, Arapahoe or Kiowa camp.
1869?
Albumen print
Blackmore Collection
Courtesy Palace of the Governors Photo Archives , Santa Fe (NMHM/DCA), 058658

photograph taken around 1869 by William S. Soule (1836-1908), from 1869 until 1875 the photographer at Fort Sill, Indian Territory (near Lawton, Oklahoma), of women and children outside tipi in a Cheyenne, Arapahoe or Kiowa camp. Blackmore's most significant use of photography in the field took place in September 1871 when he visited Taos in New Mexico at the time of the Indian feast of San Geronimo on the 30th September. Blackmore noted in his diary the following day that he had had photographs taken of the Apache Indians.[45]

These photographs – a series of at least fourteen – were taken by Orloff R. Westmann (1833-1886), a German immigrant, whose studio was in Elizabeth Town, a gold mining town northeast of Taos. However,

45 Blackmore Diary No.3 p.34.

while copies of these images were to find their way into the collections of the Smithsonian, Blackmore did not exploit these images as part of a publication and he does not appear to have commissioned other similar photographic campaigns in the field.

One of the most detailed accounts we have of the photographic activities with which Blackmore was involved is recorded in the diary of Sidford Frederick Hamp (1855-1919), who was William Blackmore's nephew.[46] Sidford's mother Margaret Hamp, sister of Mary Sidford, William's wife, lived in Bedford and was one of Blackmore's 'personal pool' of investors. In 1871 she acquired, via William, a £100 investment in the Mountain Base Investment Fund related to the construction of the Denver and Rio Grande Railway. In 1872 she also had membership certificates in the National Land and Improvement Company related to the opening up of the Arkansas Valley. At the age of 17, Sidford Hamp accompanied his uncle in 1872 on a sixth month visit to the USA. This included Hayden's expedition to Yellowstone. On 30th May he noted 'at 8.30 I went with Mr. Shindler, the Indian artist, to see the Indians photographed . . . . About 8 were taken' including 'Slow Buffalo.'[47] On 3rd June Sidford again noted he went with Shindler to see more Indians photographed, though again he fails to mention at which studio. Hamp became more closely involved with the photography on Hayden's expedition. On 4th July he wrote; 'I was photographed in a tent today, just to try something in the photographing machinery. Mr. Jackson, is the best photographer I know.' On the 21st July Hamp noted that

46 Margaret Sidford (born 1830) married Francis Hamp a widower with three children on June 8th 1854. Her son whom she named Sidford was born in 1855 and she went on to have two more children. The family moved to Bedford at some time. Sidford was only 10 years old his father died. At the suggestion of her brother-in-law William, in June 1877 Margaret took her three sons and one daughter to the recently founded city of Colorado Springs at the foot of Pike's Peak. Sidford followed a few months later. There he worked for *The Gazette* as a reporter and then editor. I thank Ann Ferriera for this information. More biographical information on Sidford Hamp is available in his entry in *Who's Who in America. A Biographical Dictionary of Notable Living Men and Women*, 1903 p. 637.

47 This is probably 'Slow Bull' (Ta-Tan-Kah Hun-Ki-Sh-Neh) whose portrait appears in *Photographs of Red Cloud and Principal Chiefs of Dacotah Indians taken on their visit to Washington, D. C., May, 1872 by Alex. Gardner for Trustees of Blackmore Museum, Salisbury, England.*

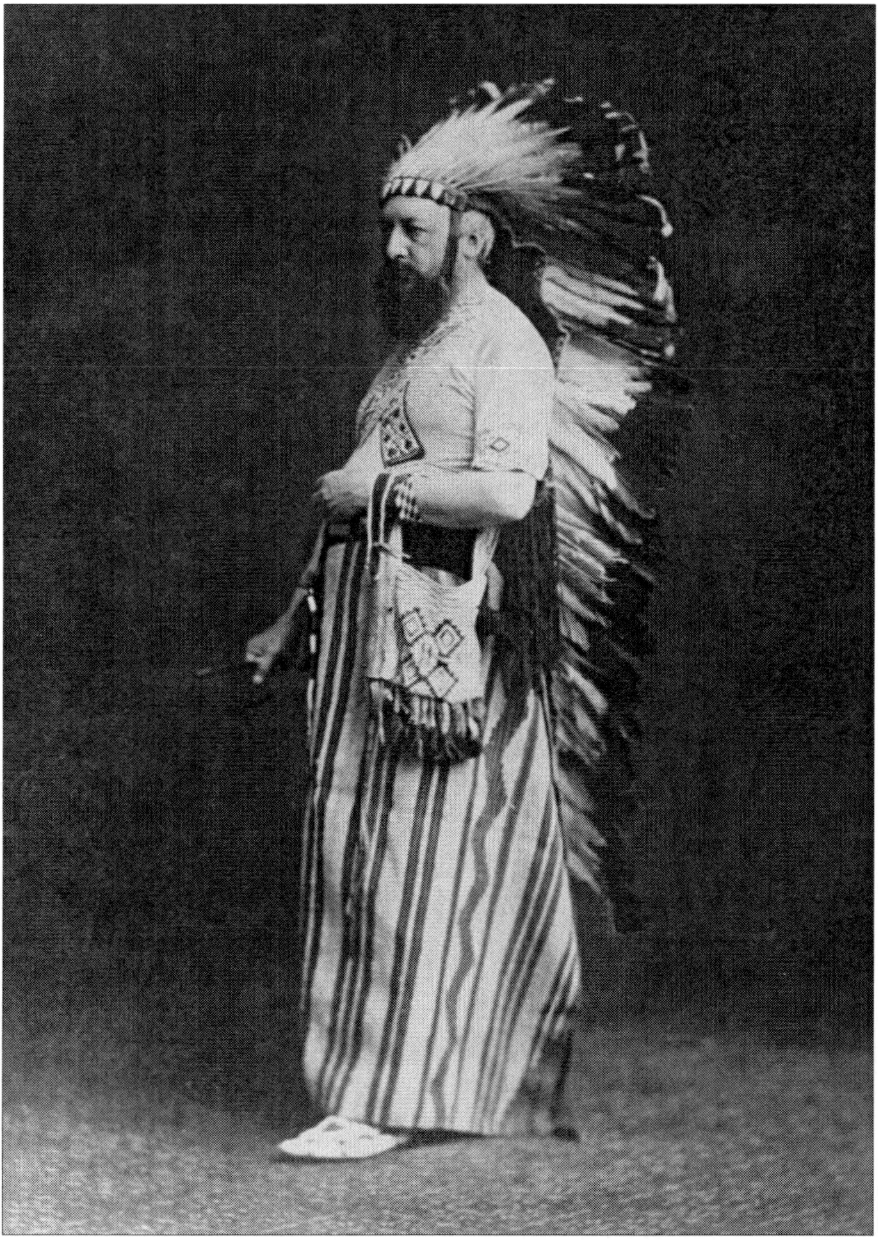

Blackmore dressed as Sioux Indian Chief
Albumen Print
Sidford Hamp Collection, W American Heritage Centre (AHC)
University of Wyoming

Jackson had photographed the camp that day and there are other similar references to Jackson photographing on 5th, 16th and 24th August. Sidford also bought photographs to send his family in England. He noted on 1st November, 'We went back to Salt Lake today, and I wrote a letter to Mother and one to Nell, and sent a few photos back.' He bought more photographs on the 14th November in Washington, D.C. as he returned home to England.[48] In 1877 Sidford Hamp's family moved to Colorado Springs for health reasons where he later joined them. Hamp authored a number of books for the youth market, short stories, plays, and opera librettos, many set in Colorado.

In the 1870s Blackmore's obsession with North America Indian culture led him to have himself photographed in Sioux Indian regalia, including a head dress and blanket, possibly given to him by Red Cloud (1822-1909), a war leader of the Oglala Lakota (Sioux) in June 1872.[49] The only known copy of this image is in the Sidford Hamp Collection, American Heritage Centre, University of Wyoming. It is possible that Blackmore was made an honorary member of the Sioux tribe as a result of his meetings with Red Cloud in the summer of 1872. It is also possible that the photographer was Alexander Gardner. It seems unlikely that no other copy of this image existed and that William would have kept copies for his own collection or to distribute to family and friends. The head dress worn by Blackmore is visible in a photograph in the Salisbury & South Wiltshire Museum of Humphrey Blackmore seated in the Blackmore Museum. It appears in the wall cabinet behind Humphrey and is now in the Pitt Rivers Museum in Oxford.

The work of some twenty-eight photographers were to be found in Blackmore's photographic collection in the British Museum. These included Antonio Zeno Shindler (1823-1899), Alexander Gardner (1821-

48 Herbert Oliver Brayer, 'Exploring the Yellowstone with Hayden, 1872, Diary of Sidford Hamp', *Annals of Wyoming*, Volume 14, Number 4, October 1942 pp.253-298.

49 Blackmore Diary No.5, 15th June 1872 'met Red Cloud in train, gave me his blanket.' Blackmore had probably first met Red Cloud in 1868. He noted in his diary 'Red Cloud was at school at St. Louis – writes and speaks English – ? half breed.' Blackmore Diary 16 p.10

1882), William S. Soule (1836-1908), Jeremiah Gurney (1812-1886) and Son, Orloff R. Westmann (1833-1886), Dr. William Abraham Bell (1841-1920) and James D. Hutton (c.1828-1868). The Blackmore photograph collections also included a range of commercially available carte de visites and stereoscopic views. Not all of these were true documentary images. One of a number of carte de visites by Edric L. Eaton of Omaha, Nebraska in the Blackmore Collection at the British Museum depicts – within a studio setting – a tableaux vivant grouping of two North American Indians recreating the killing and scalping of a white man.[50]

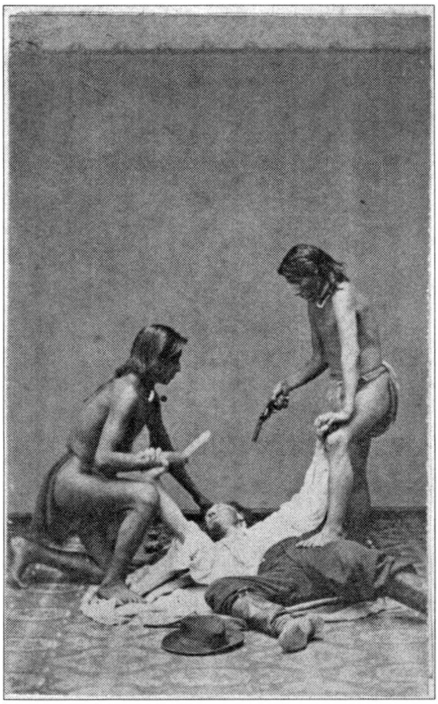

Studio tableaux vivant of two North American Indians recreating the killing and scalping of a white man. Photographed by Edric L. Eaton.
Carte de visite
Albumen print
Blackmore Collection Album 9
Courtesy of The Trustees of the British Museum

50 British Museum AN107395001. This and the other carte de visites by Soule have the advertisement of the distributor E. Lovejoy, 87 So. Clark St. Chicago.

By 1876 part of the topographic views in Blackmore's extensive photographic collection was described in the London periodical *The Field* as 'the most beautiful collection in the world, illustrative of the natural features of the Yellowstone river and its surroundings.'[51] These were presumably views taken by William Henry Jackson though where the reviewer had seen the photographs is unclear. When Blackmore started collecting images for this part of his photograph collection must be left to conjecture. Jackson's first connection with the US Geological Survey was as an unpaid photographer on Hayden's 1870 Wyoming survey, a twenty-man expedition to South Pass, Fort Bridger, Henry's Fork, and back to Cheyenne, and his first systematic photographic campaign in the Yellowstone region took place the following year. So the likelihood is that Blackmore began collecting views of Yellowstone on his visits to the USA in 1871 and 1872. A number of these photographs in Blackmore's collection were used as the basis of some of the illustrations to the published account of the visit of the traveller, journalist and author Windham Thomas Wyndham-Quin, Earl of Dunraven (1841-1926) to the Estes estate and Upper Yellowstone region in 1874. Blackmore had joined this party by invitation. The wood engraved illustrations include a number of portraits including Vannerson and Cohner's portrait of the Pawnee chief Pi-ta-ne-sha-a-du (Man and Chief).[52]

Following William Blackmore's death the topographic views from his collections subsequently disappeared without trace. What might have represented part of the collection was sold at the sale of the remainder of the collection of Humphrey Blackmore's estate in Salisbury in a three day house sale on the 2nd, 3rd and 4th March, 1932.

51 *The Field*, London, 25th November 1876 as cited by Colin Taylor, ''Ho, for the Great West!' Indians and buffalo, exploration and George Catlin: the West of William Blackmore' in Barry C. Johnson, *'Ho for the Great West!' and other original papers to mark the 25th Anniversary of the English Westerners' Society*, Eatome Ltd. for The English Westerners' Society, London 1980 p.18.

52 'I take this opportunity of thanking my fellow-countryman, Mr. William Blackmore, for his goodness in allowing me to use in illustration some specimens selected from his beautiful collection of photographs of the Yellowstone district and Geyserland.' Earl of Dunraven, *The Great Divide: Travels in the Upper Yellowstone in the Summer of 1874*, Chatto & Windus, London 1876 p.xiii. Dunraven was one of William Blackmore's investors at the time of the capitalist's death.

The sale contained 'A bound album of photographs of the Yellowstone National Park and Views in Montana and Wyoming territories by W. H. Jackson, photographer, issued by the United States Department of the Interior Geological Survey of the Territories' dated 1873 together with 'A portfolio of 15 mounted photographs published by the United States Geological Survey of the Territories.[53]

Unlike his library, no printed catalogue of Blackmore's photographic collection was produced and it is not clear that he ever intended to publish one. How Blackmore stored and managed his photographic collection also remains obscure. There is no evidence of a photograph register or for a classification or a numbering system. No catalogue or checklist has been found to date. The photographs acquired by the British Museum in 1931 arrived in a set of some forty-one contemporaneous folding 'portfolios' and a box containing photographs labelled as 'William Blackmore'. These portfolios had no markings on them though the photographs appear to be sorted by Native American tribes. They may have been used to pack and transport the photographs rather than representing the manner in which Blackmore intended them to be stored.[54]

How often and within what context Blackmore exhibited his photograph collection in public settings has yet to be fully established. Blackmore is known to have exhibited and discussed his by then extensive collection of photographs at the December 1868 meeting of the American Ethnological Society in New York.[55] At the time of this meeting he bought a carte de visite portrait of George Folsom, the

53 These items formed part of lot 347 of the auction held at Humphrey's former home, Vale House in Salisbury, by Woolley & Wallis, a local Salisbury auctioneer.

54 The 'Disposal book of the Salisbury South Wilts and Blackmore Museum No. 1 1928-1952' reports the disposal of 'Photographs of North American Indians and miscellanea' given to the Department of Ceramics and Ethnography of the British Museum. It is dated 24th February 1932. For a more detailed account of classification of mid 19th century photographic archives, see Anthony J. Hamber, 'Building Nineteenth-century Photographic Resources: The South Kensington Museum and William Blackmore', *Visual Resources*, Vol. 26, no. 3 September, 2010 pp. 254-273.

55 Brayer, *op. cit.* Volume I, p.57 citing a letter from Henry R. Stiles, Recording Secretary, American Ethnological Society, to Blackmore dated 4th December, 1868. Blackmore 0068.

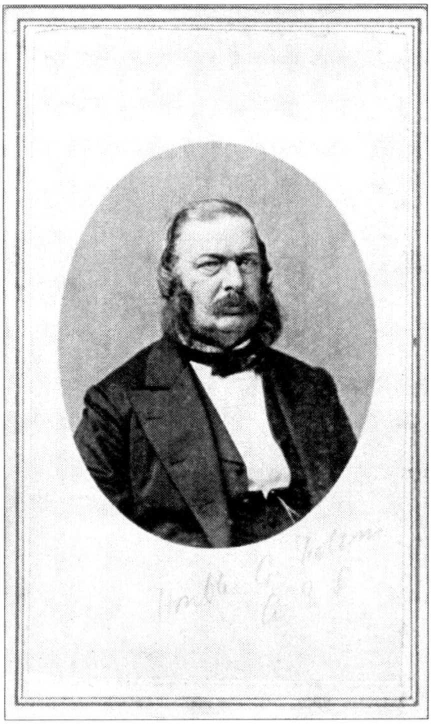

George Folsom, Third President of the American Ethnological Society of New York.
"December 5. 1868."
Photographed by R. A. Lewis.
Carte de visite
Albumen print
Blackmore carte de visite album
Courtesy of Salisbury & South Wiltshire Museum

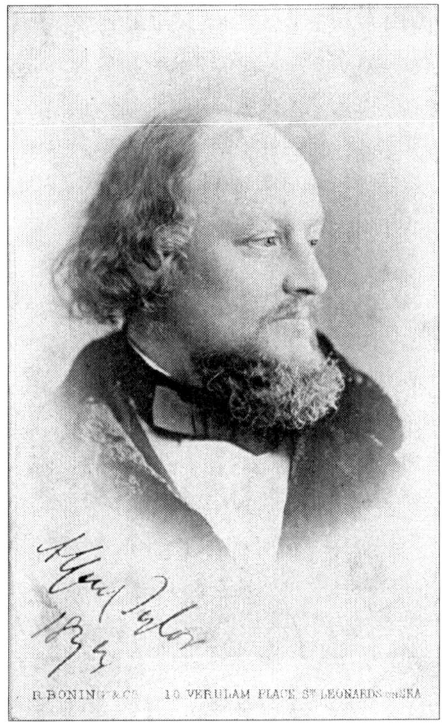

Alfred Tylor (1824-1884)
Photographed by Robert Boning, 10 Verulam Place, St. Leonards on Sea.
Carte de visite
Albumen print
Blackmore carte de visite album
Courtesy of Salisbury & South Wiltshire Museum Edwin Macy.

President of the American Ethnology Society.[56] In 1876 Blackmore lent 'Photographic Views taken in Colorado and New Mexico, including Aztec Ruins and Portraits of Natives' to the Royal Society in London for inclusion in the society's annual conversazione held on 5th April.[57] It is

56 The photograph is in one of the carte de visite albums held by the Salisbury & South Wiltshire Museum.

57 The conversazione checklist in the library of the Royal Society records that these were displayed in Room III. These ruins in question were considered during the

worth noting that at the first Royal Society conversazione held on the 27th April 1872 A. Tylor exhibited 'Photographs of Landscape Scenery, Geysers, and Mud-Springs in the Region of the Yellowstone River, explored by F. Hayden, United States' Government Geologist.'[58]

PHOTOGRAPHY AND THE BLACKMORE MUSEUM

The Blackmore Museum was founded at a time of the rapid expansion of commercial photography. This was reflected by the rise in the number of commercial photographers, a wide range of commercially available photographs and the increase in the application of photography for professional and scholarly purposes. There was also a rapidly emerging middle class with associated disposable income to purchase photographs.

By the early 1860s the major national museums in Britain – such as the South Kensington Museum and British Museum – had adopted photography to provide a number of services including collections documentation, to provide a new form of visual resources for collections management and for commercial publication at affordable prices.[59] While in 1868 Blackmore hired the artist and photographer Antonio Zeno Shindler of Washington, D.C. to copy his collection of photographs of Native Americans for the Smithsonian Institution, he made no such formal arrangement in Salisbury. Nor is there any evidence that local Salisbury photographers were regularly used to undertake work on behalf of the Blackmore Museum.

By the mid 1860s there were at least twelve commercial photographers active in Salisbury.[60] At least one of these Edwin Macy,

1870s to be 'Aztec', but were not. They might have been the Anasazi ruins of the Pueblo people in Mancos Canyon, Colorado.

58 The library of the Royal Society has the checklist for this *conversazione*. The photographs were exhibited in Room I. A. Tylor was probably the geologist Alfred Tylor (1824-1884). The anthropologist Sir Edward Burnett Tylor (1832–1917) was his younger brother. Blackmore knew Edward Tylor well. Another connection is that Alfred Tylor took over the lease of Shepley House in Carshalton from Blackmore in 1870.

59 See Anthony J. Hamber, *'A Higher Branch of the Art' – Photographing the Fine Arts in England 1839-1880*, Gordon & Breach, Amsterdam, 1996.

60 E. Whitlock – active from the mid 1850s; William Thomas Pitcher – active from 1855 and with a studio in St. Ann Street from 1859; James W. Miell – who opened a

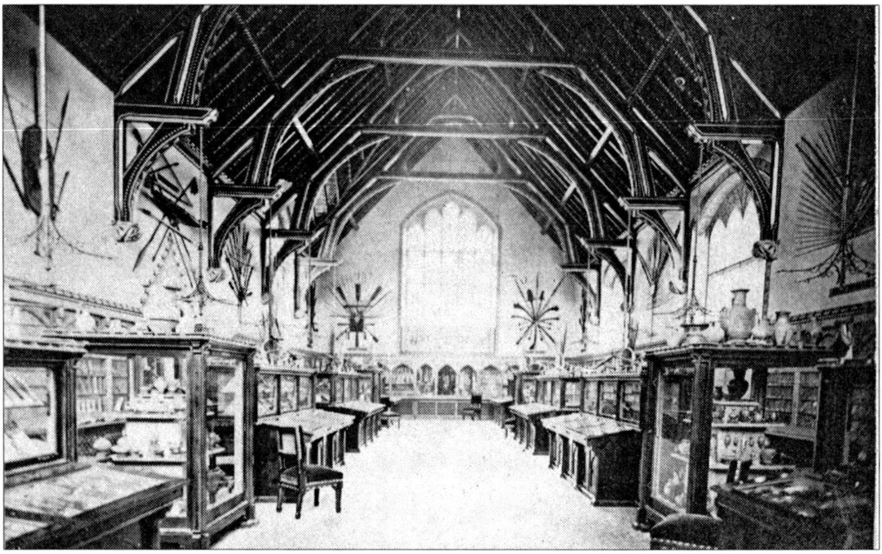

Interior view of the Blackmore Museum c.1870
Photographed by Edwin Macy
Carte de visite
Albumen print
Author's collection

created a carte de visite format view of the interior of the completed Blackmore Museum, thus dating it to after 1867. Whether Macy was commissioned by the Blackmore Museum or this image formed part of a series has yet to be established. Blackmore used copies of this image to give to friends and acquaintances. A small pocket box containing twenty-eight copies of this carte de visite is to be found amongst the Blackmore papers at the Salisbury & South Wiltshire Museum.[61] However it is unclear whether this image was made commercially available. Probably

studio in Catherine Street in 1859; Henry Brooks – whose studio in the High Street opened in 1859; Edmund Rogers – who commenced in a studio De Vaux Place in 1865; J.E. Neville – with a studio in the High Street from 1865; C.J. Witcomb and Son – whose studio opened at 47 Catherine Street during the 1860s; Frederick Treble – who opened a studio in Catherine Street in the early 1860s; Thomas Edwards – who opened a studio in St. Ann Street during the 1860s; Edwin Macy – whose Wiltshire Photographic Rooms, Town Mill House, St. Thomas Churchyard opened in 1865; C.P. Gearing – with a studio in the High Street from 1867; and J.E. Neville – with a studio in the High Street from 1865.

61 S&SWM Box 'Photographs of Wm Blackmore and Mary Blackmore Ref No 1732'.

larger format photographs were also used by Blackmore as a marketing tool to spread knowledge of the existence of his museum. In 1868 – a year in which he donated 'a series of photographs of American Indians', to the Smithsonian[62] - the institution received from Alma B. Bond a donation of two interior photographic views of the Blackmore Museum.[63] In 1875 the report of the Peabody Museum of Archaeology and Ethnology recorded that it had received during 1874 a 'Photograph of the Blackmore Museum, Salisbury, England. – From Mr. W. Blackmore.'[64]

From the limited extant material it would seem that William Blackmore and Edward Stevens may at one stage have had a preference for the services of Frederick Treble.[65] In 1863 Stevens took 'Flint Jack', an itinerant knapper and creator of a wide range of forgeries, to Treble's studio for him to be photographed (above, page 117).[66] During the 1860s and 1870s Blackmore had his portrait taken by a number of photographers. James Owen of Salisbury probably took the last portrait of the financier in July 1877.[67] Photographic portraits of Edward Stevens

62 'Report of the Secretary', *Annual Report of the Board of Regents of The Smithsonian Institution*, Washington, D. C., 1869 p.27.

63 SPC BAE 4801 01015000 and SPC BAE 4801 01014900. Who Alma B. Bond was and how she acquired these photographs has yet to be clarified.

64 '7624, Photograph of the Blackmore Museum, Salisbury, England. – From Mr. W. Blackmore.', *Eighth Annual Report of the Peabody Museum*, Harvard, 1875 p.16. I thank Patricia Kervick, Associate Archivist at the Peabody Museum, for confirming these details.

65 Born around 1830, Treble operated photographic studios in Nottingham, Yeovil, Salisbury, Hastings, London, Brighton and Norwich during his career. See http://freepages.genealogy.rootsweb.ancestry.com/~brett/photos/emtreble.html accessed on 25th July, 2010.

66 *The Reliquary, Quarterly Archaeological Journal and Review*, October, 1867 p.74. This formed an article (pp.65-76) 'Flint Jack; A memoir and An Appeal.' by Llewellynn Jewitt F.S.A.

67 William Blackmore had his portrait taken in Salisbury by James Owen in July 1877. There are both carte de visite and Cabinet format photographs from this session. The cartes de visites would have been mainly used by Blackmore as mementoes to give to friends and acquaintances. Amongst Mary Blackmore's photographs in the S&SWM are portraits of both William and Mary in carte de visite and Cabinet formats by Elliott & Fry of Baker Street, London. Both hand annotated envelope in Box 'Photographs of Wm Blackmore and Mary Blackmore Ref No 1732'.

taken during different periods of his life survive in the Salisbury & South Wiltshire Museum.

Edward Stevens' role in developing the photographic collections of the Blackmore Museum remains unclear as do their scale and scope at the time of William Blackmore's death in 1878. In 1868 Stevens gave some insight into the museum's photography collections in a letter cited in an article titled 'Photography as an aid to archaeology' by J. Henderson.[68] Stevens wrote that 'photographs of forms of clubs, spears, ornaments, tools and weapons etc. are useful and valuable to us. We also collect photographs of the aborigines of various countries, and for this nothing is equal to photography, because artistic license is impossible. He further noted 'I had a flint hatchet photographed yesterday, but for such objects photography is not very useful, as the yellows come out too dark.'[69] Only a handful of such photographs have been to date located.

Stevens was also in receipt of photographs of archaeological digs since in a letter to *The Times* in January 1868 regarding prehistoric remains found in gravel beds near Malton, Yorkshire, Stevens wrote 'judging from a photograph of the gravel-beds in question, all the stones which constitute the gravel are much water-worn, whereas the hatchet itself, which is assumed to be part of the bed . . . is not rolled at all.'[70] While there is a photograph in the collections of the Society of Antiquaries that

68 The author was probably the collector and archaeologist John Henderson (1797-1878), FSA. In 1868 Henderson privately published *Works of Art in Pottery, Glass and Metal in the Collection of John Henderson, MA, FSA.* Cundall and Fleming, London, 1868. Each copy contained twenty Albumen print photographs as illustrations. Henderson bequeathed, a substantial collection of Egyptian, Etruscan, Greek, and Roman antiquities to the Ashmolean Museum, Oxford and he left collections of decorative art, glass, and arms, as well as important watercolour drawings to the British Museum.

69 J. Henderson, 'Photography as an aid to archaeology', *Journal of the Photographic Society*, No.192 18th April, 1868 pp.37-40 as cited by Elizabeth Edwards, *Raw Histories – Photographs, Anthropology and Museums*, Berg Publishers, Oxford, 2001 p.55. The article was reprinted in *The Illustrated Photographer*, 24th April 1869 pp.139-140.

70 *The Times*, 3rd January, 1868.p.8. The S&SWM has a photograph by Budtz Muller & Co. of [Copenhagen] that has been annotated by Edward Stevens 'Photograph of a block, one third natural size, from the shell-mound of Meilgaard, near Grenaa in north-west Jutland, The original block is preserved in the Royal Copenhagen Museum of Northern Antiquities, at Copenhagen.'

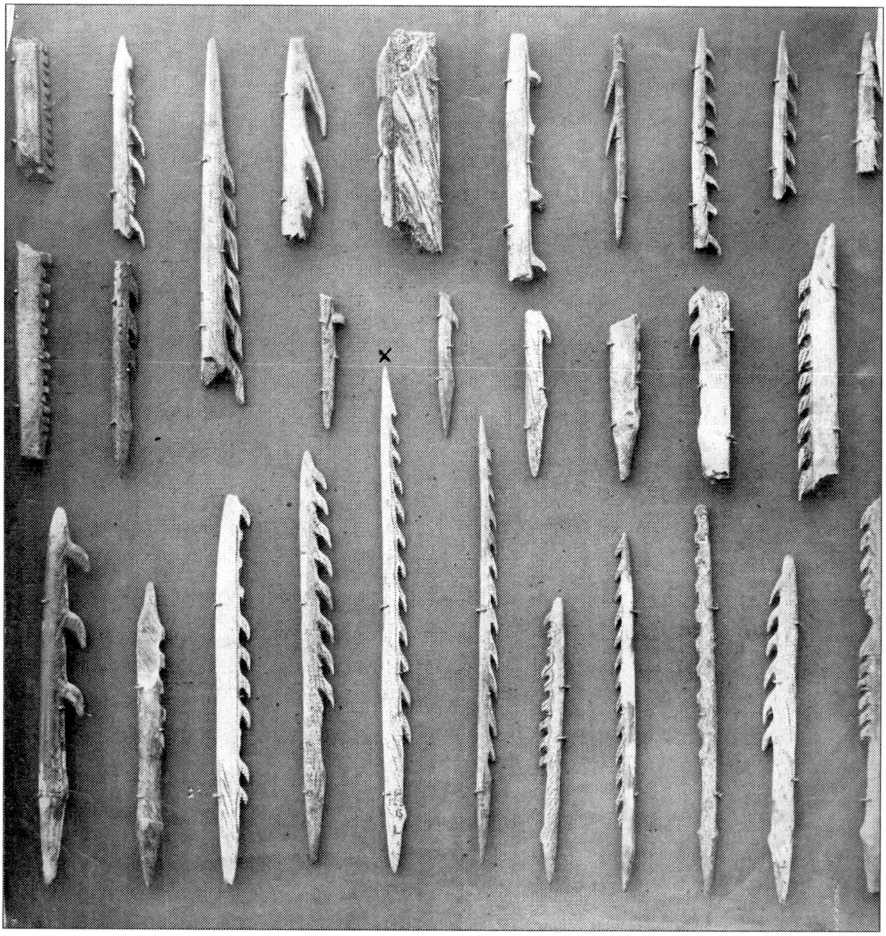

29 harpoon heads mounted on a board
Albumen print
Courtesy of Salisbury & South Wiltshire Museum

was taken during the excavations at Elm Grove, Milford Hill in 1864. The first implement from this site was found by Humphrey Blackmore on 27th April, 1864 and during the following summer months further excavations were undertaken by James Brown, a local tobacconist and amateur archaeologist. It has yet to be established which excavation campaign has been recorded in this photograph, who the photographer was, or the identity of the two men and one woman recorded. There is no copy of this photograph amongst the Blackmore Museum papers.

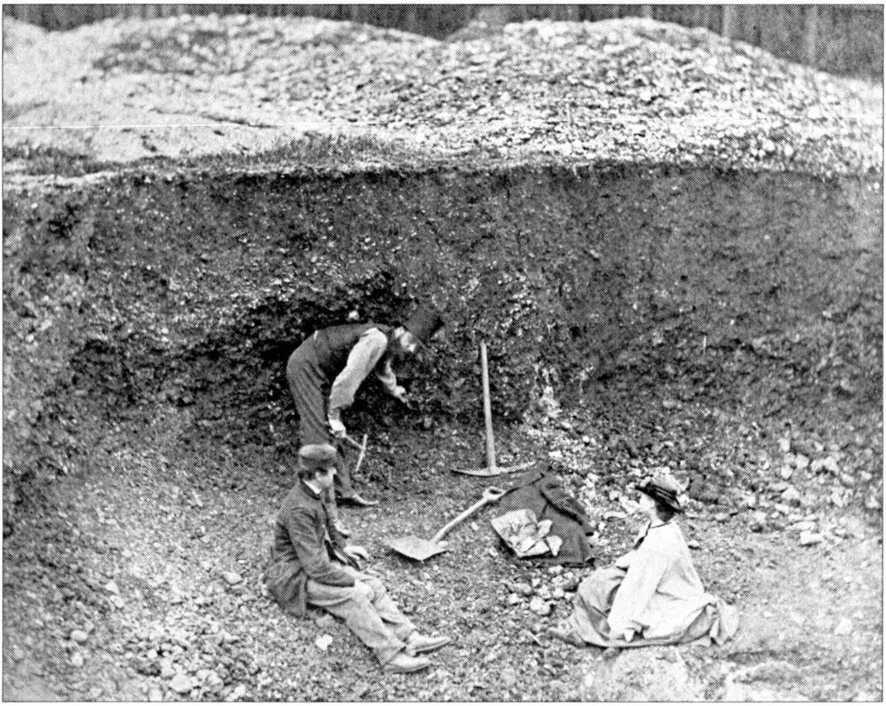

Photograph of Gravel pit on Milford Hill, Salisbury showing the spot where a finely chipped pointed flint implement was dug out in the presence of James Brown on 13th June 1864.'
Albumen print
Courtesy of the Society of Antiquaries, London

Blackmore did form a photographic collection of other 'aboriginal' people but it does not seem to have been large in either scale or scope. In 1867, in his address at the opening of his museum in Salisbury, he stated that Edward Lamb, an English merchant of Buenos Aires, had sent 'by the last mail a collection of photographs of some of the aborigines of South America.'[71] These are probably the thirteen photographs in the album titled 'Ethnology' that remains in the collections of the Salisbury & South Wiltshire Museum. The images are a mixture of Argentinian, Amerindian, possibly Guyana/Brazilian, and Mexican natives. One of the photographers may have been the Italian-born photographer

71 *Some Account of the Blackmore Museum – Part I. The opening Meeting*, H.F. & E. Bull, Devizes; Bell & Daldy, London ; J.R. Smith, London 1868 pp.66-67.

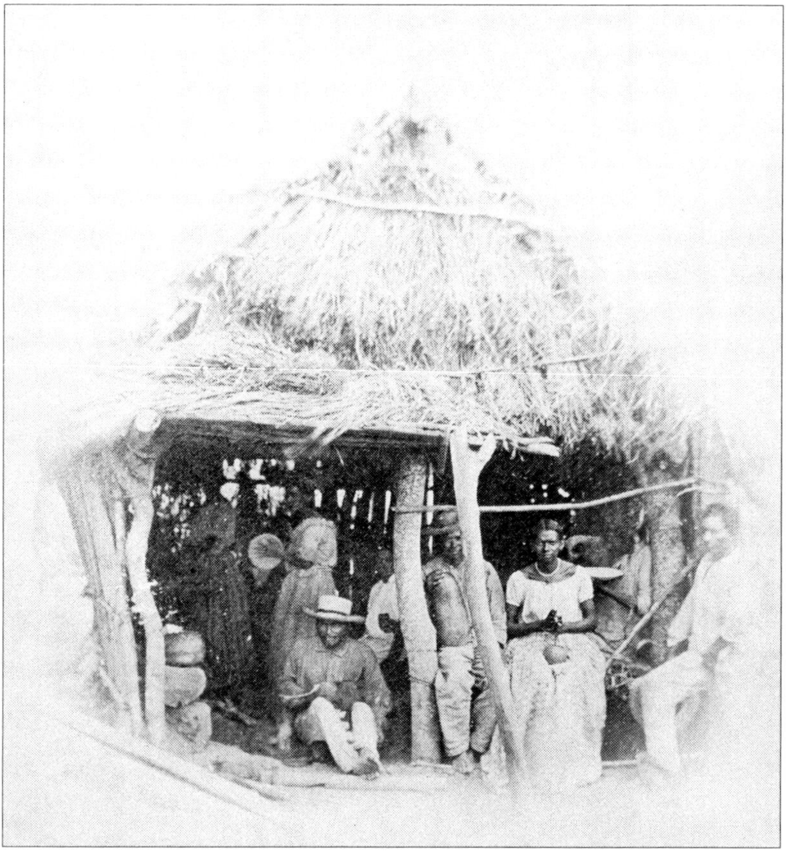

South American family group in their hut. Before 1867. Possibly photographed by Benito Panunzi (1819-1894)
Albumen print
Blackmore "Ethnology" album
Courtesy of Salisbury & South Wiltshire Museum

Benito Panunzi (1819-1894) who had arrived in Argentina in 1862. Finding that Buenos Aires had reached saturation point in terms of professional photographers he ventured into the nearby provinces in search of new subject matter to record. He documented examples of rapidly disappearing indigenous populations.[72] Quite what purpose

72 I thank Harry Persaud for his suggestions as to the range of ethnic types and Steven Joseph and Tristan Schwilden for helping to identify Panunzi as one of the likely photographer of some of these images. See Luis Priamo, *La fotografía italiana en la Argentina. Siglos XVIII / XIX. Benito Panunzi.*, Fundación Proa at http://www.proa.org/exhibiciones/pasadas/italianos/fotografia/fotografia.html. Another possible

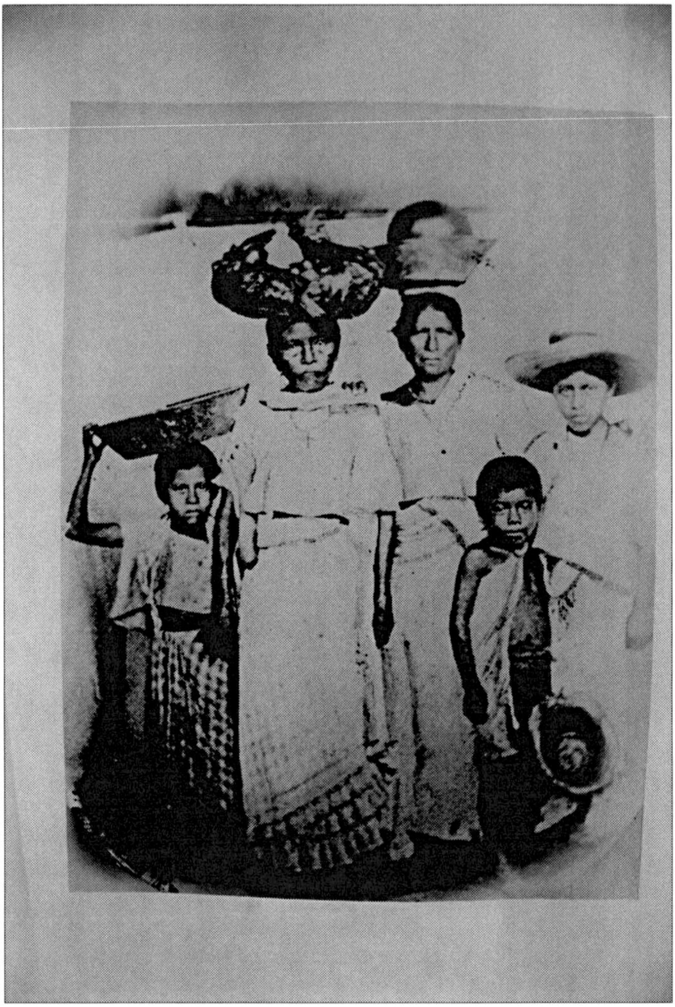

Group of standing South American women and children. Before 1867.
Possibly photographed by Benito Panunzi (1819-1894)
Albumen print
Blackmore "Ethnology" album
Courtesy of Salisbury & South Wiltshire Museum

the 'Ethnology' album had – or even when it was made up – remains unknown since the photographs are mounted separately on the recto of

creator of these photographs is the French-born photographer Esteban Gonnet (1830-1868). I also thank Abel Alexander who suggests that some of the photographs are of natives of the Guianas. Email to author date 13th June, 2010.

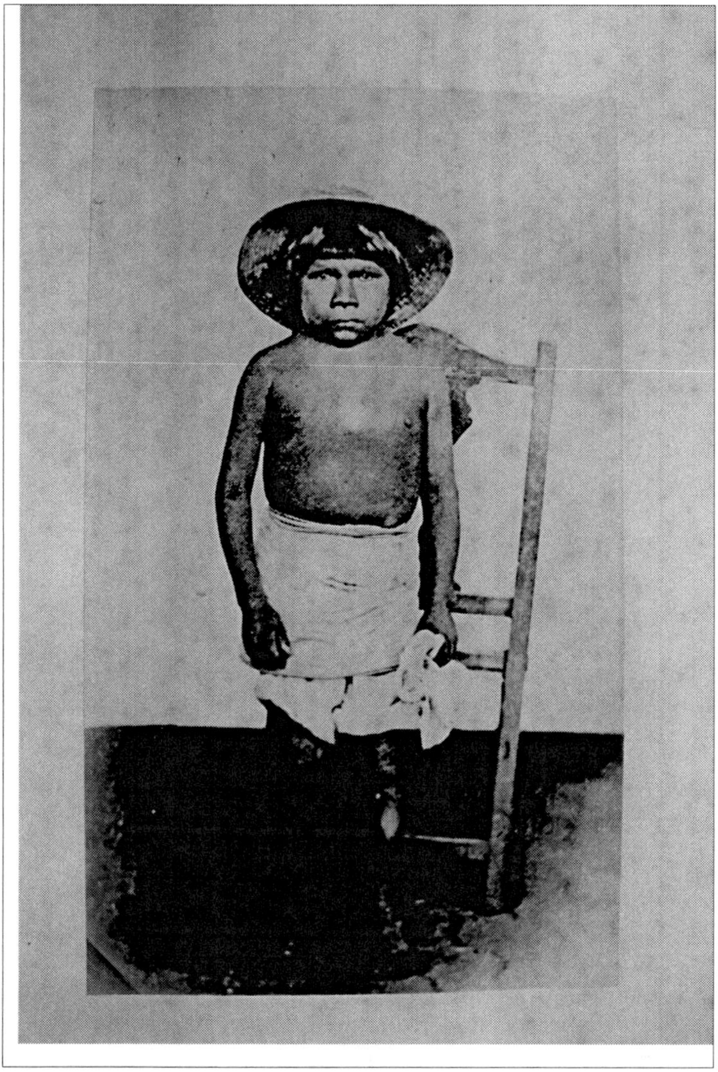

Small South American boy standing before a chair. Before 1867. Possibly photographed by Benito Panunzi (1819-1894)
Albumen print
Blackmore "Ethnology" album
Courtesy of Salisbury & South Wiltshire Museum

each folio and there are no annotations that might cross reference it to any other source.

No other photographs of other 'aboriginal' people have been located from the collections originally held in the Blackmore Museum

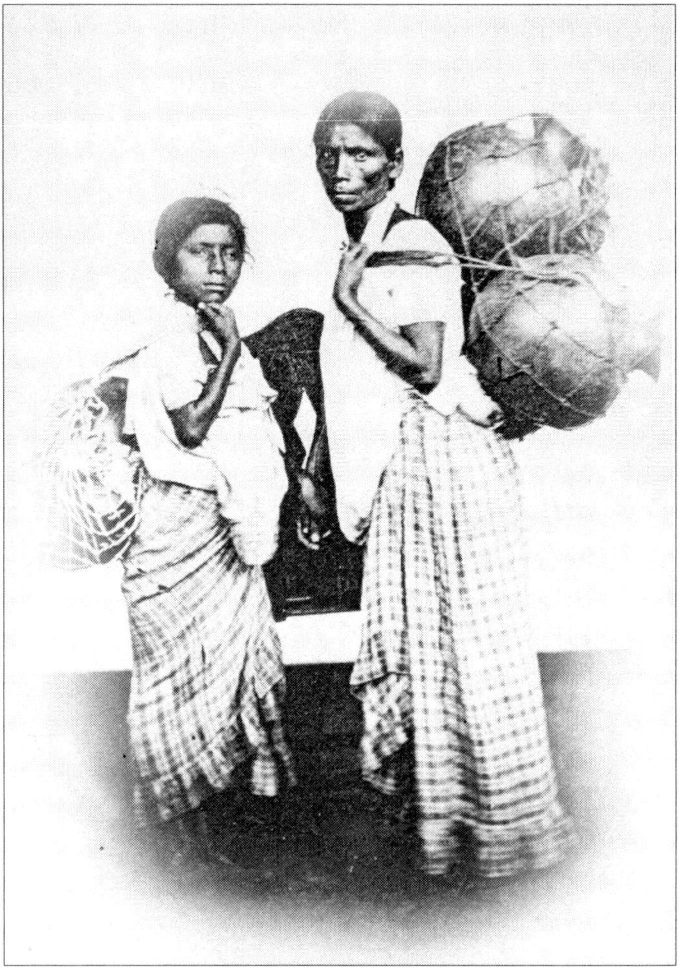

South American woman and girl with burdens. Before 1867. Possibly photographed by Benito Panunzi (1819-1894)
Albumen print
Blackmore "Ethnology" album
Courtesy of Salisbury & South Wiltshire Museum

though Blackmore noted in March 1872 that he owed the New York booksellers J. Sabin & Sons US$16. 2c. – the equivalent of three Guineas – for photographs of 'colored Ministers.'[73] However, Blackmore resolutely maintained a complete focus on North American natives and does not

73 Wiltshire and Swindon History Centre 776/642. The entry refers to 'Henry's a/c' which may be Joseph Henry of the Smithsonian.

seem to have had any interest in building a comparative collection of ethnographic photographs of races of the World.

There are tantalising references to other now lost parts of Blackmore's photographic collection. In an entry in his 1868 diary Blackmore refers to 'Mr. Griggs Photographs'. This was probably William Griggs (1832-1911) the inventor of a photo-chromo-lithographic printing process and who had set up a photolithographic printing works in Peckham in that year. Until 1878 Griggs was contracted as a photographer and printer to the India Office and had printed the photographs illustrating Forbes Watson's *The Textile Manufactures and the Costumes of the People of India. With Plates, exhibiting numerous coloured photographs by J. Forbes Watson, M.A., M.D., F.R.A.S., &c. Reporter on the Products of India to the Secretary of State for India in Council,* published by William Allen in London in 1866. Each copy was illustrated with nine mounted photographic plates made up of composite photographs. The photographs had been carefully chosen to illustrate styles and modes of wearing traditional items of clothing. Seven of these were by the Albumen process while one each was by the 'Photochromo' and photolithographic process – thus showing Griggs' proficiency in a range of innovatory printing processes. One specific capability that Griggs had displayed in producing the images for this publication would have been particularly relevant to William Blackmore. In a review of the book in the *British Journal of Photography* in January 1867 it was noted that Griggs had successfully copied and manipulated many 'old and half-faded photographs of bad quality.'[74] Blackmore's photograph collection undoubtedly contained images of variable quality similar to those that Griggs had copied.

Little is known of the practicalities of the Blackmore Museum's photographic collections; how they were stored and managed; whether they were regularly used and by whom; and whether they were placed on public display. For instance, which photographs were kept in Salisbury and which were distributed between initially his home in Hooton outside Liverpool, the Blackmore Museum, Shepley House and then Belgrave

74 See *British Journal of Photography*, 11th January 1867 p.17 and Ray Desmond, *The India Museum 1801-1879*, HMSO, London, 1982 p.98.

Mansions? Other than the three hundred photographs loaned to the Smithsonian, did Blackmore keep a collection of photographs in the USA, and if so where was it located? The lack of a photograph register – such as was held at the South Kensington Museum – also makes the detailed chronology of when photographs were acquired problematic.

A letter from Edward Stevens to Blackmore in 1864 indicated that the intention was to display photographs in the proposed library of the Blackmore Museum to 'make it look like the Drawing Room of a Scientific Man' that would be 'at the disposal of the Scientific visitor.'[75] This does not clearly indicate whether photographs would be held in portfolios or whether some would be framed and hung on the walls. Stevens' aspirations were somewhat thwarted by the fact that the majority of Blackmore's photographs – and glass negatives – were kept at the Smithsonian Institution for several years while Shindler copied them. In late 1871 probably the majority of the photographs were sent to Salisbury though some copy prints, the Daguerreotypes and the glass negatives remained in the Smithsonian. While Blackmore's 'great series of photographs of American Indians' in Salisbury was noted in 1892 it remains unclear whether it was regularly or significantly used for research or publication.

Given that acquisitions of North American objects ceased after Blackmore's and Stevens's untimely death in 1878, and that there were copy prints of the Blackmore collection in the Smithsonian , there was little need for American scholars to travel to Salisbury specifically to view the photograph collection.[76] In parallel there did not seem to be any British scholars who wished to avail themselves of the resource. It would appear that since William Blackmore was the driving force behind both the acquisition of photographs of North American Indians and the photographic publications of the Trustees of the Blackmore Museum –

75 Letter dated 2nd April 1864 as cited by R. W. H. Willoughby 'The Salisbury & South Wiltshire Museum: Founded 1860', *Wiltshire Archaeological and Natural History Magazine*, Volume 57 Number CCVIII, Devizes, 1960 p.315 end note 52. It should be noted, as previously mentioned, that Stevens himself hung framed, signed photographic portraits of noted archaeologists in the library in his home.

76 Frederick Starr, 'Anthropological Work in Europe', *The Popular Science Monthly*, May, 1892 p.71.

the entire production of which was undertaken under his direction in the USA – no cataloguing of these images took place in Salisbury. The state in which the photographic collections were received in 1932 at the British Museum seems to support this.

Given Blackmore's interest in photography it might seem surprising that he did not use the medium to illustrate Edward Stevens' catalogue of the collection of flints in the Blackmore Museum – *Flint Chips: A Guide to Historic Archaeology, as illustrated by the collection in the Blackmore Museum, Salisbury* published in 1870. For instance a photographic view of the interior of the museum – such as Macy's carte de visite view – might have formed a suitable frontispiece. One possible reason might have been the sizeable print run and the additional cost of including photographic illustration. Another form of publishing might have been either loose photographs of the most significant items in the collection or portfolios of photographs of parts of the collection. The fact that no Salisbury photographer appears to have considered photographs of artefacts within the Blackmore Museum as worth adding to their stock probably underlines the perceived lack of demand by the general public. Technical difficulties – as evidenced by Edwards Stevens – in reproducing some items would have been another key consideration.

PHOTOGRAPHIC PUBLICATION OF THE TRUSTEES OF THE BLACKMORE MUSEUM

One of William Blackmore's most significant projects was to become a photographic publisher in the form of the imprint of 'The Trustees of the Blackmore Museum'. The imprint had a somewhat grand title given that there were only three trustees; William, his brother Humphrey and his brother-in-law Edward Stevens. Evidence suggests that William was entirely responsible for these photographic publications; their design, editorial control and practicalities and cost of production. Another point worth bearing in mind is that the most significant publication connected with the museum – Edward Stevens' *Flint Chips* catalogue of 1870 – did not bear the imprint of the museum's Trustees.

Three photographic publications of the Trustees of the Blackmore Museum are known and date to 1865, 1871 and a series of 1872 respectively and they are linked together by a number of common themes. Firstly, these were loose mounted prints in a portfolio that might be bound into volumes. There was no accompanying text though each publication appears to have had a printed title page and a single contents page listing the photographic plates. Their layout matches traditional prints in that the photographs are mounted on larger sheets of heavier stock and have printed captions and credits. However, none of the photographs have printed numbers – though some of the prints in the Blackmore Collection in the British Museum have numbers in manuscript annotations in Blackmore's hand. All three of the publications are dated in the printed credits to 1865, 1871 and 1872 respectively. The 1872 series is the most ornate in terms of having a decorated border frame within which the Albumen prints are mounted.

Secondly, all the images are formal studio portraits. These vary between full and half length seated portraits to full length standing portraits. In some instances multiple views – full face and profile – have been taken.[77] Thirdly, all the portraits are almost exclusively male. Native American Indian women accompanied their men folk to Washington and were part of the social scene and Alexander Gardner did photograph three Brulé 'squaws' that were published.[78] Mary Blackmore met with two of the Oglala Lakota (Sioux) squaws accompanying their chief Red Cloud on his delegation to Washington in May and June 1872 and presented them with gifts.[79] That Blackmore did not commission more photographs to be taken individually of North American Indian women who formed part of the delegations visiting Washington, D.C. seems a curious omission since there are other photographs of such women in their natural habitat in the Blackmore collection.

77 It was claimed by De Lancey Gill (1859-1940), a photographer for the Bureau of American Ethnology, that Indians preferred full-length, full face portraits 'with two eyes, and a whole mouth' shown. See Joanna Cohan Scherer, *A Danish photographer of Idaho Indians: Benedicte Wrensted*, University of Oklahoma Press, Norman, 2005 p.145 endnote 101.

78 See the description of the set of images in the Beinecke Library below.

79 Herbert Oliver Brayer, 'Exploring the Yellowstone with Hayden, 1872, Diary of Sidford Hamp', *Annals of Wyoming*, Volume 14, Number 4, October 1942 pp.253-298. Quotation from p.261.

A final over arching consideration is that to date it has not been possible to establish how many copies of these publications were made up, what constitutes the complete list of which individuals and institutions acquired them or whether the photographs were ever made commercially available. Since no related text publications ever appeared under the imprint of The Trustees of the Blackmore Museum, one must ask what indeed were the aims and objectives of this endeavour?

1865 BLACKMORE MUSEUM PORTFOLIO OF PHOTOGRAPHS

Blackmore prepared images for publication a mere two years after his first visit to the USA and these appeared in 1865. What inspired him to embark on such a venture remains unclear but it may have been the vacuum that had resulted from the failure of state funding for such a venture via either the Bureau of Indian Affairs of the Department of the Interior or the Smithsonian Institution.

An undated list of photographs in the British Museum entitled *Photographs of some of the principal chiefs of the North American Indians, Taken when they have visited Washington as Deputations from their Tribes. Probably Photographed from 1850 to 1863.* was published by The Trustees of the Blackmore Museum and represents the contents page of the 1865 Blackmore Museum portfolio publication of photographs. These images had all been taken by Julian Vannerson and Samuel Cohner of the studio of James E. McClees in Washington, D.C. The provenance of the photographs can be identified as from the studio of McClees from the distinctive floral design on the carpet on which each subject sits or stands. The list contains the names of thirty Native American Indian chiefs from eleven tribes. While the printed contents page gives a date range of 1850 to 1863, as mentioned previously, the photographs that were published by Blackmore were all taken by Vannerson and Cohner between 1857 and 1858 in the McClees Studio.[80]

Neither McCLees nor Vannerson received any printed credits in the 1865 Blackmore Museum publication. This was probably due

80 BM, A30/1715-44.

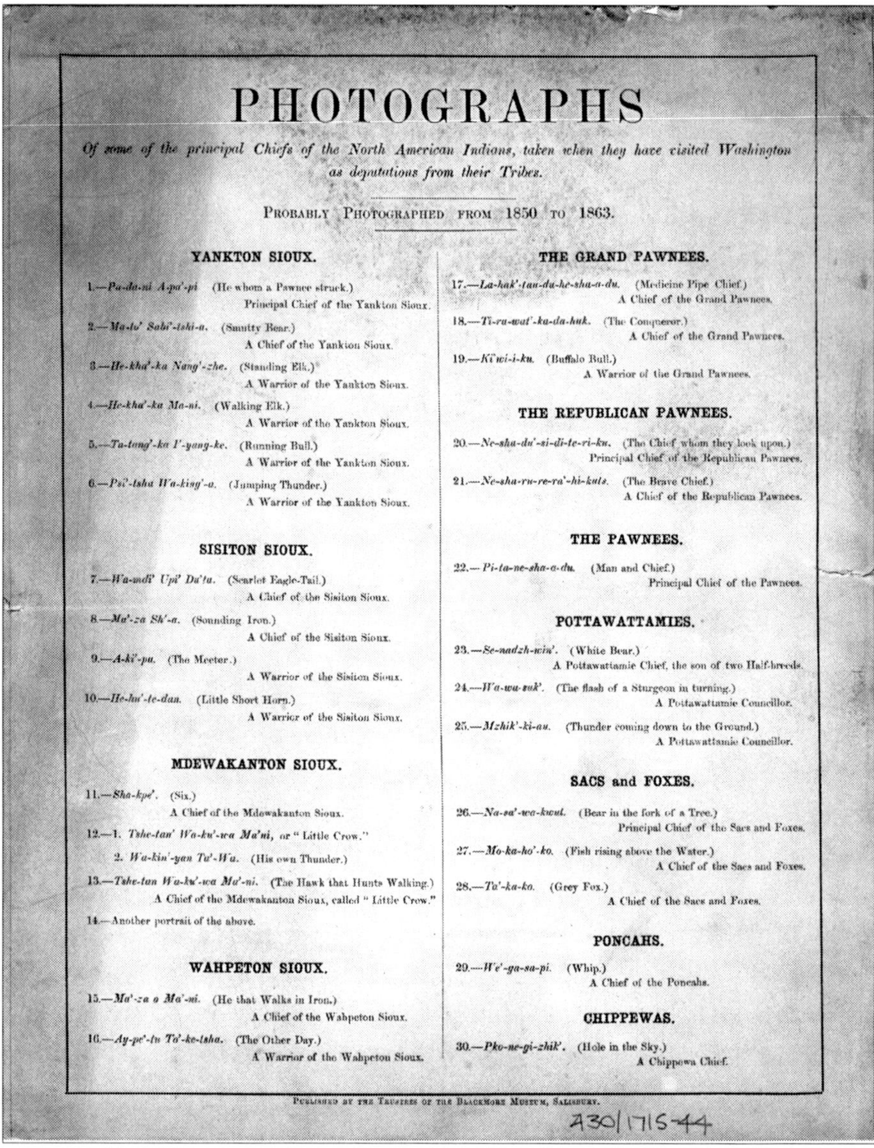

PHOTOGRAPHS

Of some of the principal Chiefs of the North American Indians, taken when they have visited Washington as deputations from their Tribes.

PROBABLY PHOTOGRAPHED FROM 1850 TO 1863.

YANKTON SIOUX.

1.—*Pa-da-ni A-pa'-pi* (He whom a Pawnee struck.)
Principal Chief of the Yankton Sioux.

2.—*Ma-to' Sabi'-tshi-a.* (Smutty Bear.)
A Chief of the Yankton Sioux.

3.—*He-kha'-ka Nang'-zhe.* (Standing Elk.)
A Warrior of the Yankton Sioux.

4.—*He-kha'-ka Ma-ni.* (Walking Elk.)
A Warrior of the Yankton Sioux.

5.—*Ta-tang'-ka I'-yang-ke.* (Running Bull.)
A Warrior of the Yankton Sioux.

6.—*Psi'-tsha Wa-king'-a.* (Jumping Thunder.)
A Warrior of the Yankton Sioux.

SISITON SIOUX.

7.—*Wa-mdi' Upi' Du'ta.* (Scarlet Eagle-Tail.)
A Chief of the Sisiton Sioux.

8.—*Ma'-za Sh'-a.* (Sounding Iron.)
A Chief of the Sisiton Sioux.

9.—*A-ki'-pa.* (The Meeter.)
A Warrior of the Sisiton Sioux.

10.—*He-hu'-te-dan.* (Little Short Horn.)
A Warrior of the Sisiton Sioux.

MDEWAKANTON SIOUX.

11.—*Sha-kpe'.* (Six.)
A Chief of the Mdewakanton Sioux.

12.—1. *Tshe-tan' Wa-ku'-wa Ma'ni*, or "Little Crow."
2. *Wa-kin'-yan Tu'-Wa.* (His own Thunder.)

13.—*Tshe-tan Wa-ku'-wa Ma'-ni.* (The Hawk that Hunts Walking.)
A Chief of the Mdewakanton Sioux, called "Little Crow."

14.—Another portrait of the above.

WAHPETON SIOUX.

15.—*Ma'-za o Ma'-ni.* (He that Walks in Iron.)
A Chief of the Wahpeton Sioux.

16.—*Ay-pe'-tu To'-ke-tsha.* (The Other Day.)
A Warrior of the Wahpeton Sioux.

THE GRAND PAWNEES.

17.—*La-hak'-tau-du-he-sha-a-du.* (Medicine Pipe Chief.)
A Chief of the Grand Pawnees.

18.—*Ti-ra-wat'-ka-da-huk.* (The Conqueror.)
A Chief of the Grand Pawnees.

19.—*Ki'wi-i-ku.* (Buffalo Bull.)
A Warrior of the Grand Pawnees.

THE REPUBLICAN PAWNEES.

20.—*Ne-sha-du'-si-di-te-ri-ku.* (The Chief whom they look upon.)
Principal Chief of the Republican Pawnees.

21.—*Ne-sha-ru-re-ra'-hi-kuts.* (The Brave Chief.)
A Chief of the Republican Pawnees.

THE PAWNEES.

22.—*Pi-ta-ne-sha-a-du.* (Man and Chief.)
Principal Chief of the Pawnees.

POTTAWATTAMIES.

23.—*Se-nadzh-win'.* (White Bear.)
A Pottawatiamie Chief, the son of two Half-breeds.

24.—*Wa-wu-suk'.* (The flash of a Sturgeon in turning.)
A Pottawattamie Councillor.

25.—*Mzhik'-ki-au.* (Thunder coming down to the Ground.)
A Pottawattamie Councillor.

SACS and FOXES.

26.—*Na-sa'-wa-kwut.* (Bear in the fork of a Tree.)
Principal Chief of the Sacs and Foxes.

27.—*Mo-ka-ho'-ko.* (Fish rising above the Water.)
A Chief of the Sacs and Foxes.

28.—*Ta'-ka-ko.* (Grey Fox.)
A Chief of the Sacs and Foxes.

PONCAHS.

29.—*We'-ga-sa-pi.* (Whip.)
A Chief of the Poncahs.

CHIPPEWAS.

30.—*Pko-ne-gi-zhik'.* (Hole in the Sky.)
A Chippewa Chief.

PUBLISHED BY THE TRUSTEES OF THE BLACKMORE MUSEUM, SALISBURY.

PHOTOGRAPHS Of some of the principal Chiefs of the North American Indians, taken when they have visited Washington as deputations from their Tribes. PROBABLY PHOTOGRAPHED FROM 1850 to 1863. Published by The Trustees of the Blackmore Museum, Salisbury [1865]
Blackmore Collection Album 30
Courtesy of The Trustees of the British Museum

to the fact that Blackmore had purchased the photographic glass plate negatives of the photographic studio of Robert W. Addis (d.1874), who in turn had acquired them when he had taken over the studio of James Earle McClees.[81] Blackmore possibly considered that as the owner of the negatives the copyright was his.[82] The precise date when Blackmore acquired the negatives is not known but it was presumably during his 1863 visit to Washington since Addis appears to have closed his establishment in 1864 and moved to San Francisco.[83] It was not until 1867 that Antonio Zeno Shindler (1823-1899), acquired the Addis Gallery and it was around this time, probably during his second visit to the USA in 1868, that Blackmore hired him. Thus to all intents and purposes this 1865 publication is a reissue of McClees' 'Indian Gallery' of 1859.

Only one of the portraits is a full length standing portrait – Tshe-tan Wa-Ku'wa Ma'-ni, (The Hawk that Hunts Walking, or Little Cow) (1810-1863), a chief of the Mdewakanton Dakota. The remaining twenty-nine portraits depict the sitters in a chair, probably the result of technical considerations such as the sitters keeping still while long camera exposures took place.A full set of these images is contained in the 'Ethnology' album in the Salisbury & South Wiltshire Museum, though this album contains only mounted, uncaptioned prints.

The production of this 1865 publication raises central considerations about Blackmore's photographic publications since it would appear that like the 1871 and 1872 publications it was produced in the USA. The negatives acquired by Blackmore from Addis in 1863 never found their way to England, though it is probable that William did have copy prints made – possibly by Shindler – to examine at his home in Shepley House or his museum in Salisbury. Who printed the

81 A manuscript note by Blackmore in Album 37 from his collection, now held in the Department of Africa, Oceania and the Americas, British Museum refers to the purchase from Addis.

82 I thank Paul Richardson Fleming for this insight. Email to the author 2nd June 2010.

83 For a short biography of Addis see Peter E. Palmquist and Thomas R. Kailbourn, *Pioneer Photographers of the Far West: A Biographical Dictionary, 1840-1865*, Stanford University Press, 2002 p.79.

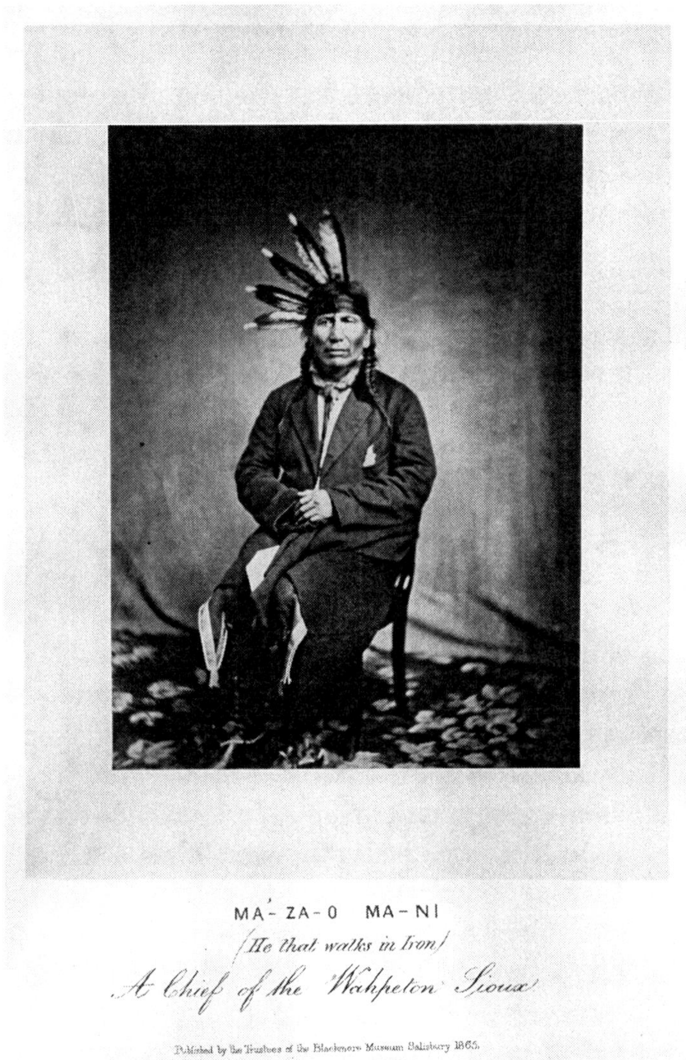

Ma-za-o Ma-ni (He that walks in Iron) A chief of the Wahpeton Sioux.
Photographed 1857-1858 by Julian Vannerson and Samuel A. Cohner at the James E. McClees Studio, Washington D.C.
Plate 15 of *PHOTOGRAPHS Of some of the principal Chiefs of the North American Indians, taken when they have visited Washington as deputations from their Tribes. PROBABLY PHOTOGRAPHED FROM 1850 to 1863.* Published by The Trustees of the Blackmore Museum, Salisbury [1865]
Blackmore Collection Album 35
Courtesy of The Trustees of the British Museum

captioned mounts and printed contents list and then assembled the publication remains unknown but production was probably undertaken entirely in Washington, D.C.

How many copies of the 1865 portfolio were produced and how extensively they were distributed may never be established. Very few examples have been located and the assumption is that they were made up in an *ad hoc* manner and distributed probably on a case by case basis to either individuals or institutions. There are two identical sets of the 1865 portfolio assembled by Blackmore himself in the collections of the Pitt Rivers Museum in Oxford. One set was sent to Edward Burnett Tylor (1832-1917), a founding figure of the science of social, or cultural anthropology, by Blackmore and is inscribed 'a gift from Wm. Blackmore.'[84] In 1855 Tylor had travelled to the United States and spent several months exploring the Mississippi river valley. The following year he met Henry Christy on an omnibus in Havana, Cuba and became interested in anthropology. It is unclear whether Tylor formed a significant collection of photographs.

The other set was donated to the Pitt Rivers Museum by the Salisbury, South Wilts and Blackmore Museum by its 'controller', Frank Stevens, in 1933.[85] In both sets, many mount cards do have the letterpress captions and Trustees of the Blackmore Museum imprint underneath, but a number do not. Both sets have the printed list of sitters. The Newberry Library has thirteen photographs from this publication and the British Museum has twelve.

The 'gift' of a set of photographs to Edward Burnett Tylor begs the question as to which other individuals and institutions received such donations from William Blackmore. This remains unresolved though clues are likely to be found in the names of professional colleagues

84 I thank Chris Morton, Curator of Photographs and Manuscripts, Pitt Rivers Museum for this information. Email to author 30th March, 2010.

85 I thank Elizabeth Edwards and Chris Morton for this information. The papers of Henry Balfour at the Pitt-Rivers Museum in Oxford includes S14 – a typed letter from Frank Stevens, Salisbury, South Wilts and Blackmore Museum, 8th August 1933 referring to his sending a series of Native American photographs (1998.129) belonging to William Blackmore for the Museum. Stevens also sent a further photograph of 'Flint Jack' (Edward Simpson).

referred to in Blackmore's opening address of the Blackmore Museum and the list of those individuals and institutions who had donated items to the museum as listed in Stevens' 1870 *Flint Chips* catalogue. Tracing extant copies of the photographs and establishing their provenance has proved to be a frustratingly unrewarding task for historians.

As regards the reception of the 1865 set one is again faced with a blank. The photographs were not sold commercially. No reviews have been found or mention in either primary or secondary sources. Similarly, they do not appear to have been exhibited. If William Blackmore was undertaking this publication as a discrete market testing exercise then it appears to have been on such a small scale that he can have learned little. For the next five years following his 1865 publication Blackmore does not seem to have had any scheme to publish further photographs though he continued to collect examples when in the USA.

Three years after the 1865 Blackmore Museum's first original photograph publication appeared, William made his first trip to the 'Great West'. He for first time saw and met with Native Americans in their habitat. Significantly, he became aware of a range of photographers located in the West who had documented Native Americans and thus he had direct access to a wide range of commercially available photographs. He availed the opportunity to exploit both sources. In September 1868 he was in Omaha, Nebraska and ordered two dozen photographs of North American Indians and local views from the local photographer Jackson Brothers. One of the Jacksons was William Henry, who had settled in Omaha the previous year and set up in business with his brother Ed. William Henry Jackson would subsequently be part funded by Blackmore to accompany the Englishman and Hayden on Hayden's 1872 expedition to the Yellowstone area. As mentioned previously, Blackmore subsequently formed a now lost collection of Jackson's views of Yellowstone.

While on his expedition through the 'Great West' during the autumn of 1868 Blackmore began outlining his vision for a substantial photographic publication. Earlier that year *The People of India. A series of photographic illustrations, with descriptive letterpress, of the races and tribes of Hindustan, (by Meadows Taylor,) originally prepared under the authority of the Government of India, and reproduced by order of the Secretary of State for India ... Edited by J. F. Watson and J. W. Kaye.* published by W.H. Allen and Co. of London began publication. It was to appear in eight volumes between 1868 and 1875. Suggestions for this publication had been made by John Forbes Watson (1827-1892), Reporter for the Products of India at the India Office, in a memorandum to his colleague John William Kaye (1814-1876), secretary of the political and secret department of the India Office, dated 18th July 1863. Two years later its impending publication was mentioned in the periodical press.[86] Though it is unclear whether Blackmore had seen this reference or had been influenced by it, the commencement of publication of *The People of India* triggered him to use this publication as a template for a series of North American Indian portrait volumes.

Blackmore noted in his diary in October 1868 his intention was to publish a set of six to ten volumes of 'Photographs of North American Indians' with fifty photographs in each. The 'Intention to devote 6 to 8 photos to each tribe.' Significantly, Blackmore noted that the prints should be printed using the Carbon print process 'so as not to fade.' The series was to cost around two Guineas per set and would be limited to an edition of three hundred copies, one hundred of which were destined for the USA. Blackmore noted 'To be similar to photos of aboriginal Tribes in India' – a clear reference to Watson and Kaye's *The People of India.* The letter press was to be by both Blackmore and Ferdinand Hayden.[87] Later on this trip, Blackmore noted a proposed 'Book of photographs of N. A. Americans'. 'Photograph[s] to be by Gardner [i.e. Alexander Gardner]' [88]

While Blackmore was aware of the instability of photographic prints made by the Albumen process, he did not avail himself of other photographic processes such as photolithography. In 1867 George

86 India Office Records/L/E/6/37, item 39 in the Oriental and India Office Collections, British Library, and *Athenæum*, No.1945, 4th February, 1865 p.165 ('Our Weekly Gossip' – mention of publication 'this summer' 400 photographs in five volumes).

87 Blackmore Diary No.17 p.16. The entry is dated to around 18th October when Blackmore was near Laramie, Wyoming.

88 Blackmore Diary No.17 p.39.

Catlin's *O-kee-pa, a Religious Cermony and Other Customs of the Mandans* had been published by Trübner and Co. in London and in an American edition of the same year by J.B. Lippincott of Philadelphia. The thirteen illustrations were coloured photolithographs by Simonau & Toovey of Brussels. With his other contacts with leaders in photomechanical printing, such as William Griggs, Blackmore was interested in learning more about the possibilities, but yet again did not drive to a definitive conclusion the consideration as to which photographic process best met his aims and objectives.

Blackmore's focus from the time of his 1868 trip to the USA was primarily on assisting the Smithsonian Institution in building its photographic archive. In this year some three hundred photographs from his collection were loaned to the Smithsonian and Shindler was employed to copy these images. These led to the display in 1869 of 301 photographs that comprised the first photographic exhibition at the Smithsonian that are listed in the associated catalogue *Photographic Portraits of North American Indians in the Gallery of the Smithsonian.* Whether this project directly impacted on Blackmore's plans for further publications by the Trustees of the Blackmore Museum remains unclear.

1871 BLACKMORE MUSEUM PORTFOLIO OF PHOTOGRAPHS

Curiously, given Blackmore's exposure to the 'Great West' on his trip in the autumn of 1868 and his acquisition of a wide range of photographs of Native Americans, this did not significantly change the style or coverage of the publications of the Trustees of the Blackmore Museum. His plans for a large-scale publication outlined in his 1868 diary were not Blackmore's next publishing venture.

In 1871 a second series of photographs was published by the Trustees of the Blackmore Museum. This differed significantly from the 1865 publication since the photographs were the result of what appears to have been a specific commission from Blackmore. This set records the chiefs of the Cheyenne, Arapaho, and Wichita who, on their return home from a delegation visit to Washington, D.C. in May 1871, were given a grand reception at the Cooper Institute in New York on the 1st June to which Blackmore was invited. Blackmore arranged for them to be photographed at the studio of Jeremiah Gurney & Son in Fifth Avenue later that month. Quite why Blackmore did not commission photographs to be taken in Washington, D.C. has yet to be established.

While again the photographs were mounted on heavier stock with printed captions and credits, no printed title page or list of contents has been located for this series. All photographs are approximately 5¾ x $4^7/_8$ inch Albumen prints mounted on 10 x 12 inch card indicating that Blackmore had not progressed his ideas on exploiting the Carbon print process. There are printed captions and credits including 'Photographed June 1871, by J. Gurney & Son, Fifth Avenue, New York, for the Trustees of the Blackmore Museum, Salisbury'. This is significant in as much as the caption details the date of creation, which was unusual. One may presume that Gurney produced the photographic prints and Blackmore arranged for the printing of the mounts.

It is unknown how many photographs formed this 1871 Blackmore Museum publication. From the photographs from this set that have been located four sitters have been identified. There are eight photographs in the British Museum (Blackmore Collection), twelve photographs in the Beinecke Library at Yale University, four photographs in the Blackmore Collection in Santa Fe and a set of twelve photographs was offered by Cowan's auction house in 2005.[89] Significantly, there are four views per sitter for two of the identified sitters; 'Bird Chief' and 'Buffalo Goad.' These are made up of a full face and profile view in both full length and half length.Whether this convention was established by Gurney or as a result of the instruction of William Blackmore is unknown.

If Blackmore had been aware that his 1865 publication was in essence a reissue of Vannerson and Cohner's photographs for McClees' Indian Gallery he does not seem to have made any significant attempt to market and promote the photographs by Gurney as a unique Blackmore Museum publication. Again, the photographs do not appear to have

89 *Historic Americana* 16th, 17th & 18th November 2005 lot 692. Sold for US$40,250. In 1849 Jeremiah Gurney (1812-1886) opened the first photograph gallery in the USA at 189 Broadway, New York.

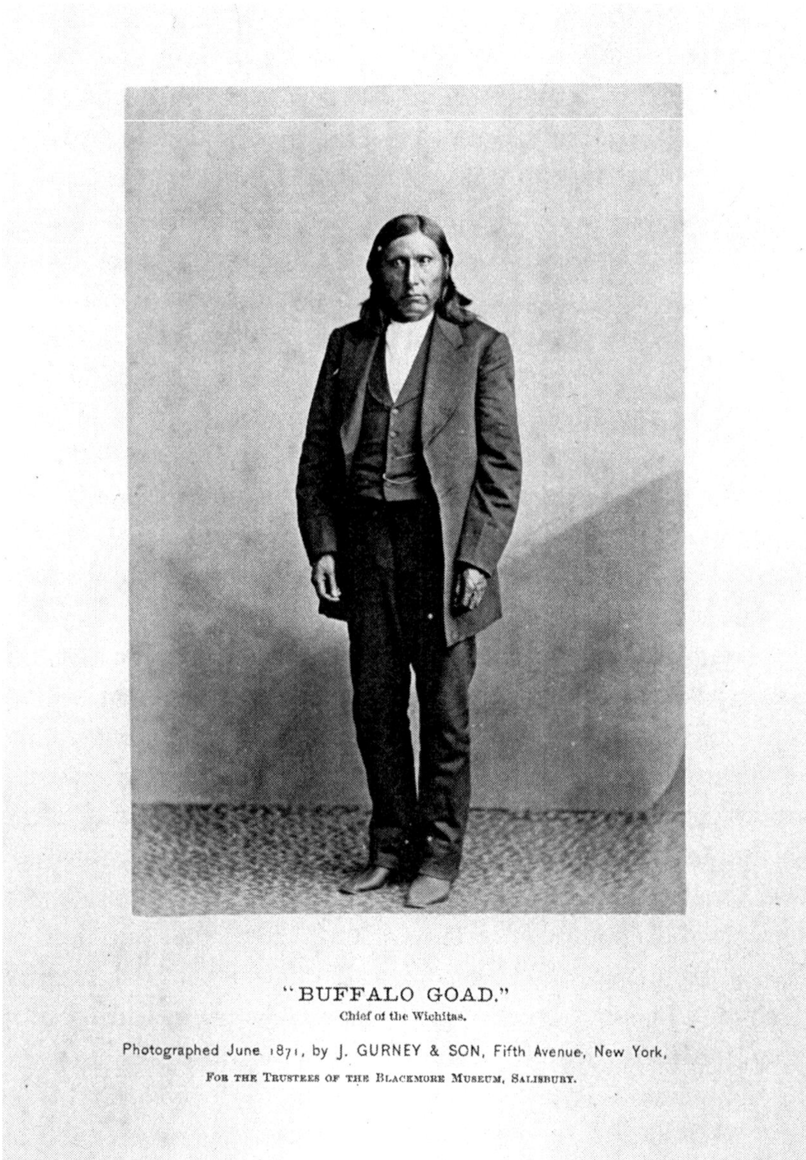

Buffalo Goad,
Chief of the Wichitas 1871
Photographed (full face) "June 1871, by J. Gurney & Son,
Fifth "Avenue, New York.
Albumen print
Blackmore Collection Album 30
Courtesy of The Trustees of the British Museum

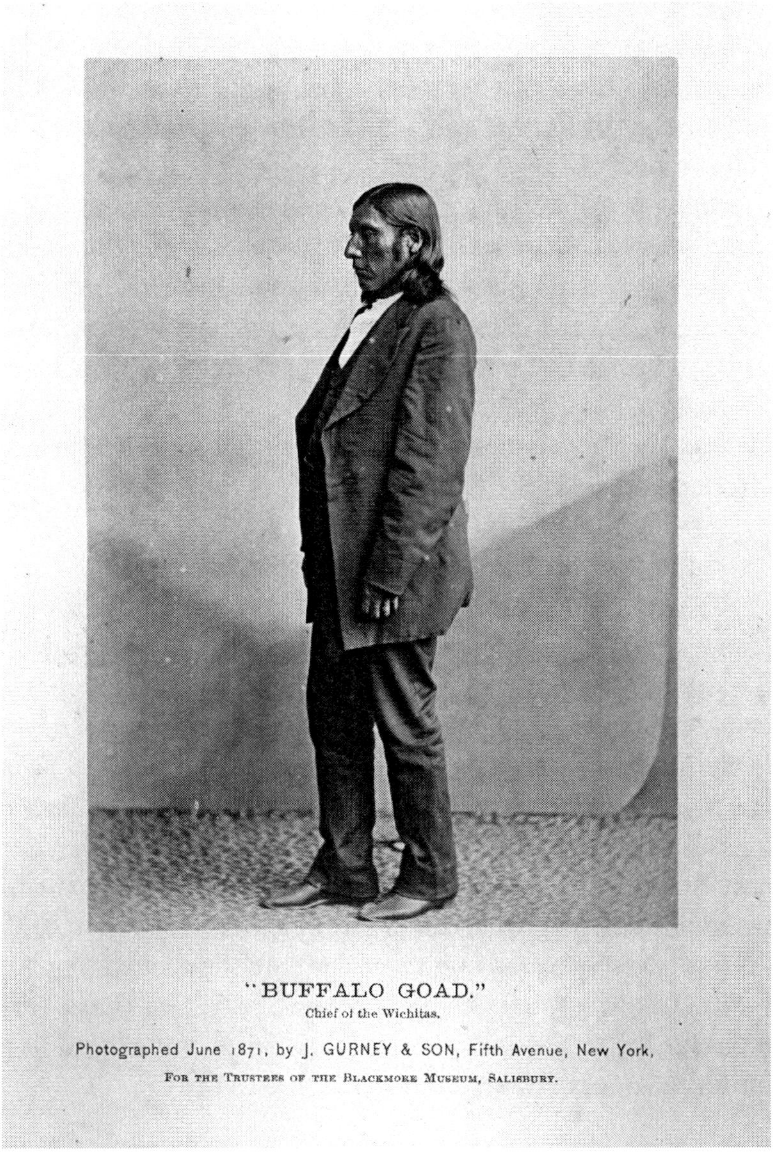

Buffalo Goad,
Chief of the Wichitas 1871
Photographed (in profile) "June 1871, by J. Gurney & Son,
Fifth Avenue, New York."
Albumen print
Blackmore Collection Album 30
Courtesy of The Trustees of the British Museum

been made commercially available, no record has been found that they were exhibited and no contemporary reviews have been found. However, the photographs from this set were subsumed into the collections of the Smithsonian Institution and would subsequently appear in albums created by or for Ferdinand Hayden.

Another possible publication was under consideration in 1871 as Blackmore was in contact with George Catlin discussing the possibility of reproducing through photography some two hundred images from Catlin's second Indian Gallery. Catlin discussed the use of some of the possible permanent and photomechanical processes by then available, but this came to nothing.[90] This proposed publication will be discussed in more detail in the chapter on Blackmore, the Smithsonian Institution, Richard Dodge and Catlin.

1872 BLACKMORE MUSEUM PORTFOLIO OF PHOTOGRAPHS

The most substantial photographic publications of the Trustees of the Blackmore Museum appeared in 1872 and parallels the height of Blackmore's influence in Washington, D.C. This was also a period in which Blackmore's disposable income was at its apogee and he could indulge himself in his publishing ventures. By this date Ferdinand Hayden had taken increasing responsibility for the archive of photographs of North American Indians and also arranged for photographs of the visiting Indian delegates to be taken in studios in Washington, D.C.

It has been estimated that some ten portfolios containing around two hundred and forty-one photographs were published by the Trustees of the Blackmore Museum as part of a series that commenced in 1872. The Smithsonian Institution online catalogue states;

> In 1872, the Office of Indian Affairs contracted Gardner to photograph the American Indian delegates to Washington, D.C. These images, representing nineteen tribes, were then compiled by English collector William Henry Blackmore into ten albums and exhibited at the

90 George Catlin to Blackmore 12th December, 1871. Fray Angélico Chávez History Library Blackmore 0407. As cited in Dippie (1991) p.523 endnote 77.

Smithsonian. The original negatives were eventually transferred to the Bureau of American Ethnology and then the Smithsonian Institution.[91]

To date no publicly published record has been found of the exhibition of the ten albums at the Smithsonian though this does not imply that they did not exist.

The photographs for the 1872 series were taken by Alexander Gardner in the photographer's Washington, D.C. studio. It is likely that Blackmore either formally commissioned them or came to a contractual arrangement with Gardner to publish a selection of photographs under the imprint of the Trustees of the Blackmore Museum. The existence of multiple views of the same sitter – in some cases there are at least four portraits of most of these Indian leaders – followed the convention used by Gurney for Blackmore's 1871 publication. The photographs measure 5 ¼ x 4 inches on mounts 12 x 10 inches – yet again Albumen rather than Carbon prints – and were separately mounted within highly decorated coloured lithographed and 'gilt' frames in the same design as Gardner's own publications. Some images have printed captions and credits. Title pages and contents pages are known for a number of titles in this series which represented the most deluxe format of Blackmore's publications.

Piecing together the different portfolios that made up the 1872 publications of the Trustees of the Blackmore Museum is complex and may never be achieved. However, it is worth noting what can be deduced from existing material.

What appears to be the first publication in the series was *Photographs of Red Cloud and Principal Chiefs of Dacotah Indians taken on their visit to Washington, D. C., May, 1872 by Alex. Gardner for Trustees of Blackmore Museum, Salisbury, England*; it contains a printed title page and a printed Contents page.[92] The title page was printed by Gibson Brothers of

91 Paula Fleming stated this number in her catalogue entry for the portfolio of *Red Cloud & His Braves* auctioned by Cowan in December 2007. See endnote 78. However, a definitive list of these ten portfolios has yet to be fully established. See the Smithsonian online catalogue for catalogue number P10142.

92 The copy in the Beinecke Library at Yale University has thirty-one photographs, WA Photos 394. MIT has a copy with thirty-one photographs, E89.G226 1872, stating that seven plates are missing. A copy in the Cincinnati Historical Society Library

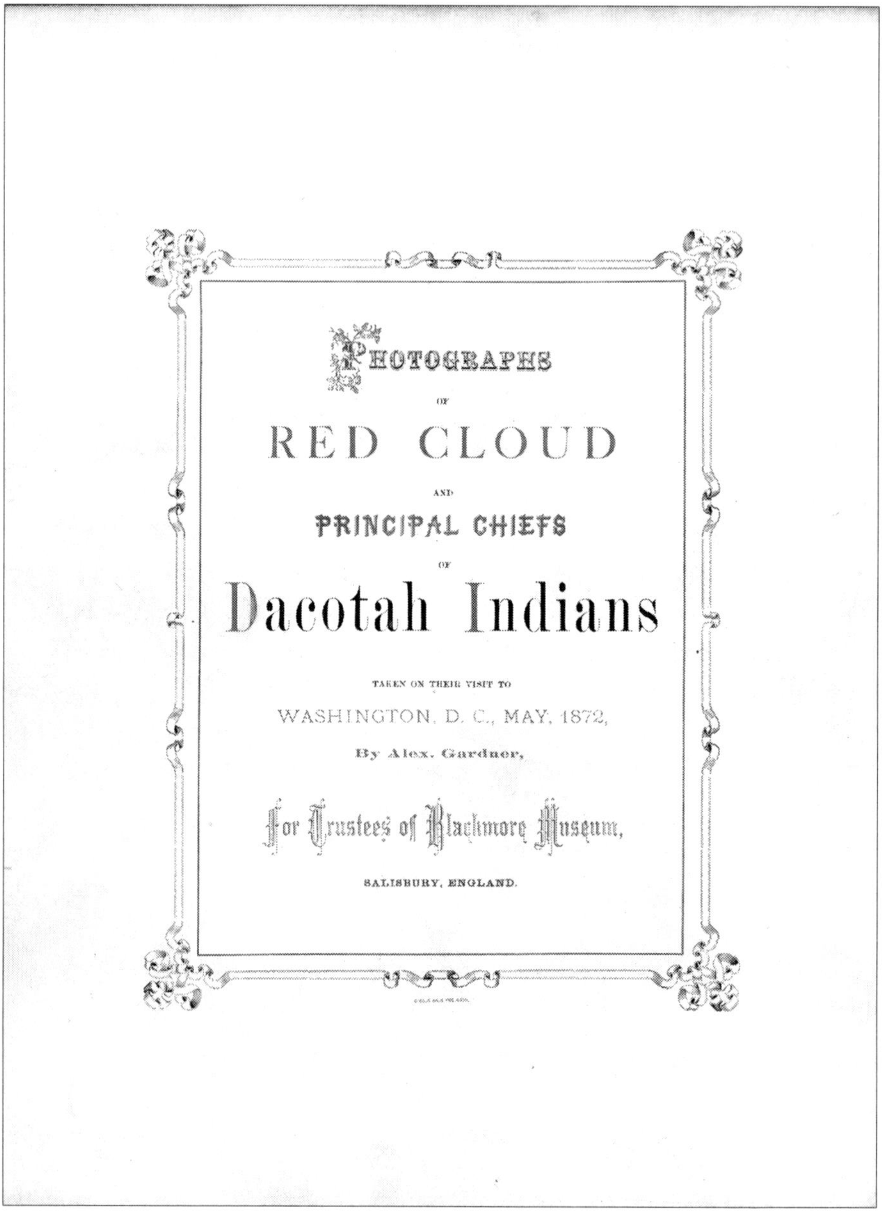

PHOTOGRAPHS

OF

RED CLOUD

AND

PRINCIPAL CHIEFS

OF

Dacotah Indians

TAKEN ON THEIR VISIT TO

WASHINGTON, D. C., MAY, 1872,

By Alex. Gardner,

For Trustees of Blackmore Museum,

SALISBURY, ENGLAND.

Printed title page of *Photographs of Red Cloud and Principal Chiefs of Dacotah Indians taken on their visit to Washington, D.C., May 1872, By Alex. Gardner, for Trustees of Blackmore Museum, Salisbury, England.*
Blackmore Collection Album 1
Courtesy of The Trustees of the British Museum

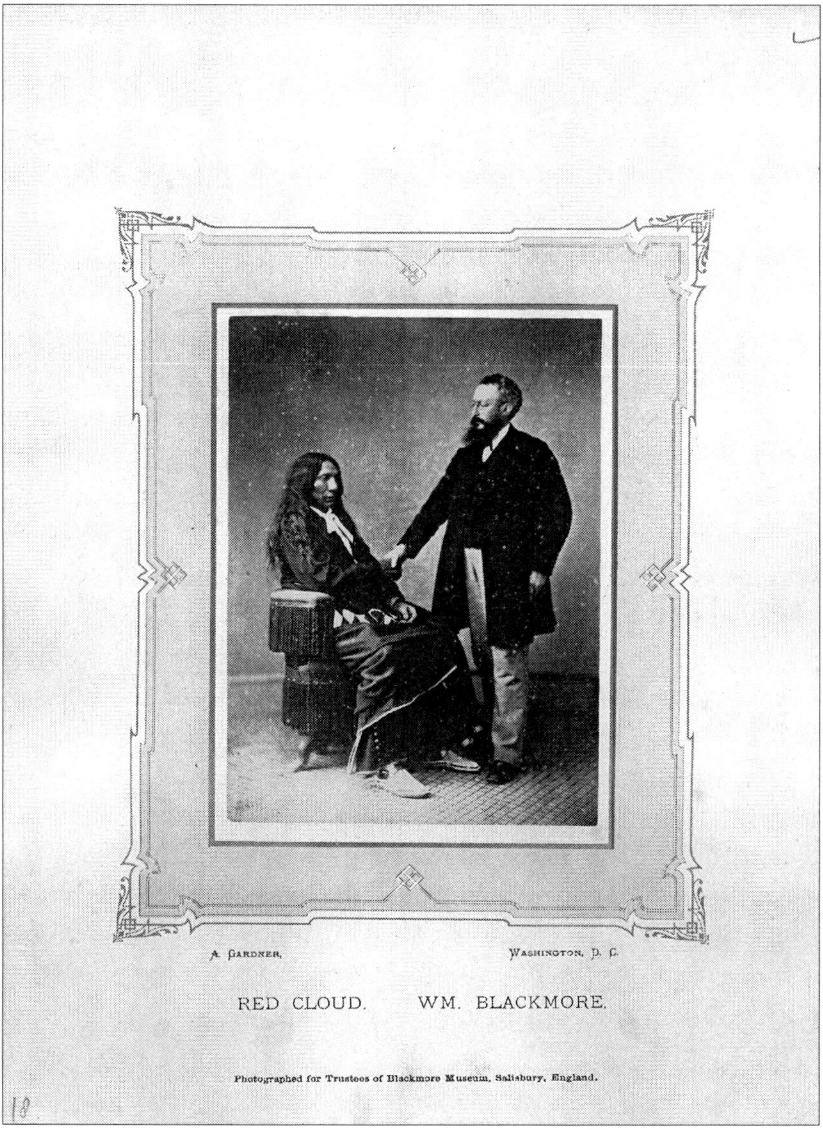

Red Cloud (Ma-kpe-ah-lou- tah) & William Blackmore from *Photographs of Red Cloud and Principal Chiefs of Dacotah Indians taken on their visit to Washington, D.C., May 1872, By Alex. Gardner, for Trustees of Blackmore Museum, Salisbury, England.*
Albumen print
Blackmore Collection Album 1
Courtesy of The Trustees of the British Museum

Washington, D.C.[93] The list of seventeen sitters plus the double portrait of Blackmore with Red Cloud is printed within a standard Gardner litho-printed mount. However, the images are not numbered in the Contents list and there is no printed credit to the Blackmore Museum on the list. The copy of this list in the British Museum has been annotated by William Blackmore in pencil numbering the photographs '1' to '18'. The mounts of the prints themselves do contain a credit 'Photographed for [the] Trustees of [the] Blackmore Museum.' However, there is no printed date of creation as there was on mounts of photographs of the 1871 publication.

The Blackmore Collection in the British Museum contains a number of Contents pages that match the standard Gardner litho-printed mount format. One of these lists nine plates numbered 18 to 26. It has the printed credits of Alexander Gardner. The page has been annotated in pencil by Blackmore 'Apaches of Arizona.'[94] No title page has been located for this publication.

Another Contents page in the British Museum has twenty-one plates numbered 27 to 47, that is the continuation of the numbered series. It has the printed credits of Alexander Gardner. The page has been annotated in pencil by Blackmore 'Brulé Sioux'.[95] The Beinecke Library holds ten images from this series dating to around June 1872– including Black Crow (Kan-Gah-Sa-Pah), Charge On The Hawk (Tske-Tan-Vua-Tak-Pah), Spotted Tail (Tshin-Tah-Ge-Las-Kah), Swift Bear (Ma-To-Lousah), Two Strike (Num-Ka-Chpah), White Eyes (Ish-Tah-Skah), and White Thunder (Vua-Ke-Ah-Skah). Unusually for the photographs in the Blackmore Museum publication there are images of Brulé women.

also has thirty-one photographs, R.B. 970.2 G226, 1872. There is a copy of this title containing thirty-four photographs in the Huntington Library, callmark 422000. This copy was acquired at an auction of Sotheby Parke-Bernet, 19th June 1973 lot 343.The copy in Cornell University Library was originally owned by William Henry Jackson and has thirty-five photographs, E99.D1 G22 ++ as does the copy in the Library of Congress , LOT 11790 (H) [P&P] (a copy previously owned by President James A. Garfield (1831-1881)).

93 It would appear that all the publications of the Trustees of the Blackmore Museum were created in their entirety in the USA.

94 BM, AN605096001.

95 BM, AN605083001.

These consist of the individual, but unnamed, 'squaws' of Spotted Tail, Thigh (Tsheh-Sha-Lah), and Two Strike.[96] Again, no title page has been found for this publication.

A third Contents page in the British Museum has four plates numbered 121 to 124. It has the printed credits of Alexander Gardner. This set records leaders from the Ute tribe.[97] Yet again, no title page has been found for this publication.

Another, but incomplete, Blackmore Museum publication was offered at auction by Cowan's in 2007. *Yanctonai, Sans Arc, Blackfeet & Uncpapa Sioux under charge of Col. J. C. O'Connor, U.S. Agent, taken during their visit to Washington, D.C. September 20, 1872 by Alexander Gardner for the Trustees of the Blackmore Museum, Salisbury,* printed by Gibson Brothers Press, Washington. The contents page of this publication listed fourteen sitters – each with two poses.[98] Three of the photographs are numbered; Running Antelope (51), Bear Ribs (52) and Thunder Hawk (53). The session at Gardner's studio at which these Indian leaders were photographed was noted in the *Washington Evening Star* on 20th September, 1872;

> Real American Red Men. The Sioux chiefs, and their party . . . are at least as noble specimens of savage and hardy nature as have ever yet visited the cities of the pale face. Any first-class artist or sculptor would never tire of their powerful and massive forms, the gnarly and luxuriant amplitude of their limbs and chests, and the antique and homely fascination of their physiognomies, calling to mind the best profiles of Egyptian and Assyrian antiquities, but more splendid even than they, and in some respects ahead even of the Greek, and absolutely unapproachable as pronounced aboriginal portraits, with all the eloquence of silent but most vital expression, deep-cut lines, and the great eyes of the superior birds and animals. The inherent and athletic royalty of the man of the woods and mountains, amid all the general deprivations and squalor of

96 Yale University, Beinecke Rare Book and Manuscript Library, Call Number WA Photos 25. These photographs were purchased for the Beinecke Library from William Reese Co. on the Walter McClintock Memorial Fund, 1996.

97 BM, AN607023001.

98 Cowan, Western & Historic Americana, 6th and 7th December, 2007 lot 55a.

> the race, is triumphantly vindicated by these natural kings, in shapes that make the types and samples of our civilized manhood, in America and Europe, shriveled and puny in comparison . . . This forenoon the chiefs are being photographed at Gardner's establishment, on the avenue. They appeared just before noon in all their war-paint, bears' claws and eagles' feathers, with much scarlet cloth and fringe . . .[99]

The Beinecke Library at Yale University holds one of the most significant collections of photographs related to the Blackmore Museum publications, *Photographs of Indian delegations, consisting of Kiowas, Comanches, Apaches, Arrapahoes, Caddoes, Wichitas, Wacos, Keechies, Towoccaroes, and Delawares, under charge of Captain Henry E. Alvord, Special Indian Commissioner. Taken by Alex. Gardner, Washington*. This delegation visited Washington and New York in October 1872. The Beinecke copy has twenty-six photographs of which four have the printed credit of Trustees of the Blackmore Museum. The remaining twenty-two photographs are in the same format, within the same decorative frame. Another copy of this title with forty-four portraits of thirty-one Indians is held in the Massachusetts Institute of Technology (MIT) library.[100] The plates in this copy have printed numbers. The number range is from 80 to 120 though the MIT copy lacks plates 80, 82, 84, 94, 95, 97, 106, 111, 114, 177 and 120.

Another volume in the Beinecke is titled *Photographs of Teton Sioux Indian Delegation consisting of Oncapapa, Chawana, Cut-head and Tachana. Under Supervision of Maj. A. J. Simmons, U.S. Agent, taken by Alex. Gardner, Washington, D.C., 1872*. It contains thirty-six Albumen prints. This style and format is consistent with the Blackmore Museum publications on having a title page and the same standard frame for the list of Contents – with printed credits – which in this case has eighteen plates numbered 62 to 79.[101] This title evidences the fact that while

99 As cited in the Cowan's online catalogue entry accessed 10th August, 2010.

100 Callmark E89.G225 1872.

101 Yale University, Beinecke Rare Book and Manuscript Library, Call Number WA Photos 395. The copy was donated in 1899 by Professor Othniel Charles Marsh (1831-1899), Professor of Paleontology at Yale. Marsh was the nephew of George Peabody (1795-1869) and was influential in persuading his uncle to establish the Peabody

contents pages from Gardner's series of portraits do list the sitters, they do not necessarily indicate that there are multiple views of an individual sitter. This is complicated by the lack of printed numbers of the matching photographic mounts. One explanation might be that the mounted photographs were also made available as loose, unnumbered prints.

From the above one can deduce that at least one hundred and twenty-four photographs by Gardner were published though how they were split between Gardner's own imprint and that of the Blackmore Museum has yet to be established. Close examination of the photographs in the Blackmore Collection now held at the British Museum indicates that the images were part of a working and reference collection for the Englishman. They are extensively annotated in pencil in William's hand. No complete sets of the Blackmore Museum publications have been located and no evidence that the Museum itself ever held a complete set.

The Beinecke Library also holds an album with a manuscript title page – 'Photographs of Indians selected from the collection in the possession of the U.S. Geological Survey of the Territories / Prof. F.V. Hayden in charge. Representing 70 different tribes'. This album is from the Collection of William Robertson Coe (1869-1955) donated to Yale University in 1948. It contains some six hundred and sixteen photographs – mounted six to a page – and would appear to have been assembled in 1876-1877 from images in the collection of the United States Geological and Geographical Survey of the Territories. The images in the photographs were originally created between 1851 and 1876, and the Yale University Library catalogue states 'The images were created for ethnographic portfolios of the Blackmore Museum, Salisbury, England.'[102] The album does contain a print of Gardner's photograph of Blackmore with Red Cloud and others from the 1872 series, copies of some of Easterley's Daguerreotypes, photographs from the McClees studio series published in 1865 under the imprint of the Trustees of the Blackmore Museum

Museum of Natural History at Yale in 1866. In the same year Peabody funded the Peabody Museum of Archaeology and Ethnology at Harvard. It is possible that this album was a gift from William Blackmore to Marsh.

102 WA Photos Folio 54.

and the imprint's 1871 Gurney images. One may assume that this album was created partially from copy photographs made by Antonio Shindler from images loaned by Blackmore to the Smithsonian Institution.

Further evidence of the scale and scope of Blackmore's vision and his collaborative working relationship with the Smithsonian is found in the Prefatory Note to the *Descriptive Catalogue of Photographs of North American Indians by W. H. Jackson, Photographer of the* [Geological] *Survey* published in 1877 in which Ferdinand Hayden stated that there were some one thousand negatives and wrote that;

> The greater portion of the whole collection is derived from the munificent liberality of William Blackmore, esq. of London, England, the eminent anthropologist who has for many years studied closely the history, habits, and manners of the North American Indians. The Blackmore portion of the collection consists of a number of small lots from various sources; and it is Mr. Blackmore's intention to enlarge it to include, if possible, all the tribes of the North American continent.[103]

As with the 1871 publication the various photographs of the 1872 series do not appear to have been made commercially available, they were not exhibited and no contemporary reviews have been found. Which individuals and institutions received copies also remains unclear.

BLACKMORE'S USE OF PHOTOGRAPHY FOR BUSINESS VENTURES

By the late 1860s photography was being increasingly used to promote a variety of business interests aimed at exploiting the agricultural, mineral and commercial wealth of the American West. The parties included railway companies, those involved in land grants and a variety of government sponsored organizations.

Blackmore's interest in such images is reflected in a series of cartes de visites by the Salt Lake City photographer Charles William Carter (1832-1918) of buildings and industries in Utah around Little

103 W. H. Jackson, *Descriptive Catalogue of Photographs of North American Indians*, Government Printing Office, Washington, 1877 p.iv.

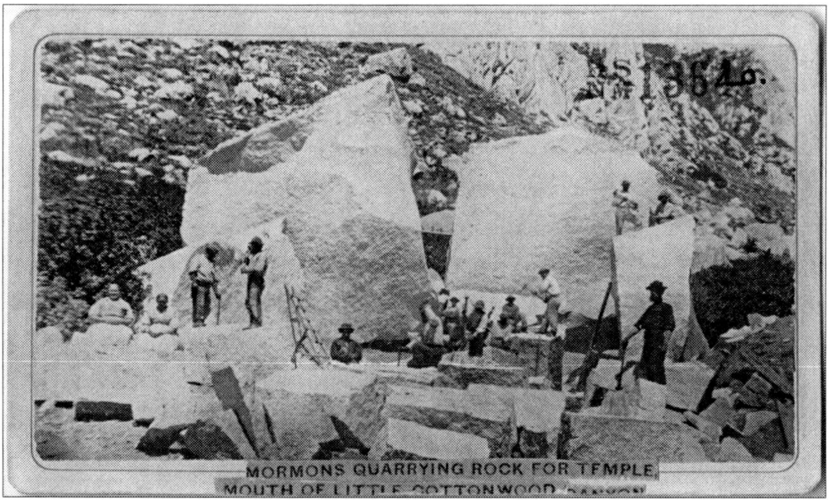

Charles William Carter.
Mormons Quarrying Rocks for Temple, Mouth of Little Cottonwood Canyon [Utah] 1870?
Carte de visite. Albumen print
Blackmore Collection
Courtesy Palace of the Governors Photo Archives , Santa Fe (NMHM/DCA), 065075

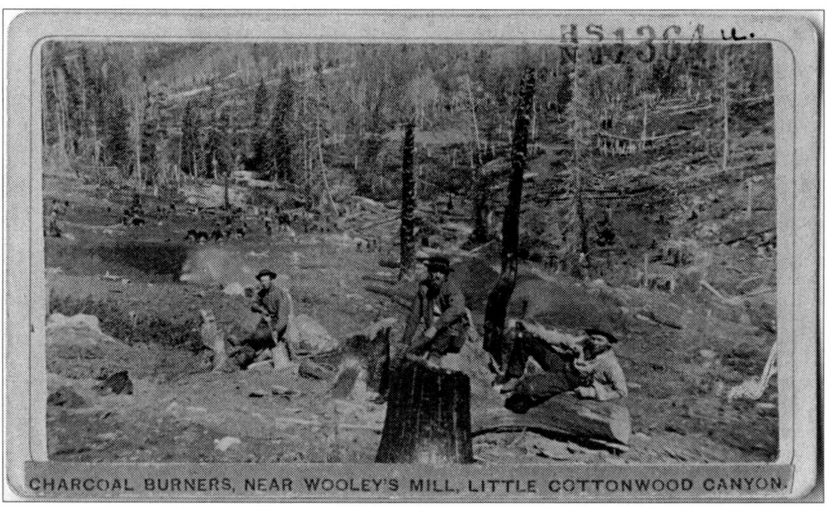

Charles William Carter.
Charcoal Burners near Wooley's Mill, Little Cottonwood Canyon [Utah] 1870?
Carte de visite. Albumen print
Blackmore Collection
Courtesy Palace of the Governors Photo Archives , Santa Fe (NMHM/DCA), 065069

Cottonwood Canyon, and the Emma Hill mine near Ophir City, South-West of Salt Lake City. These are now held in Santa Fe.

There are few clues as to what triggered Blackmore's interest in illustrating his business publications with photographs. In 1869 his *Colorado: Its Resources, Parks, and Prospects as a New Field for Emigration; with an account of the Trenchara and Costilla Estates, in the San Luis Park* was published in London. This is a substantial and complex publication that appeared in two 'editions'; a standard edition published by Sampson Low, Son, and Marston in London and a 'Privately Printed' edition. This was a book of two hundred and seventeen pages rather than the shorter pamphlets more associated with such 'booster' publications aimed at stimulating interest in land grants. It contained reports by a variety of authorities on the agricultural and mineral wealth of Colorado. Ferdinand Hayden, given the integrity of his scientific reputation, produced a curiously exaggerated survey to market the land grant's agricultural and mineral potential. However, this was the first and only time Hayden undertook such commercial work for Blackmore.

Both the editions and individual copies have different numbers of photographs. Copies with one, four, five, eight or twelve photographs have been noted. The private edition in two volumes – had a maximum of twelve photographs – and the trade edition by Sampson, Low, Son, and Marston of London, a maximum of five photographs. The most commonly found copies are the Sampson Low containing a single photograph, a frontispiece portrait of William Gilpin (1813-1894), first Governor of Colorado, that cost 15s. A survey of copies of both editions of this title held in public and academic libraries indicates that many are Blackmore presentation copies. E. G. Squier owned a copy and another was presented to the Library of Congress by B. Moran, the U.S. Secretary of Legation at London and an associate of Blackmore.[104]

The photographs selected by Blackmore were a mixture of views of streets and buildings in Denver and views of the Garden of the Gods and Monument Park, near Colorado Springs, best known for its geology and colorful sedimentary rock formations. What informed the selection

104 *Catalogue of the library of E. G. Squier*, 1876.

criteria is not clear. The following list of photographic illustrations is taken from a copy offered by William Reese Company in 2004 and represents the largest number of photographs found in any copy.

> 'Corner of F and Blake Streets, Denver,'
> 'Portrait of William Gilpin, Governor of Colorado,'
> 'Corner of Blake Street, Denver,'
> 'Platte Canon, to the South of Denver,'
> '7 Street, Denver, Looking towards Platte River,'
> 'View, Garden of the Gods, Colorado,'
> 'Episcopal Seminary, Denver,'
> 'View, Garden of the Gods, near Colorado City,'
> 'Corner of F and Holliday Streets, Denver,'
> 'Garden of the Gods, Colorado,'
> 'Sand Rocks in Monument Park, Colorado,'
> 'Big Rock, in Monument Park.'

The inclusion of city views would appear to be a ploy to encourage potential investors that while there were opportunities to exploit the rich and untapped agricultural and mineral resources of Colorado, civilisation, in the form of cities such as Denver, already existed.

Colorado: Its Resources, Parks, and Prospects was cited at the time of its publication in a number of journals in the Netherlands, Germany and France, three key target markets for Blackmore and his involvement in the United States Freehold Land and Emigration Company Limited – formed to encourage emigration, particularly from Holland and Germany.[105] However, while in 1869 Blackmore also published German and French language editions of short prospectus titles, he appears not to have produced photographically illustrated issues of *Colorado: Its Resources, Parks, and Prospects* in any foreign language editions. However, there is evidence that Blackmore subsequently used photography to

105 Such as a review by Reinhart Pieter Anne Dozy (1820-1883) in *De Gids: nieuwe vaderlandsche letteroefeningen*, 1871 p.193; *Zeitschrift der Gesellschaft für Erdkunde zu Berlin*, 1869 p.628 ; *Petermanns Mitteilungen*, 1870 p.119; *L'année géographique. Revue annuelle des voyages de terre et de mer ainsi que des explorations, missions, relations et publications diverses relatives aux sciences géographiques et ethnographiques*, 1870 p.168.

document other estates. Brayer referred to a photographer commissioned by Blackmore in 1871 being at work documenting the Costilla estate.[106]

There was almost universal scepticism from contemporary reviewers of *Colorado: Its Resources, Parks, and Prospect* as to the actual opportunities being described. In August 1869 the *Standard* newspaper of London followed this theme, though it did state;

> The book before us is a compilation from the reports and letters and works of many men of high scientific attainments and unexceptionable character, both in the United States and this country. But for this we should be inclined to deem the whole account exaggerated and highly coloured, if not fabulous.[107]

None of the reviews located by the author has included detailed reference to the photographic illustrations.

Blackmore may have acquired additional, but now lost, photographs of topography and industries in the 'Great West' but he did not exploit photography to illustrate any of his subsequent business publications and there are no references to his use of photography in business meetings.

THE DISPERSAL OF WILLIAM BLACKMORE'S PHOTOGRAPH COLLECTIONS

In the absence of a photograph register, the scale and scope of William Blackmore's multiple photographic collections at the time of his death and their ultimate fate may never be fully established. The collection was probably originally distributed across at least three sites; Washington,

106 Letter from Newell Vicary Squarey to Blackmore 27th October, 1871. As cited by Brayer, *op.cit.*, Volume I p.114. Newell Squarey (1813-1891) was the uncle of Andrew Tucker Squarey, Blackmore's partner in the Liverpool law firm of Duncan, Squarey and Blackmore. Newell was recorded as a wine merchant in the 1841 census of Barford St. Martin. He was elected a member of the Pharmaceutical Society in 1847. He became an experienced English stockraiser and was appointed resident assistant to William Gilpin (1813-1894), former Governor of Colorado and the Managing Director of the Costilla Estate. Newell Squarey is also recorded as having donated two stone and flint weapons from Jamaica to the Blackmore Museum. Edward Thomas Stevens, *Flint Chips, A Guide to Pre-Historic Archaeology*, Bell & Daldy, London; Brown and Co., Salisbury, 1870 p.239.

107 *The Standard*, Thursday 19th August, 1869 p.4.

D.C., the Blackmore Museum in Salisbury and his residences, such as Shepley House and then his apartment in Belgrave Mansions in London. Another consideration is the differentiation between the photographs that were considered part of the collections of the Blackmore Museum as opposed to William Blackmore's private collection.

As mentioned previously, a substantial number of copy prints and glass negatives remained in the Smithsonian Institution together with what appears to be all but one of Blackmore's collection of ten Daguerreotypes. These were integrated into the Smithsonian's holdings following Shindler completing his contract for Blackmore and the transfer of the photographic holdings of the Interior Department in 1879. The photographs originating from Blackmore's photographic collection became largely anonymous until Paula Fleming published her 'Shindler catalogue' in 2003. Whether other parts of the Blackmore photo collection remained in the USA is unknown.

The history of the Blackmore photograph collection in Salisbury during the period from 1878 until the death of his brother Humphrey in 1929 is one of dormant latency. It is assumed that some of the Blackmore photographs distributed between London and Salisbury were brought together in the Blackmore Museum. While the 1892 reference to the 'great series of photographs of American Indians' has been noted previously, no serious scholarly exploitation of the resource was to take place until a century after William Blackmore's death when Colin Taylor examined the collection in the British Museum and published his findings in 1980.[108]

With no specific interest in the ethnology of North American Indians and the comparatively unstructured nature of his brother's photographic collection it is possible that Humphrey Blackmore gave away some of his brother's photographs as gifts. These may be the source of some of the photographs originating from the Blackmore collections offered through auction houses and book dealers.

108 Colin Taylor, 'Ho, for the Great West!' Indians and buffalo, exploration and George Catlin: the West of William Blackmore' in Barry C. Johnson (ed.), *'Ho, for the Great West!' and other original papers to mark the 25th Anniversary of the English Westerner's Society*, Eatome Ltd. for the English Westerners' Society, London, 1980 pp.8-49.

After Humphrey Blackmore's death the vast majority of Blackmore's collection of photographs of North American natives was acquired by the British Museum following a decision made in February 1932 by the management and trustees of the Salisbury & South Wiltshire and Blackmore Museum.[109] The background as to how and why the set of one hundred and twelve photographs acquired by the State Historical Society of New Mexico was separated from the portfolios given to the British Museum remains unknown but probably reflects how fragmented the Blackmore's photograph collection had become by the 1930s and the delineation between the collections of the Blackmore Museum and William's own collection.[110]

Curiously, while Blackmore's donated photographs to a number of major institutions in the USA, such as the Smithsonian Institution and the Peabody Museum, he appears not to have donated photographs to the British Museum or the British Museum Library. The British Museum lists some fifty-seven artifacts donated by William Blackmore covering the years 1866 (some items came from the Squier and Davis collection), 1868 (again some of the Squier and Davis collection), 1872 (Santa Cruz islands and Pacific). Today, including the one thousand two hundred or so photographs, the British Museum has in excess of two thousand four hundred artifacts originating from the collections of William Blackmore and the Blackmore Museum.[111]

Another apparent anomaly is that the Blackmore Museum appears not to have held a complete set of its own photographic publications. Whether copies of these were amongst the three tons of books sent to auction in the 1934 as described in more detail in the chapter on the Blackmore Museum has yet to be established but it is unlikely that they would have been considered of any significant value since there was

109 Disposal Book of the Salisbury & South Wiltshire and Blackmore Museum No. 1 1928-1952. 24th February 1932, '*Photographs of North American Indians and miscellaneous. Notes, newspaper cuttings & pamphlets, ethnographical material & various North American objects. Bundle of spears etc. (Blackmore Museum) 1 paddle & small N. American implements*'.

110 I thank Tomas Jaehn of the Fray Angélico Chávez History Library for supplying a typescript descriptive list of these images.

111 See the British Museum Web site at http://www.britishmuseum.org/research.aspx.

little interest in such items at this time.

Nevertheless, there was what appears to have been a significant residue of William's photographic collections that remained in Salisbury after the major de-accessioning of the early 1930s, including the 'Ethnology' album still held at the Salisbury & South Wiltshire Museum, several carte de visite albums and other items. As mentioned previously, in 1933 Frank Stevens gifted a volume of the 1865 portfolio of Vannerson and Cohner photographs to the Pitt Rivers Museum in Oxford. Herbert Brayer wrote to Frank Stevens in May 1942 asking 'Incidentally, whatever happened to Mr. Blackmore's fine collection of Indian photographs?'[112] Presumably Stevens explained that the bulk had been acquired by British Museum. Yet there were other volumes of photographs still being held in the Blackmore Museum.

Brayer kept in contact with the Blackmore Museum in the period after World War II while he continued his research for his biography of Blackmore and the surviving correspondence sheds light on what photographs remained in Salisbury. In a letter to Hugh Shortt, the curator of the Salisbury, South Wiltshire and Blackmore Museum, in August 1948 Brayer wrote 'With reference to the framed photographs on glass, tinted, and the other photographs and albums, I should be most happy to take these over from Mr. Stevens, and in fact am quite anxious to have them . . . Please say to Mr. Stevens that this is a serious and firm offer . . .'[113] It is unknown whether Brayer did acquire any of the Blackmore photographs he referred to and since the papers of Blackmore's American biographer have not been located by the author this cannot be corroborated.

In 1951 the Ayer Collection at the Newberry Library in Chicago acquired an original Daguerreotype portrait of the mercenary, merchant, fur trader and scalp hunter James Kirker (1793-1852). This had been sourced from an unidentified book dealer who had in turn allegedly acquired it from the Blackmore Museum.[114] This would seem

112 Letter dated 12th May, 1942 in S&SWM, Blackmore Museum Papers.

113 Letter dated 20th August, 1948 in S&SWM, Blackmore Museum Papers.

114 Dolores Ann Kilgo, *Likeness and Landscape: Thomas M. Easterly and the art of the Daguerreotype*, Missorri Historical Society Press, St. Louis, 1994 p.141. A copy is held in the Missouri Historical Society.

to indicate that at least one Daguerreotype in the Blackmore collection did find its way to Salisbury. On 9th March 1953 an 'unspecified number of photographs of North American Indians' were sold to the Newbery Library.[115] The provenance of those photographs with the Blackmore Museum imprint sold at auction also begs more questions; particularly centring on which individuals and institutions acquired or were donated copies.

Blackmore's substantial collection of topographic views of the Yellowstone area has disappeared without trace. Similarly, the photographs of 'forms of clubs, spears, ornaments, tools and weapons' referred to by Edward Stevens in 1868 – and a collection presumably extended over the following decade until Stevens' death – have been lost.

Fortunately, though distributed amongst a number of public and independent collections, the majority of Blackmore's photographic collections are available for analysis. Thus his achievements and legacy may continue to grow as scholars become aware of his role and its significance to a generation of anthropologists, ethnologists and archaeologists and associated institutions active in the third quarter of the nineteenth century.

115 Letter from Hugh Shortt, Director of the Salisbury Museum to Walter L. Fertig dated 3rd April 1973. SSWM Blackmore Museum Papers file 2. In 1911, Edward E. Ayer (1841-1927), a Chicago businessman, donated more than 17,000 pieces on the early contacts between American Indians and Europeans. A number of the photographs of American Indians published by the Trustees of the Blackmore Museum form part of the Ayer collection. These may have been acquired through the Ayer endowment fund.

7
Blackmore, American Institutions and Scholarship

William Blackmore has remained a comparatively overlooked figure in the institutional history of the American West. Yet in the decade that followed his second visit to the USA in 1868 he formed a wide range of successful and productive relationships with prominent individuals and institutions on both the East Coast and the Western Territories. The failure of his business ventures and his untimely death blighted his legacy and obscured his activities, the significance of his influence and the impact of his achievements.

Probably no better evidence of Blackmore's interpersonal skills and ability to build friendships and social networks can be found than in his business dealings in the USA. Politics – with both an upper and lower case 'p' – ran through William Blackmore's activities. He clearly identified the matrix of politicians, civil servants, businessmen and public and private institutions within which he would have to work to achieve success. By leveraging the high level contacts of his uncle John Lambert to open doors in the corridors of power in Washington, D.C., Blackmore was able to lobby politicians and civil servants and this in turn enabled him to secure a critical part of the foundations for his business dealings and the engine to help drive them. He was aware of how significant certain public institutions would be to his achieving success and understood the critical interrelationships they had with the other elements of the post Civil War American establishment. The Smithsonian Institution was a key entity linking together many of Blackmore's commercial and private objectives. The US Army was another institution that Blackmore had built links with during his 1863 trip to America and was to utilise to his benefit. His specific interest in the culture of North American Indians added another dimension that he successfully exploited within the mix of his social network to further his aims and objectives. This linked US government policy and its delivery through a number of government departments, agencies, institutions such as the Smithsonian, and artists favoured within official circles. Blackmore became a master at what has been termed the 'politics of patronage.'[1]

The breadth and depth of Blackmore's social network in North America was remarkable. In this chapter a small set of individuals who formed a prominent part of this network will be examined. These are Joseph Henry (1797-1878), the first Secretary of the Smithsonian Institution; Ferdinand Hayden (1829-1887), a geologist and US Army surgeon who in 1856 was engaged under the United States government to undertake series of investigations of the one hundred and nine Western Territories and in 1867 became geologist-in-charge of the United States Geological and Geographical Survey; three of the leading American artists of the nineteenth century, George Catlin (1796-1872) painter, author and traveller who specialized in portraits of Native Americans and their way of life; Thomas Moran (1837-1926), the English-born artist who is now the most prized of American 19th-century painters; and William Henry Jackson (1843-1942) the photographer, and another prominent member of the band of 'men of the West', Colonel Richard Irving Dodge (1827-1895) of the US Army.

Blackmore was both strategic and tactical in the manner in which he engaged with artists and institutions. However, while he had a profound personal interest in the Native American Indians and the threat to their way of life it would be mistaken to believe that he merely exploited this interest to benefit his business interests. Of all his network relationships within the establishment in Washington, D.C. none was more representative of Blackmore's approach than his dealings with Joseph Hayden, the Smithsonian Institution and through this the link with the artist George Catlin.

1 This chapter owes much to Brian W. Dippie's *Catlin and His Contemporaries: The Politics of Patronage.*, University of Nebraska Press, Lincoln, 1990. The section on Catlin is largely based on this study.

JOSEPH HENRY AND THE SMITHSONIAN INSTITUTION

Blackmore's relationship with the Smithsonian Institution was in somewhat stark contrast to the position he took with respect to the major British institutions, specifically the British Museum. In his opening address at his eponymous museum, Blackmore made an oblique reference to the 'rival claims of the British Museum and Liverpool' to establish an institution to hold his collections. That Blackmore chose to place his collection in a purpose built museum in his home town perhaps indicated an appreciation that the 'munificence' of any bequest to the British Museum would be overshadowed by the recent bequest of the Christy collection while Liverpool boasted the collection of Joseph Mayer. Blackmore did not exclude the British Museum from his network. He knew Augustus Franks reasonably well and donated a limited number of objects to the British Museum. However, he did not forge the strong working relationship with the national museum that one might have expected. Another consideration was how connections with major British institutions could benefit Blackmore's wide ranging objectives. Crudely they could add comparatively little value, while the Smithsonian could.

The Smithsonian Institution was created as the result of a bequest of the British mineralogist and chemist, James Smithson (1765-1829) who had never even visited the USA. Smithson wished to 'found at Washington, under the name of the Smithsonian Institution, an establishment for the increase and diffusion of knowledge among men.' In 1838, following a dispute of Smithson's will, eleven boxes containing 104,960 gold sovereigns were shipped to Philadelphia and minted into dollar coinage worth US$508,318.

On 10th August 1846, following eight years of frequently heated debate, an Act of Congress signed by President James K. Polk (1795-1849) established the Smithsonian Institution as a trust to be administered by a Board of Regents and a Secretary. In the same year the noted architect James Renwick, Jr. (1818-1895) won the competition to build the Smithsonian Institution. Renwick worked closely with the Smithsonian Building Committee to create a building in Romanesque style that included an art gallery, a library, a chemical laboratory, lecture halls, and museum galleries. This was constructed in red sandstone between 1847 and 1855 and was popularly known as the 'Castle'.

The remit of the Smithsonian was wide encompassing 'all objects of art and of foreign and curious research and all objects of natural history, plants, and geological and mineralogical specimens belonging to the United States.'[2] The Smithsonian became the principal scientific institution for the US Federal government and subsequently dozens of government agencies with research missions emerged.

Within six months of Congress passing the Act to enable the creation of the Smithsonian the newly appointed Regents established a plan of operation and outlined their interpretation of the character of the national museum. Critically the Board of Regents stated that while ethnology and anthropology were not specifically named in the Act they were as important subjects as natural history.[3] This was quickly reflected in the publications of the Smithsonian Institution – the first of which was Ephraim G. Squier and Edwin H. Davis' *Ancient Monuments of the Mississippi Valley* published in 1848.[4] Knowledge of these developments would have been available to Blackmore through the full set of the Smithsonian's publications held in the library of the Historic Society of Lancashire and Cheshire.

Joseph Henry (1797-1878) was appointed in 1846 as the first Secretary of the Smithsonian Institution. A physicist, Henry had been appointed Professor of Mathematics and Natural Philosophy at The Albany Academy and in 1832 became a Professor of Natural Philosophy at Princeton. Henry's principle achievement was the discovery of the electromagnetic phenomenon of self-inductance.[5] He was to establish a

2 From the Act of Incorporation passed by the US Senate on 10th August, 1846.

3 'Inception and History', *Report on the Progress and Condition of the U. S. National Museum for the Year Ending June 30*, 1910 p.9.

4 Ephraim G. Squier, Edwin H. Davis, *Ancient Monuments of the Mississippi Valley: Comprising the Results of Extensive Original Surveys and Explorations*, Smithsonian Contributions to Knowledge 1, Washington, D.C., 1848.

5 See *A Memorial of Joseph Henry*, Government Printing Office, Washington, D. C., 1880; Thomas Coulson, *Joseph Henry, his Life and Work*, Princeton University Press, Princeton, 1950 and Albert E. Moyer, *Joseph Henry: The Rise of an American Scientist*,

close working relationship with Blackmore that proved to be fruitful to both parties.

The Smithsonian Institution only received part of its funding from the US Federal Government and Henry forged strong links with US politicians and bureaucrats and lobbied for full state funding. In February 1863, Henry was named on a three-member board charged with advising the US government on scientific matters. He advised the Permanent Commission of the Navy Department as part of the evaluation of proposed warship designs, signalling systems, inventions of torpedoes, underwater guns and other ordnance. In its most active period, the Commission met as frequently as three times a week, often at the Smithsonian Building. However, Henry was fully aware that the Smithsonian should not fall into the hands of partisan politicians through the appointment of politicians to the Board of Regents. This was a tricky balancing act.

Henry had a clear vision of what he believed the Smithsonian should be and adroitly and successfully exploited threats and opportunities as and when they appeared. The period of the American Civil War is particularly relevant since a spate of events led Henry to address a number of issues and thereby formed the characteristics of the institution as Blackmore first properly experienced it in 1868. When the federal government hesitated in paying interest on the Smithson bequest, Henry reminded it of its solemn obligation. When public buildings in Washington were threatened by the nearby fighting of the American Civil War, he asserted the institution's private status. When a fire damaged the Smithsonian Building, Henry used it to eliminate functions he saw as secondary to the core mission of the Smithsonian. The military repaired the roof and he divested the institution's library to the Library of Congress. With his vision of an institution devoted to the support of basic research and dissemination of its findings throughout the world, he took the interruptions and embarrassments caused by the war and used them to further realise his vision, a vision which Blackmore could align with his own aims and objectives.[6]

Smithsonian Institution Press, Washington, D. C., 1997.

6 See Kathleen W. Dorman, "'Interruptions and Embarrassments': The Smithsonian

The Smithsonian Institution was governed by a Board of Regents consisting of the Vice-President and Chief Justice, three Senators, three members of the House of Representatives, and six private citizens chosen by Congress. Quite how Blackmore built and exploited relationships with Regents remains to be unravelled. However, one Regent was of particular significance to the English financier. General William Tecumseh Sherman was a Citizen Regent from 1871 until 1883 and Chairman of the institution's Building Committee. Blackmore knew Sherman well having first met him during his 1863 visit to America and again in 1868. Sherman had a professional background that linked him to Blackmore. He had established the branch bank of Lucas, Turner, and Company in San Francisco in 1853 and worked for the same bank in New York for a short period between 1857 and 1858, when the bank failed. In 1858 he moved to Leavenworth, Kansas where he practiced law until the following year when he was appointed the first superintendent of the Louisiana State Seminary of Learning & Military Academy in Pineville, Louisiana. Following his prominent military career during the American Civil War Sherman played a central role in Indian affairs – as part of the Indian Peace Commission (founded in 1867) – and thus various aspects of the settlement of the West.[7] In 1869 Sherman was made Commanding General of the US Army and one of his main concerns was the protection of the construction and operation of the rapidly expanding railway network from attack by hostile Indians. Having access to Sherman's support within the Smithsonian and his high ranking connections in Washington, D. C. gave Blackmore another configuration of his matrix of social networking.

1848 Henry specifically selected and edited the Smithsonian Institution's first publication, Ephraim G. Squier and Edwin H. Davis' *Ancient Monuments of the Mississippi Valley*. This represented a substantial decision for Henry since the first publication in the Smithsonian

Institution during the Civil War' at http://siarchives.si.edu/history/jhp/Civilwar.htm#49 accessed on 27th August 2010.

7 Sherman was at this time commander of the Military Division of the Missouri. See Robert G. Athearn, *William Tecumseh Sherman and the Settlement of the West.*, University of Oklahoma Press, Norman, 1956.

Contribution to Knowledge series would set a benchmark for the future reputation of the institution. The fact that William Blackmore was later to purchase the Squier and Davis collection was highly significant to Joseph Henry since he had not actively recommended that Squier and Davis' collection be purchased by the US government for the nation. Henry's stance on this collection was somewhat at odds with the written statement he made in 1854:

> Among the objects which should be collected and preserved with care, are the remains of the specimens of the arts of the aboriginal inhabitants of this county, the contents of mounds, and the stone implements found on the surface of the earth. The implements and industrial products of the present tribes of Indians should also be gathered as the materials for the advance of the new and interesting science of ethnology. Of the contents of mounds, but a limited amount of specimens exist; and as these are not, like the spontaneous productions of nature, constantly in the process of reproduction, every article should be diligently sought for, and carefully preserved. Some additions have been made to the collections in this line.[8]

The creation of a photographic gallery of North American Indians was another objective that linked the Smithsonian and William Blackmore. It also evidenced the phase change introduced by the advent of photography and the preferences and priorities shown by the Institution, specifically with respect to Catlin's 'Indian Gallery'.

During the 1820s Thomas Loraine McKenney (1785-1859), until 1822 second superintendent of Indian Trade in Georgetown, then port of entry for the District of Columbia, and the first superintendent of Indian affairs between 1824 and 1830, conceived the idea of forming an official government collection of portraits of prominent Indians who visited the capital. Charles Bird King (1785-1862), a leading Washington portrait painter, was commissioned and his depictions of the leaders of at least twenty tribes were reproduced as hand coloured lithographs in Thomas McKenney and James Hall's three-volume classic, *History*

8 *Eighth Annual Report of the Board of Regents of the Smithsonian Institution*, Washington, 1854 p.220

of the Indian Tribes of North America, published in 1837, 1842 and 1844 respectively. The work was republished in a different format edition – with addenda – a number of times up until 1870. Blackmore owned a copy of the first edition of each of the three volumes.[9]

King's paintings were donated by McKenney to the National Institute for the Promotion of Science and the Useful Arts founded in Washington, D.C. in 1840. The National Institute was bedevilled by politics and subsequently disbanded, its collections being transferred to the Smithsonian Institution between 1857 and 1862. King's portraits were displayed among similar paintings by the New York artist John Mix Stanley (1814-1872) in a gallery containing two hundred and ninety-one paintings of Native American portraits and scenes.[10] This Picture Gallery in the Upper Main Hall was already installed by 1858 when the photographers Langenheim, Lloyd & Co. of the American Stereoscopic Co. recorded a number of general views that were made commercially available.[11] It would seem likely that during his visits to Washington in late 1863 and early 1864 Blackmore visited the Smithsonian and saw the gallery of Native American portraits and scenes. Whether he met Joseph Henry or Mix Stanley at this time has yet to be established. However, there are five photographs of paintings by John Mix Stanley in the Blackmore Collection in Santa Fe; *Snake in the Grass, Gambling for the Buck, Indian Telegraph, Young Chief* and *Hunters.*[12]

9 See Shirley H. Bowers, ''Captured on Canvas': McKenney-Hall's History of the Indian Tribes of North America', *The Florida Historical Quarterly*, Volume 71, No.3, January, 1993 pp.339-347.

10 Smithsonian Institution catalogues refer to one hundred and fifty-two paintings by Stanley and one hundred and thirty-nine by King. Mix Stanley also used the Daguerreotype. In 1843 he and his partner Caleb Sumner Dickerman (1819-1882) were reported to have taken a significant number of Daguerreotype portraits of Indians in Fort Gibson, Oklahoma and took ten portraits of John Ross (Guwisguwi) (1790-1866), a prominent Cherokee, and his family. These may have been used as the basis of subsequent paintings. These Daguerreotypes may have been lost in the 1865 fire at the Smithsonian. See Peter E. Palmquist and Thomas R. Kailbourn, *Pioneer Photographers from the Mississippi to the Continental Divide. A Biographical Dictionary, 1839-1865*, Stanford University Press, Palo Alto, 2005 p.205.

11 See Smithsonian Institution SI.2004.020 and SI.2004.021.

12 These are by an anonymous photographer and are numbered 65033 to 65036 and 65044.

On January 24, 1865 a fire destroyed the paintings in the Smithsonian's Picture Gallery, though five of the paintings by Bird were saved. Those images that were destroyed remain recorded through McKenney's lithograph collection. This disaster posed a number of questions for the Smithsonian. Stanley had exhibited his paintings at the Smithsonian for fourteen years without receiving any fee or other financial gain, there being, in Stanley's eyes at least, a tacit understanding that the Smithsonian would one day purchase them. The question of compensation was a pressing issue. Should there be a new Picture Gallery populated with paintings similar to those by King and Stanley that had been lost? If so, what options were available? Should resources be focussed on a different type of gallery of North American Indians?

In 1867 Joseph Henry again suggested the use of photography to document North American Indians. In a letter to Lewis V. Bogy (1813-1877), the Commissioner of Indian Affairs, dated 20th February, Henry put forward a number of considerations. Firstly, following the 1865 fire, there was no official government collection of Indian portraits and previously the Commission had originally funded the creation of the portrait gallery now lost. Photography would be cheaper than painted portraits. Another advantage of photography was that the negatives could be preserved and copies made at a low cost to anyone who desired them. Henry proposed making facial portraits where the subjects were bareheaded. This would remove the problem of headdresses obscuring the sitter's physiognomy and the tendency of artists to emphasize dress. The suggestion fell on deaf ears and Bogy made the comment when passing on the letter to Orville Hickman Browning (1806-1881), the Secretary of the Interior, that any funding should come from the Smithsonian itself since its mission was to diffuse useful knowledge. Henry himself appears not even to have had the satisfaction of a reply from either Bogy or Browning.[13] Joseph Henry was therefore left with something of a predicament – and William Blackmore was to provide a timely solution. Henry and Blackmore could therefore be considered kindred spirits in their objectives to document the rapidly disappearing North American Indian. Blackmore was also

13 See Herman J. Viola, *Diplomats in Buckskins: A History of Indian Delegations in Washington City*, University of Oklahoma Press, Norman, 1995 pp.180-2

aware of the constant struggle facing Henry regarding the Smithsonian's financial resources, its split funding and how he could support a mutual objective.

Probably in 1868, during his second visit to the USA, Blackmore hired the artist and photographer Antonio Zeno Shindler (1823-1899), of Bulgarian or Romanian extraction, who was listed as a painter and draftsman in Philadelphia in the early 1850s before settling in Washington in April 1867. Shindler then acquired the studio of Robert W. Addis (d.1874), who had previously acquired the business of James Earle McClees (1821-1887) for whom he had worked as an operator. The purpose of Shindler's contract was to make copies of Blackmore's photographs and negatives that had been lent to the Smithsonian, Subsequently ninety-five of the three hundred and one photographs that formed the 1869 exhibition of Photographic Portraits of North American Indians in the Gallery of the Smithsonian Institution were provided by Shindler from Blackmore's collection.

The 1869 exhibition of photographs formed the Smithsonian's first photographic exhibit, and probably the first in any American museum.[14] Blackmore also hired Shindler to make oil paintings of some of the photographic images. This seemed a curious, somewhat counter-intuitive commission from Blackmore and it is possible that he

14 These images are documented in the catalogue *Photographic Portraits of North American Indians in the Gallery of the Smithsonian Institution* (1867) The photographs, presumably printed c.1869, are albumen prints trimmed into ovals and mounted on Addis Gallery stock. Each photograph is identified by a reference number corresponding to the printed Smithsonian catalogue, and the titles and identifications are drawn from a manuscript list included with the Shindler Collection at the American Philosophical Society (usually, but not always identical to the entries in the printed catalogue). This collection contains photographs no. 1-104, with the exception of nos. 48, 54, 60, 67, 75, 76, 83, 88, and 95. The dates of these photographs were taken from Paula Richardson Fleming's *Native American Photography at the Smithsonian: The Shindler Catalogue* (2003), and names and other information were checked against her work. See A. Zeno Shindler American Indian Photograph Collection at http://www.amphilsoc.org/mole/view?docId=ead/Mss.970.1.Sh6-ead.xml A significant number of the photographs in the British Museum from the Blackmore Collection have small printed labels stuck to the mounts of the photograph. These refer to Shindler making copies in 1869. It has not been possible to date conclusively these printed labels and connect them to the Smithsonian exhibition.

was considering building an 'Indian Gallery' of painted portraits for his museum in Salisbury. However, Shindler appears to have worked slowly. Blackmore became increasingly concerned about the time taken by Shindler to make these copies and wrote to the Hayden in December 1869 complaining about the delays and failure to return his 300 photographs. He did so again in June and July 1870 and again in March 1871.[15] As a result of his persistence, in late 1871, a significant proportion of the photographs were sent to Blackmore in England. However, some of the images – such as all but one of the Daguerreotypes and all the glass negatives – were not returned and remained at the Smithsonian where, following Blackmore's untimely death and the lack of follow up by his executors, they were subsumed into the institution's wider photographic holdings.[16] Thus Blackmore's ultimate aim of housing his entire photographic collection in his eponymous museum was never to be realised.

An indication as to how well Henry and Blackmore got on – and how effectively Blackmore could use his contacts – is reflected in a letter Henry wrote to William Worth Belknap (1829-1890), Secretary of War, supporting Blackmore's request for a military escort to investigate the San Juan countryside northeast of the San Luis Valley that straddles Colorado and New Mexico. Henry wrote on the 17th April 1872;

> I beg leave respectfully to commend the petition of Mr. Blackmore, for a military escort, to your favourable consideration. He is an English gentleman of wealth and influence; a generous patron of science both in his own and in our country; he has established from his private funds a public museum in Salisbury, England, and has made valuable donations to the Smithsonian Institution. He has made large investments in our mineral lands and whatever facilities you can give him in the way of his explorations will tend to the advancement of the knowledge of our Western Domain.[17]

15 Paul Richardson Fleming, *Shindler Catalogue*, Smithsonian Books, Washington and London, 2003 p.6.

16 *ibid.*, p.6. Shindler's painted copy portraits probably did not reach Salisbury until late 1874 or 1875.

17 As cited in Brayer, *op.cit.*, volume I, p.185.

As Henry indicated, Blackmore had donated a wide range of items to the Smithsonian Institution. In 1868 Blackmore donated 'a series of photographs of American Indians', a model of Stonehenge (by Mr. Brown of Amesbury, a well known local guide to the monument), a number of electrotype copies of ancient medals and a copy of a privately published book by Thomas Inman titled *Ancient Faiths embodied in ancient names.*[18] The model of Stonehenge and other artefacts were placed on display in the Institution's galleries.[19] The Smithsonian Institution Research Information System also lists two interior photographic views of the Blackmore Museum donated in 1868 by Alma B. Bond.[20] In 1870 Blackmore donated stone artefacts from the drift of Thetford, in the Valley of the Little Ouse, England (ace. 1846). In 1872 he donated a second collection (ace. 2371) from four localities in England and from one in Italy. These represented some of the first archaeological material acquired for the Smithsonian Institution from Europe.[21] Blackmore also donated an Aboriginal Australian boomerang from the Yaraldi Tribe

18 A list of thirteen items is listed in the entry for 16th November 1868 in Blackmore Diary No.17. It is assumed that the 'photographs' mentioned were those taken of visiting delegates by Vannerson and Cohner in the winter of 1857-1858.

19 'Report of the Secretary', *Annual Report of the Board of Regents of the Smithsonian Institution*, Washington, D. C., 1869 p.27. Thomas Inman, *Ancient Faiths Embodied in Ancient Names: Or an Attempt to Trace the Religious Belief, Sacred Rites, and Holy Emblems of Certain Nations By an Interpretations of the Names Given to Children by Priestly Authority or Assumed by Prophets, Kings, and Hierarch*, London and Liverpool, 1868. The model of Stonehenge was allocated National Museum of Natural History accession number 1826 with anthropology catalogue number 9634. It is no longer part of the collection. However, the English newspaper editor and author William Morris (1826-1891) noted that on a visit to the Smithsonian in 1874 he 'was much interested in noticing that some of the cases were devoted to specimens from Wiltshire, more particularly from the 'drift,' the contributions being principally from the Blackmoor [sic] Museum, Salisbury. Amongst the specimens, there was a model of Stonehenge, by Mr. Brown, of Amesbury, the well-known guide.' William Morris, *Letters Sent Home. Out and Home Again by way of Canada and the United States.*, Frederick Warne, London [c.1875] p.341. This book was based on letters which had been originally published in 1874 in the *Swindon Advertiser*, of which Morris was editor.

20 SPC BAE 4801 01015000 and SPC BAE 4801 01014900.

21 Michael D. Petraglia, Richard Potts, *The Old World Paleolithic and the Development of a National Collection*, Smithsonian Contributions and Studies Series, 2004 p.64.

acquired near Lake Alexandrina, south-east of Adelaide.[22]

Soon after its opening, the Blackmore Museum became of interest to a number of prominent members of the American establishment such as Dr Charles Rau (1826-1887), the Belgian-born archaeologist. Rau, whose contributions to the publications of the Smithsonian Institution first appeared in 1863, wrote to Joseph Henry at the Smithsonian on 15th December 1868 stating of Blackmore, 'Through him, I think, we shall enter into pleasant relations with the prominent archaeologists of England.'[23] This comment gives an insight into how those in the Smithsonian considered Blackmore could assist the Institution. Blackmore had a network of high ranking scholarly contacts in Britain and Europe and Henry and his colleagues relished the opportunity to tap into this resource.

By 1870 Blackmore had established himself as a primary benefactor of the Smithsonian Institution with the associated privileges. Assistant Secretary Spencer Fullerton Baird (1823-1887) wrote to Blackmore on 11th June;

> Our duplicates are, now, somewhat numerous and no one has a better right to the first choice from among them than yourself. If we could only look forward to a speedy visit from you and have you make the selection for yourself it would be a source of the highest gratification to us.[24]

Blackmore sent twenty copies of Stevens' *Flint Chips* catalogue to the Smithsonian and in a letter in June 1870 stated 'You ask me to indicate what I should like you to send me for the Blackmore Museum. I shall be very glad if you send me all your publications relating to Archaeology and Ethnology.'[25] These copies of *Flint Chips* sent to Washington, D.C. were soon exhausted and Assistant

22 Smithsonian Institution catalogue number 12262.

23 Michael Petraglia and Richard Potts, *op.cit.*, p.64. Rau's name and publications featured prominently in Edwards Stevens' *Flint Chips* published in 1870, which also listed Rau as a donor to the Blackmore Museum.

24 As cited in Michael Petraglia and Richard Potts, *op. cit.*, p.67.

25 Letter from Blackmore to Henry date 17th June 1870 as cited in Michael Petraglia and Richard Potts, *op.cit.*, pp.65-8.

Secretary Spencer Fullerton Baird, wrote to Edward Stevens stating that:

> The copies of the 'Flint Chips' sent by Mr. Blackmore have, all, been distributed and we shall, therefore, be much pleased to have the additional ones to which you refer in order to supply a number of establishments where they will be highly prized.[26]

The donation of copies of *Flint Chips* acted as both a marketing tool for Blackmore but also aligned with his aims to 'spread knowledge.' One of the reciprocal benefits was that the Blackmore Museum received Smithsonian publications, as part of its international exchange system. The Blackmore Museum continued to be included on the International Exchange list of the Smithsonian Institution more than two decades after William's death and at a point when his museum was no longer actively engaged in the study of or publishing on Americana.[27]

Joseph Henry was scheduled to visit the Blackmore Museum – to which the Smithsonian had donated objects – in the summer of 1870 while on a three month tour of Europe though it is unknown whether he met Blackmore himself.[28]

In 1872 the Smithsonian made a significant donation to the Blackmore Museum, Joseph Henry writing to Edward Stevens on the 11th June of that year indicating that ethnological objects were being sent:

26 As cited in Michael Petraglia and Richard Potts, *op. cit.,*, p.65.

27 *International Exchange list of the Smithsonian Institution corrected to September, 1903*, Smithsonian, Washington, 1904 no. 9473 p.349. Also listed under Salisbury institutions were the College of Agriculture, the Hampshire Down Breeders' Association and 'Philatelic Journal of Great Britain.'

28 Letter from Baird to William Blackmore dated 11th June 1870. 'Profr. Henry has just left us for a visit to Europe and one of his principal anticipations of pleasure, during his three months absence, was in visiting your museum at Salisbury.' As cited in Michael Petraglia and Richard Potts, *op. cit.*, p.65. Edward Stevens, *Flint Chips*, p.xxi.

> It gives us much pleasure to announce . . a box containing a number of originals and casts of ethnographical objects selected from the duplicates in the Smithsonian Institution, and intended as a present to the Blackmore Museum. We are under so many obligations to Mr. Blackmore for services rendered the Institution, from time to time, that we are very happy in being able to make even this slight return.[29]

Blackmore subsequently reciprocated and in the same year donated a number of flint implements and some casts of hand axes and scrapers to the Institution.

Blackmore's donations to the Smithsonian continued. In 1874 he donated to the Institution a portfolio of photographs of objects in the British Museum. This was part of the series of over nine hundred photographs commissioned by the solicitor Charles Harrison and taken by Stephen Thompson that began publication in 1872.[30] Blackmore knew Harrison since they were both engaged that year on the case of the British civil engineering partnership of Samuel Morton Peto (1809-1889) and Edward Betts (1815-1872) against the Republic of Bolivia regarding a breach of an 1864 contract related to railway construction, shipments of guano – a fertilizer, and mining concessions in Bolivia. Harrison appears to have been one of the investors who may have purchased the assets of Peto and Betts related to this contract with the Bolivian government.[31]

The death of both William Blackmore and Edward Stevens in 1878 broke the collaborative link with the Smithsonian Institution.

29 As cited in Michael Petraglia and Richard Potts, *op. cit..*, p.67.

30 *Annual Report of the Board of Regents of The Smithsonian Institution*, Washington, D. C., 1874 p.29. The entry refers to objects from Nineveh and presumably formed part of Part III [Plates 350-595] of the *Assyrian Series*, selected and catalogued by Samuel Birch and George Smith, of the British Museum. There were in total 245 plates. 2s. 6d. each, mounted or £30. 12. 6d. complete in three portfolios. Joseph Henry of the Smithsonian transmitted this series of photographs to President Ulysses S. Grant. Letter from Henry to Grant dated 25th November 1873 in John Y. Simon, (ed.) *The Papers of Ulysses S. Grant: 1873. Volume 24*, Southern Illinois University Press, Carbondale, 2000 p.483.

31 Harrison's name is listed in a document dated August 1873. Wiltshire & Swindon History Centre 776/644.

Humphrey Blackmore had no burning passion for Americana and would appear to have done little to maintain and foster the relationship with the Institution. Blackmore's significant role in the Smithsonian's history was left unacknowledged in the published history of the institution's first half century though there was reference to the significance of the photograph collection held in the Bureau of American Ethnology. 'Advantage has been taken of every opportunity to make or acquire photographs of Indians and their works; and the files now include about twenty-five hundred portraits, with some twenty-five hundred groups, houses, ceremonials, and other subjects.'[32] William Blackmore might have given a wry smile.

FERDINAND HAYDEN

Ferdinand Vanderveer Hayden (1829-1887) represents a key type of US government official with whom Blackmore built a successful and productive professional relationship and thereby met a wide range of business and private aims and objectives. Hayden was also a key component of the matrix of politicians, government officials and railways and land grant investors who were in the symbiotic relationship that was instrumental in opening up the 'Great West' for settlement and commercial exploitation.

Hayden graduated from Oberlin College in 1850 and then from the Albany Medical College in 1853. He would appear to have abandoned medicine almost immediately and was engaged by James Hall (1811-1898), the palaeontologist and New York State Geologist, to explore the White River Bad Lands of South Dakota. In the summer of 1853 Hayden explored this area of Dakota on the expedition led by Fielding Bradford Meek (1817-1876), a geologist of the U.S. Geological and Geographical Survey of the Territories and who was appointed the Smithsonian's first full-time palaeontologist in 1858. Subsequently, the Smithsonian was involved in Hayden's 1854-1855 Missouri River Expedition which was funded mainly at his own expense.[33] This expedition included a find of

32 George Brown Goode (ed.), *The Smithsonian Institution, 1846-1896. The History of its First Half Century.*, City of Washington, 1897 p.395.

33 F. Martin Brown, 'Hayden's 1854-55 Missouri River Expedition', *The Denver*

unusual teeth uncovered and collected at the confluence of the Missouri and the Judith Rivers. These were later determined by the paleontologist Joseph Leidy (1823-1901), then professor of Anatomy at the University of Pennsylvania, to whom Hayden supplied fossils, to be those of the dinosaurs Trachodon, Troodon and Deinodon, and thus it represented the first confirmed discovery of dinosaur remains in North America.

During the 1850s a variety of individuals who had no affiliation with the Smithsonian or any appointed role on an organized government expedition aided the development of the Institution's collections. However, Hayden represented one strand of the strategic approach of Spencer Fullerton Baird, the Assistant Secretary of the Smithsonian, in building up a network of collectors. Baird gave special attention to US army and US navy officers since their duties often took them to distant, isolated and unexplored regions and, crucially, they were largely funded by other parts of the US government.[34]

During 1855 and 1856 specimens continued to be added to the Smithsonian's collection as a result of Baird's collectors working in the field. These included the results of a number of surveys; the United States-Mexico boundary (1848-1855); the North Pacific Exploring Expedition of the early 1840s under the US naval officer Captain Cadwalader Ringgold (1802-1867); the expedition to the Parana, Paraguay, Vermejo and Uruguay Rivers, under Captain Thomas J. Page, U.S.N. in 1853; the California coastal exploration headed by Lieutenant William P. Trowbridge (1828-1892), also of 1853, and various other U.S. Army expeditions and the Pacific railroad route (five surveys undertaken between 1853-1855).[35]

In 1856 Hayden was engaged under the United States government, and commenced a series of investigations of the one hundred and nine Western Territories. He accompanied Gouverneur Kemble Warren (1830-1882), a civil engineer in the Corps of Topographical Engineers of

Westerners Roundup, Volume 27, 1971 pp.3-66.

34 James G. Cassidy, *Ferdinand Hayden: entrepreneur of science*, University of Nebraska Press, 2000 p.21.

35 *Annual Report of the Smithsonian Institution for the year 1855*, p. 42 and *Annual Report of the Smithsonian Institution for the year 1856* pp.48-54.

the US Army, on his expedition to Nebraska.[36] In the first month of this expedition Hayden sent some two hundred and ninety-one specimens back to the Smithsonian. Hayden was later to distribute other specimens, photographs – including stereoscopic views – to friends, colleges and schools, such as Wooster College and his alma mater, Oberlin.[37] Warren took part in studies of possible transcontinental railroad routes, creating in 1857 the first comprehensive map of the United States west of the Mississippi. This required extensive explorations of the vast Nebraska Territory, including Nebraska, North Dakota, South Dakota, part of Montana, and part of Wyoming. Hayden's early survey works in the area of the Yellowstone and Missouri rivers was documented in his *Geological Report of the Exploration of the Yellowstone and Missouri Rivers in 1859–1860*, published in 1869.

In the winter of 1856-1857, Hayden became one of the earliest members of the Megatherium Club – a group formed by a number of somewhat boisterous young scientists who worked, lived and partied at the Smithsonian.[38] The bohemian trait displayed in Hayden's youth resonated with Blackmore who was happy to muck in with the lifestyle required of the explorers of the 'Great West' and whose family reported he had a bohemian streak in him.

Hayden, like many military contemporaries, built a public career from the experiences gained while on active service during the American Civil War. Soon after the outbreak of the war, he enlisted as a surgeon of volunteers and was posted to South Carolina where his medical ability coupled to his management and interpersonal skills led to his rapid promotion. He returned to Washington in February 1864 and served as an assistant medical inspector. In October of that year he was assigned to the Army of the Shenandoah in Winchester, Virginia as chief medical officer for the region, reporting to General Philip Henry Sheridan (1831-

36 Throughout his travels in the western frontier, Warren assisted Smithsonian Secretary Joseph Henry with efforts to create the first network of systematic weather observations in the United States.

37 James Conaway, *The Smithsonian: 150 Years of adventure, discovery, and wonder.*, Smithsonian Books, 1995 p.81.

38 See http://www.150.si.edu/chap3/club.htm accessed on 16th August 2010.

1888). Hayden remained there until May 1865 when he resigned from the army with the brevetted rank of lieutenant colonel. Needing to find a regular income, Hayden secured the post of professor of Mineralogy and Geology in the University of Pennsylvania, a position secured for him by Joseph Leidy. Hayden held this post until 1872.

The post Civil War period is partly characterised by Congress reacting to external pressures to support financially the 'Great Surveys' and thereby meet the needs of those groups flooding across the Mississippi to the 'Great West' to find a better life. A number of acts of Congress

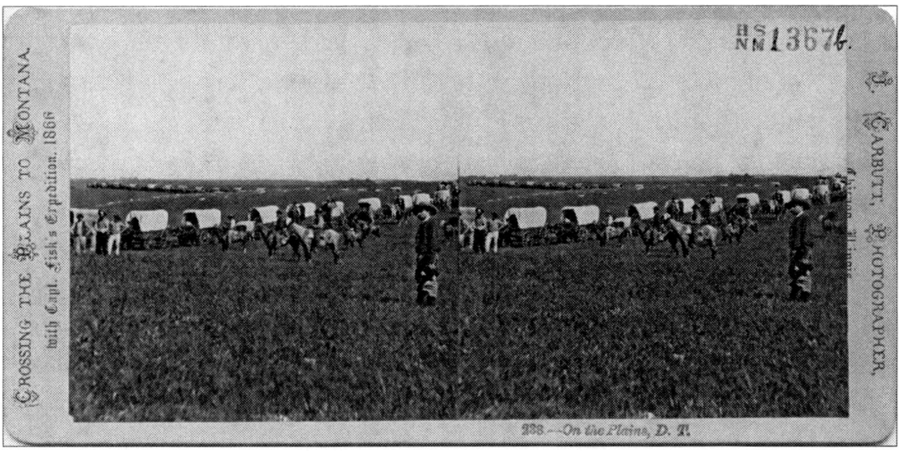

William H. Illingworth and George Bill.
No. 238 On the Plains, D[akota] *T*[erritory]. 1866. Stereoscopic view from the series
Crossing the Plains to Montana with Captain Fisk's Expedition 1866
Published by John Carbutt
Albumen prints. Blackmore Collection
Courtesy Palace of the Governors Photo Archives , Santa Fe (NMHM/DCA), 065054

stimulated this migration. The ninety-four million acres of land grants related to the Pacific Railroad Act enabled the speedy construction of the Union Pacific, Central Pacific, Northern Pacific, Santa Fe, and Southern Pacific railroads. Under the famed Homestead Act, settlers were each able to obtain for free a one hundred and sixty-acre homestead, the final total claimed being almost two hundred and ninety million acres. These settlers and speculators sought the opportunities of comparatively cheap and commercially exploitable land and the mineral wealth that would be opened up by the rapidly expanding railroad network.

Hayden has been described as adroitly seizing opportunities to multiply his markets; as a 'salesman who achieved remarkable success selling Congress something it was not always sure it wanted: science.'[39] An obituary of Hayden noted that 'In dealing with the public men of the country he was so frank, forcible and direct that it was impossible to suppress or resist him.' 'He was a warm personal friend of some of the highest officials in the Government, who never failed to support strenuously and successfully his surveys.'[40] Hayden was adept at effectively handling the demands of a range of stakeholders, particularly the hands of those on Capitol Hill that fed him. Blackmore subtly blended his business interests with those of Hayden to the benefit of both.

As mentioned previously, in 1865 Ferdinand Hayden had made a suggestion to the American Philosophical Society and the American Academy of Natural Sciences that photography be more strategically used to document the North American Indian tribes.[41] He was to become instrumental in developing the official use of photography on the 'Great Surveys' and the building of photographic collections in Washington, D. C., notably at the Smithsonian.

In 1867 Hayden was appointed geologist-in-charge of the United States Geological and Geographical Survey of the Territories, a position Baird had proposed him for.[42] From Hayden's subsequent twelve years of labour and annual survey journeys there resulted a valuable series of some fifty volumes covering natural history and economic science including topography, geology, paleontology, ethnology, philology, botany and 'kindred sciences'. In 1877 Hayden's *Geological and Geographical Atlas of Colorado and Portions of Adjacent Territory* was published 'presenting the results of the field work of 1873, '74, '75 and '76, covering he entire State of Colorado and adjacent portions of Utah, Arizona

39 James G. Cassidy, *op. cit.*, p.110.

40 J. P. Lesley, 'Obituary Notice of Ferdinand Vandevere [*sic*] Hayden, M. D., Ph. D., LL. D.', *Proceedings of the American Philosophical Society*, Volume 25, No. 127, January - June, 1888 pp. 59-61.

41 Mike Foster, *Strange Genius: The Life of Ferdinand Vanderveer Hayden*, Roberts Rinehart Publishers, Niwot, 1994 p.138.

42 James G. Cassidy, *op. cit.*, p.xii.

and New Mexico . . . .'[43] The atlas contained twenty sheets consisting of sixteen maps, two geological sections and two panoramic views. These maps became useful to railroad builders such as Blackmore's business colleagues William Jackson Palmer (1836-1909) of the Denver & Rio Grande Railroad and the Colorado 'booster' William Gilpin.[44] However, by the time they were published Hayden's maps were of little use to Blackmore who was by then on the verge of bankruptcy.

In 1869, the same year in which he first officially commissioned William Henry Jackson, Hayden decided to exploit photographic illustration in his *Sun Pictures of Rocky Mountain Scenery* published the following year.[45] To illustrate this book, he selected thirty of the photographs taken by Andrew J. Russell (1830-1902), the official photographer of the Union Pacific Railway, of the geological formations in the Rockies, the Sierra Nevadas, Wyoming, Utah and California. These photographs had appeared in a larger format in *The Great West Illustrated* published in 1869.[46] Russell used a mammoth plate camera (21 x 15 inch) for much of his work. His best known photograph shows the joining of the rails at Promontory Summit, Utah on 10th May, 1869 where the United States' first Transcontinental Railroad was officially completed. Hayden intended his book to be used as a guide to the geological formations along the train route from Cheyenne to Salt Lake City.

43 Contents page of *Geological and Geographical Atlas of Colorado and Portions of Adjacent Territory*, Department of the Interior, [Washington, D.C.] 1877.

44 Richard A. Bartlett, *Great Surveys of the American West*, University of Oklahoma Press, Norman, 1962 p.103.

45 Ferdinand Vanderveer Hayden, *Sun Pictures of Rocky Mountain scenery: with a description of the geographical and geological features, and some account of the resources of the great West; containing thirty photographic views along the line of the Pacific Rail Road, from Omaha to Sacramento*, Julius Bien, New York, 1870. Five hundred copies were printed and Blackmore owned a copy.

46 *The Great West illustrated in a series of photographic views across the Continent: taken along the line of the Union Pacific Railroad, west from Omaha, Nebraska: with an annotated table of contents, giving a brief description of each view, its peculiarities, characteristics and connection with the different points on the road. Volume 1.*, Union Pacific Railroad, New York, 1869. There were fifty photographs in this title. The preface stated that the volume 'is calculated to interest all classes of people, and to excite the admiration of all reflecting minds as to the colossal grandeur of the Agricultural, Mineral and Commercial resources of the West are brought into view.'

Blackmore probably first met Hayden in Laramie in September 1868 and the Englishman and his business partner, the soldier, civil engineer, industrialist and philanthropist General William Jackson Palmer soon commissioned the geologist to survey the San Luis Valley area making up the Sangre de Cristo Land Grant. Hayden then spent several months gathering information which he submitted in a five page report. This was subsequently published in Blackmore's most significant business publication, *Colorado: Its Resources, Parks, and Prospects* together with Hayden also providing one of the laudatory reports that appeared in the associated prospectus for Blackmore's business vehicle, the Colorado Freehold Land and Emigration Company (Limited), which was published in July 1869. Other notable contributors to the prospectus included Joseph S. Wilson, Commissioner of the General Land Office and William Maxwell Evarts (1818-1901), the former Attorney General of the United States. However, Hayden never again created commissioned reports for Blackmore, perhaps aware of not only a conflict of interests but also Blackmore's tendency to exaggerate when discussing the opportunities related to his extensive land grants.

By 1870 close friendship between Blackmore and Hayden was evident and Hayden was listed as a donor to the Blackmore Museum.[47] In 1871 Blackmore allocated US$10,000 of shares in the Colorado Freehold Land and Emigration Company (Limited) to Hayden and gave Hayden US$500 as a wedding gift 'as a slight recognition of my appreciation of your valuable services to me in inspecting and reporting on the Sangre de Cristo Grant.'[48] Their mutual interest in education was behind Blackmore's proposal in November 1871 to set up jointly with Hayden a college and museum 'devoted in the Physical Sciences especially Geology.' Hayden was to be the 'President' and become 'the professor Huxley in fact of America', Blackmore stating that he was willing to donate the land he owned known as the Garden of the Gods, outside Colorado Springs, for this purpose.[49]

47 Stevens, *Flint Chips* 1870 p.xxii.

48 Letter dated 18th February 1871. As quoted in Brayer, *op. cit.*, Volume I, pp.99-100.

49 Letter dated 18th November 1871 as quoted in Brayer, *op. cit.*, Volume I, p.180. Blackmore co-owned the land with his business associate James Archer. There may

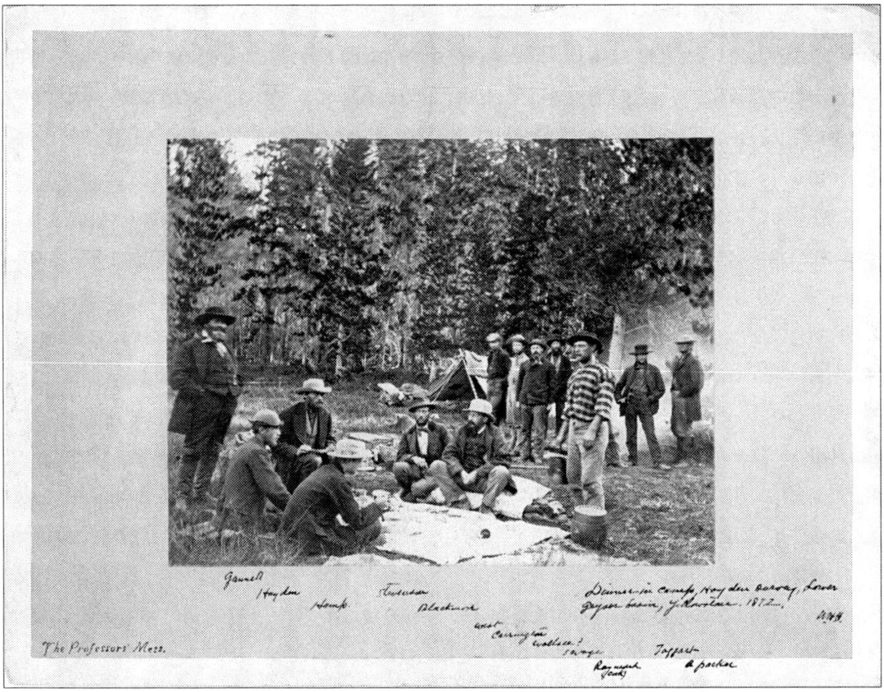

William Henry Jackson.
"The Professor's Mess" Lower Geyser Basin, Yellowstone Park, August 1872.
Albumen print
Smithsonian Institution Archives (SIA),George P. Merrill Collection, SIA2010-3558.
This photograph includes Henry Gannett, astronomer; Ferdinand Vandiveer Hayden, survey leader; Sidford F. Hamp, Blackmore's nephew acting as Assistant Cartographer; James H. Stevenson, executive officer and Hayden's deputy; William Blackmore, W. A. West, Campbell Carrington, zoologist; Griffith, Joseph Savage, of the Kansas Academy of Science; John Raymond, the cook; and William R. Taggert, assistant geologist.
George P. Merrill Collection

have been some politics behind this decision and how it related to the Morrill Land-Grant Colleges Act of 1862. Under this act, each state was allocated 30,000 acres of public land for each Senator and Representative, the numbers being based on the census of 1860. The land was then to be sold and the money from the sale of the land was to be put in an endowment fund which would provide support for the colleges in each of the states.

In 1872 Blackmore played a substantial role in Hayden's second expedition to Yellowstone. He not only part funded the expedition, and helped with the expenses of the expeditions photographer, William Henry Jackson, but he accompanied the group together with his nephew Sidford Hamp, who was given the position of Assistant Cartographer. Mary Blackmore also accompanied her husband on this trip to the USA but did not join her husband on the more extreme ventures into the Yellowstone area. Blackmore's diaries document how he relished this raw and untouched environment and enjoyed living rough in the forests of the Yellowstone. One photograph entitled 'The Professor's Mess' taken on this expedition records a meal taken by key members of the group at the Lower Geyser Basin, Yellowstone Park, in August 1872.

Hayden expressed his closeness to Blackmore by a heartfelt act following the death of Mary Blackmore in July 1872 while her husband accompanied him on his exploration of the Yellowstone region. He named the mountain outside Bozeman at the foot of which Mary Blackmore was buried as Mount Blackmore.

The relationship between Blackmore and Hayden was not without some public controversy. In 1873 Hayden undertook a survey of part of Colorado funded by Congress and including coalfields near Trinidad and Raton. In 1875 the findings were published as the *Report upon the Southern Coal and Iron Fields of Colorado Territory*. The author was James Terry Gardner (1842-1912), Hayden's second in command. Hayden may have suggested Gardner write the report in order to mask his own role as head of the survey. The report significantly benefitted Blackmore and his business partner General William Jackson Palmer and was to cause a small scandal.[50]

The details of Hayden and Blackmore's collaborative project to build a photographic gallery of North American Indians for the Smithsonian Institution has yet to be fully documented. As mentioned previously, Blackmore's death resulted in the link being broken and the Englishman's role being lost to subsequent historians. Hayden did not publish a memoir or autobiography and one must leave to

50 Celinda Reynolds Kaelin, *Pikes Peak Backcountry: The Historic Saga of the Peak's West Slope*, Caxton Press, Caldwell, 1999 pp.101-2.

conjecture as to whether had he done so he would have acknowledged and documented in detail his friendship and professional collaborative achievements with Blackmore.

THOMAS MORAN (1837-1926)

Hayden appreciated the role that 'artists' should play on his surveys, both to document and to market the lands he explored. Both painters and photographers accompanied him on his surveys either as guests or as direct or indirect employees. They could provide both documentary and 'booster' images that were used to justify the expense of his surveys and to illustrate the popular press and official reports.

There was in the late 1860s and early 1870s the paradox introduced by a point of inflection in imaging systems and reprographics. Photography was expanding the portfolio of processes that could be employed by the likes of Hayden, and the geologist seemed to be well aware of this and the relative costs and benefits. The new medium would supplement and then replace the market for the 'painted' and hand drawn image. The cost of photography was declining and this was accompanied by the rise in photomechanical processes, such as photolithography – that was extensively exploited for the reproduction of maps – and the Collotype.

After the 1870 Washburn–Langford–Doane Expedition to Yellowstone, Jay Cooke of the Northern Pacific Railroad financed Nathaniel Pitt Langford (1832-1911) to undertake a speaking tour in which he gave a vivid account of Yellowstone. Langford's itinerary included Virginia City, Helena, New York, Philadelphia and Washington D.C. On 19th January 19, 1871 Ferdinand Hayden attended one of Langford's speeches in Washington, D.C. and was inspired to conduct his next geological survey in the Yellowstone region. After extensive lobbying Hayden received a US$40,000 appropriation from Congress for a geological survey into the Yellowstone region of north western Wyoming, an expedition Blackmore was invited to join but due to business commitments could not. On this trip Hayden was accompanied by a team of thirty-two including Henry W. Elliot of the Smithsonian, the private secretary of Joseph Henry, the artist Thomas Moran and the photographer William Henry Jackson.

Thomas Moran was born in Bolton in England on 12th February 1837 and his family emigrated to America in 1844, settling in Kensington, Pennsylvania where he became a teenage apprentice to the Philadelphia wood-engraving firm Scattergood & Telfer. Following two years of training, Moran began to produce illustrations and watercolours. In the 1860s he produced a variety of works, including landscape 'fantasy' pictures, often working with his brothers, Edward, also an artist, and John, a photographer. In 1867 Moran exhibited his landscape painting *Children of the Mountain*, at the Exposition Universelle in Paris. He was also producing lithographs of landscapes around the Great Lakes in the 1860s. On a study trip to England in 1862, Moran was introduced to the work of J. M. W. Turner and later acknowledged Turner's influence on his subsequent use of colour and selection of landscapes. Moran returned again to Europe in 1866.

Moran became one of the chief illustrators of *Scribner's Monthly*, a periodical that published its first issue in November 1870. In 1871, Scribner's acquired a story called 'The Wonders of Yellowstone' and assigned Moran to illustrate this tale from the Montana territory by Nathaniel Pitt Langford.[51] The article appeared in the May/June 1871 issue of *Scribner's Monthly*. Fired with a desire to visit Yellowstone, Moran sought out backers. Scribner's Publishing Company of New York City gave its support but Moran's initial financial backing came via Alvred Bayard Nettleton (1838-1911), a business associate of Jay Cooke, who was involved in the financing of the Northern Pacific Railroad.[52] Jay Cooke

51 The Cook–Folsom–Peterson Expedition of 1869 was the first organized expedition to explore the region that became Yellowstone National Park. It had no photographer. Later Langford wrote that 'It is much to be regretted that our expedition was not accompanied by an expert photographer: but at the time of our departure from Helena, no one skilled in the art could be found with whom the hazards of the journey did not outweigh any seeming advantage or compensation which the undertaking promised.' Nathaniel Pitt Langford, *Diary of the Washburn Expedition to the Yellowstone and Firehole Rivers in the Year 1870*, St. Paul, 1905 p.122. A Private Moore was the expedition's artist.

52 Nettleton became the official agent and Chief Financial Manager for the Northern Pacific on 20th March, 1872. See *Northern Pacific Railway Company. Secretary's Department. Unregistered Letters Received and Related Records, undated and 1864-1876.*Minnesota Historical Society, St. Paul. http://www.mnhs.org/library/findaids/m0459.pdf accessed 31st August, 2010.

having learned of Moran's interest agreed to loan the artist US$500 and Scribner's matched Cooke's loan, thereby enabling Moran to join Hayden in Virginia City, Montana. Moran promised Cooke twelve watercolours of Yellowstone as a return on his investment. Blackmore saw the set of Moran's field sketches when they were shown in Washington, D.C. in the winter of 1871. In May 1872 Blackmore was to commission Moran to paint a series of sixteen aquarelles of Yellowstone. That Moran completed the set for Blackmore sooner than the set previously promised to Jay Cooke seems to have been the result of the intervention of Hayden. Following the death of Mary Blackmore during the expedition, Hayden suggested to Moran that he might try hard to complete the pictures since Blackmore wished the aquarelles to be a sort of monument to the memory of his late wife.[53]

Moran was an integral part of Blackmore's entourage that met in Washington, D.C. and then headed for the 'Great West.' Sidford Hamp noted that he breakfasted with Moran and Hayden in their hotel in Washington, D.C. on 25th May 1872.[54] Hamp and Blackmore were to share many adventures during the expedition to Yellowstone, William, Moran and Langford being made 'honorary members of the U. S. surveying company' on Friday 16th August.[55]

The contemporary reception of Moran's aquarelles commissioned by Blackmore has been described previously. Blackmore's commission – a tactical example of the politics of patronage – combined the growing kudos of the artist's 1871 views of Yellowstone, Moran's role on an official government expedition and perhaps some rivalry between Blackmore and Jay Cooke. However, Blackmore was not to employ Moran again – though his series of aquarelles were to become some of the most celebrated views of Yellowstone and the Englishman went to the trouble and expense of publishing a printed catalogue of them.[56]

53 Thurman Wilks, *Thomas, Moran: Artist of the Mountains*, University of Oklahoma Press, Norman, 1998 p.105.

54 Herbert Oliver Brayer, 'Exploring the Yellowstone with Hayden, 1872, Diary of Sidford Hamp', *Annals of Wyoming*, Volume 14, Number 4, October 1942 p.261.

55 *ibid.*, p.279.

56 *Catalogue of water-colour drawings of the Yellowstone region, great national park of the United States, painted by J [i.e. T.] Moran, for William Blackmore; and list of photographs by W.H. Jackson*. [n.p., n.d.].

Though displayed at the Blackmore Museum and at the Royal Society in London the role they played there after William's death has yet to be fully established. Their subsequent rise to iconic status would have more than pleased Blackmore.

WILLIAM HENRY JACKSON (1843-1942)

William Henry Jackson was born in Keeseville, New York on the 4th April, 1843. A talented water-colourist, in 1858, he found work as a retoucher for a photographic studio in Troy, New York, and he worked there for the next two years picking up a knowledge of cameras and darkroom techniques. In October 1862, at the age of 19, he joined the 12th Vermont Infantry, and made views of camp life, sending sketches home to his family. He subsequently fought in the Unionist Army at the Battle of Gettysburg during the American Civil War.

Jackson returned home after the Civil War and recommenced his photographic career with some success. However, following a decision to break off his engagement to a Miss Carolina Eastman in Vermont, he boarded a train in 1866 and travelled to the end of the Union Pacific railway at Omaha, Nebraska where in the following year he and his brother settled and set up as commercial photographers. The Jackson brothers ventured out of Omaha and photographed North American Indians; Osages, Otoes, Pawnees, Winnebagoes and Omahas. In 1869 Jackson had received a commission from the Union Pacific Railroad to record the scenery along the route of the railway, some of the photographs being intended for a promotional publication while others were made available in stereoscopic view format.

Hayden first met William Henry Jackson at his studio in Omaha in early July 1870. However, Blackmore had met Jackson considerably earlier than Hayden. In September 1868, on his first visit to the 'Great West', the Englishman had visited Omaha and in his diary had noted that he visited Jackson's studio and purchased photographs of North American Indians and views of the route of his trip.[57]

57 Blackmore Diary 16. The order was made on the 20th September, 1868. The only copy located is in the Ayer Collection of the Newberry Library, Chicago. Call Number Ayer 290.B5875.

In August 1870 Jackson joined that summer's expedition led by Hayden of the U.S. Geological Survey through Wyoming and Colorado. Jackson then became the official photographer to several of Hayden's surveys until these ended in 1879. Hayden initially only paid Jackson's expenses but, crucially, he allowed him to keep his negatives, or perhaps a duplicate set. This was in many respects a win-win situation for both Hayden and Jackson. Hayden did not have to find the full funding for Jackson and benefitted from the marketing of his surveys through commercial sales of Jackson's photos. Jackson, while having to invest his time, had his expenses paid and could maximise the sale of his photographs – and he did this most effectively. His photographs were to appear in a range of publications, from stereoscopic and large plate photographs, through illustrations in official reports of the surveys, to booster books such as the 1878 edition of *Crofutt's Transcontinental Tourist Guide*.[58]

Following his return from Yellowstone in late 1871 Hayden was contacted by a vice-president of the Denver & Rio Grande Railway company who requested one thousand eight by ten inch photographs by Jackson of 'at least one of the pictures you have taken along the route of our road, if I can get them at cost . . . ready to paste in a book.'[59] This was further evidence of the business use of photographs of the Yellowstone though whether Blackmore, as the chief financier of the Denver & Rio Grande Railway, knew of or had any involvement in this plan is unknown.

In his official report for 1873 Hayden stated that an account of his surveys of 1870 and 1871 would be published: 'vol. IV, part 1 will contain about one hundred illustrations, printed by the albertype process from photographic negatives taken by Mr. Jackson.' These Albertypes (a trade name for the Collotype process licensed by its inventor Joseph Albert of Munich) were printed by Edward Bierstadt of New York who in 1870

58 See Peter Bacon Hales, 'American Views and the Romance of Modernization', in Martha A. Sandweiss (ed.), *Photographs in Nineteenth-Century America*, Amon Carter Museum; Harry N. Abrahams, Inc., Fort Worth; New York, 1991 p.217. Jackson's photographs had already been used to illustrate the 1868 edition *of Crofutt's Transcontinental Tourist's Guide.*

59 As quoted by James G. Cassidy, *op. cit.*, p.232 This was possibly Robert H. Lamborn (1836-1895).

had acquired the licensing rights for the process in the United States. However, the Bierstadt works suffered a fire in 1874 that ended the project, though at least four incomplete sets in portfolio format have been located.[60] It is again worth pointing out that Blackmore is likely to have been aware of Hayden's use of the Albertype and yet although conscious of the issues of impermanence of the Albumen process never actually took the step of exploiting photomechanical reproduction in the publications of the Trustees of the Blackmore Museum.

Hayden later wrote a detailed account justifying the use of photography in his annual report for the year 1875. It is quoted here in full since it encapsulates Hayden's views and gives details of the practicalities behind, and current state of, the photographic holdings;

> In 1870, a photographer was attached to the Survey, and the results arising therefrom have fully proven the wisdom of thus adding a most useful art to the organization. An unthinking public might imagine that the employment of photography in connection with the work of the Survey is more ornamental than useful, and that the sole business of the photographer is to secure in the field a number of pictures merely to please the eye, and not for practical and scientific use. This idea is so at variance with those believed to be popularly entertained as to practical economy, that it seems worth while to enumerate some of the many, useful applications photography may be put to. Although in its infancy, it has been so successfully applied to many branches of Government work that it is now considered a necessity of any well organized expedition or in any office where there is any considerable amount of illustrating or designing, notably so with the English and continental governments,

60 The set in the David A. Hanson collection at the Sterling and Francine Clark Art Institute Library has fifty-five plates; a copy in the Denver Public Library has thirty-four plates; there is a set in the National Museum in Washington and another was sold at Metropolitan Auctions in New York in 1995. See http://maca.cdmhost.com/cdm4/document.php?CISOROOT=/p1325coll1&CISOPTR=1888&REC=16 accessed on 30th August, 2010. Another example of the use of photomechanical illustration to geological surveys is Nathaniel Southgate Shaler, *Memoirs of the Geological survey of Kentucky / N.S. Shaler, director.*, University Press, Cambridge,1876 that contained seven Albertype plates of fossils by E. Bierstadt of New York and a similar number of Heliotypes of Indian artefacts (arrow head, axe heads, etc.) by James R. Osgood of Boston.

where large schools of instruction are supported for the sole purpose of turning out skilled employees. In our own country, photography was first used to any extent by the Government during the war in securing series of illustrations for the Surgeon-General and Engineer bureaus, and since then for the reproduction of the drawings of the Supervising Architect, and other work of like nature for the United States Treasurer's office. This establishment is the nearest approach to those maintained at Woolwich, Berlin, Paris, and Vienna, but is insignificant in comparison with them.

After the close of the war, the previous good services of photography in the field recommended it to the exploring and surveying expeditions, and it was extensively employed by them. A photographic corps was attached to the Survey in 1870, and it has continued its use ever since. Besides, the constant and important use made of these illustrations in the preparation of the geological and topographical reports, copies of them are now used by professors in all the principal colleges of the land to illustrate their geological teachings.

The photographic work has been under the direction of Mr. W. H. Jackson, an experienced landscape-photographer, who has made an average of 400 negatives each year, ranging in size from the stereoscopic up to plates 20 by 24 inches square. The first year the work lay entirely within Wyoming and Utah Territories. In 1871 and 1872, the expeditions to the Yellowstone regions afforded opportunities that were not lost, and the splendid series of photographs then secured have retained their popularity to this day. In 1873, 1874, and 1875, the work was transferred to Colorado, and the operations of the first season were confined to the mountain-ranges bordering the Middle and South Parks and the Elk Mountains beyond. It was on the trip of 1873 that Mr. Jackson made one of his greatest successes, in securing a fine view of the Mountain of the Holy Cross. In 1874, the views covered a much greater range of subjects, taking in the Parks, the San Juan Mountains, and the remarkable ancient ruins south of the La Plata Mountains. These ruins were first brought to the notice of the world through the photographs made of them by Mr. Jackson. The interesting results secured the previous year justified the sending of Mr. Jackson to the same region again in 1875, but extending his journey down the hitherto unexplored San Juan to the mouth of the Rio de Chelly, and then to the Moquis Pueblos in Arizona, many interesting ruins were discovered, which were fully described and illustrated in the

Bulletin and also the Annual Report for that year. Returning from Moqui via the De Chelly, the plateau country between the Sierra Abajo and La Plata was found to contain many interesting ruins, and was thoroughly photographed. An interesting feature in connection with this season's work was the success attending the production of a series of 24 by 20 inch negatives of the most prominent points in the San Juan Mountains, the very first plate of this size ever made among the Rocky Mountains.

From the two thousand or more negatives made during these preceding six years, we must ascertain what return they have made for the time and money expended upon their production, and entirely aside, too, from their aesthetic qualities, and the pleasure which lovers of the beautiful and picturesque may derive from them. They have done very much, in the first place, to secure truthfulness in the representation of mountain and other scenery. Twenty years ago, hardly more than caricatures existed, as a general rule, of the leading features of overland exploration. Mountains were represented with angles of sixty degrees inclination, covered with great glaciers, and modeled upon the type of any other than the Rocky Mountains; the angular lines of a sandstone mesa, represented with all the peculiarities of volcanic upheaval, or of massive granite, or an ancient ruin with clean-cut, perfectly squared and jointed masonry, that would be creditable to modern times. The truthful representations of photography render such careless work so apparent that it would not be tolerated at the present day.

One of their most evident practical uses is in securing faithful views of the many unique and remarkable features of newly explored territory, that are subsequently to be reproduced, by engraving, in the Reports. Especially to be noted in this line are the views of the remarkable hot-spring deposits of the Yellowstone National Park, where the exceedingly intricate and delicate tracery of the incrustations, that would defy the most expert pencil, is readily secured in all its varied forms. So it is also with the great cañons, grand waterfalls, impressive mountain masses, the craters of old volcanoes, and beds of ancient lakes, the faulting and folding of the strata, and many other features, of which the geologist finds it necessary to have accurate representations for the illustration of his subjects. To the topographer, also, it is of great assistance in enabling him to represent correctly the surface of the country upon his map; panoramic views for that purpose being made from the summits of the highest peaks.

In ethnography, it gives us faithful portraits of the varied families of oar great Indian population, representing with unquestioned accuracy the peculiar types of each, their manners of living, dressing, occupations, and mythical inscriptions. In archaeology, how important it is that the uncompromising lens portrays the at present almost inaccessible ancient ruins of the Southwestern Territories! These photographs can be sent all over the world, and practically answer the purpose of a personal inspection. The photographs of the ancient ruins have been of great assistance in the construction of the models of the remarkable cliff-houses that have been prepared by some of the members of the Survey. In the office, the uses of photography are manifold: copying the maps of the topographers to a given scale for the engraver or photo-lithographer, and also rare documents or pictures; the production of views for the stereopticon for lectures; and for enlarged transparent photographs on glass from small originals, whereby the minutest feature of rock structure, the varied details of an old ruin, or the grand and imposing mountain mass, are brought so vividly before the eye that they can be studied to much better advantage than in nature, the mind being in rest, and far from the perplexities of the surroundings.

The total number of negatives in the possession of the Survey are now nearly four thousand. Of these, upward of twelve hundred are of Indians photographed from life, representing the most prominent individuals from seventy-four different tribes. The great Sioux family is in this manner well represented, and among them are Red Cloud, Spotted Tail, and Sitting Bull. The Apaches, Comanches, Cheyennes, Utes, Navajoes, etc., are also well represented by excellent negatives, showing not only their personnel, but many of their customs.[61]

61 *Annual Report of the United States Geological and Geographic Survey of the Territories embracing Colorado and Parts of Adjacent Territories: Being a Report of Progress of the Exploration for the Year 1875.* , Government Printing Office, Washington, D. C., 1877 pp.21-3. Hayden wrote; 'During the latter part of the season of 1874, Mr. W. H. Jackson, the photographer of the United States Geological Survey, in connection with Mr. Ernest Ingersoll, visited the south western portion of Colorado for the purpose of photographing the ruins which rumor had placed in the cañons of the Mesa Verde and about El Late. The season was far advanced, and there was but little time for investigation, yet the eight days that were actually devoted to the subject brought to light, a group of ancient habitations so novel in their construction and position that they have excited a very general interest. The results of the trip, as published in Bulletin No. 1, second series, of the Survey, have already been widely distributed.

Hayden had a particular interest in stereographic imagery and Jackson was already aware of the potential of this format that had become popular during the 1860s. The photographer travelled with three formats of camera – a stereographic camera (for stereoscopic cards), a 'whole-plate' or 8 x 10 inch plate-size camera, and even larger 18 x 22 inch camera. Jackson published a number of sets of stereo views of Yellowstone. One set of forty views was titled 'Scenery of the Yellowstone, 1871.'[62] Hayden provided Charles Bierstadt, brother to the artist and a leading manufacturer of stereographic cards, with copies of William Jackson's expedition photographs. E. & H. T. Anthony of New York sold at least two sets of Jackson's stereo views of Yellowstone.

The decision made by Blackmore to help fund Hayden's 1872 expedition – including the provision of equipment for Jackson and a commission to Moran that would offset the artist's costs – evidences a number of interrelated facets of the Englishman's character. Blackmore's interest in the geographic wonders of an unexplored part of the Great West; support for Hayden as a friend; the prestige of involvement in a US government survey; development of his business interests; and possibly competing against a business rival in Jay Cooke.

Moran's watercolours together with bound volumes of Jackson's photographs from the 1871 expedition were used by Hayden to lobby Congress for the Yellowstone as a national park. A year later, Hayden was instrumental in convincing Congress to establish Yellowstone as the first U.S. National Park, aided by the stunning large-format photographs taken by William Henry Jackson.

It would seem likely that Jackson – or perhaps Hayden – would have given Blackmore a set of the photographs he had taken in Yellowstone on the 1872 survey and this is supported by the reference in *The Field* in

The illustrations secured by photography, and then reproduced by photolithographic processes, have done much to, popularize and render familiar the leading features of the subject, and, showing as they do all the phases of the eccentric methods of these ancient builders, has made them an authority, and they have already been reproduced in a number of later publications.' *Ibid.* p.12

62 See http://www.yellowstonestereoviews.com/publishers/jackson.html accessed on 17th August 2010. The National Archives in Washington D. C. hold a significant number of unpublished Jackson Yellowstone stereo views.

1876 to Blackmore owning 'the most beautiful collection [of photographs of Yellowstone] in the world.' [63] Blackmore seems to have given Jackson a copy of the 1872 Blackmore Museum publication *Photographs of Red Cloud and Principal Chiefs of Dacotah Indians*, a copy with Jackson's signature is now held by Cornell University Library. Blackmore's set of Jackson's photographs appear to have been considered part of his personal collections and were inherited by Humphrey Blackmore. How extensive this set was remains unclear. Some photographs by Jackson were sold at the house sale of the final part of Humphrey's estate in March 1932.

Hayden formed a number of international professional contacts through which to disseminate photographs including the Royal Anthropological Institute in London. Blackmore may well have been instrumental in enabling these for his friend. In February 1877 the Institute passed, 'A special vote of thanks . . . to Professor Hayden for his present of an album (which was exhibited at the meeting) containing photographs of the Indians of North America, representing 70 of the principal tribes.'[64] This album – which contains some six hundred photographs – may have contained images from the Blackmore collection and also supports the suggestion that Ferdinand V. Hayden and William Blackmore planned to publish a national album of photographs.[65] Whether Jackson was formally involved in this project has yet to be established.

63 *The Field*, London, 25th November 1876 as cited by Colin Ford, ''Ho, for the Great West!' Indians and buffalo, exploration and George Catlin: the West of William Blackmore' in Barry C. Johnson, *'Ho for the Great West!' and other original papers to mark the 25th Anniversary of the English Westerners' Society*, Eatome Ltd. for The English Westerners' Society, London 1980 p.18.

64 *Journal of the Archaeological Institute*, Vol. VII, 13th February, 1877 p. 2. The album is in the collection of the Royal Anthropological Institute. I thank Dr Arkadiusz Bentkowski, former RAI Photo Curator, for confirming this and that there are no photographs in the collection categorically related to Blackmore. Email to author 9th August, 2010.

65 See description of Manuscript 4420 in Bureau of American Ethnology-United States National Museum Photographs of American Indians. http://www.nmnh.si.edu/naa/guide/appx_g.htm accessed on 30th August, 2010.

RICHARD IRVING DODGE

William Blackmore appreciated at an early stage of his business career in America that the US military was central to achieving success. He had made significant efforts to build contacts with senior Union army officers during his first visit to the USA. In early 1864 Blackmore left Washington, D. C. and with the permission of the Secretary of War, Edwin McMasters Stanton (1814- 1869) visited the Army of the Potomac, the major Union Army in the Eastern Theatre of the American Civil War. In the field, he met for the first time a number of Generals including William Tecumseh Sherman (1820-1891), George G. Meade (1815-1872), Philip Henry Sheridan (1831-1888), John Gibbons (1827-1896) and numerous other officers and was to develop additional contacts on subsequent visits, particularly on his long expeditions to the 'Great West.'

The US Army offered high level contacts within the corridors of power in Washington, D. C.; it implemented Government policy such as the Indian Peace Commission; it had the ability to protect Blackmore as he went on expeditions in the new territories opened up in the West; it could provide information on various aspects of North American Indians; and it also could provide him with entertainment – particularly Buffalo hunting, which William participated in with great enthusiasm and no little success. One US Army officer who encapsulated such a range of William's interests and who became a close friend was Richard Irving Dodge.

Richard Irving Dodge (1827-1895) was born and raised on a farm in rural Surrey County in North Carolina and commissioned in 1848. He retired as a colonel in 1891 after forty-three years of active service in the United States Army, having evidenced his versatility in a number of senior duty officer roles. He commanded the camp of instruction at Elmira, New York, in August and September 1861. In October 1861 he was transferred to Harrisburg, State Capital of Pennsylvania, and served as mustering and disbursing officer for the remainder of the Civil War. Dodge then spent some twenty years in military service on the Great Plains thereby learning much about North American Indians as well as exploiting the abundant opportunities for hunting and fishing. He subsequently became a popular authority on the Great Plains as the author of two books; *The Hunting Grounds of the Great West* (published in the USA under the title *The Plains of the Great West and Their Inhabitants*) (1877) *Our Wild Indians* (1883).

Dodge gave a vivid insight into the great changes seen in the Great American West during his lifetime when he wrote;

> When I was a schoolboy my map of the Unites States showed between the Missouri River and the Rocky Mountains a long and broad white blotch, upon which was printed in small capitals 'The Great American Desert – Unexplored.'[66]

The changes that Dodge was to evidence in his two books were the result of the impact of new explorers, settlers, prospectors, railroads and the plethora of surveys of the New Territories and the effect these had on the indigenous population – both human and animal. To protect settlers travelling to the American west the US Army set up camps and forts along the favoured routes. However, the North American Indians suffered as a result of these incursions and their numbers began to drop significantly. Similarly, hunters were to have a catastrophic impact on the vast herds of buffalo that represented the sole subsistence of the Plain Indians – shelter, clothing, food and fuel. At the time of Christopher Columbus (c.1451-1506) there may have been as many as one hundred and twenty-five million buffalo in the 'Great West' and some quarter of a million Indians. In 1867 conservative estimates put the number of buffaloes in the trans-Missouri region at fifteen million. [67] From the early 1870s meat packers saw the business potential of buffalo meat and animals were slaughtered to help feed railway construction crews and supply – via the rapidly expanding rail network – the East coast market. Buffalo hides also became of value as new tanning techniques enabled the soft and spongy pelts to be turned into usable leather. As a result,

66 Richard Irving Dodge, *The Hunting Grounds of the Great West: A description of the plains, game, and Indians of the Great North American Desert*. Chatto & Windus, London, 1877 p.3.

67 Mari Sandoz, *The Buffalo Hunters: The Story of the Hide Men*. Second edition, University of Nebraska Press, Lincoln, 2008 p.xii.

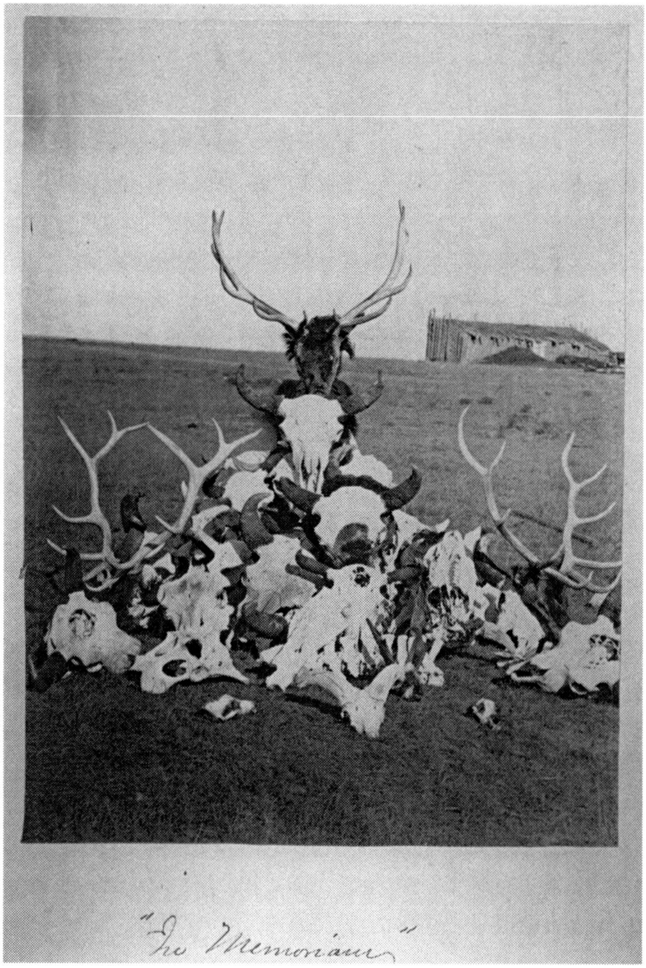

William Henry Jackson.
"In Memoriam." 1870.
Carte de visite
Albumen print
Blackmore Collection
Courtesy Palace of the Governors Photo Archives, Santa Fe (NMHM/DCA), 065031

by the end of the 1880s, the population of buffalo had dwindled and numbered but a few hundred. Dodge was a witness and participant to these changes which he documented in a number of diaries.[68]

68 These have been edited and published by Wayne R. Kime. For an account of the

Blackmore may have first met Dodge on his trip to the USA in 1863 though their first meeting of any consequence took place in Fort Sanders in Laramie in September 1868. The Englishman was part of the official inspection party certifying the satisfactory progress on the construction of the Union Pacific Railroad. The fort had originally been constructed to protect travellers on the nearby Overland Trail from Indian attacks. Later the garrison was given the task of protecting the workers of the Union Pacific railroad when it arrived in the spring of 1868. Dodge met Blackmore again in Washington in late 1871.

There is no evidence that Blackmore was a particularly keen huntsman before he first travelled to the 'Great West' in 1868. However, he soon became addicted to the hunting opportunities offered in America, largely as a result of his contact with Richard Dodge. The scale of the 'sporting' opportunity and the benchmark of a successful hunt on the 'Great Plains' were extraordinary. They lasted days, sometimes weeks, and the slaughter of as many of the living creatures encountered as possible seemed to be the sole purpose of the endeavour.

On his first trip to the 'Great West' in September 1868 Blackmore had participated in a brief buffalo hunt organised by General Henry Beebee Carrington (1824-1912) at Fort Sedgwick near Julesburg, in the north-east corner of Colorado. Also participating in this hunt was Colonel Edward Bridges, of the Grenadier Guards, allegedly a noted big game hunter in India and South Africa. Bridges became a member of Blackmore's investment pool in Colorado and New Mexico land and he may have been instrumental in whetting William's appetite for hunting on the 'Great Plains.'

In October 1872 Dodge organised a hunt for Blackmore. Dodge's hunting companions included the traveller, journalist and author Windham Thomas Wyndham-Quin, Earl of Dunraven (1841-1926), who also knew Blackmore, and Colonel Bridges. Venturing out from Fort Dodge the party accumulated a staggering total of 1,262 head including

arrival of the professional buffalo hunters see 'The Hide Men Come to Adobe Walls', Chapter 1 in T. Lindsay Baker and Billy R. Harrison, *Adobe Walls: The History and Archaeology of the 1874 Trading Post*, Texas A and M University Press, College Station, 1986.

one hundred and twenty-seven buffalo, a number of antelope, turkeys, game birds, two badgers, seven racoons and eleven rattlesnakes, among other species. Dodge described this hunt as the 'most delightful and successful' he had ever made, concluding that 'our appetites for murder had apparently been fully satiated.' The following day Blackmore took part in a hunt of buffalo and got lost chasing a gigantic buffalo bull. Dodge was impressed by the cool and calm way in which the Englishman had got out a map and compass and orienteered himself back up the Arkansas River, crossed it and eventually arrived at Fort Dodge some thirty miles away. [69] During this trip Dodge discussed accompanying Blackmore on hunting trips to Africa – where the Englishman had business interests – and to India, where Blackmore had family.[70]

However, Blackmore was clearly made aware during his 1872 hunt with Dodge of the significant impact it was having on the ecosystem and he expressed concerns for the rapidly diminishing herds of buffalo that were being slaughtered for their pelts. He noted that while on his 1872 visit to the region one hundred miles south of Fort Dodge 'we were never out of sight of buffalo', the following year 'the whole country was whitened with bleached and bleaching bones, [and] we did not meet with buffalo until we were well into Indian territory, and then only in scanty bands.'[71] He persisted with publicly raising the issue of the wanton and wasteful slaughter of buffalo – differentiating between the illegitimate slaughter for hides against the legitimate slaughter for food – and wrote a letter to the London *Field, Farm and Garden* periodical

69 Richard Irving Dodge, *The Hunting Grounds of the Great West: A description of the plains, game, and Indians of the Great North American Desert.* Chatto & Windus, London, 1877 pp.61-2. Curiously Dodge did not mention Blackmore by name, merely reporting his hunt with three English men. The following year a hunt over nearly the same ground bagged 1,142 head. *Ibid.* p.118.

70 Wayne R. Kime, *Colonel Richard Irving Dodge: the life and times of a career army officer*, University of Oklahoma Press, Norman, 2006 p.165. In October 1873 Dodge organised a fourteen day, two hundred and four mile buffalo hunt in southwest Kansas. In 1874 Blackmore accompanied Dodge on a ten day hunting trip along the South Platte River.

71 Richard Irving Dodge, *The Hunting Grounds of the Great West: A description of the plains, game, and Indians of the Great North American Desert.* Chatto & Windus, London, 1877 p.xvii.

dated 23rd October, 1876. Significantly, this letter was reprinted almost in its entirety in Ferdinand Hayden's official report for his survey of 1875. Blackmore wrote that Dodge had told him of an instance where one hundred and twelve carcasses of dead buffalo killed by one man in three-quarters of an hour had been found in a semicircle of two hundred yards radius. The comparisons made by the Englishman with the equivalent level of livestock in Europe were stark. In three years more buffalo had been killed than there were cattle in Holland and Belgium, or the equivalent of three-quarters of the cattle in Ireland, or half of the cattle in Great Britain. Blackmore concluded in almost the style of a 21st century business consultant in his concise and punchy summary;

> 1 Loss of the good and nutritious meat of upward of 3,000,000 of buffalo
> 2 Loss of revenue to the United States of $15,000,000, assuming that a reasonable tax of $5 had been imposed on each pelt.
> 3 Principal Indian tribes of the plains being deprived of their annual supply of food for the winter, and only receiving short rations on their reservations, driven on the war-path.
> 4 Cost of Indian wars in the lives of the citizens of the United States and money [sic]
> 5 Pioneer settlers deprived of their winter food. Prior to 1870 the western settlers, from Eastern Kansas to the base of the Rocky Mountains, looked to the buffalo as their winter store-house.[72]

Blackmore might be accused of being repetitive in that he regurgitated many of the same statistics again and again in his published writings. However, in the dire circumstances there was nothing wrong in the repetition.

In the spring and summer months of 1875, Dodge led an escort of over four hundred troopers accompanying the US Geological Survey backed expedition of the geologists Henry Newton and Walter P. Jenney into the Black Hills of the Dakotas. The objective was to determine the

72 *Annual Report of the United States Geological and Geographic Survey of the Territories embracing Colorado and Parts of Adjacent Territories: Being a Report of Progress of the Exploration for the Year 1875.* , Government Printing Office, Washington, D. C., 1877 pp.556-8.

truth of rumours of gold started by General George Armstrong Custer (1839-1876) the previous summer. The confirmation of gold from this survey led to a significant increase in the numbers of prospector miners that in turn led to the Great Sioux War of 1876-1877.

Aware of his friend's interest, Dodge had written to Blackmore in January 1875 requesting his help and advice on a project to publish a book on the Indians of the Plains since he considered there was an audience for such a compilation of his experiences that might be published first in England and then in the USA.[73] Given Dodge's political stance as a supporter of the US Army's point of view, his commander, General Philip Henry Sheridan, backed the publication since it advanced the political interests of the army and extended the contribution of army officers to the contribution to knowledge. This last aspect formed a link with the Smithsonian Institution.

Blackmore loved the big game hunt of the 'Great Plains' and considered that this subject and curiosity around the North American Indian would be of particular interest to British readers.

He accepted Dodge's invitation and was to play a crucial role in publishing the subsequent book. A detailed account of the history of the editorial and production processes behind this title has been given by Wayne R. Kime. It is, however, worth highlighting some of the key aspects.[74]

Dodge understood little about the components of publishing; about the subtle linguistic differences between English and the American variant, about composing, printing and marketing a popular volume. Blackmore had acquired experience from his numerous business publications and in 1869 had overseen the publication of his 'booster' book, *Colorado: Its Resources, Parks, and Prospects*. That Blackmore took on this project underlines both his interest and his commitment. He was a busy businessman who by 1875 had significant concerns about his finances. Evidence suggests Blackmore was a willing and active collaborator and financial sponsor.

73 Wayne R. Kime, *Colonel Richard Irving Dodge: the life and times of a career army officer*, University of Oklahoma Press, Norman, 2006 pp.180-1.

74 Kime, *ibid.*, Part 4, Chapter 13.

Blackmore's funding of the project and his experience in publishing provided a solution to Dodge's predicament. The Englishman negotiated with two London publishers, Sampson Low – who had published his 1869 Colorado title – and Chattos & Windus. The publication of the forthcoming title was advertised in British newspapers such as *The Examiner* and priced at 24s.

The level of detailed interest and comment taken by Blackmore in Dodge's draft text is evidenced by his making no less than one hundred and thirty-four changes. He also took the liberty of Anglicising Dodge's text. The American edition had 1,921 changes to the words in the manuscript Dodge had originally sent Blackmore.[75] Significantly, Blackmore did support the inclusion of several pages that described the sexual license and brutality of the 'noble savage.'

Blackmore may have considered that Dodge's book might include photographic illustrations – or perhaps the American author hoped it would. In June 1876 Dodge sent to Blackmore photographs for possible use as illustrations for *The Hunting Grounds*.[76] However, the only photographic illustration in the finished publication was a photographic frontispiece half-length portrait of Dodge.

On his dedication page Dodge described Blackmore as a 'keen sportsman, genial companion, firm friend with whom I have passed many happy hours on 'The Plains' and to whose favourable appreciation of my campfire stories the inception of the work is principally due, this book is affectionately inscribed by the author.'[77] A second British edition appeared in 1878. The American edition was titled *The Plains of North America and Their Inhabitants* and was published by G. P. Putnam in New York. The title was the preferred one of the author but which had been changed for the English edition as a result of Blackmore's intervention.

Blackmore ensured that *The Hunting Grounds of the Great West* was widely reviewed and organised the strategic distribution of

75 Kime, *ibid.*, p.547 endnotes 41 and 46

76 Kime, *ibid.*, p.546 endnote 27

77 Dedication page of *The Hunting Grounds of the Great West: A description of the plains, game, and Indians of the Great North American Desert*. Chatto & Windus, London, 1877.

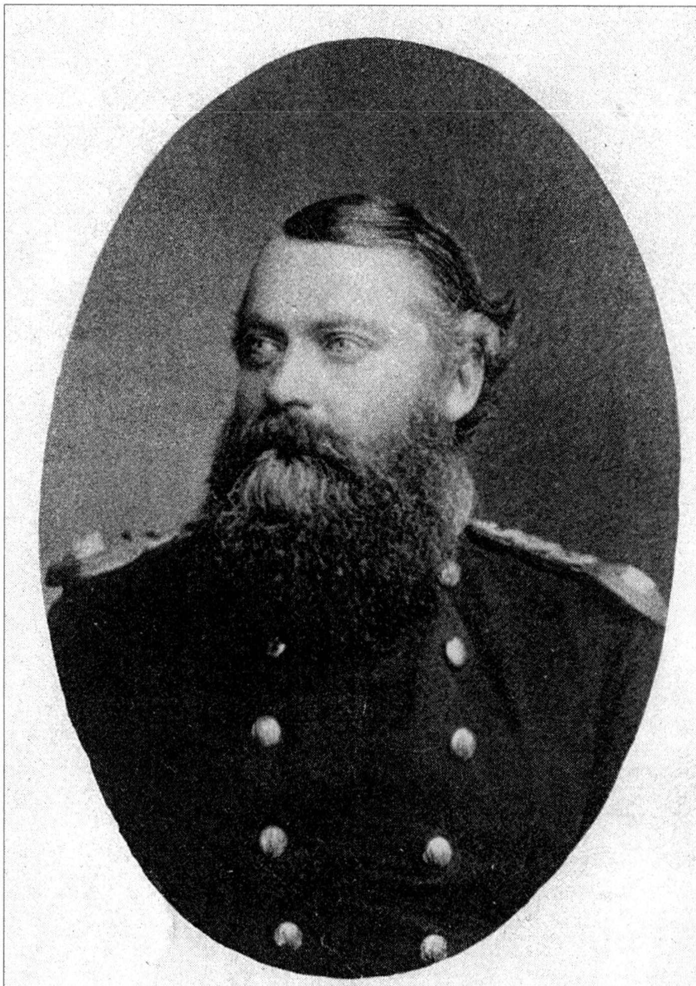

Colonel Richard Irving Dodge (1827-1895)
Frontispiece to *The Hunting Grounds of the Great West: A description of the plains, game, and Indians of the Great North American Desert.* Chatto & Windus, London, 1877.

complimentary copies. It received generally good reviews though British readers were somewhat more critical than their American equivalents with respect to the chapters involving Indian stealing, scalping and their brutality toward captives. Chatto & Windus adroitly quoted in its advertisements from the best review it could find. The *Edinburgh Daily*

Review had stated that 'Since Catlin, no such valuable work has appeared as this.'[78] How Blackmore reacted to this review is not recorded.

While enthusiastically reviewed in America, sales were initially disappointing. Nevertheless, the seven hundred copies of the first impression sold out by July 1877 and Blackmore's precarious financial situation seems not to have prevented him from preparing a second British edition which appeared in 1878.

Dodge's gratitude to Blackmore was reflected in a significant donation he made to the Blackmore Museum. This was a scalp fragment taken from the youngest son of Dull Knife (c.1810-1883), a Cheyenne, given to Dodge in December 1876 by Frank White, a Pawnee Indian scout who had won it in the recent Dull Knife Fight – or Battle of Bates Creek – near the North Fork of the Powder River in Wyoming. There was some significance in this gesture since Frank White had given Dodge the understanding that the giving of a scalp sealed the two men as something like brothers.[79]

Though Dodge gave an effusive dedication to Blackmore in *The Hunting Grounds of the Great West* his loyalty to his 'firm friend' was not built on solid foundations. Probably reflecting Blackmore's fall from grace, Dodge did not even mention his English friend and patron in his *Our Wild Indians: Thirty-three Years Personal Experience Among the Red Men of the Great West* published in 1883.[80]

78 The quotation formed part of the publisher's advertisement that appeared in *The Examiner*, Saturday 30th December, 1876 p.1483.

79 The Dull Knife Fight took place on 25th November 1876 between a contingent of 4th U. S. Cavalry led by Colonel Ranald Slidell Mackenzie (1840-1889) and a group of Cheyenne led by Dull Knife and Little Wolf (c.1820-1904). Frank White was one of Mackenzie's large contingent of Pawnee, Arapaho and Lakota scouts. Wayne R. Kime, *The Powder River Expedition Journals of Colonel Richard Irving Dodge*, University of Oklahoma Press, Norman, 1997 p.26 and p.99 and Wayne R. Kime, *Colonel Richard Irving Dodge: the life and times of a career army officer*, University of Oklahoma Press, Norman, 2006, p.256. The scalp fragment in now in the British Museum, Department of Africa, Oceania & the Americas, Registration number: Am1983,Q.194.

80 Richard Irving Dodge, *Our Wild Indians: Thirty-three Years Personal Experience among the Red Men of the Great West.. A Popular Account of their Social Life, Religion, Habits, Traits, Customs, Etc. with Thrilling Adventures and Experiences on the Great Plains and in the Mountains of Our Wide Frontier.* .A. D. Worthington, Hartford, Conn, 1883.

CATLIN AND BLACKMORE

The origins of Blackmore's interest in the North American 'noble Red Man' remain obscure though as has been noted he claimed that this began around 1846. It is possible that in the early 1840s he had seen an exhibition of the works of George Catlin (1796-1872) American painter, author, traveller and showman whose portraits of Native Americans and their way of life combined with his show to had been influential during this period.

Catlin was a generation older than William Blackmore and the artist's heyday was in the 1840s. By the 1860s – when the Englishman's interest in North American Indians began in earnest – Catlin was an old man nearing the end of his life. Catlin's position had become increasingly historiographic. His glory days were well behind him and though he continued to create works of art based on his early experiences of the 'Great West', the environment within which he tried to operate had fundamentally changed. The interrelationship between Catlin and Blackmore included the new dynamics of the post Civil War opening of the West, the politics of patronage in Washington, D.C. that saw Catlin continually frustrated and thwarted by his rivals, and new forms of image making and reprographics. Their common bond was the documentation of the vanishing Indian population of the Great Plains of the American West.

Catlin's career was dominated by a perpetual struggle to obtain patronage and secure a home for his Indian Gallery. He had made five trips to the 'Great West' between 1830 and 1836 following the trail of the Lewis and Clark expedition of 1804–1806, the first United States government sponsored overland expedition to the Pacific coast and back. He visited fifty tribes living west of the Mississippi River from present day North Dakota to Oklahoma. In the late 1830s Catlin then formed his Indian Gallery of paintings and artefacts and toured this to major cities such as Pittsburgh, Cincinnati, and New York. However, the costs of running the gallery were not being matched by the receipts from the American paying public and Catlin resolved to take his collection across the Atlantic for a tour of what he considered would be the more lucrative

European capitals.

Having arrived in London in late 1839, in January 1840 Catlin leased the largest room within the Egyptian Hall, in fashionable Piccadilly, in which he displayed his Indian Gallery of nearly six hundred paintings of Native American subjects, together with the vast collection of native artefacts and costumes. Catlin lectured and demonstrated Native American hunting practices and employed a number of locals to dress up in 'Red Indian' garb and create *tableaux vivants*.

In 1841 Catlin published his *Letters and Notes on the manners, customs, and condition of the North American Indians* in London. In 1844, again in London, he published twenty-five coloured lithographic plates, entitled *Catlin's North American Indian Portfolio. Hunting Scenes and Amusements of the Rocky Mountains and Prairies of America*. The printed catalogue of the library of the Blackmore Museum indicates that William owned a copy of both of these publications though when he acquired them is unknown. Catlin's original intention was to produce four portfolios of twenty-five plates each, disseminating his images more widely than he could by displaying his oil paintings. However, Catlin did not make a profit from this first portfolio and no more were to appear.

The Indian Gallery remained in the Egyptian Hall until 1842 when Catlin's lease expired. He then moved his Gallery for a short period to an open air venue in Vauxhall Gardens on the South bank of the River Thames and then to Liverpool. From 1843 Catlin took his Gallery on tour around Britain accompanied by a group of Ioway, North American Indians – he also employed a band of Ojibwas from Canada. These Indians had been brought to England by the American showman Arthur Rankin (1816-1893). Venues for Catlin's shows included Birmingham, Newcastle-upon-Tyne, Edinburgh, Dundee, Perth, Glasgow, Dublin, Liverpool and Manchester.[81] In December 1843 his company performed

81 This itinerary has been assembled from references in George Catlin, *Catlin's notes of eight years' travels and residence in Europe with his North American Indian collection with anecdotes and incidents of the travels and adventures of three different parties of American Indians whom he introduced to the courts of England, France and Belgium*. London, 1848. It is not complete and identifying exactly where Catlin exhibited and performed his shows may never be established.

at Windsor Castle before Queen Victoria and Prince Albert. Catlin was back in London at the Egyptian Gallery in 1844. In 1845 He then toured in France and Belgium where his company performed before King Louis-Philippe of France at the Tuileries on 21st April, 1845 before returning, once again, to London in 1848.[82]

A Daguerreotype of six Ojibwas Indians who had been employed by Catlin during the years of his shows in Great Britain and Continetal Europe is now in the collection of the Chicago History Museum. The subjects are Maungwadaus (The Great Hero), Awunnewabe (Bird of Thunder), Waubuddick (The Elk), Ujejock (The Pelican), Uhwuasiggeezighgookkway (Woman of the Upper World) and Noodinnokay (The Furious Storm). The dating of this Daguerreotype has yet to be firmly established. A copy photograph of this Daguerreotype in the Smithsonian Institution is accompanied by a note stating that it was taken in 1851 in North America. There is no evidence that this Daguerreotype might have been taken in England during the Ojibwas engagement with Catlin.[83] However, the Ojibwas themselves exploited photography during their stay in London where they were befriended by a Mr. Saunders.

They loved him, and when they were again in their own land it would

82 For an account of this itinerary see Christopher Mulvey, 'Among the Sag-a-noshes: Ojibwa Indians with George Catlin in Europe. Indians and Europe, 1843-1848' in Christian Feest (ed.), *An Interdisciplinary Collection of Essays.*, University of Nebraska Press, Lincoln and London, 1999 pp.153-276,

83 The Smithsonian Institution catalogue entry reads: *From a daguerreotype deposited in the Chicago Historical Society with the following letter: 'This certifies to my purchase from A-wun-ne-wa-be, now known as Chief John T. Henry of the Munsey Reservation, Ontario, Canada, of the daguerreotype of the six Ojibbeway Indians who visited Queen Victoria and King Louis Philippe in 1845-46, in charge of George Catlin, who exhibited these Indians in England and France at the time. The personages were identified to me in the picture by the chief, and recorded in his own handwriting as attached herewith; noting those that are still alive, the chief remembering his age is 79 years. This picture, which is unique from the fact that but one was taken, was made in 1851 – five years after their return from England – and bears the date on the back of the original frame with signature of Maun-qua-daus, the Great Chief. This picture was purchased by me at the home of the chief on July 2, 1903, and the names given by the chiefs as written below correspond with the titles given of these Indians on page 294 of Catlin's Ojibbeway and Iowa Indians published in London in 1852, giving account of the reception to the Royalties and their various exhibitions in Europe.' (Signed /Walter C. Wyman.) Chicago, October 1, 1903.*

> be pleasant to see him still. They wished to have his face (meaning a portrait). They would then be able to show to their tribe the man who had been a father to them! The old gentleman kindly complied with the request and the Ojibbeways, at their own expense, procured a Daguerreotype likeness, which will, doubtless, for many years hereafter, be handed down as a heirloom in the forests of the far West.[84]

It is unclear to what degree the great showman Catlin exploited photography during the 1840s while in Europe, though later in his life he adopted novel photomechanical processes to reproduce his works. November 1843 Catlin's show was in Manchester and it was reported that the Indians were photographed. 'The Indians were greatly surprised at the 'mystery' by which portraits were obtained in so very short a time.'[85] As previously mentioned, the following year Antoine Claudet (1797-1867) photographed the Rankin/Catlin troop of Ojibwas in London and these images were copied as engravings by Vizetelly Brothers to produce illustrations for a booklet by Charles Stuart (1783-1865), *A Short History and Description of the Ojibbeway Indians now on a visit to England with correct likenesses, engraved from daguerreotype plates, taken by M. Claudet.*[86] Whether the group of Objiwa was photographed in any other British town during Catlin's tours during the 1840s remains to be established. Similarly, what role Catlin played in such activities is unclear.

In 1849 Catlin received the support of Senator William L. Dayton (1807-1864) of New Jersey who moved for an amendment to the Civil and Diplomatic Appropriation bill by proposing the insertion of an item of US$5,000 as the first of ten annual payments to purchase Catlin's Indian Gallery. This was unsuccessful. Catlin's financial situation steadily declined and he took up other employment. In early 1850

84 *A Short History and Description of the Ojibbeway Indians now on a visit to England*, London 1844 pp.19-20. This pamphlet has been attributed to Arthur Rankin.

85 *Manchester Guardian*, 22nd November, 1843 p.4 as quoted in Kate Flint, *The Transatlantic Indian, 1776-1930.*, Princeton University Press, Princeton and Oxford, 2009 p.60-61 and p.305 endnote 26.

86 Charles Stuart, *A Short History and Description of the Ojibbeway Indians now on a visit to England with correct likenesses, engraved from daguerreotype plates, taken by M. Claudet.*, [n.p.] London, 1844.

Catlin was appointed Superintendent of the Texas Department of the newly merged Universal Emigration and Colonization Company with the United States Land Company. He toured the English Midlands lecturing on the benefits of emigration to this part of the USA. In April 1850 George Adams the agent of the United States Land Company for Gosport and Portsmouth placed an advertisement in the *Hampshire Telegraph and Sussex Chronicle* which outlined Catlin's role;[87]

> An arrangement has been made with Mr. George Catlin (who is well known to the public by his writings on the Western States, and by his delineations of Indian character) to proceed in a short time, with the aid of suitable persons associated with him, to establish the first settlement, upon a large tract of valuable Prairie Land, well known to him as a most favourable position for Emigration, in the centre of one of the Western States of America, under a title direct from the Government, which has been legally transferred to one of the Directors, and duly registered in his name in the proper office of that country; and measures will be taken to secure the most moderate costs to Emigrants, and without any profit to the company, the means of easy and rapid transit, both by sea and afterwards by land, to the place of destination, with every attention to their health and comfort.

An advertisement in *The Essex and General Advertiser* in July 1850 identified the destination as Milam County, Texas.[88]

Whether Blackmore attended any of the lectures given by Catlin or was aware of his role in promoting land sales in America is unknown. Blackmore may have been familiar with the Universal Emigration and Colonization Company since one of the banks acting for it was the Liverpool Borough Bank. In addition, the United States Land Company had an agent in Liverpool whom Blackmore may have been aware of.

Catlin was scheduled to sail from Liverpool with the first group

87 Advertisements including George Catlin's name were placed in the provincial press by local agents. *Hampshire Telegraph and Sussex Chronicle*, 27th April, 1850 p.2.

88 *The Essex and General Advertiser*, 12th July, 1850 p.1. Advertisement placed by George Sansom, local agent of the Universal Emigration and Colonization Company.

of emigrants in early September 1850.[89] However, he appears to have resigned this post in August and did not sail to America as scheduled.[90]

Presumably disillusioned, Catlin returned to another business venture aimed at exploiting his collection. In 1851 he submitted proposals to the Ethnological Society of London for a floating Museum of Mankind with his collection as the centrepiece, and went so far as to invite his patron Sir Thomas Phillipps (1792-1872) to become a director. Catlin continued to lobby the US government for patronage, hoping Congress would purchase the Indian Gallery as a legacy for future generations. However, Catlin's financial situation now plunged him into bankruptcy in 1852. Joseph Harrison (1810-1874), a Philadelphia industrialist, then stepped in, paid Catlin's debts and acquired the Indian Gallery in the same year. Catlin's family returned to the USA and in 1854 he sailed alone to South America. For the next six years, accompanied by various companions, guides, and interpreters, he travelled extensively throughout the continent on and off until 1860. He returned to England, Belgium, France, and Prussia on visits during the 1850s but had to do so anonymously since he was still liable for his debts in these countries.

Continuing to seek out additional forms of income, during a brief stay in Brussels over the winter of 1857 to 1858, Catlin registered a design for 'improvements in the construction and propelling of steamers.'[91]

In 1860 Catlin returned to Europe and settled in Brussels where he lived in two scantily furnished rooms at 8 Rue de Brabant, in a relatively obscure part of the city beside Brussels Nord railway station. He painted a large number of images of North American Indians similar in subject to those he had lost to creditors a decade earlier – his

89 *The Huddersfield Chronicle and West Yorkshire Advertiser*, Saturday, 17th August, 1850 p.8.

90 The first ship of emigrants was reported to have sailed as scheduled in September 1850 though there is another report that it sailed to Galveston in July 1851 and George Catlin was stated to have been on board. See *The Plough, the Loom, and the Anvil*, July, 1851 p.22.

91 Dated 20th February 1858 in 'Provisional Protection', *Mechanic's Magazine*, 12th March, 1858 p.262. In 1843 Catlin had been granted a British patent for his invention of 'Certain Improvements in the Construction of Vessels for Navigation, Designed to Prevent the Loss of Life in Case of Shipwreck or Other Accidents at Sea.' This patent, no. 9878, was granted for a period of 14 years.

Cartoon Collection. Between 1864 and 1865 Catlin produced a series of watercolours – based on field notes and sketches – which depicted several episodes of the O-Kee-pa ('Buffalo Dance') ceremonial of the Mandans, a Native American tribe that historically lived along the banks of the Missouri River in present-day North and South Dakota. Eight of these watercolours were subsequently deposited in the British Museum.

Evidence suggests that it was not until after his first visit to the USA that Blackmore actively collected Native American artefacts. By the early 1870s Blackmore was seen as a potential sponsor by a number of artists, one of whom was George Winter (1809-1876), an English-born American painter noted for his portraits of Native Americans and other figures of the American frontier. Correspondence between Blackmore and Winter dating to 1871 survives, though it does not appear that Blackmore acquired any of the artist's work and the discussions were primarily around Winter's desire to find a publisher in England.[92]

In 1865 the Philobiblion Society of London published fifty copies of *An Account of an Annual Religious Ceremony Practised by the Mandan Tribe of North American Indians*. This sixty-seven page publication was based on a written account of Mandan ceremonies based on a lecture Catlin had given to the society. The Philobiblion Society published the account without Catlin's permission, and he denied authorship and attempted, unsuccessfully, to have all copies surrendered. Blackmore had been deeply involved in this publication, though Catlin was unaware of this. Blackmore appears to have had access to Catlin's text and watercolours prior to their being deposited in the British Museum and had five of the descriptive captions copied. Some sixty years later, Blackmore's nephew Frank Stevens informed L. J. P. Gaskin, then Librarian of the Horniman Museum in London, that his uncle had 'provided the cost of publication.' Some fifty copies had been printed and several of these

92 See Brian W. Dippie, *Catlin and His Contemporaries: The Politics of Patronage.*, University of Nebraska Press, Lincoln, 1990 p. 421 and endnote 76 on p.523 in which letters from Blackmore to Winter dated 6th August and 9th November 1871 and Winter to Blackmore of 9th August 24th November 1871 and 5th March 1872 are cited. These are held in the George Winter Papers, Tippecanoe County Historical Association, Lafayette, Indiana.

had been held in the Blackmore Museum.[93] In 1867 Catlin's *O-KEE-PA: A Religious Ceremony: and other customs of the Mandans,* was published by Trübner and Co. in London and in the same year an American edition by J.B. Lippincott of Philadelphia costing US$4.00. The thirteen illustrations were coloured photolithographs by Simonau & Toovey of Brussels. Catlin referred to this process as 'phototypography' and was later to suggest to Blackmore it be exploited to produce a photographic publication of his new Indian Gallery.

During the early 1840s Catlin had found an English sponsor in the form of the bibliophile Sir Thomas Phillipps who had loaned the American money on a number of occasions, often with Catlin's paintings used as collateral. This sponsorship was maintained until around 1860. How Catlin became aware of William Blackmore is not clear. It may have been that Blackmore found Catlin. Always on the lookout for sponsors Catlin clearly considered Blackmore both as a potential patron and as a publishing collaborator.

In Brussels in 1870 Catlin began exhibiting his Cartoon Collection which he had recreated from his Indian Gallery largely from memory. It closed the following year without much success. In early 1871 Blackmore visited Catlin in Brussels and purchased for £125 one of Catlin's albums. Catlin was grateful for Blackmore's support and gave him a copy of his recent books – *Last rambles amongst the Indians of the Rocky Mountains and the Andes* (1868), *The lifted and subsided rocks of America: with their influences on the oceanic, atmospheric and land currents, and the distribution of races* (1870), and *Shut your mouth and save your life* (1870) – together with an original portrait of the explorer Alexander von Humboldt (1769-1859).[94]

93 See L.J.P. Gaskin, 'A Rare Pamphlet on the Mandan Religious Ceremony, in the Library of the Horniman Museum' *Man*, No. 131, September 1939 pp.141-142 and Colin Taylor, 'William Blackmore: A 19th Century Englishman's contribution to American Indian ethnology', in Christian F. Feest (ed.), *Indians and Europe. An Interdisciplinary collection of Essays.*, University of Nebraska Press, Lincoln, 1999 p.332.

94 Only *The lifted and subsided rocks of America* is listed in the 1871 printed catalogue of the library of the Blackmore Museum. The portrait of Humboldt has not been located.

The money Catlin received from Blackmore enabled him to travel to New York in late 1871. In a letter dated 12th December 1871 Catlin wrote to Blackmore requesting a loan of £100.[95] This was Catlin's first return to the USA in thirty-one years and he was confident enough in Blackmore's desire to acquire his gallery that he stated to the New York Historical Society that an 'English nobleman' [i.e. Blackmore] was prepared to pay US$40,000 for his collection on demand.[96]

In 1871-1872 the two discussed a photographic publication of Catlin's second Indian Gallery which eventually totalled some 500 works. Catlin wrote to Blackmore on the 12th December 1871 outlining the proposed publication. It would be a limited edition of one hundred copies consisting of two volumes, each containing one hundred photographic plates and one hundred pages of text. The illustrations should be created by the 'phototypography' process – possibly Simonau & Toovey's photomechanical process employed to create the colour illustrations for Catlin's 1867 work *O-KEE-PA, a Religious Ceremony and Other Customs of the Mandans*. However, Catlin appears to have been discussing production of the proposed publication in Antwerp, where Joseph Maes (1838-1908) had set up a collotype photomechanical printing establishment.[97] The estimated cost would be £10 14s. per set.

However, it is worth considering Blackmore's activities and projects at this time and thus the context within which he considered Catlin's business proposition. Firstly, by 1871 Blackmore had visited the Great West on several occasions and thus seen North American Indians in their natural habitat. The mystic of Catlin's images would have been diluted. Blackmore was at this point committed to photographic publishing – significantly publishing photographs from life, rather than exploiting the medium to reproduce works of art such as Catlin's.

95 Blackmore Collection, Fray Angelico Chavez History Library, Santa Fe Box 3 Folder 5.

96 See Brian W. Dippie, *Catlin and His Contemporaries: The Politics of Patronage.*, University of Nebraska Press, Lincoln, 1990 endnote 76 on p.523.

97 Blackmore Collection, Fray Angelico Chavez History Library, Santa Fe Box 3 Folder 5. For Simonau & Toovey and Joseph Maes see Steven F. Joseph, Tristan Schwilden and Marie-Christine Claes, *Directory of Photographers in Belgium 1839-1905. Volume I – Text.*, Museum voor Fotografie, Antwerp, 1997.

He was in the process of publishing the photographs of chiefs of the Cheyenne, Arapaho, and Wichita who, on their return home from a delegation visit to Washington, D.C. in May 1871, had visited the studio of Jeremiah Gurney in New York. Blackmore was already planning his own 'Indian Gallery' and in 1872 would publish a series of portfolios containing photographs by Alexander Gardner, though these were not made commercially available. In addition, about this time Blackmore commissioned Antonio Shindler to create oil paintings from a set of sixteen photographic portraits in the Englishman's collection. This series was completed around 1874 and was put on display in the Blackmore Museum. Though comparatively small in number, it might be considered as the start of a small scale 'Indian Gallery' to rival that of Catlin. When Catlin obtained news of Blackmore's plans he wrote to Blackmore in December 1871 stating 'I am at a loss to know how it may affect the 200 photos which I am anxious to put out.'[98]

Blackmore was not unsympathetic towards Catlin's plight and discussed the artist's situation with Spender F. Baird, Assistant Secretary of the Smithsonian, prompting an offer to Catlin for him to use the institutions' facilities. In early 1872 Catlin travelled to Washington, D.C. at the invitation of Joseph Henry, the first secretary of the Smithsonian. Until his death in Jersey City, New Jersey later that year, Catlin worked and lived in a room in the Smithsonian 'Castle' given to him by Henry.

In October 1872, with still no signs that the Smithsonian would purchase his work, Catlin packed up his paintings and had them shipped to Jersey City. He died two months later on the 23rd December 1872.

Joseph Harrison's widow presented Catlin's original Indian Gallery to the Smithsonian Institution in 1879. Much of the collection had been damaged from the poor conditions in which it was stored. It was not until 1912 that Catlin's heirs sold the Cartoon Collection to the American Museum of Natural History in New York. Today Catlin's Indian Gallery is recognized as a great cultural treasure, offering rare insight into native cultures and a crucial chapter in American history. However, that chapter was a generation before that of William Blackmore.

98 Museum of New Mexico, Santa Fe HSNM 0407.

Dippie considered Catlin's character as one of 'pride, fortitude and indomitable will' stating 'who could doubt he would one day rout his detractors and win lasting renown?'[99] In a number of respects this also mirrored the situation in which William Blackmore found himself during the last few years of his life. Neither necessarily achieved their goals within their respective lifetimes. Catlin received posthumous recognition, though his legacy was ensured through the private benefaction of the Harrison family rather than state funding. Blackmore played a small but significant role in achieving this for Catlin.

Quite how Blackmore considered Catlin and what type of relationship he should form with the artist remains unclear. Normally decisive in his thoughts and actions, Blackmore was uncharacteristically reticent to commit to funding Catlin's publishing ventures or acquiring his Cartoon Collection. Possibly Blackmore saw Catlin as a two-edged sword; an enviable history surrounding his shows and Indian Gallery, but also a liability, a bankrupt clinging to a reputation that did not align with either the Englishman's or Smithsonian's primary objectives. He may also have possibly considered Catlin as something of a threat. If Catlin succeeded in selling his gallery to the Smithsonian this might push Blackmore's aim to create a photographic gallery of Native Americans into the shadows.

There remains an irony that Catlin identified and exploited the benefits of new photomechanical reprographic processes in an effort to promote his work while Blackmore did not. Had Catlin lived longer and Blackmore formed a suitable and acceptable business proposition for both of them, they might have collaborated further. However, it seems unlikely that William Blackmore would ever have met Catlin's ultimate goal by purchasing his Cartoon Gallery. It fell outside his matrix management of his social network and could not be configured effectively within his view of the wider politics of patronage in Washington, D.C.

99 Brian Dippie, *Catlin and His Contemporaries: The Politics of Patronage.*, University of Nebraska Press, Lincoln and London, 1990 p.318.

8
Conclusion

As individual activities William Blackmore's professional and personal pursuits were not unique amongst his contemporaries. There was a plethora of English and European financiers involved in exploiting the business opportunities offered by the development of the Great West. Similarly, there were archaeologists, anthropologists and ethnographers working on various aspects of North American Indians. Photography had been acknowledged as a key tool in capturing portraits of Native Americans and their lifestyles by a number of Blackmore's contemporaries. However, few of Blackmore's contemporaries combined such a range of activities so significantly, delivered results so quickly and achieved such significant outputs.

By the early 1870s Blackmore was involved in a bewildering number of interrelated business ventures and a myriad of other investments distributed across Great Britain, mainland Europe and North America . These included land holdings, railways, mineral mines, a Welsh colliery and telecommunications.

In his personal life, Blackmore was clearly affected by the loss of his wife Mary in July 1872 during their visit to the USA. He wrote in his diary at the end of this trip;

> I, having bathed in the Pacific & visited N. Mexico, hope to get back once more to Old England. I feel I cannot say 'Home' again for I feel that none is left for me.[100]

100 Blackmore Diary No. 7 Saturday 17th August, 1872.

However, William was subsequently not without some happy – although apparently complicated – romantic moments. By late 1872 Blackmore appears to have formed a close – probably romantic – attachment to a woman he refers to in his diary as 'Ellie'. On 1st April 1873 he noted 'Ellie mine three months ago today' and on the 18th April 'Ellie wrote to R. breaking off the engagement.' For the entry for Saturday 17th January 1874 he noted 'Arrived in Paris. Saw Ellie. Bliss.' and the following day he recorded in his Diary 'Extreme Bliss .... Very, very dangerous'. This last comment perhaps indicates the possible scandal if the relationship was to be made public. Blackmore noted her birthday was on 15th March. Who Ellie was remains to be determined though the 'R.' referred to might have been one of Blackmore's investors, Robert E. Randall with whom he had a problematic business relationship and whose name appears regularly in Blackmore's diary during this period.

Ellie appears to have been residing in Paris at this time and her name appears regularly in Blackmore's diary until his embarkation on a boat to New York on 26th August 1874. Whether this relationship forms part of the 'Bohemian life' that Brayer alluded to may have to be left to conjecture. It certainly points towards him willing to take significant risks. Ellie's central role in Blackmore's life does not appear to have continued in the last few years of his life. However, the Blackmore papers in the Wiltshire & Swindon History Centre include a version of William's will dated 25th November 1872. This document has been heavily defaced and the corner that would have contained William's signature has been torn off, though the signatures of Henry Johnson and P. Shepheard, Blackmore's clerks, are still legible indicating that this was not a draft document. It refers to Humphrey being bequested £5,000 but also notes an Eleanor [defaced with illegible middle and surname] of Philadelphia as the other beneficiary and executor. It would thus appear that after his death, William's family retrospectively superseded this will in order to secure Humphrey as the sole executor.

The decline of William Blackmore was to a certain extent precipitated by the economic depression that began in 1873 and was to continue in the USA until 1879. The Englishman's strategy was not to halt new investments and to consolidate and exploit his existing holdings. From around 1875 this financial recession impacted on Blackmore's business and private interests – such as the Blackmore Museum and some of his art collection. The stress of his disintegrating investments and the financial liabilities they represented began to take effect and by the summer of 1877 Blackmore's health began to fail. The cumulative effect of overwork, lack of rest and general overindulgence in what Brayer referred to as a 'Bohemian life'– particularly intemperate 'use of alcoholic beverages' and 'strong liquor' – were taking their toll. There are uncorroborated family stories that William, following the collapse of his business empire, had accompanied his client Charles Darwin on a trip to the Far East where he become addicted to opium.[101] Darwin was certainly not one of Blackmore's clients and it is unlikely one will ever be able to establish whether the financier had slipped into opium addiction.

One critical impact of this was on Blackmore's relations with key players within the financial houses of London on which he relied.[102] Another factor was that he was increasingly incapable of effectively managing his business interests in the USA, and his brother Humphrey and assistant Henry Johnson worked as best they could to keep the show on the road.

Blackmore spent the summer of 1877 convalescing in Torquay but suffered sunstroke which set back his recovery. Yet in December of that year he wrote to his sister Blanche Boyle stating the he was immersed in writing up the text for a history of New Mexico.[103]

In March 1878 Blackmore suffered serious concussion following a fall from a London omnibus. Brayer's account of the last day of William's life states that on the morning of 12th April Blackmore had gone to his library to read his morning mail when the quiet of his Belgrave Mansions apartment was suddenly shattered by the report of a revolver. Brayer reported that Henry Johnson, Blackmore's trusted assistant, found William slumped over his desk. The morning mail

101 Letter, undated, sent in 1998 from Carole Ann Farley of El Paso, Texas – a descendant of Henry Blackmore and Charlotte Polhill – to Ken Blackmore. I thank Ken Blackmore for supplying a copy of this letter and giving permission for it to be quoted.

102 Brayer, *op.cit.*, Volume I p.311.

103 Letter dated 1st December 1877. Boyle papers as cited by Brayer *op.cit.*, Volume I pp.311-313.

probably had brought yet more financial problems that had tipped the balance. Though still alive, William Blackmore was mortally wounded and died some five and a half hours later.

However, Brayer's description does not match the details outlined in the documents and statements made at Blackmore's inquest which took place on 15th April.[104] Humphrey Blackmore travelled from Salisbury to give evidence. Curiously, his name does not appear in the official list of witnesses at the inquest. Similarly, Henry Johnson was not called as a witness. Two witnesses who gave evidence and claimed to have found Blackmore were members of the staff of Belgrave Mansions; Walter Cooper, a waiter, and Emma Rose, a housemaid. Cooper stated that he had been called to William's rooms but the door was locked – which was most unusual. Having knocked and called out several times, Cooper declared that Blackmore opened the door himself but he was staggering and therefore Cooper put him onto a bed.

Blackmore's doctor, Dr. Henry Montague Duncan, who lived a short distance away from Belgrave Mansions at 139 Buckingham Palace Road, was another witness and gave the coroner a written statement in a letter dated 12th April, presumably written late in the evening of William's death. According to Duncan, a 'Dr. Black' first attended William Blackmore at the urgent request of the manager of Belgrave Mansions – but hoped he would not be called upon to give evidence in the inquest. This reluctance was probably due to a mixture of the illegality of suicide and dealing with a professional colleague's patient. Who Dr Black was is unclear but Duncan assured his medical colleague that his [Duncan's] evidence would be sufficient and that he would write a letter to the coroner, Charles Bedford, giving an account of events. The letter stated that Duncan attended Blackmore from shortly after 4.00pm – when William is reported to have shot himself – until he died at 9.30pm.

What is curious is that while Blackmore lived for some five hours after he shot himself, no attempt was made to take him to hospital. He was laid on a bed in his apartment while Dr. Duncan attended to

104 The inquest documents and verdict are held in Westminster Abbey Muniments.

him. Again, a combination of a fatal wound and the stigma of suicide may have been the reason for this. The verdict of the inquest was 'That deceased destroyed himself when in a state of temporary insanity.'

However, the implications of his death almost immediately became apparent. Blackmore's inquest documents include several letters from George Barker, of the insurer G. Barker & Co. of Mark Lane, London E.C. requesting a copy of the verdict of the inquest and also the name and contact details of Blackmore's doctor. This was presumably related to one of Blackmore's life insurance policy though it has yet to be established that these were eventually paid out.[105]

Brayer summarised the reasons for Blackmore's failures that led to his bankruptcy. These centred on;

- His failure to recognise changes in US Government land policy after 1873
- Over extending his land grant holdings during the world-wide economic depression
- Lack of his own funds to develop the land grants
- Lack of concentration on a single business investment at a time
- Inability to delegate authority to competent representatives and then support their decisions
- Failure to appreciate that it took years to develop lands, mines and railroad before any profit could be made

Evidence suggests that Blackmore's lack of concentration on a single business venture was mirrored in some of his other pursuits – though there may have been mitigating circumstances due to the busy business life he led. For instance Blackmore's objective in becoming a photographic publisher was not entirely successful or fully realised during his lifetime; he undertook three speculative photographic publications characterised by short print runs that bordered on 'vanity' publishing. His collecting of three paintings by Rossetti in a few years in the 1860s failed to blossom into a commitment to build a collection of

105 Humphrey Blackmore mentioned that one of William's life insurance policy was for £5,000 and that this would pay off some of his brother's immediate debts. Brayer, *op.cit.*, Volume I p.319.

British paintings and his set of Moran aquarelles was a one off. Similarly, his set of sixteen paintings by Shindler copied from photographs did not turn into a substantial Indian Gallery.

However, William could sometimes delegate successfully. He tasked much of the work of the Blackmore Museum to his industrious brother-in-law Edward Stevens and the 1870 publication of Flint Chips showed their professional partnership at its best and most influential. Quite what might have been achieved had Blackmore continued to be a prosperous entrepreneur and Stevens had lived longer one can only speculate.

Given his significance it is surprising that there is no obituary of William Blackmore in *The Times* though the *Athenæum* recorded his 'untimely death' that 'will be much regretted in a large scientific circle.'[106] The President of the Anthropological Institute of Great Britain and Ireland noted Blackmore's passing in his annual address and stated that 'we have lost a discerning and liberal promoter of anthropological science.'[107] The *Salisbury and Winchester Journal* published a half-column obituary in the issue of Saturday 20th April 1878 and referred to his death 'after a short illness.' Though Blackmore had been elected a council member of the Ethnological Society of London in 1866 he received a comparatively short obituary in the society's journal. Similarly, the published account of the 1878 meeting of the Wiltshire Archaeological and Natural History Society gave but passing mention of his demise, an extraordinary position to have taken given the lengths the Society had gone to a mere decade before when it had published the two volume *An Account of the Blackmore Museum, Salisbury* and lauded the Museum's benefactor.

The paucity of extensive obituaries for William Blackmore reflect the mid-Victorian moral and legal ramifications of the nature of his death. Suicide remained illegal in England and Wales until 1961 and the social stigma attached to suicide by the Victorians probably lies behind the paucity of references to his passing. Families 'shrank from the stigma' and tried hard to conceal a suicide whenever they could.[108]

106 A note in 'Scientific Gossip', *Athenæum*, No.2634, 20th April 1878.p.513.

107 *The Journal of the Anthropological Institute of Great Britain and Ireland*, Vol. 8, 1879, p.423.

108 See Michael MacDonald and Terence Murphy, *Sleepless Souls: Suicide in Early*

In certain respects, William Blackmore's death forms a significant case study of the manner in which Victorian society dealt with the suicide of a prominent contemporary.

By far the greatest consideration at the time of his death was that of William's financial situation. In the year leading up to William's suicide, Humphrey Blackmore had been supported by Henry Johnson, William's legal assistant and in whom William increasingly confided. Johnson was also an investor in some of William's trust lands investments, in 1875 subscribing £100 for shares in the Mora Grant purchase. From the spring of 1877 Johnson, together with Humphrey Blackmore, endeavoured to keep knowledge of William's poor health becoming public and at the same time maintain the status quo in William's similarly ailing trust land developments.

An indication of the seriousness of William's financial constraints is found in a letter written in November 1877. In this William acknowledged a loan of £360 from Humphrey and stated that he was selling bronzes, some watercolours and furniture to service the loan. On the 29th December William acknowledged the loan of £3,000 'or thereabouts monies which you have at various times advanced to me, or expended on my behalf.'[109]

Humphrey's character was of a very different nature to that of his elder brother. He was neither a businessman nor a risk taker. Though he was cautious, he had invested significantly in William's business ventures. Brayer considers Humphrey should have been bolder in his attempts to shore up his brothers remaining assets in the USA. However, Humphrey was happy to attempt to manage the remains of William's business interests from the provincial city of Salisbury and showed no appetite to visit the USA in order to sort matters out.

On William's death the complexity of his finances clearly posed a significant set of challenges to Humphrey Blackmore and Henry

Modern England, Oxford University Press, Oxford, 1990 p.351 and Barbara Weiss, *The Hell of the English. Bankruptcy and the Victorian Novel,* Associated University Presses, Cranbury, NJ, 1986.

109 Letter written in Salisbury on 8th November, 1877. Wiltshire & Swindon History Centre 776/579.

Johnson. It was more than two years before his will was proved on 4th December 1880. Humphrey Blackmore used an 1878 Letts diary as a notebook in which he listed William's debts as £17,715 10s. 9 ½d. of which £7,840 1s. 4d. was unsecured. William also owed a variety of other creditors some £7,844 7s. 6½d. of which £5,043 11s. was owed to his friend and professional partner in Liverpool, Andrew Tucker Squarey.[110] It is likely that there were other debts.

The background to the financial issues was documented by Humphrey in a letter to his brother in law Arthur Boyle written in July 1878. Humphrey stated that while he had located William's will, he was not inclined to offer it for probate because of the muddled status of the estate and the impending rush of creditors which would result from the recording of his late brother's testament. He added that advice from John Senior, his brother in law, and his uncle Edward Blackmore, was against 'proving the will.' In the event William's will remained unproven until John Horatio Lloyd (1798-1884), QC,[111] an elderly and cautions creditor, devised a ruse by which Humphrey was compelled to probate the will in order to protect his own interests in the Land Company of New Mexico; this Humphrey considered was a potential 'golden goose' that might save William's hopelessly insolvent estate.[112] The probate form signed by Humphrey and witnessed by Henry Johnson, stated that William had a personal estate of under £2,000 at the time of his death. The will itself is dated 17th April 1873 and the sole beneficiary is Humphrey Blackmore. It bears all the hallmarks of a document created in retrospect – particularly given the contents of William's will of November 1872 – and does not include William's signature.

On his forty-sixth birthday on 2nd August 1873 – and a year after the death of his wife Mary – Blackmore rather morbidly yet prophetically wrote in his diary;

110 Wiltshire & Swindon History Centre 776/579.

111 John Horatio Lloyd became known as the chief authority in all legal matters connected with railways and was employed as counsel for almost all the railways in the United Kingdom. He devised the well-known security called 'Lloyd's Bonds' without which a large proportion of the mid Victorian railways could not have been constructed.

112 This account is based on Brayer, *op.cit*, Volume I, pp.318-329.

> My birthday – 46 – How many years longer, if any, have I to live? I have never wished for a long life but have always desired to die in the full possession of all my faculties mental and bodily and have fixed as it were 50 as the limit beyond which even the strongest and most vigorous of us begin to deteriorate. This only gives me a few years more and 'The night cometh when no man can work.' May I utilise the remainder of my life long or short. Come life come death, I trust I shall be equally prepared.[113]

While great business opportunities still lay ahead of him, Blackmore's 'golden years' were behind him. The decline that overcame him was only a matter of years away.

Herbert Brayer made two perceptive comments on William Blackmore in a letter written while he was researching the Englishman;

> Yes, Blackmore in many ways was a 'conceited and objectionable man', but it sometimes takes men of that ilk to plow the ground and make it ready for those who will come after to sow the seed.[114]

From the perspective of the early 21st century one might wonder how William Blackmore was able to keep so many 'plates spinning'. Ultimately, he didn't. His pyramidal business empire imploded as a result of a number of interrelated events and he failed to ensure his eponymous museum had a secure and long-term funding stream. Bankruptcy and suicide were the final nails in the coffin of Blackmore's status and legacy. He plummeted from the lofty heights of reputational prominence and in doing so was entirely dislocated from a fitting position amongst the pantheon of 'men of mark' of the mid Victorian era. Simply put, he fell off the scholarly radar. Today, many works on the historiography of anthropology, ethnology, archaeology and photography that should rightfully include reference to his significance fail to do so. In spite of his weaknesses and the circumstances of his untimely demise, Blackmore deserves better.

113 Blackmore Diary No.6, 2nd August 1873 p.87.

114 Letter to Hugh Shortt dated 3rd January, 1947 in Blackmore Museum Papers in the S&SWM. It is unclear whom Brayer was quoting when he used the phrase 'conceited and objectionable man.'

Bibliography

Reports

Annual Reports of the Blackmore Museum
Annual Reports of the Salisbury & South Wilts Museum
Annual Reports of the United States Geological and Geographical Survey of the Territories
Annual Reports of the Board of Regents of the Smithsonian Institution

Newspapers

The Times
Salisbury & Winchester Journal
The Hampshire Advertiser
The Liverpool Mercury

Periodicals

Wiltshire Archaeological and Natural History
Hatcher Review
Sarum Chronicle
Transactions of the Historic Society of Lancashire and Cheshire
Proceedings of the Literary and Philosophical Society of Liverpool
Journal of the British Archaeological Association
Journal of the Anthropological Institute of Great Britain and Ireland
Journal of the Ethnological Society of London

Abbott, Edith. *Historical Aspects of the Immigration Problem. Select Documents*, University of Chicago Press, Chicago, 1926.

Altick, Richard. *The Shows of London: A panorama history of exhibitions, 1600–1862*, The Belknap Press of Harvard University Press, Cambridge, Mass. and London, 1978.

Anderson, Nancy. *Thomas Moran*, National Gallery of Art; Yale University Press, Washington; New Haven, 1997.

Arrington, Joseph Earl. 'Henry Lewis' Moving Panorama of the Mississippi River', *Louisiana History: The Journal of the Louisiana Historical Association*, Vol. 6, No. 3,Summer, 1965 pp. 239-272.

Baker, T. Lindsay and Harrison, Billy R. *Adobe Walls: The History and Archaeology of the 1874 Trading Post*, Texas A and M University Press, College Station, 1986.

Bandelier, Adolph F. *The Southwestern Journals of Adolph F. Bandelier*, University of New Mexico Press, 1966.

Barnhart, Terry A. 'The Hamilton Davis collection of American Antiquities', *Journal of the History of Collections*, Volume 16, Number 2, 2004 pp.59-87.

Bartlett, Richard A. *Great Surveys of the American West*, University of Oklahoma Press,

Norman, 1962.
Belchem, John. (ed.). *Liverpool 800: Culture, Character & History*, 2006.
Bennett, Mary. 'A Check List of Pre-Raphaelite Pictures Exhibited at Liverpool 1846-67, and Some of Their Northern Collectors,' *The Burlington Magazine*, Volume 105, No. 728, Victorian Art. Painting, Furniture, Sculpture November, 1963 pp.486-495.
[Blackmore Museum] *Account of the Blackmore Museum – Part I. The opening Meeting,* H.F. &E. Bull, Devizes; Bell & Daldy, London ; J.R. Smith, London 1868.
[Blackmore Museum] *Account of the Blackmore Museum – Part II. Report of the Blackmore Museum* H.F. &E. Bull, Devizes; Bell & Daldy, London ; J.R. Smith, London 1868.
Blair, Mary Ellen. *A Life Well Led: The Biography of Barbara Friere-Marreco Aitken British Anthropologist,* Sunstone Press, Santa Fe, 2008.
Bowden,Mark. *Pitt Rivers: The Life and Archaeological work of Lieutenant-General Augustus Henry Lane Fox Pitt Rivers,* Cambridge University Press, Cambridge, 1991.
Bowers, Shirley H. "Captured on Canvas': McKenney-Hall's History of the Indian Tribes of North America', *The Florida Historical Quarterly,* Volume 71, No.3, January, 1993 pp.339-347.
Bradshaw's Railway Manual, Shareholders' Guide and Official Directory.
Brayer, Herbert Oliver. 'Exploring the Yellowstone with Hayden, 1872, Diary of Sidford Hamp', *Annals of Wyoming,* Volume 14, Number 4, October 1942 pp.253-298.
Brayer, Herbert Oliver. *William Blackmore: A Case Study in the Economic Development of the West; Volume I –The Spanish Land Grants of New Mexico and Colorado 1863-1878; Volume II - Early Financing of the Denver & Rio Grande Railway and Ancillary Land Companies 1871-1878,* Bradford-Robinson, Denver, 1949.
Brinkerhoff, Roeliff. *Recollections of a Lifetime,* The Robert Clarke Company, 1900.
Brown, F. Martin. 'Hayden's 1854-55 Missouri River Expedition', *The Denver Westerners Roundup,* Volume 27, 1971 pp.3-66.
Cassidy, James G. *Ferdinand Hayden: entrepreneur of science,* University of Nebraska Press, Lincoln, 2000.
Catlin, George. *Catlin's notes of eight years' travels and residence in Europe with his North American Indian collection / with anecdotes and incidents of the travels and adventures of three different parties of American Indians whom he introduced to the courts of England, France and Belgium.* London, 1848.
Caygill, Marjorie and Cherry, John. (eds.). *A.W. Franks – Nineteenth-century Collecting and The British Museum,* British Museum Press, London, 1997.
Chandler, John. *Endless Street,* Hobnob Press, Salisbury, 1983.
[Christy Collection] *Guide to the Christy collection of Prehistoric Antiquities and Ethnography. Temporarily placed at 103, Victoria Street, Westminster.,* Trustees of the British Museum, [London], 1868.
Chung, Yun Shun Susie. 'Prehistoric Narratives in County Archaeological Museums in Mid-Nineteenth Century England', *Stanford Journal of Archaeology,* 2002.
Clark, Carol. *Thomas Moran – Watercolours of the American West,* University of Texas Press, Austin, 1980.
Clark, Graham. *Prehistory at Cambridge and Beyond,* Cambridge University Press, Cambridge, 1989.
Coulson, Thomas. *Joseph Henry, his life and Work,* Princeton University Press, Princeton, 1950.
Crittal, Elizabeth. (ed.). *A History of the County of Wiltshire: Volume 6,* Victoria County

History, London, 1962.

Cross, D. *Salisbury: a history and celebration*, Frith Book Co. for Ottakar's, Teffont, 2004.

DeMaillie, Raymond. "Scenes in the Indian Country': A Portfolio of Alexander Gardner's Stereographic Views of the 1868 Fort Laramie 'Treaty Council'", *Montana, The Magazine of Western History*, 31, 1981 pp.42-59.

Desmond, Ray. *The India Museum 1801-1879*, HMSO, London, 1982.

Dippie, Brian W. *Catlin and His Contemporaries: The Politics of Patronage*, University of Nebraska, 1990.

Dodge, Richard Irving. *The Hunting Grounds of the Great West: A description of the plains, game, and Indians of the great North American Desert.* Chatto & Windus, London, 1877.

Dorsey, George A. 'Notes on the Anthropological Museums of Central Europe', *American Anthropologist*, New Series, Volume 1, No. 3, July, 1899 pp. 462-474.

Doughty, Oswald, and Wahl, John Robert. *Letters of Dante Gabriel Rossetti, Volume II: 1861-1870*, Oxford University Press, Oxford, 1965.

Dunraven, Earl of. *The Great Divide: Travels in the Upper Yellowstone in the Summer of 1874*, Chatto & Windus, London 1876.

Edwards, Elizabeth. *Raw Histories - Photographs, Anthropology and Museums*, Berg Publishers, Oxford, 2001.

Feest, Christian F. (ed.), *Indians and Europe. An Interdisciplinary Collection of Essays*, University of Nebraska, Lincoln, 1999.

Fleming, Paula Richardson, and Luskey, Judith. *The North American Indians in Early Photographs*, Dorset Press, New York, 1986.

Fleming, Paula Richardson. *Native American Photography at the Smithsonian – The Shindler Catalogue*, Smithsonian Books, Washington and London, 2003.

Flint, Kate. *The Transatlantic Indian, 1776-1930.*, Princeton University Press, Princeton and Oxford, 2009.

Forbes, J. Watson and Kaye, John William. *The People of India. A Series of photographic Illustrations with Descriptive Letterpress, of the Races and Tribes of Hindustan*, William H. Allen and Co., London, 1868.

Foster, Mike. *Strange Genius: The Life of Ferdinand Vandeveer Hayden*, Roberts Rinehart Publishers, Niwot, 1994.

Fredeman, William E. *The Correspondence of Dante Gabriel Rossetti – The Chelsea Years 1863-1872, Volume III 1863-1867*, D.S. Brewer, Cambridge, 2003.

Gaskin, L.J.P. 'A Rare Pamphlet on the Mandan Religious Ceremony, in the Library of the Horniman Museum' *Man*, No. 131, September 1939 pp.141-142.

Gillam, P. M. S. *A History of General Practice in and around Salisbury*, Salisbury Medical Bulletin, Supplement to Number 97, January 2000.

Glenn, James R. 'The 'Curious Gallery': The Indian Photographs of the McClees Studio in Washington, 1857-1858, *History of Photography*, Volume 5, No.3, July 1981 pp.249-262.

Goldney, Frederick Hastings. *A History of Freemasonry in Wiltshire*, Virtue & Co., London 1880.

Goode, George Brown. (ed.). *The Smithsonian Institution, 1846-1896. The History of its First Half Century.*, City of Washington, 1897.

Greenwell, W. *'Grimes Graves': A Paper read at the Blackmore Museum at the Seventeenth Annual Meeting of the Wiltshire Archaeological and Natural History Society*, Frederick

A. Blake, Salisbury [1870].

Greenwood, Thomas. *Public Libraries: a history of the movement and a manual for the organisation and management of rate-supported libraries*, Cassell & Co., London, 1891.

Greeley, Horace. *Art and Industry as Represented in the Exhibition at the Crystal Palace New York —1853–4*, Redfield, New York, 1853.

Hales, Peter Bacon. 'American Views and the Romance of Modernization', in Martha A. Sandweiss (ed.), *Photographs in Nineteenth-Century America*, Amon Carter Museum; Harry N. Abrahams, Inc., Fort Worth; New York, 1991.

Hallett, Michael. 'The Manchester-Liverpool Circle', *The PhotoResearcher*, Number One, October 1990 pp.7-13.

Hamber, Anthony J. *'A Higher Branch of the Art' – Photographing the Fine Arts in England 1839-1880*, Gordon & Breach, Amsterdam, 1996.

Hamber, Anthony J. 'Building Nineteenth-century Photographic Resources: The South Kensington Museum and William Blackmore', *Visual Resources*, Vol. 26, no. 3 September, 2010 pp. 254-273.

Hart, Robert. *The I.[nspector] G.[eneral] in Peking. The Letters of Robert Hart Chinese Maritime Customs 1868-1907*, Volume One, Belknap Press, Harvard, 1975.

Hart, Robert. *Archives of China's Imperial Maritime Customs: confidential correspondence between Robert Hart and James Duncan Campbell, 1874-1907*, Foreign Languages Press, 1993.

Haskins, Charles. *The History of Salisbury Infirmary*, Salisbury & District Infirmary & Hospital League, Salisbury, 1922.

Heathcote, Bernard & Heathcote, Pauline. *A Faithful Likeness. The First Photographic Studios in the British Isles 1841-1855*, Lowdham, 2002.

Henderson, J. 'Photography as an aid to archaeology', *Journal of the Photographic Society*, No.192 18th April, 1868 pp.37-40.

[Henry, Joseph] *A Memorial of Joseph Henry*, Government Printing Office, Washington, D. C., 1880.

Hinkley, Caroline Lawson. *Thomas Moran: Artist of the Mountains*, 2nd edition, University of Oklahoma Press, Norman, 1998.

Howells, Jane. 'Salisbury's 1852 'Great Exhibition'', *Sarum Chronicle*, 2, 2002 pp.25-34.

Hume, A. *The Learned Societies and Printing Clubs of the United Kingdom*, G. Willis, London, 1853.

[International Congress of Prehistoric Archæology: 1868] *International Congress of Prehistoric Archæology: Transactions of the Third Session which opened at Norwich on the 20th August and closed in London on the 28th August, 1868*, Longmans, Green, and Co., London 1869.

Jackson, W. H. *Descriptive Catalogue of Photographs of North American Indians*, Government Printing Office, Washington, 1877.

van Keuren, David K. 'Museums and Ideology: Augustus Pitt Rivers, Anthropological Museums, and Social Change in Later Victorian Britain', *Victorian Studies*, Vol. 28, No. 1 (Autumn, 1984), pp. 171-189.

Kilgo, Dolores Ann. *Likeness and Landscape: Thomas M. Easterly and the art of the Daguerreotype*, Missorri Historical Society Press, St. Louis, 1994.

Kime, Wayne R. *The Black Hill Journals of Colonel Richard Irving Dodge*, University of Oklahoma Press, Norman, 1996.

Kime, Wayne R. *The Powder River Expedition Journals of Colonel Richard Irving Dodge*,

University of Oklahoma Press, Norman, 1997.
Kime, Wayne R. *The Indian Territory Journals of Colonel Richard Irving Dodge*, University of Oklahoma Press, Norman, 2000.
Kime, Wayne R. *Colonel Richard Irving Dodge: The Life and Times of a Career Army Officer*, University of Oklahoma Press, Norman, 2006.
King, J.C.H. 'A Century of Indian Shows: Canadian and United States Exhibitions in London 1825-1925,' *European Review of Native American Studies* 5,1991 pp.35-42.
Lane Fox, Augustus. 'On the Principles of Classification Adopted in the Arrangement of His Anthropological Collection, Now Exhibited in the Bethnal Green Museum.' *The Journal of the Anthropological Institute of Great Britain and Ireland*, Volume 4, 1875 pp.293-308.
Langford, Nathaniel Pitt. *Diary of the Washburn Expedition to the Yellowstone and Firehole Rivers in the Year 1870*, St. Paul, 1905.
Levine, Philippa. *The Amateur and The professional; Antiquarians, Historians and Archaeologists in Victorian England, 1838-1886*, Cambridge University Press, 1986.
Lewis, Robert M. 'Wild American Savages and the Civilized English: Catlin's Indian Gallery and the shows of London', *European Journal of American Studies*, 1, 2008.
Linkman, Audrey. *Professional Photographers in Liverpool 1851-1900*, The PhotoHistorian Supplement No.98, 1992.
Little, B. M. *A History of Libraries in Salisbury, 1850-1922*, M.Phil dissertation, Polytechnic of North London, 1980.
MacDonald, Michael, and Murphy, Terence. *Sleepless Souls: Suicide in Early Modern England*, Oxford University Press, Oxford, 1990.
MacGregor, Arthur. *A Summary Catalogue of the Continental Archaeological Collections in the Ashmolean Museum: Roman Iron Age, Migration Period, Early Medieval*, British Archaeological Reports International Series 674, Archaeopress, Oxford, 1997.
Macleod, Dianne Sachko. *Art and the Victorian middle class - Money and the making of cultural identity*, Cambridge University Press, Cambridge, 1996.
Marillier, Henry Currie. *Dante Gabriel Rossetti, An Illustrated Memorial of His Art and Life.*, George Bell & Sons, London, 1899.
McEvansoneya, Philip.'William Blackmore, Patron of Dante Gabriel Rossetti', *Review of the Pre-Raphaelite Society*, 9, Spring 2001 pp.9-17.
McEvansoneya, Philip. 'William Blackmore, Patron of Dante Gabriel Rossetti and Robert Moran, and ethnographer of the United States', *Journal of Pre-Raphaelite Studies*, (12), 2003 p.62-73.
McEvansoneya, Philip. 'Dante Gabriel Rossetti's 'Hamlet and Ophelia' and its patron.', *The Burlington Magazine*, Number 1273, Volume CLI, April 2009 pp.219-223.
Middleton, A. B. *The Benefits of Sanitary Reform as shown at Salisbury, as shown at Salisbury in nine years' experience therof: a paper read before the British Association for the Advancement of Science, at Bath, September 17th, 1864*. Simpkin & Co., London, 1864.
Morand, Anne. *Thomas Moran, The Field Sketches, 1856-1923*, University of Oklahoma, Norman, 1996.
Morris, Edward, and Roberts, Emma. *Liverpool Academy and Other exhibitions of Contemporary Art in Liverpool, 1774-1867: A History and Index of Artists and Works Exhibited.*, Liverpool University Press, Liverpool, 1999.
Mulvey, Christopher. 'Among the Sag-a-noshes: Ojibwa Indians with George Catlin in

Europe. Indians and Europe, 1843-1848' in Christian Feest (ed.), *An Interdisciplinary Collection of Essays.*, University of Nebraska Press, Lincoln and London, 1999.

Musty, John. 'The Catlin affair: the dispersal of the Blackmore Museum library, Salisbury', *Hatcher Review*, Volume 3, Number 26, Autumn 1988 pp.303-310.

Newman, Ruth and Howells, Jane. *Salisbury Past*, Phillimore & Co Ltd, Chichester, 2001.

Northy, T. J. *The Popular History of Old & New Sarum*, Wiltshire County Mirror & Express' Co., Salisbury, 1897.

O'Dwyer, Frederick. *The Architecture of Deane and Woodward*, Cork University Press, Cork, 1997.

Palmquist, Peter E., and Kailbourn, Thomas R. *Pioneer Photographers of the Far West: A Biographical Dictionary, 1840-1865*, Stanford University Press, 2002.

Palmquist, Peter E. and Kailbourn, Thomas R. *Pioneer Photographers from the Mississippi to the Continental Divide: A Biographical Dictionary, 1839-1865*, Stanford University Press, 2005.

Petch, Alison. 'Chance and Certitude: Pitt Rivers and his first collection', *Journal of the History of Collecting*, 2006 pp.249-256.

Petraglia, Michael, and Potts, Richard. *The Old World Paleolithic and the Development of a National Collection*, Smithsonian Contributions and Studies Series, Washington, D.C., 2004.

Picton, James. *Memorials of Liverpool Historical and Topographical including A History of the Dock Estate*, Longmans, Green, and Co., London, 1873, Volume I pp.660-661.

Priamo, Luis. *La fotografía italiana en la Argentina. Siglos XVIII / XIX. Benito Panunzi.*, Fundación Proa at http://www.proa.org/exhibiciones/pasadas/italianos/fotografia/fotografia.html.

Purvis, Bruce. *Salisbury: the changing city*, Breedon Books, 2003.

Rivett-Carnac, J. H. *Many Memories of Life in India at Home and Abroad*, William Blackwood, Edinburgh ; London : W. Blackwood, 1910.

Rossetti, William Michael. *Dante Gabriel Rossetti as Designer and Writer*, Cassell & Company Limited, London, 1889.

[Salisbury; Exhibitions] *Catalogue of the Salisbury Exhibition of Local Industry, Amateur Productions, Works of Art, Antiquities, Objects of taste, Articles of Vertu, etc.,Opened on the Twelfth of October 1852, James Bennett,[Salisbury] [1852].*

[Salisbury; Exhibitions] *Catalogue of the Temporary Museum, Pictures, Works of Art, &c., exhibited at The Council Chamber Salisbury, At the Conversazione given by the Salisbury Literary & Scientific Institution and Salisbury and South Wilts Museum, on Thursday, 23rd January, 1862, and following days.*, Bennett, Salisbury [1862].

[Salisbury Infirmary] *The History of Salisbury Infirmary*, Salisbury & District Infirmary & Hospital League, Salisbury, 1922.

[Salisbury & South Wiltshire Museum] *Catalogue of the Salisbury & South Wilts Museum*, Bennet, Salisbury, 1864.

[Salisbury & South Wiltshire Museum] *Proceedings of the Inauguration of the Salisbury and South Wilts Museum*, Bennett, Salisbury, 1864.

Sandoz, Mari. *The Buffalo Hunters: The Story of the Hide Men*. Second edition, University of Nebraska Press, Lincoln, 2008.

Saunders, Peter R. *Channels to the past: the Salisbury drainage collection*, Salisbury & South Wilts Museum, Salisbury, 1986.

Scherer, Joanna Cohan. *A Danish photographer of Idaho Indians: Benedicte Wrensted,*

University of Oklahoma Press, Norman, 2005.
Smith, James. *Wilton and Its Associations*, George Brown, Salisbury and J. B Nichols & Son, London, 1851.
Squarey, Lavinia M. *Family Records and Pedigrees*, Bennett Brothers, Salisbury [1909].
Starkey,Pat. (ed.). *Riches into Art – Liverpool Collectors 1770-1880. Essays in honour of Margaret T. Gibson.*, Liverpool University Press, Liverpool, 1993.
Starr, Prof. Frederick. 'Anthropological Work in Europe', *The Popular Science Monthly*, Volume XLI, May to October 1892 pp.54-72.
Steele, Francis E. *Present-Day Banking: Its Methods, Tendencies and Characteristics.*, Butterworth, London, 1909.
Stevens, Edward T. *Flint Chips: A Guide to Historic Archaeology, as illustrated by the collection in the Blackmore Museum, Salisbury.*, Bell and Daldy; Brown and Co., and F.A. Blake, London and Salisbury, 1870.
Stevens, Frank. *The Salisbury Museums 1861-1947: A Record of Eighty-Six Years of Progress* Bennett Brothers, Salisbury [1948].
Stevens, Frank. *The Salisbury Museums, 1861-1947: A Record of Eighty-Six Years of Progress*, 2nd edition, Salisbury, 1954.
Strong, Thomas Augustus. *Bruton Register. A Calendar of the Master and Pupils, &c., from 1826 to 1890*, Frowde, 1894.
Taylor, Colin F. "Ho, for the Great West!' Indians and buffalo, exploration and George Catlin: the West of William Blackmore' in Barry C. Johnson, *'Ho for the Great West!' and other original papers to mark the 25th Anniversary of the English Westerners' Society*, Eatome Ltd. for The English Westerners' Society, London 1980 pp.8-49.
Taylor, Colin F. 'William Blackmore: A 19th Century Englishman's contribution to American Indian Ethnology', in Christian F. Feest (ed.), *Indians and Europe. An Interdisciplinary Collection of Essays*, University of Nebraska, Lincoln, 1999 pp.321-336.
Taylor, Colin F. 'The 'Tall Bear' Drawings in the William Blackmore collection at the British Museum', *European Review of Native American Studies*, Volume 18, No,2, 2004 pp.1-12.
[Taylor, Colin F.] *Colin Taylor: Ethnologist of the Plains Indians. A Memoir: 1937-2004; Recollections by his Friends. A Bibliography of his Work. Edited by Barry C. Johnson.*, Bartletts Press, Birmingham, 2006.
Thompson, D. 'Queenwood College, Hampshire; A mid-19th century experiment in science teaching', *Annals of Science*, Volume 11, Number 3, Number 3/September 1955 , pp. 246-254.
Thompson, M. W. *Catalogue of the correspondence and papers of Augustus Henry Lane Fox Pitt Rivers,,, in the Salisbury & South Wiltshire Museum*, Royal Commission on Historical Manuscripts, 1976. [Typescript]
Torrens, Hugh S. 'A Wiltshire Pioneer in Geology and his Legacy: Henry Shorto III (1778-1864), Cutler and Fossil Collector of Salisbury' *Wiltshire Archaeological And Natural History Magazine*, Volume 83, 1990 pp. 170-189.
Treuherz, Julian. 'Aesthetes in Business: The Raes and D. G. Rossetti', *The Burlington Magazine*, Vol. 146, No. 1210, January, 2004 pp. 13-19.
Twitchell, Ralph Emerson. *The Leading Facts of New Mexico History*, Volume 4, The Torch Press, Cedar Rapids, 1917.
Viola, Herman J. *Diplomats in Buckskins: A History of Indian Delegations in Washington City*, University of Oklahoma Press, Norman, 1995.

Who's Who in America. A Biographical Dictionary of Notable Living Men and Women, A.N. Marquis & Company, Chicago, 1903.

Weiss, Barbara. *The Hell of the English. Bankruptcy and the Victorian Novel*, Associated University Presses, Cranbury, NJ, 1986.

Wilkins, Thurman. *Thomas Moran –Artist of the Mountains*, 2nd edition. University of Oklahoma Press, Norman, 1998.

Willoughby, R. W. H. 'The Salisbury and South Wilts Museum: Founded 1860.', *Wiltshire Archaeological and Natural History Magazine*, Volume 57 Number CCVIII, Devizes, 1960 pp.307-315.

Willoughby, R. W. H. 'The Blackmore Museum.', *Wiltshire Archaeological and Natural History Magazine*, Volume 57 Number CCVIII, Devizes, 1960 pp.316-321.

Wilson, David Mackenzie. *The British Museum; A History.*, British Museum Press, London, 2002.

Wood, R. Derek. *The Daguerreotype in Liverpool in 1839: Ste Croix, A. Abraham and J. B. Dancer.* at http://www.midley.co.uk/sourcetexts/liverpool_dag1839_wood.htm.

Yanni, Carla. *Nature's Museums: Victorian science and the architecture of display*, Princeton Architectural Press, New York, 2005.

Index

Lightning Source UK Ltd.
Milton Keynes UK
UKOW030439111012

200381UK00001B/10/P

9 781906 978105